Digital Culture & Society

Vol. 7, Issue 2/2021

Olga Moskatova, Anna Polze, Ramón Reichert (eds.)
Networked Images in Surveillance Capitalism

The journal is edited by
Pablo Abend, Mathias Fuchs, Ramón Reichert,
and Karin Wenz

Editorial Board
Maria Bakardjeva, David Berry, Jean Burgess, Mark Coté,
Colin Cremin, Sean Cubitt, Mark Deuze, José van Dijck, Delia
Dumitrica, Astrid Ensslin, Sonia Fizek, Federica Frabetti, Orit
Halpern, Irina Kaldrack, Denisa Kera, Lev Manovich, Janet
H. Murray, Jussi Parikka, Lisa Parks, Dominic Pettman, Rita
Raley, Richard Rogers, Julian Rohrhuber, Marie-Laure Ryan,
Mirko Tobias Schäfer, Jens Schröter, Trebor Scholz, Tamar
Sharon, Roberto Simanowski, Nathaniel Takcz, Geoffrey
Winthrop-Young, Sally Wyatt

[transcript]

Indexed in EBSCOhost databases

Bibliographic information published by the Deutsche Nationalbibliothek
The Deutsche Nationalbibliothek lists this publication in the Deutsche National-bibliografie; detailed bibliographic data are available on the Internet at http://dnb.d-nb.de

© 2022 transcript Verlag, Bielefeld

All rights reserved. No part of this book may be reprinted or reproduced or utilized in any form or by any electronic, mechanical, or other means, now known or hereafter invented, including photocopying and recording, or in any information storage or retrieval system, without permission in writing from the publisher.

Cover layout: Kordula Röckenhaus, Bielefeld
Typeset: Mark-Sebastian Schneider, Bielefeld

ISSN: 2364-2114
eISSN: 2364-2122
Print-ISBN 978-3-8376-5388-5
PDF-ISBN 978-3-8394-5388-9

Content

Introduction
Networked Images in Surveillance Capitalism
Olga Moskatova, Anna Polze and Ramón Reichert   5

I Image Platforms

Kind of Blue
Social Media Photography and Emotion
Michelle Henning   31

Embedding Heterogenous Forms of Surveillance in China's Autocratic Networked Media
How the Government Supports and Controls Platforms, Companies, Online Celebrities, and Users
Cornelia Bogen   55

Black Squares and Gucci
Networked Images and the (In)Visibility of Surveillance
Sascha Hosters and Silke Roesler-Keilholz   97

Automating Platform Spectators
Algorithmic Montage and Affective Scroll in TikTok
Alexandra Anikina   119

II Datafication and Operative Images

Seeing Like a Border
Biometrics and the Operational Image
Mark Andrejevic, Volcic Zala   141

Doing Google Maps
Everyday Use and the Image of Space in a Surveillance Capitalism Centrepiece
Peter Gentzel, Jeffrey Wimmer, Ruben Schlagowski   159

The Invisualities of Capture in Amazon's Logistical Operations
Armin Beverungen   185

III Automated Vision

Apple Memories and Automated Memory-Making
The Networked Image Inside the iPhone Chip
Gabriel Pereira   205

Images of Resistance
Thinking about Computer Vision AI in Surveillance Capitalism through Images of Marielle Franco
Vinicius Ariel Arruda dos Santos, Bruno Moreschi, Amanda Jurno, Didiana Prata, Monique Lemos, Lucas Nunes Sequeira   229

IV Gaze, Normalization, Subjectivation

The Digital, Capitalist Gaze
Jens Schröter   247

Nudged to Normal
Images, Behaviour, and the Autism Surveillance Complex
Daniela Wentz   265

V Methodological Reflections

Detained through a Smartphone
Deploying Experimental Collaborative Visual Methods to Study the Socio-Technical Landscape of Digital Confinement
Carolina Sanchez Boe and Henry Mainsah   289

Urban Data Analytics as Research Topic, Method and Ethical Concern
Daniel Trottier, Ju-Sung (Jay) Lee and John Boy   311

Biographical Notes   329

Introduction
Networked Images in Surveillance Capitalism

Olga Moskatova, Anna Polze and Ramón Reichert

In 2020, in the middle of a world-wide pandemic, the artist and hacker Thomas Webb launched an online exhibition called "Exercise in Hopeless Nostalgia" at König Galerie. For this, Thomas Webb created a virtual multiplayer game-world in nostalgic 8-bit-aesthetics – a "World Wide WEBB" inviting users to travel to Berlin, Osaka and Kanagawa, to visit the simulated exhibition rooms of the gallery, and to interact with other gamers or the artist's featured digital artworks. Creating a digital space for social interaction and art reception during the pandemic, the digital exhibition was of course commenting on the transformation of private and professional activities under the conditions of distant socialising. While doing so, it was also a reflection on the economies and the mechanisms of today's networked images and digital spaces for social interaction: The game was advertised, among other places, on Instagram and could be played in a regular web browser or in the Instagram app. Before starting the game and choosing their avatars, the gamers were asked to enter their Instagram usernames and, thus, to reveal their digital identity. The game was driven by an artificial intelligence that analysed the decisions made and the real-time data produced during the game. The AI used the personality test developed by Cambridge Analytica in order to deduce one of the 16 possible personalities, and to personalise the further gameplay by offering tailored information from the "real world". While Cambridge Analytica harvested data of Facebook users to sway the US-presidential election in 2016, "Exercise in Hopeless Nostalgia" is less about data privacy, and more about the commodification of everyday online activities and networked visual practices. Webb's aim was to mimic data-mining strategies without monetising them (Webb/Reese 2021). The game and the artworks presented in it, such as *Rainfall* (2018) or *Depressed Twitter* (2017), explored a virtual world where data could be a common property and shared good, not monopolised by big companies, where users would have control over their data without being exploited by technologies (Webb 2021). After successfully completing the game, insights into the gathered data and algorithms were offered to the gamers.

Inviting the user to engage experientially, aesthetically and interactively with dataveillance, Thomas Webb's exhibition intervenes into the discourse on digital, data-driven economies that prevail on the web, social media and image sharing platforms such as Instagram. Capturing personal data in exchange for free services such as image sharing, phatic communication, online playing, or real-time streaming is now ubiquitous in networked media, and recently led to diagnoses of surveillance and platform capitalism (Zuboff 2019; Srnicek 2017). In social media discourse, dataveillance and data mining have been criticised as new forms of digital work and capitalist exploitation for some time (cf. Allmer 2015; Andrejevic 2012; van Dijck 2014; Fuchs 2013; Scholz 2013; Trottier 2012). While Webb's game and artworks subversively and reflexively engage with economic surveillance, everyday networked images usually form a constitutive part of platforms and their extractive mechanisms. With the general transformation of the open web into an ecology dominated by commercial platforms (Hands 2013; Helmond 2015; Langois/Elmer 2013; Gillespie 2018), platformisation and economic surveillance are also redefining digital visual culture, facilitating new forms of images, everyday practices and online visibility, while expanding the logics of social media to the rest of the web. From social photos (Jurgenson 2019), selfies and image communities on the internet to connected viewing, playing and streaming, and video conferencing during the Corona pandemic – the digital image is not only predominantly networked (Rubinstein/Sluis 2008) but also accessed through platforms (van Dijck 2013; van Dijck et al. 2018) and structured by their economic imperatives, data acquisition techniques and algorithmic processing. Today, participation and commodification are closely linked to the production, circulation, consumption and operativity of images and visual communication, raising the question of the role networked images and aesthetics play for and within the proliferating surveillance capitalism.

Linking images and surveillance automatically brings traditional concepts such as the panopticon and its numerous modifications into play, since they rely on optical and visual metaphors (Haggerty 2006; Buschauer 2016). In his famous analysis of the panopticon, Michel Foucault showed to what extent power can be exercised through visuality and so produce specific subjects. However, as frequently noted (Deleuze 1992; Haggerty/Ericson 2000; Kammerer/Waitz 2015), this form of power seems incapable of fully grasping the dynamics of networked digital media technologies. Today, not only media but also the techniques of surveillance and control are increasingly networked and unobtrusive. In surveillance and platform capitalism, many of their contemporary forms do not rely on the visible demonstration and internalisation of the gaze, but on automated data-based and algorithmic forms of control that are motivated economically. They are not "salient", but "silent" (Introna/Wood 2004) and even "calm" technologies (Weiser/Brown 1997) that proliferate in everyday life and diffuse through environments. Although the relationship between visuality and surveillance is being transformed, images are nevertheless an important part of post-panoptical media assemblages and their silent forms of power. Since many successful economic platforms and our everyday networked practices are image-based, an evaluation of surveillance capitalism that takes media differences seriously becomes decisive.

This special issue thus invites the examination of questions about digital economies from a media-specific and media aesthetics point of view. The ground-breaking work on digital economies and economic surveillance on social media and networked media, exemplified by authors such as Zuboff, Srnicek, Andrejevic, Fuchs or Trottier, rarely considers aesthetic issues, or differentiates between the types of medialities actually involved in the media constellation called "social media". However, this kind of issue concerns media studies in the first place. This is not to say that political, social and economic problems of capitalist surveillance should be replaced by a focus on aesthetics. On the contrary, one of the characteristics of media studies and their methodologies is that they enable us to integrate different facets and to relate aesthetics to economies as well as to technologies of power, subjectivation and social formations.

This special issue therefore aims to interrogate the manifold relationships between economic surveillance and networked images, and to identify their intersections. In particular, it focuses on the tension between a visual aestheticisation of capitalism and the anaesthetisation of images or/and surveillance techniques, i.e., on the dynamics between visibility and invisibility. On the one hand, it asks to what extent and using which aesthetic strategies images can create incentives for, and stabilise surveillance capitalism, i.e., how they contribute to its aestheticisation. On the other hand, it is interested in the transformation of pictoriality in post-panoptical, ambient media environments, resulting in forms of the anaesthetisation of images. Closely linked to the problems of anaesthetisation is the question of whether and how the regimes of the gaze are transformed in apparatuses of dataveillance and algorithmic control, and what kind of subjectivities are produced within them.

Platform Surveillance

Before questioning the aesthetics and anaesthetics of surveillance capitalism, it is helpful to introduce and contextualise the main notions and concepts guiding this special issue and the contributions to it. While economic surveillance has been known and problematised for several decades, Zuboff's (2015; 2019) diagnosis of "surveillance capitalism" attracted a lot of attention, offering a much-discussed "retheorization of data-driven, algorithmic commercial surveillance as instrumentarian power" (Cohen 2019: 240). By surveillance capitalism, Shoshana Zuboff means a form of digital economy and a business model that is premised upon surveillant extraction, accumulation and management of transactional and "behavioral data" (2019: 74). Its aim is to anticipate, predict and modify behaviour in order to secure profit and market – something she calls *"behavioral future markets"* (ibid.: 96). In her voluminous book and an earlier article (2015), Zuboff tries to identify and describe the main mechanisms of, and the discursive and social preconditions to this form of "informational capitalism" (Castells 2010). In her account, it was especially Google, later followed by Facebook and Microsoft, who implemented the core model of surveillance capitalism by starting to use people's search data to target them with personalised advertising. For Zuboff, surveillance capitalism benefited, among other things, from a lack of internet laws, and exceptional events such as 9/11 and the resulting expansion of security apparatuses. According to the author, surveillance capitalism poses a threat to democracy by establishing instrumentarian power, which does not aim at the *"engineering of the soul"* (Zuboff 2019: 355) as the totalitarianism of the 20th century did, but premises upon radical behaviourism and technologies of behaviour modification. By exploiting people's dependency on the internet for conducting their social and professional lives, it enforces unilateral, abusive forms of contracts, "contracts of adhesion" (ibid.: 48). It reduces human experience to measurable and observable data and raw material, and establishes a knowledge regime based on asymmetry, certainty and predictability, i.e., one that aims not at the automation of information flows, but at "the automation of the self" and "the automation of society" (ibid.: 382). By focusing on the predictive regime of knowledge and power that is based on stimuli, operates below reflexive subjectivities and capitalises on behavioural traces, surveillance capitalism shows parallels to what Antoinette Rouvroy (2013) calls "algorithmic governmentality".

The telos of surveillance capitalism is to find ever more sources for extraction of data, surpassing the model of personalised advertisement and expanding the extraction into many other online and offline sectors (Zuboff 2019: 10). Digitisation and computerisation of work, living spaces, everyday activities, health, consumption, etc., which even boomed during the recent years of the global pandemic are means to achieve this goal. Surveillance capitalists, therefore, do not simply collect incidental data; they create technologies, smart things and "ubiquitous computational architectures" (ibid.: 8) that hook and lure users into extractive applications, securing new sources for behavioural data. Zuboff compares industrial capitalism to surveillance capitalism. Whereas the former tries to intensify the means of production, the latter tries to intensify the means of gathering and modifying behaviour: "Instead of labor, surveillance capitalism feeds on every aspect of every human's experience" (ibid.: 9). Although the expansive striving for data has consequences for privacy and security, Zuboff's analysis deals with economic issues and forms of digital-capitalist exploitation. Zuboff even warns against reducing it to issues of privacy or data protection (ibid.: 90), i.e., to a simplified idea of "surveillance", minus the capitalism.

Zuboff's analysis has been rightly criticised for being techno-determinist and for affirmatively reproducing the narratives of technologists and corporations (Murakami Wood/Monahan 2019: 3), overestimating their manipulative and persuasive powers (Doctorow 2020: 12-22). Her historical and conceptual understanding of capitalism also has its flaws. In her account, "surveillance capitalism" seems to be a deviant or "rogue" form of a formerly "good", or at least "normal" or "rational" capitalism, the development of which Zuboff attributes to Thomas Edison and Henry Ford (2019: 17). The story of *The Age of Surveillance Capitalism* is very US-centred and follows a narrative of decline (Evangelista 2018: 246-247) instead of acknowledging that there is no innocent form of capitalism. Over and over, the developments seem to be attributed to the actions and reasoning of few tech-savvy capitalists, i.e., a handful of Western males, while her critique of radical behaviourism, which drives data extraction, evokes a positive image of liberal humanism, of free will and autonomy. Her very Western perspective on the rise and consequences of surveillance capitalism calls for a decentring and a supplement with accounts from non-Western countries (Evangelista 2018: 250), as offered, for example, in Cornelia Bogen's contribution to this special issue. Following Zuboff, she analyses the entanglement of surveillance capitalism and state power in China.

In a different critical reading of Zuboff, David Murakami Wood and Torin Monahan note that surveillance capitalism needs to be "defined only in conjunction with the concept of the platform" (2019: 4), thus preferring Srnicek's work on "platform capitalism" to Zuboff's. It is obvious that Zuboff's notion of "surveillance capitalism" has similarities with Srnicek's understanding of "platform capitalism". Both concepts concentrate on the digital economies of networked media and the role datafication plays in them. Focusing on players such as Google, Facebook and Amazon, while exempting Apple, Zuboff actually deals with organisational and infrastructural forms that Srnicek calls "platforms", without theoretically and discursively engaging with this notion. In contrast, Srnicek does not foreground the problems of surveillance, but without completely ignoring them. Besides offering an alternative historical account of the rise of data-driven capitalism, Srnicek especially enriches the discourse by analysing the different mechanisms and types of platforms, thus reflecting on the differences of data-driven business models and their balancing between free and paid services. Understood as intermediary digital infrastructures that enable and mediate the interaction of different actors, platforms present themselves as neutral spaces, while embodying politics (Srnicek 2017: 44, 47). Moreover, "platforms produce and are reliant on 'network effects': the more numerous the users who use a platform, the more valuable that platform becomes for everyone else" (Srnicek 2017: 45).

The idea that the two concepts by Zuboff and Srnicek could be used and thought of as complementary is acknowledged by the very term "platform surveillance" coined by David Murakami Wood and Torin Monahan in the *Surveillance & Society*-issue of the same name (2019) – a perspective that is especially productive for analysing networked and platformed images. Using the term "platform surveillance", Wood and Monahan do not only state that datafied surveillance happens on platforms; they are more interested in the ways that platforms transform social relations and produce social divisions, set the terms for individual, institutional and even governmental interaction, engender specific subjectivities, and impose the logics of platform capitalism upon more and more existing practices and institutions (2019: 1). Combining both Zuboff's and Srnicek's concepts, Murakami Wood's and Monohan's term emphasises that "surveillance is essential to the operations of platforms" (ibid.: 1-2). Their notion has the advantage of relating surveillance studies and economic analysis to platform and infrastructure studies, which has established important concepts for media studies research on networked media in recent decades. Moreover, Mukarami Wood and Monohan take the infrastructural dimension of platforms more seriously than Srnicek, thus giving an alternative account of the power structures and inner workings of surveillance and platform capitalism, literally materialising the perspective (ibid.: 3; see also the contribution by Gabriel Pereira in this issue).

Although this special issue primarily draws on Zuboff's, and to a lesser degree on Srnicek's work in order to sharpen the analytical and conceptual discussion, it does not mistake their contributions as the first to address the issues of digital-capitalists' reliance on data and dataveillance. Many scholars dealing with the Internet and social media have examined the economically motivated surveillance and the commodification of networked communication and social interaction before, offering many different concepts and notions such as "dataveillance" (Clark 1988), "informational capitalism" (Castells 2010), "capture capitalism" (Heilmann 2015), "digital enclosure" (Andrejevic 2007), "audience commodity" (Fuchs 2012) or "algorithmic governmentality"(Rouvroy 2013; Rouvroy/Berns 2013), among others. Surely, Zuboff even ignores some important contributions from media studies and surveillance studies over the last twenty years in her book (Ball 2019: 253). Therefore, in this issue, "surveillance capitalism" is not only understood as a strict reference to the work of Shoshana Zuboff, but also as an umbrella-term for a multitude of similar or comparable notions that try to analyse and grasp the logics of networked commodification, datafication, and surveillance – or what Murakami Wood and Monona called "platform surveillance". Accordingly, many contributors to this special issue not only engage directly with Zuboff's work (for one example, see Daniela Wentz's contribution in this issue), but also with related concepts, critically readdressing the conceptualisation of "surveillance capitalism", reading it, for example, through the prisms of Rouvroy's "algorithmic governmentality" and Illouz's "emotional capitalism" (2007) (see Michelle Henning's contribution to this issue), through the prism of Agre's (1994) notion of "capture" (see Armin Beverungen's contribution to this issue), or through the prism of platform and infrastructure studies (see Gabriel Pareira's paper). Nevertheless, the main objective of this special issue is not so much critique or revision of Zuboff's work, or discussing its relationship to other concepts. Instead, it is about examining the relevance of visual media for the digital economies and taking questions of aesthetics and mediality into account.

Networked Images and Aestheticisation of Capitalism

By focusing on networked images, this special issue acknowledges the transformations that have occurred in the practices, technologies and discourses of digital images in the last few decades. For a long time, digital images have been questioned with regard to the crisis of photo-theoretical guiding concepts such as referentiality and indexicality. The spatiotemporal binding of a light-sensitive carrier material no longer served as paradigm when the digital recording became reversible and its output as an image was only one of the possible manifestations of the data stored in binary form. Thus, the digital image was constantly questioned as being a "dubitative image" (Lunenfeld 2000), because the technical possibility of subsequently editing images by intervening in the pixel data set provoked doubt about their authenticity. These questions on the inherent doubt in digital images remain powerful and are even used as positive qualities by theorists and practitioners such as Hito Steyerl (cf. Steyerl 2007). In face of the contemporary digital media culture, however, they must be situated in a wide media ecology of practices. Beyond these ontological questions, multiple ways of dealing with digital images have developed: "The image was less and less a document of an external reality, but more and more part of the new forms of mediated sociality" (Cubitt et al. 2021: 68).

Especially since the mid-2000s and with the emergence of social media platforms such as Facebook, Twitter, and later Instagram and TikTok, and image sharing sites like Pinterest or Flickr (Gerling, Holschbach, Löffler 2018), the digital image has become an image destined to be shared (Rothöhler 2018a). Image sharing sites enable users to upload, tag, reference, comment and like images, attributing new forms of value, reception and circulation. By integrating digital images into Facebook for example, they have become an important stakeholder in the platform's quantification of users' expression within the like economy (Gerlitz/Helmond 2013). Within a few years, these digital actions have shaped the status of the digital image in a broad sense. Their behavioural logic has also been integrated into devices such as the smartphone, which can serve as a primary example of the networked condition of today's media. These image practices of distributed and networked visuality constitute a new point of engagement for media studies, since in the age of social media, platforms, and smartphone photography, it is not only the veracity of a snapshot or the credibility of a single image that is at issue, but rather the circulation, networking, and dissemination of an unmanageable number of images as ensembles and aggregates.

The circulatory character of networked images, with virality and memetics being their most visible manifestations, marks some shifts in visual practices and, with them, the transformations and re-organisation of power within media industries and economies. Being one of the characteristics of "participatory culture", circulation emphasises active contribution to the production, meaning and content of images as well as their redefinitions though time and space, contrasting with the top-down, centralised processes of dissemination typical of traditional mass media and the broadcasting of content (Jenkins/Ford/Green 2018: 2). Whereas this shift could be celebrated as being emancipatory and liberating in early debates (cf. Jenkins, Jenkins/Ford/Green 2018), even implying that participatory culture could break with the rules of capitalist profitability by turning towards a sharing economy (Barbrook 1998; Uhlin 2014), it is evident that spaces for online interaction, communication and consumption, such as platforms, are owned and controlled by companies that seek profit. For a regular user, participation rarely implies participating in economic decision-making and ownership (Fuchs 2014: 56). Therefore, it is short-sighted to celebrate circulatory image culture as a space free of commodification. Instead, networked images simultaneously partake in sharing economies, monetary exchanges, attention economies, like economies, and data-driven economies, i.e., they are riddled with manifold and contradictory economic logics. On platforms, visibility and popularity can be commodified in many forms, ranging from traditional advertising, product placement and influencing to using user-generated content for training proprietary algorithms to offering subscription- and fee-based models, or datafying interaction and participation. Discussing the role of images within surveillance capitalism means taking into account the different, but interconnected economic structures involved.

For example, circulatory and phatic communication seems to be crucial for generating the "network effects" (Srnicek 2017) necessary for the functioning of "platform surveillance". Circulation of content increases traffic on a platform and can attract new users or ensure the interest of existing users. Thus, images may support the reproduction and maintenance of surveillance and platform capitalism by aestheticising it: As studies on virality and mimetics have shown, not all content spreads easily; instead, spreadability relies on particular aesthetic strategies and media principles such as humour, emotionality, polarisation, scurrility or non-sense (Shifman 2014; Strick 2021; Tanni 2020). However, compactness, nudity, spectacularity, "cinematicity" (Geiger/Littau 2013; Moskatova 2020), or cuteness can also contribute to users turning to a platform, capturing attention, and prolonging browsing times on platforms. Adding to the "attention economies" (Beller 2006; Franck 1998; Goldhaber 1997; Crogan and Kinsley 2012; Terranova 2012) and experiential-aesthetic regulation online, such aesthetic strategies can reintroduce the logic of "gaze", i.e., the focused stare, into the media environments of "glance", i.e., the incidental and fleeting glimpse (Bryson 1983) or intermediate forms of active cognitive engagement with media content such as "grazing" (Creeber 2013). As such, images can serve as incentives themselves or be part of nudging interface and website aesthetics (Mühlhoff 2018), and therefore contribute to the aestheticisation of digital capitalism.

On social media, icons, buttons and graphical or textual functions enable, encourage and incite "circulatory" activities such as liking, commenting, sharing, tagging or saving, which are easily monitored, datafied, and turned into profitable images' metadata. Platformisation of images means embedding them in the omnipresent extractive and surveillant data architectures of digital capitalism. Subscription-based streaming platforms such as Amazon video or Netflix, which have monetary revenues, also still datafy spectators' behaviour and interaction with the platform and content, and rely on "behavioral surplus", among other things, for the recommendation, algorithmisation and calculated production of content

– although, in Zuboff's argumentation, companies with monetary revenues would not count as surveillance capitalists. Here, seriality comes into play. It is an important media aesthetic principle for different kind of platforms because it attracts users' attention and attaches them to content by habitualising and ritualising consumption (Moskatova 2022). On the whole, seriality pervades digital visual cultures in many forms, including serials, viral-memetic image series as well as interface serialisation by medial forms such as loops, lists, databanks or grids (Maeder/Wentz 2014).

Anaestheticisation: Calm Images

The datafication of visual culture touches upon a second important relationship between images and surveillance capitalism: that of the anaestheticisation of images. Digital images are not only visible phenomena destined to be consumed, perceived and enjoyed by humans; they are also data files destined for processing and reading by software and machines. Thus, digital images have a double existence, as aesthetic visual materialisations, i.e., displayed images, and as strings of data, i.e., image files (Rothöhler 2021, 74). The informational side of the images facilitates their data-driven commodification and may even have consequences for the very concept of the image, which turns into a "calm image". This informational side becomes relevant in many different contexts, where the extractive logics of surveillance capitalism are put in place and surpass human perception: in the Internet of Things, in automated processes on social media platforms, or in computer vision technologies, among others.

In order to outline the anaesthetic operativity of contemporary images, it is worth taking a brief detour to debates from the 1990s, when the concept of "calm technology" was conceived by Mark Weiser and John Seely Brown to point out the interweaving of computer technologies into everyday life. Since then, the term "ubiquitous computing" has been used to describe the possibilities of advanced computer technology to function automatically in any scenario without the intervention or conscious attention of users. Media scholar Kristin Veel has extended this concept to the notion of calm images, "that operate smoothly in the background" (Veel 2012: 120) in order to be of use in identification systems, police investigations, intelligence services, public institutions, marketing, or at the workplace. However, the ubiquity of such image sensor-based systems is also spreading into the domestic realm. Following current developments in smart home technologies, everyday and seemingly benign objects such as fridges, doorbells, automated windows and vacuum cleaners have also become sentient things within the Internet of Things (IoT), which are part of image networks (Rothöhler 2018; 2021). They contain integrated optical sensing technologies to address non-networked things like refrigerator contents and objects like pieces of furniture in their environment. By measuring and recording image data via optical sensor networks, they perform tasks of multimodal monitoring of spaces and living beings, and of recording, storing and circulating captured information. Generally speaking, calm images are functional image data that are neither produced by humans nor received, viewed or evaluated by humans. Thus, calm images are a service to spare human attention and cognitive capacities where data has to be collected and evaluated. Such a technological design, which enlarges the "peripheral reach" (Weiser/Brown 1995: 2) of media with the help of image sensors, performs a "subtle oscillation between service and control" (Veel 2012: 119) and calmly extends towards economic strategies of surveillance and capture by securing and expanding the surveillance-capitalists' sources for extracting behavioural data.

Similarly, on social media, networked images not only participate in an economy of attention (Terranova 2012) by aestheticising and capturing the gaze, but also in a reverse sense, by becoming invisible and, with this, operational. In line with many other positions, Anna Munster and Adrien Mackenzie have pointed out that, given the sheer number of visual expressions online, contemporary image ensembles are both quantitatively beyond human perceptual capacities and qualitatively beyond the order of representation (Munster/MacKenzie 2019). In social networks, many image operations are executed automatically by non-human agents, remaining and being treated as data. However, the fact that these images do not operate in the field of the visible does not mean that they are not prone to observation or "observation events" (Munster/MacKenzie 2019: 5). Together with the aspect of attention, the meaning of image observation undergoes a semantic and media-political expansion in the context of calm images. Numerous "impersonal, financial forms of vision" are part of these new inhuman practices of image analysis, as Emily Rosamond (2017: 113) summarises following Shoshana Zuboff.[1] Thus, images are powerful means and assets in surveillant-capitalist environments. In this way, networked images on platforms and calm images alike are not only "part of an operation" (Farocki 2004: 17) as phantom images that scan the environment or measure spaces; in a narrower sense, they are "plat-formatted in operation" (Munster/MacKenzie 2019: 9). Image files on proprietary platforms such as Facebook are "seen" directly in multiple ways: "Regardless of whether a human subject actually sees any of the 2 billion photographs uploaded daily to Facebook-controlled platforms, the photographs on social media are scrutinized by neural networks with a degree of attention that would make even the most steadfast art historian blush", states Trevor Paglen with regard to technologies like DeepFace Algorithm, DeepMask and Google's TensorFlow (Paglen 2016: 5). The influential strategy of "platform seeing" ranges from image data training, content moderation and smart genre collections to the

---

1   Emily Rosamond draws on Zuboff's article "Big Other: Surveillance Capitalism and the Prospects of an Information Civilization" published already in 2015.

integrated distribution logics of smart phones and cameras that, for example, are manifested in the production of metadata. It reaches deep into the interconnected devices, platforms and image data. In combination, these imaging operations serve and maintain a nexus of technical, cultural, economic and political manageability that lies beyond the visible. Instead, observing becomes a multiscalar activity related to capture, surveillance, extraction and commodification alike, which transforms the image from being representational and iconic to becoming processual in datafication.

Finally, computer vision constitutes another form of calm visibility, where images are not destined to be viewed by humans anymore, but are made operative by machines for machines (Paglen 2016). It is the machine-readability of digital image files that enables the automation and operationalisation of visibility. Computer-based vision or computer vision refers to systems that recognise objects in digital still and moving image material and process them accordingly. It is mainly based on pattern recognition, which must be programmed in advance. The field of computer vision has developed significantly over the last decades (Stork 2009: 9-24).[2] It became a subject of growing interest in different fields of monitoring, control procedures and surveillance activities and is used for object modelling, activity tracking, face recognition, affect recognition (see Henning and Wentz in this issue), crowd monitoring, navigation, and virtual reality, among other things. Computer vision is generally deployed in practices of monitoring, mapping and evaluation and refers to the systematic, continuous observation of a person, place, thing, or process (Huberman 2021: 337-349). In the context of surveillance, computer vision also supports the targeted surveillance of behaviour, activities, and public spaces by police or security officers using monitoring technologies to enhance the visual capabilities of operatives doing the surveillance (Nainggolan/Mustakim 2021). The relationships between networked images and computer vision are manifold: Computer vision is not only used to sort, identify, classify or optimise images on diverse social media platforms, and in smartphone cameras or apps; it often relies on networked images for its very functioning, i.e.,

---

2 Early experiments in computer vision took place in the 1960s (Manovich 1996: 229-239). In the late 1960s, computer vision was anchored in universities in connection with research on artificial intelligence. Applied research projects in the 1970s laid the first foundations for many of the computer vision algorithms that exist today, including extracting edges from images, labeling lines, non-polyhedral and polyhedral modeling, representing objects as connections of smaller structures, optical flow, and motion estimation (Kaul et.al. 2020: 807-812). Neural network models could recognise the outlines of objects, and geometric objects such as circles or rectangles were assigned to categories. Increasingly since the 1970s, computer vision has been used commercially to interpret typed or handwritten text using optical character recognition (Olague 2016: 43-47).

networked images are utilised for training the systems (Crawford/Paglen 2019). Various algorithms are applied for computer vision, but today it is mostly a *Convolutional Neural Network* (CNN).[3] Training CNNs is very memory- and computation-intensive. With the expansion of the Internet in the 1990s, large numbers of images based on databases became available online and could be analysed, which gave rise to facial recognition. Today, various public image databases are at the disposal for training computer vision models. The *Mnist* Database is one of the simplest and oldest databases and contains about 70,000 handwritten numbers in ten different classes. Another example is the image database *Coco* (Common Objects in Context), which offers a large data set – for example for object recognition and image segmentation. More than 330,000 images in 80 object categories are at hand. And the publicly accessible image database *Open Images* houses the URLs for around nine million images – also including labels. Computer vision is now closely linked to machine-based learning and artificial intelligence and benefits – also economically – from swarm intelligence on the Internet. By being used as training data for computer vision application, the networked and social media images are appropriated by companies, anaesthetised and rechannelled into an invisible "visual" culture as new economic assets (Mackenzie/Munster 2019).

Subjectivation in Surveillance Capitalism

The complex dynamics between visibility and invisibility, aestheticisation and operativity also have consequences for thinking the relationship between surveillance, power and subjectivities – a relationship traditionally dealt with in surveillance studies. Although their connection can no longer be fully accounted for by the discourse-shaping concept of panopticism, which emphasised the power of visibility, it does not mean that silent and economically motivated forms of networked surveillance eliminate power relations and processes of subjectivation, or that visibility becomes completely irrelevant for exercising power. Rather, silent and scopic forms of power can be interrelated in different ways, depending on platforms and the images they provide: For example, on social media platforms, forms of social control based on the visibility of the personal can hardly be

---

3   CNNs only came into widespread use when high-performance graphics cards and high-performance video memory became affordable. Neural networks have been used since the 1980s, but they only came into widespread use in the 2010s. They belong to what are known as *Deep Learning Neural Networks* (DLNN), which are neural networks that have several hidden layers of neurons. When DLNNs are trained, the synapse weights are optimised using computationally intensive techniques to make them perform as well as possible for specific classification or regression tasks.

separated from algorithmic sorting and recommending. They modulate visibility and invisibility as well as the associated social fears (Trottier/Lyon 2012) and thus algorithmically reconfigure scopic forms of power (Bucher 2016; Bucher 2018) and self-care (Nguyen-Trung 2020). Within these powerful regulations of the sensible, certain reconfigurations of the gaze can also be observed, which in itself is deeply embedded into capitalist logics, as Jens Schröter discusses in his contribution to this issue.

With "instrumentarian power", Zuboff herself offers a concept for analysing structures of domination in digital capitalism, emphasising the predictive automation and modification of behaviour. According to her, instrumentarism dispenses with reflexive inwardness and nudges people into profitable and exploitable conduct. Knowledge asymmetries and the power of manipulation are at the heart of her understanding of the self as produced in surveillance capitalism: instead of producing subjects, it produces predictable personalities (Zuboff 2019: 273-275). Personalisation becomes a paradigmatic example in conceiving this kind of "subjectivation" focusing on personality: Personalisation is a form of recommendation made on the basis of behavioural data. By collecting, evaluating and comparing snippets of data left by interactions, communication, consumption, or search history; by deducing or querying sexual orientation, age, political affiliation or religion, etc., personalisation calculates preferences about individual tastes and interests, and shapes them by suggesting corresponding content. That is to say, it infers personal traits, opening them to politically and economically motivated micro-targeting of behaviour, including affective modulation (see Zuboff on Facebook: 2019: 280-290; on the political and ethical stakes of behaviourism in the context of affective computing, see also the contribution by Daniela Wetz in this issue). Given the work on digital subjectivities in comparable fields of study done, for example, by Antoinette Rouvroy or Cheney-Lippold, Zuboff's account leaves many questions unasked and unresolved, like the relationships between data personalities and actual users, and, in our context, also the relationship between data and aesthetics, visibility and invisibility.

In her concept of "algorithmic governmentality", Antoinette Rouvroy (2013) famously postulates the 'evacuation' of subjectivities within data economies. She also considers personalisation as one of the main operations of this regime. However, in her account of datafied subjectivities, it is not the "personality" that forms the basis of analysis. Instead, behaviourism results in "probabilistic subject[s]" (Rouvroy 2013: 153) and desubjectivation. Algorithmic governmentality is a form of automated knowledge production, hypothesising, and regulation of future behaviour that is based on data capture, data mining and profiling (cf. Rouvroy/Berns 2013: VI-IX). The power effects of algorithmic governmentality are directed towards futurity and potentiality; they produce a "probabilistic subject" (Rouvroy 2013: 153). Algorithmic governmentality, thus, aims to minimise and manage the uncertainty associated with human action (cf. ibid.: 155). Rouvroy contrasts this regime with the neoliberal mode of governance, which produces and presupposes "hyper-subjects" who are constantly forming and optimising themselves through the processes of self-control, self-entrepreneurship and self-assessment (ibid.: 153). In contrast, algorithmic governmentality operates at the preconscious level of stimuli, alarms and reflexes, rather than putting subjects in a reflexive, intentional or interpretive relationship to themselves (cf. ibid.). According to Rouvroy, this ultimately does away with processes of subjectivation: "Algorithmic governmentality is without subject: it operates with infra-individual data and supra-individual patterns without, at any moment, calling the subject to account for himself" (ibid.: 144-145). The goal of power effects is no longer a physical individual, compliant bodies or normative conformity; more important are the statistical data doubles and the correlations found in the immanence of data (cf. Rouvroy/Berns 2013: XI-XII). These correlations dispense with the idea of statistical average, normal value or psychological motivation as regulatory mechanisms (cf. ibid.: IV-V). Discursively, they hold the promise of being more democratic and producing fewer disadvantages – because by multiplying the correlations, the individual profile can be refined further and further without referring to classic social, political, ethnic, gender or religious categories for profiling and regulation (cf. ibid.: IX). But these last points in particular seem to be problematic in at least two respects: First, the authors seem to see no relationship between data doubles and users at all. Considering the numerous fields of application of algorithmic governmentality beyond personalisation – such as education, insurance, health, or job search – and the debates about algorithmic bias and racialisation (see, among others, Gates 2014; Kember 2013; Monea 2019; O'Neil 2016; Wachter-Boettcher 2017), this decoupling of digital and physical worlds risks a theoretical depoliticisation. Secondly, with a view to actually quite diverse mechanisms of algorithmic recommendation systems (cf. Unternährer 2021), the conclusions seem incomplete and too generalising. For example, on streaming platforms, the rhetoric of algorithmic personalisation also obscures collaborative filtering and stereotypical clustering, which can reinforce gender and age biases (e.g., by correlating gender and genre) (cf. Lin et al. 2019; Unternäher 2021), among other things, and so modulates specific viewer subjects (Kellogg et al. 2020).

Cheney-Lippold offers a different and a more productive perspective on the relationship between data doubles and users. Factoring in the real consequences that data doubles have in the offline world, while acknowledging "the gaps that define the junction between datafied and nondatafied life" (2017: 179), he suggests calling subject positions and relations produced in states' and companies' apparatuses of dataveillance "algorithmic identities" (2017: 154). He sees these subject positions as multiple, i.e., the systems of datafication position the user in multiple ways by endlessly correlating profiles and data shadows with physical bodies (ibid.). It is a logic that locates and relocates identities flexibly and provisionally, depending on the data collected: it produces not subjects, but "as if" subjects (ibid.), relational associations and estimations. Cheney-Lippold, therefore, is careful not to speak of the "datafied subject", but of "datafied subject relations", emphasising that algorithmic identities do not "perfectly align with the lived experiences we have in a data world" (ibid.: 158-159). The relationship between power and subject is considered indirect, implying "identificatory messiness" and imprecision (ibid.: 171). Data shadows do not need to perfectly mirror our self-conception, experience or self-description; nevertheless, they structure and condition our possibilities for action, knowledge, access, etc. Without relying on internalisation of the gaze or symbolic interpellation presupposing a reflexive subject, the algorithmic identity is "not identified according to a pre-existing, one-to-one relationship of one's self. Rather, the subject is understood in the context of statistical estimation that fills the holes of existing data with new algorithmic approximation" (ibid.: 170). According to Cheney-Lippold, this anti-essentialist flexibility and the intermingling of technological and bodily components in data apparatuses, which render obsolete the idea of a stable, authentic, organic centre of the self, show striking and alarming parallels to posthumanist and neomaterialist conceptualisations of the self (ibid.: 162-164), making them both liberating and problematic. Extending this analysis to economic datafication and platform surveillance, the flexibility and provisionality of datafied subject positions also indicates that they reflect actual and expected consume choices: as algorithmic identities, we are what we consume or are required to consume.

Therefore, it can be assumed that datafication and algorithmic control do not suspend subjectivation, but rather complicate it and enforce both new and old ways of subjectivation and objectivation. This means that categories such as gender, age, class and race, which are gaining increasing attention in surveillance studies (Dubrofsky and Magnet 2015; Browne 2015; Conrad 2009), take on special relevance for investigations of a networked digital capitalism. For example, not all bodies are subjected in the same way to the exposure, economisation of attention, automated censorship and content moderation on popular platforms for sharing images (Gillespie 2018; Müller-Helle 2020; Roberts 2019). Nudity, female nipples, scars, bodily fluids or pubic hair, for instance, are regularly banned from Instagram (Byström et al. 2017; Gerling et al. 2018), while TikTok gets negative press for shadow banning LGBTQ-related tags or suppressing black or disabled creators – raising questions about the relationship between moderation, discrimination, normalisation and economics. Image sets that can be retrieved from social media platforms without compensation, and are destined to train algorithms, are known to demonstrate racial and gender bias or lack of diversity (Buolamwini/Gebru 2018; Crawford/Paglen 2019; Monea 2019). As Arruda dos Santos et al. show in this issue, algorithmic bias can also take the form of economic and capitalist bias, even extending into political discourses and activism (see the contribution "Images of Resistance"). Moreover, acknowledging the gaps between datafied and nondatafied lives also opens space for conceiving resistance to, and the everyday failures and imprecision of surveillance capitalism.

Apart from social media environments, the creation of "data doubles" is, to give another example, a crucial element of border control. There, it serves governmental ends in supporting transversal and calm regimes of surveillance. As the contributions by Mark Adrejevic and Volcic Zala, and by Carolina Sanchez Boe and Henry Mainsah show, micropolitical actions at different national frontiers modulate datafied subjects by monitoring their movements in online and offline spaces. Haggerty and Ericson, who not only coined the term "surveillance assemblage" but also made use of the notion of the "data double" or "data shadow", state that within these rhizomatic structures, new corporal hybrids come into being that transcend the human body to a virtual configuration of data material (Haggerty/Ericson 2000). In this context, not only a new form of policing subjectivation takes place in the sense of Rancière or Foucault, but also an objectivation that decides upon inclusion and exclusion (Rogers 2015). Boe and Mainsah, for example, help us to understand how a seemingly "mild" and "harmless" form of border enforcement via an app used by the US Immigration and Customs Enforcement, may not only shape a certain subject of the individual user but, by creating a quantified and administered "data double", also shapes the imaginary and the social visibility of the "asylum seeker". This special issue, therefore, is interested in exploring the manifold ways in which silent and scopic forms of power, aesthetics and operativity form alliances, and presents case studies observing emergent power constellations and provisional subjectivities.

Contributions

The special issue opens with a section on image platforms, which discusses the commodification of networked images on Western and Chinese social media. Against the background of current research on automated emotion recognition and sentiment analysis based on images posted on social media platforms, Michelle Henning argues for a deconstruction of the inherently positivist conception of images as given data. Instead, her article "Kind of Blue: Social Media Photography and Emotion" draws on concepts from the history of painting such as the symptom, which allows for incoherent and ambiguous readings. In order to take the symbolic action and cultural significance of networked images seriously, it is necessary to consider not only their quantifiable but also their qualitative dimension, their embeddedness in aesthetic, social and emotional realms.

The study "Embedding Heterogenous Forms of Surveillance in China's Autocratic Networked Media: How the Government Supports and Controls Platforms, Companies, Online Celebrities, and Users" by Cornelia Bogen illustrates the Chinese state's political interdependence with online platforms. The author demonstrates that China's model of media surveillance goes beyond the Western regulatory regime of surveillance capitalism, as the legal and infrastructural possibilities of state control in China run much deeper. The author makes a valuable contribution to an intercultural differentiation of the main topic of the journal.

The paper "Black Squares and Gucci: Networked Images and the (In)Visibility of Surveillance" by Sascha Hosters and Silke Roesler-Keilholz examines connected images at the intersection of fashion and social media. The authors examine social awareness campaigns on Instagram and analyse the problematic relationship between socio-political activism and the business model of global corporations and online platforms. This detailed investigation shows how political campaigns and their content become the subject of data surveillance and commercial interests.

The section closes with the article "Automating Platform Spectators: Algorithmic Montage and Affective Scroll in TikTok" by Alexandra Anikina. This paper focuses on a central site for networked images: the platform TikTok established by ByteDance. Through the development of concepts such as affective scrolling and algorithmic montage, Anikina understands spectatorship as a central part of a surveillance capitalist logic of the moving image. The author discusses how the platform captures the attention of user-spectators and how their agency is necessary for the functioning of algorithmic montage in the first place.

The papers in the second section discuss the anaestheticisation and operativity of images from different perspectives. The contribution by Mark Andrejevic and Volcic Zala considers the role that automated vision plays in the production of "operational images". In this context, the two authors support the thesis that the iconic character of visual representations is broken down into operative features by automated recording systems and thus fundamentally transformed. This new dimension of operative images opens fresh scope for action and design of the mode of governance, which the two authors aim to make visible and expressible.

In their contribution to this issue, Peter Gentzel, Jeffrey Wimmer and Ruben Schlagowski unfold the nexus between surveillance capitalism and cartographic infrastructure through an analysis of the technical development and networked visuality of Google Maps as a platform. Building on this media historical account, their paper discusses empirical findings that are based on user interviews documenting the operativity of Google Maps as well as on the development of an app that maps the "hidden cultures" of a medium-sized city in Germany.

The underlying power mechanisms of logistical media also play a decisive role in Armin Beverungen's text "The Invisualities of Capture in Amazon's Logistical Operations". Drawing on theoretical discussions and field research alike, Beverungen analyses visual and nonvisual strategies of surveillance in Amazon's warehouses. He explains in detail how the automated operability of these infrastructural spaces makes use of the barcode as a calm image embedded into networks of capture and capitalist platform seeing.

The third section deals with computer vision and its different applications in networked media. In his article "Apple Memories and Automated Memory-Making: The Networked Image Inside the iPhone Chip", Gabriel Pereira extends the concept of platform seeing from an operation based on an extractive impulse in social media to on-device image curation through Apple Memories in the iPhone. As part of Apple's ecosystem of software and hardware products, the app's infrastructure, namely the chip, serves to realise a platform and infrastructure power within surveillance capitalism. Pereira discusses how this form of power and value creation seeks to penetrate personal and intimate memories and create an affective dependency on the company's products.

How capitalist logics are inscribed in online activism and data tools is the question guiding the interdisciplinary research group from Brazil – Vicinius Ariel Arruda dos Santos, Bruno Moreschi, Amanda Jurno, Didiana Prata, Monique Lemos, Lucas Nunes Sequeira – in their practice-oriented work "Images of Resistance: Thinking about Computer Vision AI in Surveillance Capitalism through Images of Marielle Franco". To test and investigate computer vision tools, the team collected images of online activist posts on Black Lives Matter and the murder of Marielle Franco, a Brazilian Black lesbian feminist. Rather than contributing to an understanding of the structure of political movements and emancipatory demands, they describe how AI made visible the way that image content is classified as consumer objects that reinforce inherent biases and patterns of discrimination.

Issues of subjectivation and normalisation are of the key focus of the fourth section. Building on the classical theory of the gaze by Jacques Lacan, Jens Schröter discusses the notion of a digital, capitalist gaze situated in the context of contemporary media technologies such as social media and networked images. He identifies how these technologies are already deeply embedded in surveillance capitalism and proposes describing the resulting structures of the gaze as circulative and centroramatic.

In her article "Nudged to Normal: Images, Behaviour and the Autism Surveillance Complex", Daniela Wentz investigates various digital technologies that have been developed for use in autism therapy. The focus of this work is on wearables based on Google's smart glasses, which aim to teach social interaction skills to children diagnosed with autism spectrum disorder. Against this background, the paper critically analyses the role of images and their operational logic and datafication for the human-machine constellation, and shows that these technologies are not innocent but have a commercial background that the author uncovers.

The final section is dedicated to methodological reflections. In their co-authored paper, anthropologist Carolina Sanchez Boe and design scholar Henry Mainsah give insight into their collaborative method, investigating the digital confinement app SmartLink®. The app is deployed by ICE (US Immigration and Customs Enforcement) as mobile technology for border enforcement and surveillance of asylum seekers. The authors present and reflect on several approaches such as walkthroughs through the app, anthropological filmmaking, interface critique and interviews. These strategies form an experimental set of digital methods and personal alliances that not only involve Boe and Mainsah but also a participant with personal experience using the app and her lawyer.

In their contribution "Urban Data Analytics as Research Topic, Method and Ethical Concern" the authors Daniel Trottier, Ju-Sung Lee and John Boy address ethical concerns arising from a datafied urban ethnography that deals with "disparate forms of public data such as reviews, blog posts, and open data from municipalities and other organizations". The article examines the problems of public data collection in a Dutch city. The following topics are addressed: social exclusion, inequality in the data space, and the relevance of data representation for the image of a city.

References

Agre, Philip (1994): "Surveillance and Capture: Two Models of Privacy." In: The Information Society 10/2, pp. 101-27.

Allmer, Thomas (2015): Critical Theory and Social Media: Between Emancipation and Commodification. New York: Routledge.

Andrejevic, Mark (2007): "Surveillance in the Digital Enclosure." In: The Communication Review 10/4, pp. 295-317.

Andrejevic, Mark (2012): "Exploitation in the Data Mine." In: Fuchs, Christian et al. (eds.): Internet and Surveillance: The Challenges of Web 2.0 and Social Media. New York: Routledge, pp. 71-88.

Ball, Kirstie (2019): "Review of Zuboff's *The Age of Surveillance Capitalism: The Fight for a Human Future at the New Frontier of Power.*" In: Surveillance & Society 17, 1/2, pp. 252-256.

Barbrook, Richard (1998): "The High-Tech Gift Economy." In: First Monday, 3/12 (https://firstmonday.org/ojs/index.php/fm/article/view/631/552).

Beller, Jonathan (2006): The Cinematic Mode of Production: Attention Economy and the Society of the Spectacle. Lebanon, NH: Dartmouth Coll. Press.

Browne, Simone (2015): Dark Matters: On the Surveillance of Blackness. Durham/London: Duke Univ. Press.

Bryson, Norman (1983): Vision and Painting: The Logic of the Gaze. New Haven, London: Yale Univ. Press.

Bucher, Taina (2016): "Want to Be on Top? Algorithmic Power and the Threat of Invisibility on Facebook." In: Chun, Wendy et al. (eds.): New Media, Old Media: A History and Theory Reader. New York: Routledge, pp. 566-578.

Bucher, Taina (2018): If...Then. Algorithmic Power and Politics. New York: Oxford Univ. Press.

Buolamwini, Joy/Gebru, Timnit (2018): "Gender Shades: Intersectional Accuracy Disparities in Commercial Gender Classification." In: Conference on Fairness, Accountability and Transparency, pp. 77-91.

Buschauer, Regine (2016): Datavisions – On Panoptica, Oligoptica, and (Big) Data. In: International Review of Information Ethics 24, pp. 5-14.

Byström, Arvida/Soda, Molly/Kraus, Chris. (eds.) (2017): Pics or it Didn't Happen. Images Banned from Instagram. New York: Prestel.

Castells, Manuel (2010): The Rise of Network Society: With a New Preface. Chichester: Willey-Blackwell.

Cheney-Lippold, John (2017): We Are Data: Algorithms and The Making of Our Digital Selves. New York: New York Univ. Press.

Clarke, Roger (1988): "Information Technology and Dataveillance." In: Communications of the ACM 31/5, pp. 498-512.

Cohen, Julie E. (2019): "Review of Zuboff's *The Age of Surveillance Capitalism: The Fight for a Human Future at the New Frontier of Power*. Surveillance & Society 17(1/2): 240-245.

Coifman, Benjamin, et al. (1998): "A Real-Time Computer Vision System for Vehicle Tracking and Traffic Surveillance." In: Transportation Research Part C: Emerging Technologies 6/4, pp. 271-288.

Conrad, Kathryn (2009): "Surveillance, Gender, and the Virtual Body in the Information Age." In: Surveillance & Society 6/4, pp. 380-387.

Crawford, Kate/Paglen, Trevor (2019): "Excavating AI: The Politics of Images in Machine Learning Training Sets." Retrieved from: https://excavatingai.com/

Creeber, Glen (2013): Small Screen Aesthetics: From TV to the Internet. London: BFI, Palgrave Macmillan.

Crogan, Patrick/Kinsley, Samuel (2012): "Paying Attention: Towards a Critique of The Attention Economy." In: Culture Machine 13, pp. 1-29.

Cubitt, Sean et al. (2021) "Ambient Images." In: The Nordic Journal of Aesthetics 61/62, pp. 68-77.

Deleuze, Gilles (1992): "Postscript on the Societies of Control." In: October, 59, pp. 3-7.

Doctorow, Cory (2020): How to Destroy Surveillance Capitalism. New York: Stonesong Digital.

Dubrofsky, Rachel E./Magnet, Shoshana Amielle (eds.) (2015): Feminist Surveillance Studies. Durham, London: Duke Univ. Press.

Evangelista, Rafael (2018): "Review of Zuboff's *The Age of Surveillance Capitalism: The Fight for a Human Future at the New Frontier of Power*." In: Surveillance & Society 17, 1/2: pp. 246-251.

Farocki, Harun (2004): "Phantom Images." In: Public 29, pp. 13–22.

Franck, Georg (1998): Ökonomie der Aufmerksamkeit. München: Carl Hanser.

Fuchs, Christian (2012): "Dallas Smythe Today – The Audience Commodity, the Digital Labour Debate, Marxist Political Economy and Critical Theory: Prolegomena to a Digital Labour Theory of Value." In: tripleC 10/2, pp. 692-740.

Fuchs, Christian (2014): Social Media: A Critical Introduction. London: SAGE.

Fuchs, Christian (2013): "Class and Exploitation on the Internet." In: Scholz, Trebor (ed.), Digital Labor. The Internet as Playground and Factory. New York: Routledge, pp. 211-224.

Gates, Kelly (2014): "Can Computers Be Racist?" In: Juniata Voices 15, pp. 5-17.

Geiger, Jeffrey/Littau, Karin (2013): "Introduction: Cinematicity and Comparative Media." Geiger/Littau (eds.) Cinematicity in Media History. Edinburgh: Edinburgh University Press, pp. 1-18.

Gerling, Winfried/Holschbach, Susanne/Löffler, Petra (2018): Bilder verteilen. Fotografische Praktiken in der digitalen Kultur. Bielefeld: Transcript.

Gerlitz, Carolin/Helmond, Anne (2013): "The Like Economy: Social Buttons and the Data-Intensive Web." In: New Media & Society 15/8, pp. 1348–1365.

Gillespie, Tarleton (2018): Custodians of the Internet: Platforms, Content Moderation and the Hidden Decisions that Shape Social Media. New Haven, London: Yale Univ. Press.

Goldhaber, Michael H. (1997): "The Attention Economy and the Net." In: First Monday 2/4. (http://firstmonday.org/article/view/519/44).

Haggerty, Kevin D. (2006): "Tear Down the Walls: On Demolishing the Panopticon." In: Lyon, David (ed.), Theorizing Surveillance. London, Willan: pp. 23-45.

Haggerty, Kevin D./Ericson, Richard V. (2000): "The Surveillant Assemblage." In: British Journal of Sociology 51, pp. 605-622.

Hands, Joss (2013): Introduction: Politics, Power and 'Platformativity'. In: Culture Machine 14, pp. 1-9.

Heilmann, Till A. (2015): "Datenarbeit Im 'Capture'-Kapitalismus." In: Zeitschrift für Medienwissenschaft 13, pp. 35–47.

Helmond, Anne (2015): "The Platformization of the Web: Making Web Data Platform Ready." In: Social Media + Society 1/2, pp. 1-11.

Huberman, Jenny (2021): "Amazon Go, Surveillance Capitalism, and the Ideology of Convenience." In: Economic Anthropology 8.2, pp. 337-349.

Illouz, Eva (2007): Cold Intimacies: The Making of Emotional Capitalism. London: Polity Press.

Introna, Lucas/Wood, David (2004): Picturing Algorithmic Surveillance: The Politics of Facial Recognition Systems. In: Surveillance & Society 2/2,3, pp. 177-198.

Jenkins, Henry/Ford, Sam/Green, Joshua (2018) Spreadable Media: Creating Value and Meaning in a Networked Culture. New York: New York University Press.

Jones, Graeme A./Nikos Paragios/Carlo S. Regazzoni (eds.) (2012): Video-Based Surveillance Systems: Computer Vision and Distributed Processing. Wiesbaden: Springer Science & Business Media.

Jurgenson, Nathan (2019): The Social Photo: On Photography and Social Media. London Verso.

Kammerer, D./Waitz, T. (2015): Überwachung und Kontrolle. Einleitung in den Schwerpunkt. In: Zeitschrift für Medienwissenschaft 13, pp. 10-20.

Kaul, Vivek/Enslin, Sarah/Gross, Seth (2020): "History of Artificial Intelligence in Medicine." In: Gastrointestinal Endoscopy 92.4, pp. 807-812.

Kellogg, Katherine C., Valentine, Melissa A., Christin, Angele (2020): "Algorithms at Work: The New Contested Terrain of Control." In: Academy of Management Annals 14, pp. 366-410.

Kember, Sarah (2013): "Gender Estimation in Face Recognition Technology: How Smart Algorithms Learn to Discriminate." In: Media Fields Journal 7, pp. 1-10.

Kumar, Dinesh/Aadarsh, S./Kumar, Hari (2020): "Border Surveillance System Using Computer Vision." In: 2020 6th International Conference on Advanced Computing and Communication Systems (ICACCS), IEEE.

Langlois, Ganaele/Elmer, Greg (2013): "The Research Politics of Social Media Platforms." In: Culture Machine 14, pp. 1-17.

Lin, Kun et al. (2019): "Crank Up the Volume: Preference Bias Amplification in Collaborative Recommendation." In: arXiv, eprint arXiv:1909.06362.

Lunenfeld, Peter (2000): "Digital Photography: The Dubitative Image." In: Lunenfeld (ed.): Snap to Grid: A User's Guide to Digital Arts, Media, and Cultures. Cambrigde/MA, pp. 55–69.

Mackenzie, Adrian/Munster, Anna (2019): "Platform Seeing: Image Ensembles and their Invisualities." In: Theory, Culture & Society 36, pp. 3-22.

Maeder, Dominik/Wentz, Daniela (2014): "Digital Seriality as Structure and Process." In: Eludamos. Journal for Computer Game Culture 8/1: pp. 129-149.

Manovich, Lev (1996): "The Automation of Sight: From Photography to Computer Vision." In: Electronic Culture: Technology and Visual Representation, pp. 229-239.

Monea, Alexander (2019): "Race and Computer Vision." In: Sudmann, Andreas (ed.), The Democratization of Artificial Intelligence: Net Politics in the Era of Learning Algorithms. Bielefeld, Transcript: pp. 189-208.

Moskatova, Olga (2020): "Überschuss, Detail, Bewegung. Zur ortspezifischen Ästhetik und Cinematizität der GIFs. " In: nach dem film 18 (https://nachdemfilm.de/issues/text/ueberschuss-detail-bewegung).

Moskatova, Olga (2022, forthcoming): "Loop: Zur chronischen Temporalität digitaler Serialität." In: Grampp, Sven/Podrez, Peter/Wiedenmann, Nicoel (eds.), Medien | Zeiten. Interdependenzen. Wiesbaden: Springer.

Mühlhoff, Rainer (2018): "'Digitale Entmündigung' und 'User Experience Design'." In: Leviathan – Berliner Zeitschrift für Sozialwissenschaft 46/4, pp. 551-74.

Müller-Helle, Katja (ed.) (2020): Bildzensur. Löschung technischer Bilder. Bildwelten des Wissens. Berlin, De Gruyter.

Murakami Wood, David/Monahan, Torin (2019): "Editorial: Platform Surveillance." In: Surveillance & Society 17, 1/2: pp. 1-6.

Nainggolan, Era Ahmad Syahputra/Mustakim, Mustakim (2021): "Computer Vision For Monitoring The Use Of Masks In The Pandemic." In: *ITTPCOVID19* 1/1, pp. 1-11.

Nguyen, Kien Trun (2020): "Care of the Self in the Age of Algorithms: Early Thoughts from a Foucauldian Perspective." In: Journal of Science Ho Chi Minh City Open University 10/1, pp. 79-90.

O'Neil, Cathy (2016): Weapons of Math Destruction: How Big Data Increases Inequality and Threatens Democracy. New York: Crown.

Olague, Gustavo (2016): Evolutionary Computer Vision: The First Footprints. Wiesbaden: Springer.

Paglen, Trevor (2016): "Invisible Images (Your Pictures Are Looking at You)." https://thenewinquiry.com/invisible-images-your-pictures-are-looking-at-you/ (01/21/2021)

Roberts, Sarah T. (2019): Behind the Screen: Content Moderation in the Shadows of Social Media. New Haven, London: Yale Univ. Press.

Rogers, Christina (2015): "Wenn Data stirbt. Grenzen, Kontrolle, Migration." In: Zeitschrift für Medienwissenschaft 13, pp. 57-65.

Rosamond, Emily (2017): "It Sees (Notes Toward a Cultural History of Financial Vision)." In: Gloerich et al. (eds.) Moneylab Reader 2: Overcoming the Hype, Amsterdam, pp. 110–114.

Rothöhler, Simon (2018a): Das verteilte Bild. Stream, Archiv, Ambiente. Paderborn: Fink.

Rothöhler, Simon (2018b): "Calm Images: Bildproliferation und Bildlosigkeit im Internet der Dinge." In: Merkur 72, 32-42.

Rothöhler, Simon (2021): "Calm Images: The Invisible Visual Culture of Digital Image Distribution." In: Moskatova, Olga (ed.), Images on the Move: Materiality – Networks – Formats. Bielefeld: Transcript, pp. 73-86.

Rouvroy, Antoinette (2013): "The End(s) of Critique: Data-Behaviourism vs. Due-Process." In: Hildebrandt, M., de Vries, K. (eds.), Privacy, Due Process and the Computational Turn. New York: Routledge, pp. 143-168.

Rouvroy, Antoinette/Berns, Thomas 2013): "Gouvernementalité algorithmique et perspectives d'émancipation." In: Réseaux 177, pp. 163-196.

Rubinstein, Daniel/Sluis, Katrina (2008): "A Life More Photographic. Mapping the Networked Image." In: Photographies 1, pp. 9-28.

Scholz, Trebor (2012) (ed.): Digital Labor: The Internet as Playground and Factory. London: Routledge.

Shifman, Limor (2014): Memes in Digital Culture. Cambridge, MA: MIT Press.

Srnicek, Nick (2017): Platform Capitalism. Cambridge, Malden, MA: Polity

Steyerl, Hito (2007): "Documentary Uncertainty." In: Aprior 7, p. 2-3.

Stork, David (2009): "Computer Vision and Computer Graphics Analysis of Paintings and Drawings: An Introduction to the Literature." In: Xiaoyi/Nicolai (eds.), CAIP'09: Proceedings of the 13th International Conference on Computer Analysis of Images and Patterns. Berlin: Springer, pp. 9-24.

Strick, Simon (2021): Rechte Gefühle: Affekte und Strategien des digitalen Faschismus. Bielefeld: Transcript.

Tanni, Valentina (2020): Mesmetica: Il settembre eterno dell'arte. Rome: Nero Editions.

Terranova, Tiziana (2012): "Attention, Economy and the Brain." In: Culture Machine 13, 1-19.

Trottier, Daniel (2012): Social Media as Surveillance: Rethinking Visibility in A Converging World, Ashgate: Surrey/Burlington.

Trottier, Daniel/Lyon, David (2012): "Key Features of Social Media Surveillance." In: Fuchs, Christian. et al. (eds.), Internet and Surveillance: The Challenges of Web 2.0 and Social Media. New York, London: Routledge, pp. 89-105.

Uhlin, Graig (2014): "Playing in the Gif(t) Economy." In: Games and Culture 9/6: pp. 517–527.

Unternährer, Markus (2021): "Die Ordnung der Empfehlung." In: Kölner Zeitschrift für Soziologie und Sozialpsychologie 73, pp. 397-423.

van Dijck, José (2014): "Datafiction, Dataism and Dataveillance: Big Data between Scientific Paradigm and Secular Belief." In: Surveillance & Society 12/2, pp. 197-208.

van Dijck, José/Poell, Thomas/de Waal, Martijn (2018): The Platform Society: Public Values in a Connective World. Oxford: Oxford Univ. Press.

van Dijk, José (2013): The Culture of Connectivity: A Critical History of Social Media. Oxford: Oxford Univ. Press.

Veel, Kristin (2012): "Calm Imaging: The Conquest of Overload and the Conditions of Attention." In: Ekman, U. (ed.), Throughout: Art and Culture Emerging with Ubiquitous Computing. Cambridge MA.: MIT Press, pp. 119-132.

Wachter-Boettcher, Sara (2017): Technically Wrong: Sexist Apps, Biased Algorithms, and Other Threats of Toxic Tech. New York/London: W.W. Norton & Company.

Webb, Thomas (2021): "Exercise in Hopeless Nostalgia: World Wide WEBB." (https://www.koeniggalerie.com/exhibitions/30644/exercise-in-hopeless-nostalgia-world-wide-webb/).

Webb, Thomas/Reese, Julia (2021): "Paradise in 4 Megabytes: Interview with Thomas Webb." (https://www.fraeulein-magazine.eu/paradise-in-4-megabytes-interview-with-thomas-webb/).

Weiser, Mark/Brown, John Seely (1997): "The Coming Age of Calm Technology." In: Denning, P.J./Metcalfe, R. M. (eds.), Beyond Calculation: The Next Fifty Years of Computing. New York, Springer, pp. 75-85.

Weiser, Mark/Brown, John Seely (1995): "Designing Calm Technology." Xerox PARC, (http://www.ubiq.com/weiser/calmtech/calmtech.htm).

Zuboff, Shoshana (2015): "Big Other: Surveillance Capitalism and the Prospects of an Information Civilization." In: Journal of Information Technology 30, pp. 75-89.

Zuboff, Shoshana (2019): The Age of Surveillance Capitalism: The Fight for a Human Future at the New Frontier of Power. London: Profile.

Image Platforms

Kind of Blue
Social Media Photography and Emotion

Michelle Henning

Abstract

This paper considers emotion recognition and sentiment analysis in relation to social media photographs. It addresses this as part of a larger regime of surveillance and control, in which photographs are treated as symptoms for a diagnosis, and are quantified as data. Automated emotion recognition approaches are capable in principle of analysing the visual qualities of social photos insofar as these can be measured and represented numerically. In reducing the photograph to data, they select out features of the image, as a means to explain or describe a mental state that lies behind or beyond the image. To treat photographs as emotionally expressive goes against the historical idea of the photograph as objective recording. Originally, the idea that photographs could move their viewers was linked to the sense of photography as detached documentation. Today, more and more people take and share photographs as part of a larger shift in emotional culture, which places a therapeutic sense of self at the heart of economy and governance. Yet while people use mobile phone photos as a means of expressive documentation and self-representation, emotion recognition relies on a behaviourist and positivist model that is indifferent to their intentions and to culture, and which is premised on a myth of total knowledge.

Keywords

Photography, Social Media, Emotion Recognition, Behaviorism, Emotional Capitalism

Kind of Blue: Social Media Photography and Emotion

Automated techniques of mood tracking, emotion recognition and sentiment analysis are currently on the rise across several industries, drawing on massive amounts of data accumulated via people's social media feeds and mobile phone apps. They are part of new developments in artificial intelligence (AI) and affective computing (computing that concerns itself with emotion and affect). They classify and analyse text, emojis, images and video. Emotion detection algorithms also sort through data on facial, vocal and bodily behaviours supplied by cameras, microphones and other less visible sensors built into mobile phones, such as the accelerometer and gyroscope. These tools (some of which are publicly and commercially available) are machine learning systems, trained on datasets labelled by armies of low paid casualised workers including Amazon Mechanical Turk workers (Zylinska 2021: 242-249). Their uses vary and include brand reputation management, recruitment, targeted marketing, political campaigning, academic research, policing, border control and healthcare.

Emotion recognition or sentiment analysis tools are controversial for several reasons. They involve not only the identification and prediction of emotional states but, inevitably, the attempt to shape or direct them. Arguably, such tools, deployed by the social media platforms, have contributed to the heightening of political polarisation. They also raise issues of respect for privacy and for human autonomy, as participants rarely, if ever, give informed consent (Andalibi/Buss 2020; Wongkoblap/Vadillo/Curcin 2017). Furthermore, since mental health is connected to emotional expression, they may transgress laws and medical ethics relating to health data (Schneble/Elger/Shaw 2020).[1] Developments in machine learning mean that the methods by which people are classified are increasingly black-boxed and unavailable to human interpretation (Wongkoblap/Vadillo/Curcin 2017). The use of psychological profiling and facial recognition are considered particularly problematic. Facial recognition systems emerge from a biometrics industry tightly linked to state security legislation and are trained on datasets with inbuilt discriminatory assumptions about race and gender such as the ImageNet dataset (Gates 2006; Shankar et al. 2017; Crawford/Paglen 2019). Their use for purposes of emotion detection also notoriously relies on a disputed biologistic classification of discrete emotions and supposedly universal expressions, derived from the work of Paul Ekman, which also raises doubts about the validity of its results (Leys 2010). Nevertheless, the great majority of emotion detection studies now make use of facial recognition.

Profiling is used to predict people's actions, preferences or responses, as the computational sciences draw on psychological scales originally devised for therapeutic purposes (Stark 2018: 206). It has been argued that individuals are increasingly acclimatised to psychological profiles as a means of self-understanding or self-objectification – for example, via online quizzes or early internet dating sites (Illouz 2007: 75). Yet most people have no control over, and little insight into, how their social media posts are being used to construct profiles. Concerns have been raised about the "performative power" of these profiles, which provoke feelings

---

1   In 2017, a systematic review of 48 English language articles using social media for predictive analytics in mental health noted a general neglect of ethical issues by these studies, and that none of the studies used clinical diagnosis as their measure for depression, using surveys instead (Wongkoblap/Vadillo/Curcin 2017).

and engineer behaviours, often on the fly (Stark 2018: 213). Although the notion of profiling suggests something static, social media feeds can be adjusted in real time, dynamically and responsively, as part of an ongoing process of mood-tracking, which works to ensure people remain "hooked" to their devices (Davies 2017).

In the following discussion, I set out to add a new perspective to the growing literature critiquing emotion recognition, by considering the role of photographic images. Currently, the analysis of the visual qualities of photographs (as opposed to the objects depicted in them) is not a major aspect of sentiment and emotion detection and prediction. Nevertheless, scores of international university research teams have showcased projects using social media photos for "depression detection" and sometimes in relation to the identification of personality traits (some of these are discussed below). It is unclear to me to what extent such studies are also being done by the social media platforms themselves, so my examples derive from these academic studies.[2] To read them is to experience a strange historical vertigo as the discussion of "convolutional neural networks" collides with old-fashioned aesthetic strictures, and claims about faces and personality that seem to have come straight from the 19th-century pseudo-sciences of physiognomy and phrenology. If I seem impatient with such studies, it is first because many combine what I consider bad science (such as Ekman's biologistic classification of the emotions) with bad aesthetic theory, baking into their technology arbitrary judgments about what is "good" and "interesting" and what makes "aesthetic sense"; and second, because they are almost always framed as a public health good (e.g., for suicide prevention), and are at best naive regarding the other obvious applications for their methods (e.g., to discriminate against depressed people or to select "agreeable and conscientious" personality types in job recruitment).[3]

Photography and Self-Expression

The fact that social media photographs are being seen as a valid resources for this kind of study is a consequence of at least three factors. First, there is the direction taken in contemporary AI research, which supports the accumulation of vast amounts of data and inevitably takes in the huge volumes of photographs being

2   I read overviews of the field such as Wongkoblap/Vadillo/Curcin 2017, and trawled through academic databases such as PubMed and IEEE Xplore for articles and conference papers from the past five years.
3   In 2019, Business Insider reported that Facebook was using a suicide risk detection algorithm, although not in the EU, where it would breach the General Data Protection Regulation (GDPR), and that this raised concerns about data privacy (Goggin 2019). The phrase "agreeable and conscientious" is used in Liu et al.'s 2016 paper on how personality traits could be predicted through social media profile pictures.

generated daily by people with mobile phone-cameras. Kate Crawford summarises that it is now "common practice for the first steps of creating a computer vision system to scrape thousands – or even millions – of images from the internet, create and order them into a series of classifications, and use this as a foundation for how the system will perceive observable reality" (2021: 96). Studies describe these as "images collected from the wild" (e.g., Balouchian/Foroosh 2018; Vadicamo et al. 2017). The phrase "in the wild" has some specific meanings in the computer sciences, referring to data or technologies that are currently in the public domain and in public use, or no longer under the control of their makers, or to datasets that are *"not constructed and designed with research questions in mind"* (Ang et al. 2013: 39, original emphasis). Such data is also referred to as "foraged" and "found". As the metaphors suggest, social media images are considered fair game for researchers, a view underpinned by the assumption that they are reducible to "data" and are therefore merely "raw" material ripe for analysis (Gitelman 2013).

A second factor is the growth of stock photography, the influence of which is clearly evident in these datasets of images from "the wild".[4] For example, a 2018 study boasted "the largest dataset of images collected from the wild" using keyword searches on Flickr and the Bing internet search engine (Balouchian/Foroosh 2018: 1932). Yet as their own illustration reveals, the images are classic stock and stock-style images, which the search algorithms already push to the top: "happiness" is attached to photographs of white pregnant women taken in the so-called magic hour, in natural settings with shallow depth of field, their arms folded around their bellies; images of graduating students, cheering and smiling in groups, again with the background thrown out of focus; posed images of good looking, casually dressed young white people on a summer's day, grouped around a table laden with food, or around a barbecue, or gathered on a rock to watch the sunset. No-one is pulling the wrong face, no-one has their eyes closed, no head blocks another, nothing jars. These images are emphatic, promotional images, designed to *illustrate* concepts and sentiments. They tell us nothing about the emotional state of the photographer or of the person who put the image into the public space.

A third factor, and the one I will focus on here, is that people do take photographs as a means of self-expression, so that it does not seem outrageous to claim that such photographs might thereby reveal emotion. Researchers in affective computing justify their studies on the basis that people upload images to "display their sentiments and emotions" (Doshi/Barot/Gavhane 2020). It seems reasonable to judge social media photographs to be sources for emotional data, if users themselves seem to be treating them as subjective and expressive. This may seem self-evident, but as I will argue, it represents a change in the culture and practice

---

4   On stock photography and picture agencies, see Frosh 2003 and Blaschke 2016.

of vernacular photography. Conceptualising photographs as primarily media for emotional self-expression is as new as treating them as data.

For the purposes of this argument, I have artificially separated still photographs from text, emoji, graphics and video. This does not reflect the contexts in which we encounter photographs, which are increasingly hard to discern or distinguish from video (especially in the cases of "live" photographs or animated gifs), and which are invariably surrounded by text, and frequently accompanied by reaction buttons (pseudo-emoji). However, this narrowing of focus will allow me to tease out what is most distinctive about the growing trend of using photographs as a means to analyse the feelings of the people taking them. Although the idea of the photographic image as subjective and expressive may seem fairly conventional today, it stands in stark contrast to early ideas about photography as an objective, mechanical way of picturing the world.

Historically, narrative film, television and video, more often than still photography, have been understood as emotionally expressive, able to make use of the emotionality of music, storytelling and performance. In photography, the tendency of the camera to record everything without hierarchy seemed to give it both scientific objectivity and emotional flatness, even though early viewers of photographs actually responded with astonishment, horror and awe at the new technology. In the mid-19th century, theories of the aesthetic encounter largely excluded photographs, which art historians and critics tended to dismiss as affectless because authored by a machine: the photographer's status was as a mere "operator", the camera a "slavish imitator" (for a quick summary, see Brown/Phu 2014: 10-13). Photographers struggled to have their work accepted as art because of this, and the notion of an expressive or subjective photography was controversial for several decades. The pictorialist photographers of the late-19th century worked hard to give atmosphere and aura to their pictures, to imprint them with the stamp of an author, and to situate them visibly in the iconographic traditions of art. Their pictures were denigrated for their pretension, their staged effects and fakery, particularly after the rise of documentary, "straight" photography and new objectivity in the 1920s and '30s.[5]

Against my claim that (outside of certain art contexts) photography was not seen as emotionally expressive, one might point to the fact that family or vernacular photographs have always been treasured, emotionally significant objects. Throughout the 20th century, photography companies exhorted people to take photographs as a means to create a personal (though standardised) record of their

---

5 As Elspeth Brown and Thy Phu note, many writers on photography have until recently tended to disavow feeling as a legitimate aspect of photography theory and criticism despite the extensive influence of Roland Barthes' *Camera Lucida* (1980), a book that prioritises the author's own affective response to photographs (Brown/Thu 2014: 2-3).

own lives, to share experiences with people, and to keep in touch with relatives and friends at a distance. These pictures quickly became "fetishes" – objects of human attachment and superstition, worn in lockets and carried in wallets, and emotionally difficult to destroy. As Roland Barthes recognised, this emotional quality of the image was not separate from, but entirely tied to its presumed objectivity, its apparent ability to record that which has been, with very little mediation. We fetishise the physical photograph because of what it represents – superstitiously, to tear a picture of a lover is to hurt them. As well as a meditation on the emotional pull of photographs, Barthes' *Camera Lucida* is also about the difficulty in separating the photograph from its referent, from the real. Elsewhere, Barthes observed that it is precisely the emotional detachment of the camera that leads to the shocking nature of images of war and violence: the shock is inseparable from its brute factual recording (Barthes 1979). To say then, that photography was not (or not usually) a medium of subjective emotional expression is not to say that it did not provoke emotions. On the contrary, it was its presumed ability to record a scene in a way that was uncoloured by subjective vision that seemed to make a photograph capable of moving a viewer.

The historical tensions between the photograph's claim to mechanical objectivity, its uncertain position as art, and its use in popular practices of self-documentation form a backdrop to present uses of social media photography as a mode of self-expression.[6] Today, people are encouraged to photograph to communicate, not just in a deictic way ("I was/am here") but expressively ("this is how I feel"). This is not to say that the documentary aspect of the photograph has been lost; far from it – the conversational or social photograph extends the documentary function of photography. As Nathan Jurgenson says "this documentary habit burrows into consciousness. [...] Life is experienced as increasingly documentable and perhaps also experienced *in the service of* its documentation, always with the newly accessible audience in mind" (Jurgenson 2019: 12, original emphasis). But this practice of documentation is not constrained by a truth to nature or commitment to recording the facts of a situation: instead, something is documented with a view to attaching a witty caption or garnering likes, to construct an image of oneself and one's life for others, or to remind one's future self of good times. Self-expression, self-presentation and documentation are mutually connected practices. Perhaps they always have been aspects of snapshot photography, but the notion of taking a photograph as a means of subjective expression takes on a new emphasis in the context of the ability to immediately circulate the image through a mobile phone.

---

6   This is a brief and very partial summary informed by a wide range of historical-theoretical studies, too many to list here. My own take on this history is presented at length in Henning 2018.

As this brief historical summary implies, I consider mobile phone and social media photographs to be cultural artefacts. I disagree with Jurgenson's claim that art historical discourse about photographs is irrelevant to this kind of practice. Jurgenson seems to reduce art history to art appreciation and debates about aesthetic value – about "good" photographs – and he claims that "the center of conceptual gravity for describing how people communicate with images today should be less art historical and more social theoretical" (Jurgenson 2019: 9). While I sympathise with his argument that photographs need to be understood as communication media, and indeed with much of what he says about the "social photo", here I will use theories of art as well, not only because they offer nuanced ways of understanding visual culture, some of which are perfectly compatible with the social photo, but also to critique the positivism inherent in this data science approach to social media photographs via Georges Didi-Huberman's critique of positivist approaches to art history.

A New Symptomology

It is easy to imagine that the most concerning issues in relation to social media photography are to do with privacy and surveillance, given the place of cameras in surveillance and photographs in revealing private information. Certainly, emotion recognition can be understood as a significant development in what Shoshana Zuboff describes as "surveillance capitalism", where human beings are tapped or "mined" for ever hungrier data markets (Zuboff 2019). As a 2018 article describing a report by Tractica, a market intelligence firm, on this expanding "market for sentiment and emotion" enthuses:

Accelerated access to data (primarily social media feeds and digital video), cheaper compute power, and evolving deep learning combined with natural language processing (NLP) and computer vision are enabling technologists to watch and listen to humans with the intention of analyzing their sentiments and emotions. (Omdia 2018)

Being watched and listened to, without one's consent (or with little knowledge of precisely what one may have consented to), without knowledge of precisely when it is happening, and without direct access to or control over the data thus produced, nor over the various other actors to whom it is disseminated, certainly constitutes a violation of privacy, but surveillance extends far beyond this. For Michel Foucault, surveillance is a means by which bodies become subject to power, rendered "docile and knowable", their behaviours subject to "progressive objectification and [...] ever more subtle partitioning" (Foucault 1979: 172-173). For Zuboff, contemporary surveillance capitalism is premised on the extractive process of transforming experience into data, which she refers to as "rendition". She describes affective computing and sentiment analysis as "a burgeoning new domain of rendition and behavioral surplus supply operations" (Zuboff 2019: 282). This process breaks with one of the principal aspects of older modes of surveillance – the emphasis on visual observation. Matthew Fuller writes, "surveillance in the present context applies very little to acts of seeing", instead it collects traces or what Fuller calls "flecks of identity" – "a trail of triggers and tokens" (2005: 149).

A token is a small symbolic gesture or a piecemeal or partial representation, but it also has the older meaning of a *symptom*. For example, in Daniel Defoe's *Journal of the Plague Year* (1722), "tokens" describes the visible symptoms that bespoke the bubonic plague, the black swellings or "buboes". Social media photographs, reduced to data, are treated by emotion recognition AI as symptoms or tokens. Carlo Ginzburg sees "symptomology" as a mode of diagnosis using "superficial symptoms or signs, often irrelevant to the eye of the layman" (1980: 12). These are the almost imperceptible traces produced involuntarily and without conscious control. Ginzburg writes: "It is one thing to analyse footprints, stars, faeces (animal or human), colds, corneas, pulses, snow-covered fields or dropped cigarette ash; and another to analyse writing or painting or speech" (ibid.: 24). He connects the spread of symptomology across a wide range of disciplines to "the emergence of an increasingly clear tendency for state power to impose a close-meshed net of control on society" (ibid.: 24).[7]

The new surveillance would *not* be a symptomology for Georges Didi-Huberman, who conceives of symptoms in the Freudian sense, where the telling detail is not the "last word" but part of a "signifying chain, sequence or *thread*" (Didi-Huberman 2005: 231, original emphasis). For Freud, the observable symptom is never a direct expression of the unconscious but is the result of a certain work or set of processes (such as repression, condensation or displacement). To read the visual symptomatically is not to look "for some supposed explanatory 'key' to the image" but to address the "work of figurability" (ibid.: 262). Didi-Huberman uses the term to suggest how intelligibility emerges from something which does not fully cohere or which exceeds representation.[8]

In "depression detection", the social photo is treated as a means to diagnose the emotional state of the person who took or posted the photograph: it is a symptomology in Ginzburg's sense, not Didi-Huberman's (indeed, I am going to suggest Didi-Huberman's symptomological approach as a corrective or antidote to this diagnostic use of photos). The photograph is read almost as an extension of the body, like the digital traces of gestures, movements and speech. In this sense it is taken to be an "expression". This has nothing to do with the conscious self-expression of the individual. As part of a larger dataset, the photograph becomes expressive regardless of its maker's intention to express anything. This expression

---

7   Ginzburg's example is Alphonse Bertillon's anthropometric police database, which combined standardised photographs with verbal description, and later, fingerprints.
8   *Figurabilité* is a neologism used in the French translation of Freud's "The Interpretation of Dreams" for the German word *Darstellbarkeit* (Parsons 2005: xviii).

is a surface effect of something happening beneath or behind the surface. What is sought behind the image is not the author, since an author is a figure conceived as having a certain amount of interpretative authority over their own work (Barthes 1968; Foucault 1980). Nor is it the unconscious, since there is no interest in the complexity of an individual psyche here: this symptomology is indifferent to the individuals it diagnoses. It seeks to directly know their emotional or affective states regardless of intention and regardless of any unconscious drives shaping or inhibiting these. These algorithmic detectives are indifferent to the intended or imagined audience, too. The expressive photo is treated as a kind of emotional outburst thrown into the void.

Tokens are also things we *exchange*, and the people exchanging photographs on social media experience these photographs as conversational and social. This is why Jurgenson calls the practice "social photography" (Jurgenson 2019). It is this social function that makes this such a rich seam for the emotion-miners to tap, because a big part of social communication is self-expression. As Jurgenson says, "for those communicating through social images, their informational qualities are a means to the end of expression" (ibid.: 18). From the perspective of emotion detection, however, expression produces information. Yet expression is also performative, its literal content mattering less than its practice: much social photography is "phatic communication" which centres around keeping in touch, building a sense of community, through performative statements which are first of all gestures, including the gesture of taking the photograph (Frosh 2012: 133; Miller 2016: 87). This lends a deliberate triviality or lightness to social media exchange (just as people verbally exchange observations about the weather, for example). Thus, emotion recognition as a kind of "mining" of either trivial or intimate expressions may seem disproportionate or intrusive.[9]

This affective turn is starting to shift the ways in which image-data is understood. Already, writers on the digital networked image argued that the digital photographic image had become a carrier for metadata more significant than its visible content (Rubinstein/Sluis 2013). This changes now that AI can decode visible content, having been trained on datasets (frequently on ImageNet) which are effectively taxonomies of objects in images. As various writers have pointed out, the AI is subject to the human bias built into the training set, which assigns

---

9   For instance, the research participants in a study by Nazanin Andalibi and Justin Buss were asked to imagine that social media sites had analysed their posts using computational techniques to "infer their emotional states". The participants considered emotions to be intimate and personal things, nuanced and hard to understand even for the person experiencing the emotions, and several found the idea of algorithms reading their emotions through their images as creepy or scary on the grounds that they had no control over this reading and what was done with it (Andalibi/Buss 2020).

fixed meanings to visual objects in highly questionable ways (Denton et al. 2020). Now, the affective turn in the computer sciences moves the question from what images represent to what they *express*. Emotions and expression are associated with the sensual qualities of images, with embodied experience and with social relations. Nevertheless, as we shall see, the formal qualities associated with expression are not divorced from data or immune to quantification. In a digital image, they are quantities as well as qualities.

For example, colour is to a great extent a subjective perceptual experience, dependent on brains and eyes but also on culture, thus the experience of colour famously varies between language groups, between individuals, and even for the same individual from moment to moment. Yet colours are also quantifiable as different wavelengths of visible light or electromagnetic radiation and, in the context of digital media, as hue and saturation values. Several studies use these to classify images (e.g., Reece/Danforth 2017; Guntuku et al. 2019; Lin et al. 2020). In one psychological "depression detection" study, colour is described as part of "the wealth of psychological data encoded in visual social media, such as photographs posted to Instagram" (Reece/Danforth 2017: 1). The study concludes that "photos posted by depressed individuals tended to be bluer, darker, and grayer" and that depressed people were more likely to use monochrome filters (ibid.: 7-8).[10] Effectively, it claims, blue Instagram posts were a sign of the blues.

Reece and Danforth's automated analysis isolated hue and saturation values from other aspects of the photograph (such as composition and form, or what was depicted in the image, for example). Although the findings of the machine learning system correlated well with the (subsequent) diagnosis of participants as depressed, it did not correlate with the labels applied by human evaluators, and they comment "when people rated a photograph as sad, that impression was unrelated to how blue, dark, or gray that photo was" (ibid.: 9). This seemed to puzzle the researchers, since "semantically these descriptions seem like they should match well with one another, as well as link to depression" (ibid.: 9). Not only does this ignore the metaphorical character of linguistic colour expressions, it ignores the way colour meanings vary with context: a grey kitten, a blue sea, a Blue Note album cover or a black and white vintage magazine image do not necessarily convey sadness. While colours affect people's moods or emotional states, and our reactions to colours involve a strong physiological and visceral aspect, colour meanings change. In the 19th century Goethe associated bright colour with "uncivilized" peoples, and monochrome with "refinement" (Taussig 2009: 3). The

---

10 They write "when depressed participants did employ filters [which they rarely did], they most disproportionately favored the 'Inkwell' filter, which converts color photographs to black-and-white images [...]. Conversely, healthy participants most disproportionately favored the Valencia filter, which lightens the tint of photos" (Reece/Danforth 2017: 8).

colour palettes of mid-20th-century cinema were likewise sometimes deliberately restrained, to avoid accusations of vulgarity and imply sophistication (Higgins 2007; Brown 2009; Street 2011). Like mid-century cinema or 19th-century fashion, Instagram has its own changeable grammar, its own mutating sets of implicit rules and taste cultures, which impact on people's uses of the platform.

Possibly the authors of this and similar studies would respond that I am making a category error, since machine learning does not concern itself with meaning, but simply makes correlations between data, here between "blue, dark and grey" photographs and a tendency to depression. Nor is any claim being made about causation. What matters instead is merely that the correlation exists. Yet the quasi-magical ability of machine learning to find correlations across vast quantities of data gives the impression of ever-growing and exhaustive knowledge, even when (as here) the obviously cultural and linguistic nature of these correlations should give us pause. Supported by the ideological belief in the objectivity of machines and automated processes – just as in the early years of photography, mechanical objectivity is taken as what Lorraine Daston and Peter Galison (2007) call an "epistemic virtue" – these correlations are sufficient to be acted on: to treat blue and grey images as factors or markers indicating suicide risk, for example. Antoinette Rouvroy explains in an interview:

Once signals have been detected, the person in question will be treated as if they have already "contracted" the risk or already "actualised" the danger, and may then, for example, have their life insurance cancelled. It is not about acting on causes but about acting pre-emptively on effects and in a way that is beneficial to those who purchase or design the algorithm, be it to increase profits or control. (Rouvroy 2020: 1-2)

Feature Extraction

In these studies, colour is reduced to one of the "features" of an image, subjected to "visual feature extraction" alongside other visual elements – such as compositional devices, sharpness and blur, foreground and background. Features are not always objectively measurable aspects of an image (such as hue and saturation) but often very subjectively arrived at. For example, in one study, which used extracted features to "score" images for their "aesthetic sense", the features included compositional balance, whether the image follows the rule of thirds, had symmetry, "good/interesting lighting" and so on (Guntuku et al. 2019: 239). The "neural network" becomes a kind of automated photography competition jury, albeit a very rigid one with deeply traditionalist aesthetics. The study concluded that "images posted by depressed and anxious users tend to be dominated by grayscale, low arousal images lacking in aesthetic sense" (ibid.: 244). However, aesthetics are not hard and fast rules but cultural standards, subject to historical change and reinvention. The rule of thirds is a compositional device modelled on older devices such as the golden section, and lighting conventions and styles also vary historically, as do ideas about the virtues of symmetry. Specific and rather clichéd cultural expectations are thus built into the algorithm.

While a digital image is, as Bernard Stiegler (2002) explained, "discrete" in its very structure, meaning entirely amenable to disassemblage and reassemblage (which in turn makes the image able to travel), it does not disassemble as an image in the way that a sentence can be taken apart into words or a word into letters. It is up to the researcher or the AI network to decide where to make the cut, to decide what must be "extracted" and what deemed waste, to define what counts as a salient "feature". This is how something as ambiguous as an image and as fuzzy as aesthetics can enter the purview of systems which only "see" data, and for which, as Geoffrey Bowker puts it, "If it's not in principle measurable, or is not being measured, it doesn't exist" (2013: 170). Arguably, to treat photographs as data is to ignore to a large extent the explicit positions they adopt vis-à-vis the world, since "data means – and has meant for a very long time – that which is given prior to argument" (Rosenberg 2013: 36). To treat photographs as data is to assume their givenness, and to assume that the act of observing or analysing them can be culturally neutral.

In the humanities, there is a tendency to associate big data studies with a kind of distant reading, set against an older art of close reading (cf. Herrnstein-Smith 2016). Yet actually, these kinds of analyses operate at shifting scales, moving between the detail and the whole. In this regard, sentiment and emotion mining resemble the art historical approach that, as Didi-Huberman says, "postulates that the whole visible can be described, cut up into its components [...] and wholly accounted for" (2005: 231). The "whole visible" in our case is the corpus, the colossal and ever-growing accumulation of images on social media. Didi-Huberman is discussing painting, and a mode of art history in which positivism (the approach that sees knowledge as that which is scientifically verifiable) combines with a "badly-understood Freudianism" such that every detail is treated as concealing something which is "hidden behind it" (ibid.: 231). Instead of addressing the painting in its full material presence, an attempt is made to see through it, to find in the detail a motive for the painting as a whole. Here again, there is a parallel: papers in affective computing often assume that emotion is a measurable fact of the image, something embedded in it, rather than an intangible, complex and relational quality. Studies of social media images propose that images "reflect", "reveal" and "display" users' mental states, and that they can "have" emotions which can be quantified as emotion values, or that emotions are "hidden behind" images (e.g., Kim et al. 2017; He et al. 2019; Huang/Chiang/Chen 2019; Guntuku et al. 2019; Lin et al. 2020).

Cutting up, partitioning or dividing the image into "features" becomes an exhaustive exercise: witness the way different studies in the affective computing field propose new techniques, new methods to parse the visual image. Each one claims to attend to an aspect (scale, context, comparison between foreground and background) ignored by all previous studies. What Didi-Huberman says about the positivist attention to the detail in painting pertains here, too, it "verges on pure theoretical delusion" (2005: 236). It is an optimistic delusion, a belief that the image can be explained, that something as overdetermined and irreducible as a painting (or in our case a social photo) can be made "clear and distinct" (ibid.: 237). Against this, he posits the concept of the *pan,* the painterly elements that are not quite one thing or another, the points at which representation dissolves into abstraction and pigment.[11] Didi-Huberman's symptomology is thus concerned not with the symptom as an effect of a cause, but with such incoherent, ambiguous and overdetermined symptoms or signifiers.

One might object that it is inappropriate to transfer Didi-Huberman's argument about paintings by Vermeer and Brueghel to social photos which are more throwaway, more conversational, much less carefully contrived and crafted, and less tangibly material. Although he is keen to emphasise the specificity of painting, Didi-Huberman himself notes that in photographic images, the painterly "pan" finds its equivalent in the accidents and blurs that "'point' us beyond any *that-has-been*" (ibid.: 265, original emphasis).[12] So we might expect to find these elements in vernacular photographs, especially those that are *least* contrived and crafted. Although social photos may be cleaned and standardised by the mobile phone camera software and by processing within an app, and although accidental blur may be unlikely, they still retain something of the excessiveness of the photograph that early theorists noted: the non-hierarchical nature, the irrelevant detail, the odd intrusions that fail to cohere as representation. Unlike stock photos, they are non-emphatic and imperfect images, even if they aspire to the same clean mediocrity. These accidental elements are irreducible to "features", and they form an excess or waste, which cannot be accounted for in the system or quantified as data.

The theoretical delusion that an image can be exhausted by interpretation is driven by a positivism that seeks absolute knowledge and total visibility. This totalising positivism expands the technical means of collection, observation,

---

11   Didi-Huberman argues that this seeking out the detail is destructive, not just of the object, but of the observer themselves, as if they redirect toward themselves "the first, violent act of disintegration" (2005: 233). This "drama of the detail" (ibid.: 234) is perhaps too complicated to address properly here.

12   Didi-Huberman is referring to Barthes, whose concept of *punctum* is close to the concept of *pan*. These concepts differ, not because "one of the two notions originates in painting and the other in photography", but because Barthes conceives of the punctum in indexical terms: "the world reverts to depositing itself on the image" (Didi-Huberman 2005: 264). As Didi-Huberman explains, "In this sense, the punctum should be construed not as a symptom of the image, but as a symptom of the world itself" (ibid.: 265).

calculation and measurement, in the assumption that ultimately nothing can escape "capture" in the form of data. In photography theory and history, the term "positivist" is most often invoked in relation to the tendency to treat photographs as visible proofs of an external reality, but it also characterises ways in which photography and other technologies can be deployed as part of a set of protocols or procedures to suppress subjectivity and objectively yield the "facts" (Daston/ Galison 2007: 115-190). This form of positivism makes its way into data science. As Ed Finn says, the dominant computational ideology or vision is also a colonising or conquering one: "the maximalist idea that all complex systems will eventually be made equivalent through computational representation" (2017: 43).[13] The search for the sentiments and emotions "behind" images has fallen for what Didi-Huberman calls the "positivist myth of the omni-translatability of images" (Didi-Huberman 2005: 3).

Behaviourism and the Measurement of Emotions

The shift to photography as a major form of self-expression and self-presentation is taking place in the context of a larger historical change, particularly in Western capitalist countries, towards what Eva Illouz (2007) terms "emotional capitalism".[14] She describes this as a therapeutic model organised around self-reflection, soft communication skills and "emotional intelligence", which became central to the 20th-century capitalist economy, first between the 1930s and the 1970s in the United States, and then increasingly elsewhere. It replaced older distinctions between private and public spheres and between acceptable emotions (differentiated by gender), but maintained the vision of the self-interested individual (*homo economicus*), for whom "healthy" emotions are personal, not collective. Central to this new "emotional culture" is an increasing emphasis on the public performance of the private self (ibid.: 5). The prompts on social media platforms exhorting you to "share" what you are "feeling" or express what is "on your mind", are invitations to participate in such a public performance. This performance is complicated, as it has different registers, since communicating with you on the same platforms

---

13 This is despite the fact that information theory and computing begin with the idea of information as uncertainty, and are underpinned by notions of indeterminacy and probability (Finn 2017: 43). Indeed, it is probabilistic approaches to AI which have driven the mass accumulation of data regardless of its future uses (Crawford 2021: 99-103).

14 The term describes a distinct aspect of 20th-century capitalism, especially in the USA, but there is some overlap with Zuboff's characterisation of surveillance capitalism insofar as the latter makes use of the "behavioural surplus" produced through emotional expression, and elicits emotional communication in order to generate surplus.

are intimate friends, work colleagues and people you have never met – even people that you are not sure are actually people at all. The context of emotional capitalism creates a demand for self-expression, but this does not necessarily entail trying to directly communicate feelings. Instead, you may express yourself by using social media photos to represent your experiences, your tastes (including your visual aesthetic) and your ideal self-image. The image filters provided by different apps work as affect-management techniques, offering a means of adding instant atmosphere or mood but at the same time they can also be understood as indicators of taste and preference, part of this larger performance of self.

To use photography expressively involves making aesthetic and technical choices on the basis of "truth to feeling" rather than on the basis of whether the image represents the world "as it is". I refer to this as "affective realism", by which I mean any practice with photography where the measure of the photograph's realism lies in its correspondence, not with a neutrally observable reality but with subjective, felt and emotional experience. Affective realism does not necessarily require an image to conform to what is or was objectively present in the world, but rather to express the experience of an individual – in this respect it is solipsistic, since its only reference points are one's own experience and existence.[15] It contradicts the historic association of photography with a realism characterised by neutral, unfeeling or disinterested recording. The yardstick of this affective realism is not only how well the individual judges the image to correspond to their own experience and the feelings that came with that experience, but also how well it seems to communicate that to others (gleaned from reactions, comments and so on).

It is likely that many people posting social media photographs want to convey something of the world as they experience it, something of their subjective worldview, without stopping to analyse precisely what feelings they might evoke or express.[16] While people taking and posting social photos may conceive of them as a means of communicating their own subjective experience, they have not necessarily subscribed to the idea that images are about expressing emotions, nor have they necessarily set out consciously to express a specific feeling through the image. Although emotion recognition and sentiment analysis studies tend to assume that users are expressing emotions via images, the techniques themselves are indifferent to intentionality. This is because they are premised in behaviourist

---

15 My use of the term "affective realism" is related to the literary and artistic concept of realism, rather than the psychological sense, defined by Lisa Feldman Barrett and Jolie Wormwood as "the tendency of your feelings to influence what you see – not what you think you see, but the actual content of your perceptual experience" (2015).

16 An expert practitioner of affective realism would perhaps have a clear idea of what emotions they want to communicate. This suggests a practice such as that of so-called "creative photographers" who use high-end cameras and image-manipulation software to produce "expressive" images.

approaches to the emotions, which treat them as observable characteristics, rooted in the assumption that feeling and cognition are essentially discrete: our interpretation of our own feelings is no more reliable than that of an outside observer (Leys 2010: 89). Bracketed off from this are all sorts of intentions, desires and internal conflicts.

Originally, behaviours were understood as the bodily actions and expressions of an individual, but when emotion recognition algorithms are applied to social media posts, the "behaviours" are at one remove – including such things as written expression, jokes and memes, music selections, photographs and videos; things that a cultural theorist would understand as cultural artefacts, however minor or quickly produced. Culture does not simply communicate emotion directly, but makes use of complex techniques and devices such as metaphor. Since metaphors may be well-worn, deeply embedded and linked to our own embodied experience of the world, it is easy to mistake them for universal or natural forms of expression: so, a sunset can convey a pleasure in melancholy, or a solitary figure on a hill can convey loneliness. The same photo could be read as merely deictic: it points to the sunset or the figure and says "look at this!" or "we are here".

The tendency to view visual imagery as pure or direct (or "natural") emotional expression is perhaps partly a legacy of the positivist notion of the arts as a sphere dedicated purely to emotional expression, which is not knowledge-producing. This view assumes that emotion is opposed to cognition, not recognising how, as Nelson Goodman argued, "emotions function cognitively" in aesthetic experience (1976: 248).[17] Thus, the communication of emotions is assumed to be something which happens reflexively, regardless of things such as conscious intention, tacit knowledge, and newly fashionable or historically embedded modes of visual practice. Additionally, behaviourist approaches to emotion recognition conceive of emotions as able to be separated from the immediate social interaction and broader culture, and therefore disregard the situated relationship between the person responding or posting, their imagined or intended audience, and any complex conscious or unconscious motivations they may have for posting a photograph.

Rejecting the cultural specificity and diversity of emotional expression (both facial and pictorial), behaviourism universalises and naturalises human emotional behaviour while at the same time individualising it (Leys 2011: 438). Against this, I would view emotional expression as fundamentally relational, an element of the interaction between people, images and contexts. Emotions appear natural precisely because they are so deeply cultural. As Illouz argues, emotions are congealed or compacted with cultural meaning, and

---

[17] See also Brown/Phu (2014) on the relation between feeling, thinking and ethical action in photography.

it is this compact compression which confers on them their energetic and hence pre-reflexive, often semi-conscious character. Emotions are deeply internalized and unreflexive aspects of action, but not because they do not contain enough culture and society in them, but rather because they have too much. (Illouz 2007: 3)

James Elkins writes (about people crying in front of art): "strong emotions shut down our ability to reflect" (2001: 17). But even where we are "overcome" by emotion in response to a cultural artefact, this is never simply a biological response to stimuli. As Illouz suggests, the more profound the emotion, the more culturally entangled it can be. Many of the strongest gusts and waves of uncontrollable emotions are inseparable from cultural and social context, as Elkins' example of the connections between Stendhal syndrome, Romanticism and Baroque art makes clear.[18]

If the behaviourist stimulus-response model seems so poor in the face of such phenomena, its great advantage is that it works at scale. In large scale automated studies, behaviourist models seem to come into their own. There is no need to identify the intentions behind a million people clicking "like" on an image, to be able to identify characteristics that guarantee an image's likeability and enable that to be reproduced. All that is needed is for patterns to be identified and correlations made. Nevertheless, this requires emotions and their cultural expression to be translated into discrete, stable, measurable values. Following Darwin and Ekman, psychologists and neurologists have classified six to eight basic emotions. A similar classification is in operation in Facebook's current design, which includes seven possible reactions: "like", "love", "care", "haha", "wow", "sad", "angry". Human users of Facebook might see the reaction button as a means of communication, but from the platform's perspective they enable users' responses to posts to be measured and classified. The identification of discrete universal emotions allows for "commensuration", which means making qualitative differences into quantifiable ones, and "textualisation", which means "locking" emotions into texts or language (Illouz 2007: 32, 71). The Facebook reaction buttons, which (unlike emoji) have fixed textual meanings, provide a good example of how textualisation and commensuration work together.

The attempt to make emotional expression quantifiable and manipulable arrived in the mid-20th century, although the classification of emotions began

---

18   Stendhal syndrome was a set of symptoms exhibited by tourists, mostly at the Uffizi Gallery in Florence, starting in around the 1820s and manifesting in symptoms such as crying, fainting, fevers and hallucinations (Elkins 2001: 32-33). Elkins describes it as a consequence of a tourism which "sticks to the old Romantic war-horses, treating people to a heady mixture of genius worship and expectations as inflated as they are unfocused" and the first encounter with the intense, sensual and provocative aesthetics of Baroque paintings (such as those of Caravaggio) (ibid.: 35).

much earlier in Darwin's 19th-century experiments, which influenced Ekman's psychological theory of facial expressions, which in turn powerfully shapes contemporary facial recognition and emotion tracking. As Ruth Leys summarises, the supposedly basic emotions map onto universal, biologically-determined facial expressions that culture and socialisation are thought to only mask and moderate (2010: 70). Both Darwin and Ekman used sets of photographs to demonstrate and test their theories (Leys provides an extensive description and critique). This way of understanding emotions serves not only the field of behaviourist psychology, but also emotional capitalism more broadly, because it enables emotional life to be chained to "the logic of economic relations and exchange" as part of a "vast process of rationalization of intimate relations" (Illouz 2007: 6, 30). It is a precondition for the extractive approach to emotions characteristic of surveillance capitalism.

The Ruse of Personalisation

The identification of discrete universal emotions enabled them to be transformed into objects of governance, as well as fungibles or "behavioural surplus". Antoinette Rouvroy and Thomas Berns explain how "algorithmic governance" aims to regulate possible behaviours, through the transformation of our behaviour and environment into data, and through statistics (Rouvroy/Berns 2013: xiv). These processes do not produce static profiles, but dynamic "real-time" systems. Their alibi is personalisation:

They enrich our daily life's cognitive experience with dynamic and individualised informational content. Their celebrated capacity to detect, sort, evaluate and, most importantly, predict our desires and preferences, needs and propensities, and to customise and adjust deliveries, services and offers to our individual profile as if it knew us better than ourselves, spares us time and discomfort. (Rouvroy 2011: 125)

Such processes of personalisation have been critiqued for reducing people's informational horizons. This is what Eli Pariser describes as "filtering" – the production of personalised search results, news feeds and advertising that result in a narrowing of experience (Pariser 2011). Some researchers have argued that filtering has not produced the enclosure in "bubbles" that Pariser assumed, but it does not follow that personalisation is merely harmless or convenient. Instead, it is a mode of shaping conduct, tailoring people to the product rather than the other way round.[19] This idea of oppressive personalisation recalls the technical image feedback loop described by Vilém Flusser in 1985:

---

19 It does so "by tailoring sales strategies (the way of presenting the product, of pricing it, etc.) to each person's profile": i.e. market segmentation (Rouvroy/Berns 2013: xiii).

This feedback enables the images to change, to become better and better, and more like the receivers want them to be; that is, the images become more and more like the receivers want them to be so that the receivers can become more and more like the images want them to be. (Flusser 2011: 55)

Rouvroy and Berns argue that the aim is to "accelerate flows": ideally, the individual should act and respond to prompts in a reflexive fashion "without forming or formulating a desire", avoiding any detour or gap between stimulus and response (Rouvroy/Berns 2013: xiii-xiv). Digital behaviourism promises to give us what we want before we even know we want it by listening to our bodies (via involuntary expressions, unconscious actions and movements), but also by reading our photos. At the same time, it promises to furnish research with information that appears objective and rational because technologically acquired and computational, free from human bias and subjectivity, much as photography did in the 19th century. Personalisation turns out to be nothing of the sort, since the human "person" here is irrelevant.

Algorithmic governance is premised on statistical doubles with which the person has no relationship and which are at odds with their own perceptions and representations of themselves (ibid.: xvii). The mass of social media photographs is part of the raw material of these digital, statistical doubles. The myth of omni-translatability is the guiding principle of the rendition processes that turn physical existence, actions and behaviours into digital tokens or data-points.[20]

In conclusion, while there appears to be a contradiction between how photographs are increasingly understood as subjective and expressive, and the positivist and behaviourist approaches used to attend to them, I have tried to demonstrate that these two things are interdependent. The promise of photography today is to represent subjective, lived experience, and to help one express oneself or even build a sense of self – of taste, memory, appearance, connection to others – through taking, posting and sharing images. Apps and mobile phone cameras facilitate this with easy-to-use filters, colour and composition adjustments, retouching and so on. The transformation of photography into a subjective means of expression is connected to the vision of the internet as a space of personalisation. Yet personalisation is a ruse of systems that are indifferent to persons. It is used to generate an excess of "wild" data to be "mined", "harvested" or "foraged". New machine learning and AI systems, some developed on the back of spurious claims about social goods, produce unrecognisable statistical doubles whose eventual purpose is likely to be increased control over people. These systems not only simplify

---

20 The term is a little misleading insofar as these doubles are not coherent entities. The process of translation of images into data is also a process of slicing and disaggregating rather than the construction of composite doppelgangers. Or as Matthew Fuller puts it, "control has no need of individuals per se, only as referents: as scalar nodes in the flows of cash, commodity, and behavior" (2005: 152).

the emotionally and visually complex, they bracket off cultural signification or symbolic action, ignore practices of sociability and community, disregard people's own accounts of themselves and their reality, and ignore the contradictions, ambiguities and accidents inherent in the social photograph.

Acknowledgements

The author would like to thank Bernadette Buckley and Rod Dickinson for their advice and suggestions for an earlier spoken version of this paper, Jordana Blejmar and John Parish for reading and commenting on this version, and Rowan Lear for drawing my attention to the work of Antoinette Rouvroy.

References

Andalibi, Nazanin/Buss, Justin (2020): "The Human in Emotion Recognition on Social Media: Attitudes, Outcomes, Risks." In: Proceedings of the 2020 CHI Conference on Human Factors in Computing Systems, pp. 1-16.
Ang, Chee/Bobrowicz, Ania/Schiano, Diane/Nardi Bonnie (2013): "Data in the Wild: Some Reflections." In: Interactions 20/2, pp. 39-43 (https://interactions.acm.org/archive/view/march-april-2013/data-in-the-wild).
Balouchian, Pooyan/Foroosh, Hassan (2018): "Context-Sensitive Single-Modality Image Emotion Analysis: A Unified Architecture from Dataset Construction to CNN Classification." In: 25th IEEE International Conference on Image Processing (ICIP), pp. 1932-1936.
Barrett, Lisa Feldman/Wormwood, Jolie (2015): "When a Gun Is Not a Gun." In: The New York Times Sunday Review, April 17 (https://www.nytimes.com/2015/04/19/opinion/sunday/when-a-gun-is-not-a-gun.html).
Barthes, Roland (1973 [1957]): "The Great Family of Man." In: Mythologies, London: Paladin Books, pp.100-102.
Barthes, Roland (1979 [1957]): "Shock Photos." In: The Eiffel Tower and Other Mythologies, New York: Hill and Wang, pp. 71-73.
Barthes, Roland (1984 [1980]): Camera Lucida, London: Fontana.
Blaschke, Estelle (2016): Banking on Images from the Bettmann Archive to Corbis, Leipzig: Spector Books.
Bowker, Geoffrey (2013): "Data Flakes: An Afterword to 'Raw Data' Is an Oxymoron." In: Lisa Gitelman (ed.), "Raw Data" is an Oxymoron, Cambridge, Mass.: MIT Press, pp.167-171.
Brown, Elspeth H./Phu, Thy (2014): "Introduction." In: Brown, Elspeth H. Brown/ThyPhu (eds.), Feeling Photography. Durham, NC.: Duke University Press, pp. 1-25.

Brown, Simon (2009): "Colouring the Nation: Spectacle, Reality and British Natural Colour in the Silent and Early Sound Era." In: Film History: An International Journal 21/2, pp.139-49.

Guntuku, Sharath Chandra/Preotiuc-Pietro, Daniel/Eichstaedt, Johannes C./Ungar, Lyle H. (2019): "What Twitter Profile and Posted Images Reveal about Depression and Anxiety." In: Proceedings of the International AAAI Conference on Web and Social Media 13, pp. 236-246.

Crawford, Kate/Paglen, Trevor (2019): "Excavating AI: The Politics of Images in Machine Learning Training Sets." (https://excavating.ai).

Crawford, Kate (2021): The Atlas of AI: Power, Politics, and the Planetary Costs of Artificial Intelligence, New Haven: Yale University Press.

Daston, Lorraine/Galison, Peter (2007): Objectivity, Cambridge, Mass.: Zone Books/MIT Press.

Davies, William (2017): "How are We Now? Real-Time Mood-Monitoring as Valuation." In: Journal of Cultural Economy 10/1, pp. 34-48.

Defoe, Daniel (2003 [1722]): A Journal of the Plague Year, London: Penguin Books.

Denton, Emily/Hanna, Alex/Amironesei, Razvan/Smart, Andrew/Nicole, Hilary/Scheuerman, Morgan Klaus (2020): "Bringing the People Back In: Contesting Benchmark Machine Learning

Datasets." In: Proceedings of ICML Workshop on Participatory Approaches to Machine Learning (https://arxiv.org/abs/2007.07399v1).

Didi-Huberman, Georges (2005 [1990]): Confronting Images: Questioning the Ends of a Certain History of Art, Pennysylvania: Penn State Press.

Doshi, Udit/Barot, Vaibhav/Gavhane, Sachin (2020): "Emotion Detection and Sentiment Analysis of Static Images." In: 2020 International Conference on Convergence to Digital World-Quo Vadis (ICCDW), pp. 1-5.

Elkins, James (2001): Pictures and Tears: A History of People Who Have Cried in Front of Paintings, London: Routledge.

Finn, Ed (2017): What Algorithms Want: Imagination in the Age of Computing, Cambridge, Mass.: MIT Press

Flusser, Vilém (2011 [1985]): Into the Universe of Technical Images, Minneapolis: Minnesota University Press.

Foucault, Michel (1979): Discipline and Punish: The Birth of The Prison, Harmondsworth: Peregrine Books.

Foucault, Michel (1980): "What is an Author?" In: Language, Counter-Memory, Practice: Selected Essays and Interviews, Ithaca: Cornell University Press.

Fuller, Matthew (2005): Media Ecologies: Materialist Energies in Art and Technoculture, Cambridge, Mass.: MIT Press.

Frosh, Paul (2003): The Image Factory Consumer Culture, Photography and the Visual Content Industry, London: Bloomsbury.

Frosh, Paul (2012): The Poetics of Digital Media, London: Polity.

Gates, Kelly (2006) "Identifying the 9/11 'Faces of Terror': The Promise and Problem of Facial Recognition Technology." In: Cultural Studies 20/4-5, pp. 417-440.

Ginzburg, Carlo (1980): "Morelli, Freud and Sherlock Holmes: Clues and Scientific Method." In: History Workshop 9, pp. 5-36.

Gitelman, Lisa (ed.) (2013): "Raw Data" is an Oxymoron, Cambridge, Mass.: MIT Press.

Goggin, Benjamin (2019): "Inside Facebook's Suicide Algorithm: Here's How the Company Uses Artificial Intelligence to Predict your Mental State from Your Posts." In: Business Insider, January 6 (https://www.businessinsider.com/facebook-is-using-ai-to-try-to-predict-if-youre-suicidal-2018-12).

Goodman, Nelson (1976): Languages of Art: An Approach to the Theory of Symbols, Indianapolis: Hackett.

He, Xiaohao/Zhang, Huijun/Li, Ningyun/Feng, Ling/Zheng, Feng (2019): "A Multi-Attentive Pyramidal Model for Visual Sentiment Analysis." In: 2019 International Joint Conference on Neural Networks (IJCNN), pp. 1-8.

Henning, Michelle (2018): Photography: The Unfettered Image, London: Routledge

Herrnstein-Smith, Barbara (2016): "What Was 'Close Reading'?: A Century of Method in Literary Studies." In: Minnesota Review 87, pp. 57-75.

Higgins, Scott (2007): Harnessing the Technicolor Rainbow: Color Design in the 1930s. Austin: University of Texas Press.

Huang, Yu-Ching/Chiang, Chieh-Feng/Chen, Arbee LP (2019): "Predicting Depression Tendency Based on Image, Text and Behavior Data from Instagram." In: Proceedings of the 8th International Conference on Data Science, Technology and Applications (DATA), pp. 32-40.

Illouz, Eva (2007): Cold Intimacies: The Making of Emotional Capitalism, London: Polity Press.

Jurgenson, Nathan (2019): The Social Photo, London: Verso Books.

Kim, Hye-Rin/Kim, Yeong-Seok/Kim, Seon Joo/Lee, In-Kwon (2018): "Building Emotional Machines: Recognizing Image Emotions through Deep Neural Networks." In: IEEE Transactions on Multimedia 20/11, pp. 2980-2992.

Leys, Ruth (2010): "How Did Fear Become a Scientific Object and What Kind of Object Is It?" In: Representations 110, pp. 66-104

Lin, Chenhao/Hu, Pengwei/Su, Hui/Li, Shaochun/Mei, Jing/Zhou, Jie/Leung, Henry (2020): "Sensemood: Depression Detection on Social Media." In: Proceedings of the 2020 International Conference on Multimedia Retrieval, pp. 407-411.

Liu, Leqi/Preotiuc-Pietro, Daniel/Samani, Zahra Riahi/Moghaddam, Mohsen E./Ungar, Lyle (2016): "Analyzing Personality through Social Media Profile Picture Choice." In: Proceedings of the International AAAI Conference on Web and Social Media 10/1 (https://ojs.aaai.org/index.php/ICWSM/article/view/14738).

Miller, Daniel (2016): Social Media in an English Village, London: UCL Press.

Pariser, Eli (2011): The Filter Bubble: What the Internet is Hiding from You, London: Penguin Books.

Parsons, Michael (2005): "Introduction." In: César Botella/Sára Botella (eds.), The Work of Psychic Figurability: Mental States Without Representation, Hove: Brunner-Routledge, pp. xvii-xxiii.

Rosenberg, Daniel (2013): "Data Before the Fact." In: Gitelman, Lisa (ed.), "Raw Data" is an Oxymoron, Cambridge, Mass.: MIT Press, pp. 15-40.

Rouvroy, Antoinette (2011): "Technology, Virtuality and Utopia: Governmentality in an Age of Autonomic Computing." In: Mireille Hildebrandt/Antoinette Rouvroy (eds.), Law, Human Agency and Autonomic Computing, London: Routledge, pp. 119-140.

Rouvroy, Antoinette/Berns, Thomas (2013): "Algorithmic Governmentality and Prospects of Emancipation: Disparateness as a Precondition for Individuation through Relationships?" In: Réseaux 177/1, pp.163-196.

Rouvroy, Antoinette (2020): "Algorithmic Governmentality and the Death of Politics: An Interview with Antoinette Rouvroy." In: Green European Journal, March 27 (https://www.greeneuropeanjournal.eu/algorithmic-governmentality-and-the-death-of-politics/).

Rubinstein, Daniel/Sluis, Katrina (2013): "Notes on the Margins of Metadata: Concerning the Undecidability of the Digital Image." In: photographies 6/1, pp. 151-158.

Schneble, Christophe Olivier/Elger, Bernice Simone/Shaw, David Martin (2020): "Google's Project Nightingale Highlights the Necessity of Data Science Ethics Review." In: EMBO Molecular Medicine 12/3 (https://www.ncbi.nlm.nih.gov/pmc/articles/PMC7059004/).

Shankar, Shreya/Halpern, Yoni/Breck, Eric/Atwood, James/Wilson, Jimbo/Sculley, D. (2017): "No Classification without Representation: Assessing Geodiversity Issues in Open Data Sets for the Developing World." 31st Conference on Neural Information Processing Systems (NIPS 2017), Long Beach, CA, USA (arXiv preprint arXiv:1711.08536).

Stark, Luke (2018): "Algorithmic Psychometrics and the Scalable Subject." In: Social Studies of Science 48/2, pp. 204-31.

Stiegler, Bernard [1996] (2002): "The Discrete Image." In: Stiegler, Bernard/Jacques Derrida, Echographies of Television: Filmed Interviews, Cambridge: Polity, pp. 147-74.

Street, Sarah (2011): "Negotiating the Archives: The Natalie Kalmus Papers and the 'Branding' of Technicolor in Britain and the United States." In: The Moving Image: The Journal of the Association of Moving Image Archivists 11/ 1, pp.1-24.

Taussig, Michael (2009): What Color is the Sacred?, Chicago: The University of Chicago Press.

Omdia (2018): "Emotion Recognition and Sentiment Analysis." March 6 (https://omdia.tech.informa.com/OM011970/Emotion-Recognition-and-Sentiment-Analysis).

Vadicamo, Lucia/Carrara, Fabio/Cimino, Andrea/Cresci, Stefano/Dell'Orletta, Felice/Falchi, Fabrizio/Tesconi, Maurizio (2017): "Cross-Media Learning for Image Sentiment Analysis in the Wild." In: Proceedings of the IEEE International Conference on Computer Vision Workshops, pp. 308-317.

Wongkoblap, Akkapon/Vadillo, Miguel A./Curcin, Vasa (2017): "Researching Mental Health Disorders in the Era of Social Media: Systematic Review." In: Journal of Medical Internet Research 19/6, e228 (https://www.jmir.org/2017/6/e228/).

Zuboff, Shoshana (2019): The Age of Surveillance Capitalism: The Fight for a Human Future at the New Frontier of Power, London: Profile Books.

Zylinska, Joanna (2021): "Undigital Photography: Image-Making beyond Computation and AI." In: Tomas Dvorak/Jussi Parikka (eds.), Photography Off the Scale, Edinburgh: Edinburgh University Press, pp. 231-252.

Embedding Heterogenous Forms of Surveillance in China's Autocratic Networked Media
How the Government Supports and Controls Platforms, Companies, Online Celebrities, and Users

Cornelia Bogen

Abstract

The rise of platforms, datafication, and the new business model of platform capitalism have prompted scholars to carve out the differences between surveillance capitalism in authoritarian states and Western democracies. However, there has been little research about the mechanisms that authoritarian governments use to subject economic actors and users to state control and the subsequent social practices. The case studies presented here illustrate how the state's deep entanglement with platforms is meant to foster both economic and socio-political outcomes by allowing platforms to promote users' entrepreneurship and restricting their online business if they are radically indifferent to media content or Party censorship rules. Furthermore, the case studies demonstrate that China's model goes beyond the Western concept of surveillance capitalism, because the heterogeneous logics of marketisation are interconnected with types of state surveillance different from the ones described by Zuboff (2019) for democratic countries. Against the backdrop of Fuchs/Trottier's (2015) theoretical model of social media surveillance, the societal implications of categorical suspicion, social sorting, and surveillance creep play out differently. The diffusion of China's institutional setting into e-platforms provokes culture-specific narratives (Versailles literature) and social online practices utilising networked images (barrage subtitling, human flesh search) unseen in Western online publics to date. Hence, studies of surveillance mechanisms in China's digital space need to be embedded within the larger context of political economy and state control.

Keywords:

Platform Society; China; Social Media Surveillance; Networked Images; Autocratic Networked Media

1. The Interaction of Political and Economic Surveillance in China

Platformisation (i.e., the rise of platforms) has become the leading economic and infrastructural model of the social web. A shift from social network sites to social media platforms has seen datafication become even more sophisticated, and the new business model of "platform capitalism" (coined by Srnicek 2017) has emerged. This transforms the social action of interconnected businesses, advertisers, and ordinary users on online platforms into quantified data that can be commodified for real-time tracking and predictive analytics (van Dijck 2014: 198). The new model characterises capitalist internet economies not only in Western democracies (here: EU and US), but also in authoritarian capitalist countries, where state intervention is not limited by public and private goods and transgresses the principle of self-limitation of government power implied by the Rule of Law (Sallai/Schnyder 2019: 3; 13).

The top ten most valuable brands (which consist of only U.S. American and Chinese platform companies like Tencent and Alibaba) are continually seeking to drive alternative platforms out of the market and expand to other online spaces (Helmond 2015: 5). To extend their core business (i.e., everlasting data extraction), these platforms collect and process networked images to use as training examples for algorithms and image-based predictive models to predict users' future behaviour (MacKenzie/Munster 2019: 10; 17-18). However, as users have no insight into the technical infrastructure and operations of platforms, they are prevented from using self-determined reason in their interaction with digital artifacts (Mühlhoff 2018: 570-571). Due to this power imbalance between IT-firms and users, Zuboff describes "surveillance capitalism" as a form of instrumentally controlling collective behaviour that was totalistic in its ambition – in both China and the West (Zuboff 2019: 404). Other scholars used the term "neoliberal psychopolitics" to emphasise how the surveillance state and market economy go hand in hand, to foster practices of exploitation and mind-control (Byong-Chul Han 2017).

However, there is a fundamental structural difference in the entanglement of instrumentarian and state power between Western democracies and China (Zuboff 2019: 393). In the US and the EU, IT-firms possess user data, and the state moves with the firms to get access, whereas in China, the state "appears determined to 'own' this complex", and firms move with the state (ibid: 443). This is because in the US, Californian high-tech artisans promoted a neoliberal ideology to foster their social privileges (Barbrook/Cameron 1996:10), whereas in post-Mao China, a technocratic elite promoted network expansion and telecommunications for military and state surveillance purposes (Zhao 2007: 100). As a result, China's neoliberal internet economy combines commodification, public relations, and marketing with state control and socialist ideology (Fuchs 2017: 381). A public sphere with deliberative outcomes is regarded as a danger to party rule and social stability, with the potential to undermine the prestige of the government and to impede its governance (Li 2014). Hence, the Chinese government has helped national IT-companies to build native social networking platforms that allow for better control of regime-critical content (Reuter/Szakonyi 2013: 49). It follows that algorithmic control of networked images in China's authoritarian capitalism (Fuchs 2020) is not only economically but also politically motivated. Thus, scholars who have explored the institutional and cultural dimensions of the platformisation of Chinese society identify a deep entanglement between state and platforms, as well as a dynamic intersection of infrastructures, governance, and user practices (de Kloet et al. 2019).

Scholars note that the mechanisms that authoritarian governments use to subject economic actors to state control and erode the boundaries between public and private domains (in both political and economic life) have not only remained unexplored, but also differ between various authoritarian capitalist states (Sallai/Schnyder 2019: 3-4). Therefore, before we explore multifold surveillance mechanisms regulating China's online space, we first need to understand the institutional and cultural settings that enable the Chinese Communist Party to control the financial and intellectual capital of IT-firms. In a second step, case studies employing a critical discourse analysis of Chinese social media content will be discussed in order to illustrate the Chinese state's governance of platform politics in action, by shedding light on various occasions when the Chinese government either grants a certain degree of freedom to companies and users, or restricts their online activity.

First, in Western surveillance capitalism, a specialist class of software developers and data scientists owns tools to predict (computational methods) and condition (social network incentives using social pressure) collective behaviour with the goal of fostering platform growth tactics and a socially efficient collective (Zuboff 2019: 504). Such power in the hands of IT-companies is prevented by the Communist Party of China (CPC). The CPC is not only above the law in practice, but also in its control of the development of a state-dependent mercantilism. Firms in strategic and essential industries (e.g., Artificial Intelligence) are state-owned, party officials hold a personal stake in privately-owned businesses and hybrid firms, and the financial system relies heavily on state-owned banks (Witt/Redding 2012: 4-5). Hence, in China's authoritarian capitalism, Chinese companies do not enjoy the degree of freedom that firms enjoy in free-market democratic capitalism. In a capitalist system without capitalists, the knowledge (understanding the operation of the whole market and the behaviour of its actors) that IT-firms generate is subjected to state control. It follows that if IT-firms exploit their knowledge advantage by undermining the CPC's online censorship rules, they will be punished with restrictions on their business operations.

Second, the reciprocity (e.g., fair labour practices, unionisation, and collective bargaining in employment relations) that used to exist between companies and the people (i.e., employees and customers) in Western democracies is currently being eroded through structural separation of U.S. surveillance capitalists (i.e., IT-firms) from the European and U.S. American publics (Zuboff 2019: 501). China's political economy does not display this kind of reciprocity; however, platform labour poses similar challenges in China regarding monopoly, employment, wages and labour precarity, as the case of food delivery workers illustrates (Sun 2019; Doorn/Chen 2021). The growing body of literature in this field suggests that the notion of precarity (in relation to digital labour) might be different in China due to the unique historic experience under Mao's rule, when job security was ubiquitous but still meant a life in poverty (deKloet et al. 2019: 253). Furthermore, since the Communist Party already represents the interests of the proletariat, China's Federation of Trade Unions (ACFTU) is an organ of political control. For example, during workers' strikes, the ACFTU does not represent labourers' interests but instead promotes the interests of management (Witt/Redding 2012: 9). Similarly, NGOs closely cooperate with the state (Hou 2015: 81), and social protest is forbidden (Ho/Jackson 2021: 508). Despite there being no state-independent representation of workers' interests (Witt/Redding 2012:14), workers still find ways to show resistance to platform labour (Sun 2019: 319). I argue that if one assumes that productive social relationships between employers and employees do not exist in China because these are regulated by the CPC, then we are likely to overlook alternative forms for negotiations of interest in China's online public (i.e., workers' internet memes).

Third, in China we can observe a similar preference for prediction products that favour content designed to direct online users to entertainment products and sensational news. One example is the ranking system of trending topics within the popular Chinese social media platform "Sina Weibo", where celebrities can either purchase favourable positioning for a topic, or rely on their fans to generate traffic and attract public attention (Nigunigu 2021). At the same time, in authoritarian media systems, media's role is not to supervise state action, but to act as a propaganda tool serving political stability. It follows that in China's instrumentarian social order, where the asocial mode of knowledge and freedom is concentrated in the state, IT-firms cannot be radically indifferent towards media content. The Chinese government closely cooperates with platforms (who must implement censorship based on politically sensitive keywords and use advanced blocking technologies) to directly control (political) public discourse (deLisle et al.2016: 21). This helps prevent the behaviours observed with US IT-firms such as constantly attempting to surmount state laws and market constraints by consumers, competitors, employees and civil society (Zuboff 2019: 403; 504). Although scholars observe that the range of political issues allowed to be debated online in China has widened, this expansion was not to encourage public reasoning with deliberative outcomes, but to foster online consumer culture (by piquing nationalism) and people's loyalty (Jiang 2012: 84-94). Due to China's ambition to turn the country into a global power of Artificial Intelligence by 2030, it is no surprise that Chinese public discourse about government use of Artificial Intelligence for mass surveillance highlights its economic and political potency while ignoring socio-ethical implications (Zeng/Schäfer 2020: 12). If online content does not comply with the law and socialist core values as requested by the Cyberspace Administration of China, digital platforms are asked to intervene with censorship measures. It appears that Chinese IT-firms' public responsibility to promote a "healthy" internet culture and positive atmosphere (Lin/de Kloet 2019: 4) clearly goes beyond the Western model of surveillance capitalism. Ironically, the complex interplay between platformisation, datafication, networked (often image-based) practices, and the Chinese state's knowledge sharing of patient data with the public (for the sake of epidemic containment) has spurred certain forms of asocial online behaviour unseen in the West (e.g., "human flesh search", as discussed later).

2. Framework of Case Studies

As outlined previously, the concept of surveillance capitalism (with its focus on digital platforms as the dominant actor employing datafication) tends to reduce the political economy of the Internet to a narrow problem area. Against this backdrop, the focus of my analysis will be extended to explore the range of logics that are at stake in China's internet economy. This critical digital social research study applies the theoretical model of social media surveillance (Fuchs/Trottier 2015: 130) to (a) showcase how commercial social media surveillance and state surveillance interact in Chinese practice, (b) shed light on the types of incidents in which the Chinese government will either allow full autonomy to e-commerce actors, or subject economic actors and users to state control, and (c) carve out the social impact of authoritarian surveillance on online user behaviour and the social use of images on platforms.

The theoretical model is based on the assumption that social media surveillance has three societal implications: (1) permanent monitoring of citizens' social media activities (*categorical suspicion*), (2) algorithmic classification of users, which not only targets advertisements but also allocates resources to privileged individuals and discriminates against others (*social sorting*), and (3) user behaviour of habitually exposing their private lives to the public and observing other users' posts (*surveillance creep*) (Fuchs/Trottier 2015: 128-129). Against the backdrop of this model, I will discuss the diverse surveillance mechanisms and logics of marketisation in China's online space. Fuchs/Trottier's model emphasises the social, political, and lateral forms of surveillance and control going beyond the concept of surveillance capitalism, and allows us to embed China's digital economy into a wider context of political economies and state regulations. I will identify the intersections between economic and political surveillance and networked images by discussing several case studies, which are grouped here according to the dynamically intersecting parameters of "infrastructures", "governance", and "practices", as inspired by Kloet et al.'s model of the institutional and cultural dimensions of Chinese platformisation (2019).

In the *practice* section, three case studies will be presented in order to illustrate how the Chinese government not only considers instrumentarian society to be a means to work towards political and social outcomes (Zuboff 2019: 389) but also as a market opportunity. This is because certain Confucian values continue to shape China's modernity, including the crucial role of government leadership in maintaining socio-political stability *and* in providing improved material living conditions through economic growth (Tu 2002: 204-5). The Chinese government's strategy of "Mass Entrepreneurship and Innovation" (2015) views the internet's sharing economy not only as a space that provides new opportunities to IT-giants and well-established entrepreneurs to extend their core business, but also to millions of "grassroots individuals" and start-ups (Lin/deKloet 2019: 3-4). Hence, the cases discussed in this section demonstrate how the Chinese government considers rapid platformisation and datafication as tools for promoting economic growth. The first case explores how the government allows digital platforms to economically utilise public attention and user engagement in public debates (case study of Purcotton advertisement). The following two cases explore how the government allows brands and Wang Hong (web celebrities) on popular Chinese social media platforms (i.e., Weibo, Kuaishou, and Bilibili) to stimulate users to experiment with new forms of creative entrepreneurship (case study of livestreaming on Kuaishou, case study of Versailles literature). However, despite scholars' observation that the Chinese government has hesitated to implement strict rules of content regulation to promote the IT sector's economic growth (Qin et al. 2016: 5), there have recently been legal disputes between service providers and the Chinese government due to diverging interests.

The *governance section* is devoted to platform politics and the automated censorship of images. It discusses a case study (about a prominent sex scandal discussed in Chinese public discourse in 2020) to show how IT-giants that fail to maintain an equilibrium between the promotion of platform growth tactics and their public responsibility to moderate media content will have further restrictions imposed on their operational freedom in the virtual marketplace by the state. These Chinese platform operators that display their indifference to party rule by coming up with their own – not politically, but economically motivated – censorship rules will prompt state intervention. The case study is also an interesting example of how *categorical suspicion* and *surveillance creep* can backfire and not only harm users, but also those who operate social media and e-commerce platforms.

In the *infrastructure* section, the two cases not only exemplify how users employ media art and image data to stabilise surveillance capitalism, but also demonstrate the role of networked visual images in culture-specific forms of online behaviour. The first case is devoted to Chinese delivery workers' resistance to algorithmic control of their work practices by digital platforms. Although employees cannot expect their interests to be fairly represented by labour and trade unions due to China's institutional setting, delivery work has challenged traditional Chinese labour law with delivery drivers being governed, classified and surveilled by platform algorithms (*social sorting*), and the Chinese state is just beginning to investigate how to regulate these digital labour practices. While the Chinese government has allowed new forms of labour precarity to develop, it also allows digital labourers to publicly express their resistance to platform labour, provided they blame the operators and customers of food delivery platforms and not the Communist Party. I will show how delivery workers successfully use new media art (i.e., videoclip-based internet memes) to criticise surveillance capitalism and stimulate active public engagement – which, ironically, stabilises surveillance capitalism. Here, the social practice of barrage subtitling enhances the network effects that operators of video sharing sites are aiming for.

In contrast, the second case study in this section shows what kind of network effects prompt state intervention. For example, in the case of human flesh search, it is a merging of surveillance, modulation of viewing, and audience labour in times of health crisis. It shows how health data made publicly available by the government and platforms during the Covid-19 pandemic spurred a new type of human flesh search, in which online communities exposed images of patients' movements. Furthermore, this example illustrates how two social implications of social media surveillance fatefully 'enrich' each other when netizens engage in a human flesh search of Covid-19 patients (i.e., *categorical suspicion* in the form of both state and platforms monitoring smart phone users' activities to control the spread of an epidemic; *surveillance creep* in the form of exposing users' private lives).

In summary, the case studies discussed shed light on marketisation tendencies that are linked to state and social forms of surveillance that go beyond Zuboff's concept of surveillance capitalism. Applying the Fuchs/Trottier theoretical model to the Chinese context helps us to recognise that although social media surveillance in both China and the West has similar societal implications (categorical suspicion, social sorting, surveillance creep), the social effects appear to be different in China due to its peculiar institutional and cultural system.

3. Practices: How Brands and Companies Utilise User-Generated Content for Online Merchandising

3.1 Purcotton Advertisement

On January 7, 2021, the high-end daily necessity brand 'Purcotton' posted an advertisement for make-up remover-cleansing wipes online. It immediately triggered a heated online debate on the popular social media platform Weibo, especially among female netizens, because the advertisement was said to discriminate against women. In the advertisement, a man chases a young woman at night, but when she removes her make up with cleansing wipes, he walks off.

Fig. 1: Still frames from Purcotton's advertisement video

Many female Weibo users found the advertisement insulting because it not only suggested that women are ugly without make up ("The advertisement for make-up remover" 2021), but because it depicts and trivialises a gendered crime. The next morning Purcotton publicly apologised, describing it as "creative advertising", which provoked even more criticism from netizens, women's federations ("Creative advertising or insulting women?" 2021), and journalists ("China Women's Daily" 2021; "Purcotton apologises" 2021). That afternoon Purcotton published a second apology (Purcotton 2021), and deleted both the original apology and the controversial advertisement. However, commercial media (Fig. 2) and a women's newspaper (Fig. 4) provided screenshots of the deleted material (i.e., the original apology and scenes from the advertisement), and highlighted the ranking of 'PurCotton Era' ('全棉时代') on the list of trending topics on Weibo (no. 20) (Financial community network 2021) (Fig. 3). Cut versions ("Creative advertising or insulting women?" 2021) and fast motion versions of the advertisement ("China Women's Daily" 2021) were provided as well.

The case illustrates that in networked media, controversial advertisements can trigger an immediate and heated discussion among the online public. Users can quickly access the debate and the controversial content through hashtag grouping of comments and through social media platforms' ranking of trending topics. This also impacts on whether media outlets and other organisations are willing to join the debate. A company's attempt to reproduce and maintain surveillance capitalism by producing provocative, attention-seeking online ads can come into conflict with social media platforms' economic surveillance of user generated content and their efforts to transform user habits of browsing into grazing and other forms of active cognitive engagement (Creeber 2013).

Fig. 2: Commercial media; Fig. 3: Ranking as trending topic;
Fig. 4: China Women's Daily

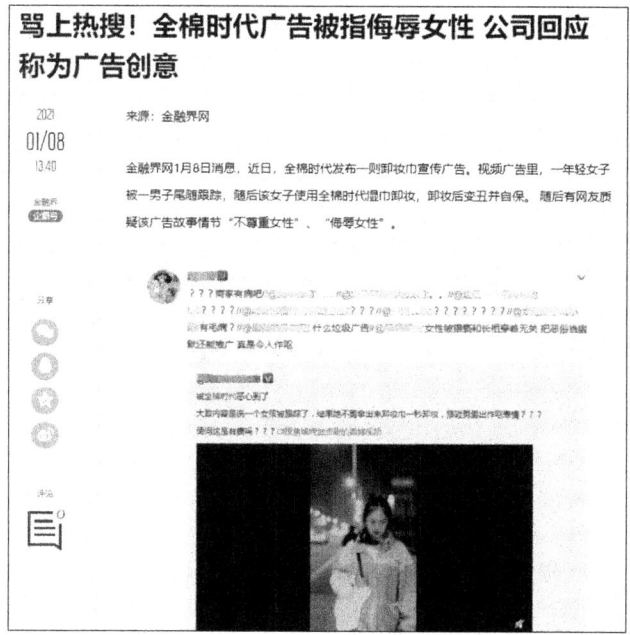

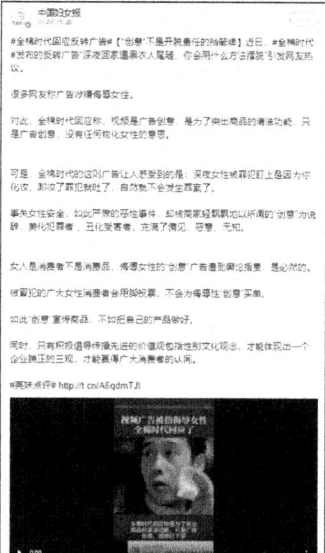

3.2 Livestreaming on Kuaishou

The social media platform Kuaishou, an algorithm-based video and live-streaming platform where registered users can upload short videos targeting second- and third-tier cities in China, took a different approach to online merchandising by making netizens into the content producers of advertisements. In 2019, the e-commerce management team of Kuaishou launched the "Kuaishou fashion product award". Bloggers were asked to upload videos in which they unpack the company's products, give tutorials on how to use certain beauty products, or show off their dressing skills when wearing fashion companies' products (Fig. 5 & 6).

Fig. 5 & 6: Participants of Kaishou fashion product award

The fashion product award became a big success, not only for the platform but also for Kuaishou anchors (who gained hundreds of thousands of additional followers), and fashion manufacturers (who saw their daily sales volumes increase). More than 70,000 users submitted 600,000 broadcasts to the competition, attracting 3.7 billion views and 130 million likes ("Hard currency" 2019). However, only the top ten bloggers that attracted the most traffic received a share of Kuaishou's revenue (traffic packages) and were offered business opportunities with respective beauty companies.

At the same time, the success of Kuaishou platform also depends on its commercial cooperation with "grassroot" content creators, mostly uneducated young Chinese living in rural areas, for whom the platform can provide a tool to build a career. While Kuaishou has been described as "democratic" because the algorithm gives users from any social stratum the chance to attract traffic with their content (Lin/deKloet 2019: 5), the operation of its algorithmic system remains invisible to users. Furthermore, content moderators need to make sure that no illegal content violates Chinese law. Kuaishou platform has already been disciplined for the distribution of harmful content, and as a result many user accounts were shut down in 2018 (ibid: 4). Hence, trying to attract as much traffic as possible, content producers are likely to engage in acts of self-censorship in order to avoid conflicts. Thus, scholars describe the special state-platform relationship as a feature that distinguishes the Chinese platformisation of cultural production from its Western counterpart (ibid: 7).

Thus, while livestreaming can empower users by stimulating creativity and new forms of creative entrepreneurship, it can also foster labour precariousness when people move from contracted labour to platform labour (de Kloet et al. 2019: 253). While service providers and brands can exploit the labour of the average user, platforms need to ensure that user-generated content is compliant with the rules of the Cyberspace Administration of China.

3.3 Versailles Literature

One of the most searched words in China in 2020 was 'Versailles literature' ('凡尔赛文学') ("Versailles Literature" 2021). Weibo user Xiaonaiqiu (@小奶球) coined this name, inspired by "The Rose of Versailles", a novel about the late 18th century French aristocracy. Versailles literature is a lifestyle narrative in which netizens present an unsatisfying image of their life on the surface, as a technique to show off their alleged wealth and high social status (Zui et al. 2020). The narrative, which suggests that a materialistic lifestyle leads to ultimate happiness, is used to promote online consumption, since its anchors implicitly advocate the purchase of certain products to achieve the supposed happiness. Instructing netizens about the main techniques, Xiaonaiqiu has become a popular lecturer on the video-sharing platform Bilibili (Little milk ball 2020, Fig. 7):

Fig. 7: Online tutorial by Xiaonaiqiu, Bilibili

In November 2020, the social media platform Douban initiated a series of online lectures instructing people how to create a proper narrative (i.e., "Versailles study group" and "Versailles open online tutorials") (Brain instructor 2020). Awards are given to those netizens who promote the narrative successfully (Zui et al. 2020). One famous but contested representative of this narrative technique is Meng Qiqi (蒙淇淇77). She received online public attention on Weibo because of how she depicted her alleged extravagant lifestyle. Meng Qiqi name drops famous brands while describing her husband's clothing style (see post from Nov. 2, 2020, Fig. 8, lower half of screenshot):

"My husband is so thrifty; he only wears $23,000 KITON suits. Even on important occasions, he just wears $5,000 ZEGNA suits to work, and always uses the same ARMANI handbag and D&G shoes".

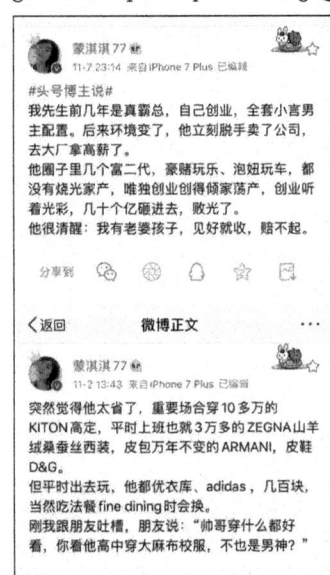

Fig. 8: Weibo posts by user Meng Qiqi

Some users express their dismay at Meng Qiqi's post and the kind of narrative she uses. This results in her blocking them, which is an act these users find even more ridiculous, as illustrated by the four screenshots below (User 'Max English name is too short' 2020, Fig. 10; User 'Iceberg Fire' 2020, Fig. 11; User 'Caribbean Big Bubble' 2020, Fig. 12).

Fig. 9: Censored; Fig. 10: User Max; Fig. 11: User Iceberg; Fig. 12: User Caribbean

Translation (Fig. 9-12): Fig. 9 (lower half): Censored user comment: "Fly your helicopter to Lhasa to see the starry sky". Fig. 10 (upper half): "I can only laugh at you! You really make me sad". (User 'Max English name is too short' 2020). Fig. 11 (upper half): "Damn, Meng Qiqi's layout is too small. That's it, you blocked me @Mengqiqi 77". (User 'Iceberg Fire' 2020). Fig. 12 (upper half): "Unbelievable. Deleted my comments and blocked me!" (User 'Caribbean Big Bubble' 2020)

Note that the first of the four user posts shown above (Fig. 9) is no longer publicly accessible and has likely been deleted by internet censors because it contains the politically sensitive word "Lhasa" (capital of Tibet). This is an example of categorical suspicion as one major implication of social media surveillance (Fuchs/Trottier 2015: 128), as this particular comment was not meant to criticise China's policy on Tibet, but was filtered out by censors anyway. Here, we can see that Zuboff's concept of surveillance capitalism is insufficient to grasp the interaction of economic interests and socio-political surveillance in the case of China.

Despite extensive user criticism, Meng Qiqi is still an opinion leader on Weibo, with hundreds of thousands of fans. Authors of Versailles literature aim to capture the attention of netizens (Hello new life 2020) by creating a fabricated image of a virtual self that flaunts its alleged wealth and high social status. If they succeed, they may be promoted by platforms, brands and merchandising companies and so be able to generate profit as an online influencer. Hence, the aesthetic and narrative strategies of Versailles literature make users turn to the platform and spend their time, either creating, admiring or criticising this content. Together, this generates the network effects needed to stabilise surveillance capitalism.

To summarise, the three case studies discussed in the practice section demonstrate that the new business model of platform capitalism in China's authoritarian state centres on enabling "grassroot" content creators to make a living through online advertisement and merchandising. The Chinese state does not intervene in the e-business activities discussed, signalling its support of the parties involved reproducing an ideology based on platforms' commodification of user content creation. Hence, against Zuboff's claim that the Chinese government regards instrumentarian society as a means to pursue political and social outcomes, the examples discussed suggest that it considers instrumentarian society as a market opportunity to be equally important. That the Chinese state is equally determined to pursue socio-political outcomes is illustrated in the next section. We will see how the Chinese Cyber Administration restricts the amount of freedom it grants to IT-companies that prioritise platform growth tactics without respecting Party rule.

4. Governance: When Social Media and E-Commerce Platforms have their Own Way with Algorithmic Censorship

The first Chinese online celebrity listed by Nasdaq in 2019 was Zhang Dayi, who started her career as an e-commerce model and established herself as a fashion entrepreneur. Operating her highly successful online store on the e-commerce platform Taobao, she interacts with her followers (and customers) by raising questions about the products she sells to increase online engagement and estimate the number of products her team should produce. Holding 13.2% of the shares, she is the chief marketing officer of Ruhan Holdings on Weibo platform, China's first ranked e-commerce company. Ruhan Holdings provides a marketing platform for online celebrities and cooperates with the online-retailing store Taobao to promote certain brands (Hangzhou Ruhan Holdings Co., Ltd. 2021). It uses the new economic operation mode of multi-channel-networks (MCN 2021) by continuously releasing professional content to promote both online celebrities and the brands these celebrities are advertising. Ruhan provides supply chain management, fabric purchases, design and pattern-making, manufacturing and production, but Zhang's task is to recruit new followers, to advertise fashion products and to stimulate user feedback on newly released products (Pan 2017). Hence, her business model is built on (a) creating audio-visual material that invites netizens to interact with her and, (b) extracting data from user engagement with the help of big data analytics (i.e., sentiment analysis). One day before Women's Day in 2019, Alibaba praised Zhang Dayi on its official Weibo account, as one of the top nine successful female "Wang Hong" practising e-commerce on Taobao and Tmall (Shandong Finance 2020). Similar to their Western counterparts, the economies of Chinese social media corporations consist of both advertising industry and financial economics, where investors purchase shares to increase market value (Fuchs 2016: 35).

Zhang Dayi is also interesting because she became involved in a major online event that illustrates the power of platforms in redefining digital visual culture: content that harms the platform's economic business is doomed to be made invisible by the platform's automated image censorship. When Dong Huahua publicly warned Zhang Dayi on Weibo not to contact her (Dong's) husband Jiang Fan anymore, netizens became curious. On April 17, 2020, Jiang Fan (Alibaba executive, Weibo's second largest shareholder, and president of Taobao Tmall) was suddenly on the list of hot topics for a sex scandal: he had cheated on his wife Dong Huahua in an affair with Zhang Dayi. Screenshots of Dong Huahua's Weibo posts show that the comment function of her Weibo account (@花花董花花) was blocked only one hour after she had posted the original message that had piqued netizens' attention (Su and Meng 2020, Fig. 13).

Due to surveillance creep, users involved in the discussion soon noticed that not only had the keyword "Jiang Fan" been removed from Weibo's hot topic list, but all related content was deleted on both the wife's (Huahuadonghuahua 2021) and the mistress' (Zhang Dayi's) Weibo account. Only two of the user comments shown in the screenshot below remained publicly accessible (i.e., the third comment by user 'Han Xiaofan' 2020, and the fourth by user 'handsome and witty lyc classmate' 2020). The first two comments (posted by the same user) have since been deleted (Fig. 14).

Fig. 13: Dong Huahua's posts on Weibo (censored)

Translation (Fig. 13): 1ˢᵗ message upper part: "Who locked the comment function of my Weibo account?" (User Dong Huhua); 2ⁿᵈ message, lower part: (@Zhang Dayi) "This is my last warning. Stop seeing my husband". (User Dong Huahua)

It is unclear why only some of these user comments have been deleted, despite all having the same meaning (i.e., expressing astonishment about the censorship of the two women's Weibo accounts). The fourth user comment even goes one step further, by relating the act of censorship to the power of capitalism, but this has not been deleted either (User 'handsome and witty lyc classmate' 2020, Fig. 14). Furthermore, user comments highlighting the economic stakes behind the ranking of trending topics are still visible on the social media platform Douban (User 'Calabash Baby' 2020). Public interest in Weibo's hashtag #Donghuahua# (i.e., 99 million readings between April 17, 2020 and June 18, 2021) can also still be retrieved ("#Donghuahua#" 2021). A year later, the topic is still being discussed by the online public (User 'Zheng went to buy shoes' 2021).

There is a commercial media article available that outlines the economic considerations behind the act of online censorship (Su/Meng 2020). It provides a screenshot of Dong Huahua's deleted Weibo posts, and points out that these had been forwarded by major Weibo big V media (i.e., Weibo accounts of verified celebrities and companies) whose official social media accounts have millions of followers. These, however, were deleted as well. Users who tried to comment on the topic would have received a notification saying "manual review required first". When asked by reporters about the rationale behind the deletions, Weibo explained that in some cases users who had replied to Dong Huahua's account deleted comments themselves, and in other cases Weibo had to shut down users' Weibo accounts entirely because of legal complaints issued by lawyers.

Fig. 14: Users comment on censorship

Translation (Fig. 14): 1st message: "What happened? Why have all these Weibo posts about Dong Huahua and Zhang Dayi been deleted?"; 3rd message: "The Weibo accounts of Zhang Dayi and Dong Huahua have all been deleted. I am so worried about it". (User 'Han Xiaofan' 2020); 4th message: "#Dong Huahua# There are more than ten new Weibo posts about this trending hashtag but Weibo comments continue to be deleted. I think capitalism is the worst!" (User 'handsome and witty lyc classmate' 2020)

Most interestingly, the journalists present net revenue statistics from Weibo advertisement and marketing, and their relation to Alibaba (Fig. 15).

Fig. 15: Weibo's net revenues and their relation to Alibaba

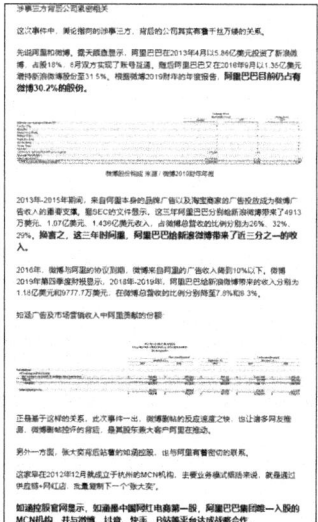

The journalists also report a deeper economic relationship between unfaithful husband Jiang Fan (Alibaba and Weibo) and mistress Zhang Dayi (Ruhan Holdings), revealing that "Alibaba currently holds 30.2% of Weibo's shares, and Ruhan Holdings is the only MCN institution that Alibaba Group has invested in". The reporters suggest that Weibo shareholder Jiang Fan's economic interests lie behind the act of censorship: when his name was brought into disrepute, he would have wanted to divert public attention away from his person to avoid any negative impact on his online businesses (Taobao/Tmall, Alibaba, Weibo).

But why would Chinese media want to highlight that the social media platform was employing forms of algorithmic and social control? Perhaps this was made publicly visible because the social media and e-commerce platforms involved had already incurred the Chinese authorities' displeasure through legal disputes within and outside China. For example, a year-long legal dispute with the Beijing Office of the Cyberspace Administration of China (CAC) accused Sina Weibo of having violated the cyberspace laws and regulations by spreading illegal information and negatively affecting the online environment ("The State Cyberspace Administration of China" 2015). In 2018, Sina Weibo was ordered to conduct a "self-inspection" and make improvements in the management of "harmful information". Weibo temporarily suspended certain functions (e.g., trending topics, 'most searched hashtags', 'Weibo Q&A', 'celebrity and soft news aggregator'), and the Beijing Municipal Internet Information Office interviewed Sina Weibo's person in charge and fined Weibo ("Dongyuan boiled wine" 2018). The Dong Huahua/Zhang Dayi/Jiang Fan incident provoked another wave of investigations by the Beijing Internet Information Office, which was following the instructions of the State Internet Information Office (Xiaoxiang Morning News's official hundred accounts 2020). Within the broader context of current policy debates on anti-monopoly and data security, Weibo has been one among other platforms (e.g., DIDI app for ride-hailing) who are being subjected to legal investigations, self-inspections and regulatory changes in China's platform economy (Chan/Kwok 2021: 14).

In summary, this example not only highlights an incident in which the state feels called into action to regulate platforms, but also shows how categorical suspicion and surveillance creep (Fuchs/Trottier 2015: 129) can backfire and not only harm users, but also those who operate social media and e-commerce platforms. Against the background of Zuboff's diagnosis of the radical indifference of U.S. American IT firms to Western democracies' inclusive economic and political institutions, this case study demonstrates that if Chinese platform operators display their indifference to party rule by coming up with their own, economically motivated censorship rules, state intervention is prompted. The case also depicts the state as being in a continuing process of contention, in which it is caught in partially dragging-on negotiations with regulatory bureaus, corporate actors, public and private sectors, and stakeholders (Hong 2017: 20), as the long-lasting legal dispute with Weibo, Alibaba and Ruhan Holdings illustrates.

Having discussed how the state controls economic actors, the final section now focuses on social actors (users) and the impact of platform surveillance on employees and patients. While these cases will highlight Chinese culture-specific forms of online behaviour that stabilise surveillance capitalism, we will also see that the power of networked images does not always play into the hands of the Chinese government.

5. Infrastructure: The Power of Networked Visual Images

5.1 Workers' Internet Memes and Young Users' Barrage Subtitling Practice between the Stabilisation and Deconstruction of Surveillance Capitalism

On-demand e-commerce platforms have reconfigured the social relationship between companies, employees, and consumers. One example of this is the food delivery industry in China. Two major players provide online meal ordering services: 'Ele.me' (backed up by the e-commerce giant Alibaba), and 'Meituan Dianping' (whose main investor is Alibaba's rival, Tencent). In contrast to other digital workers, the 3 million delivery workers are deeply embedded in digitalised platforms (Sun 2019: 309). These companies use algorithms to optimise the flexibility, scalability, and tractability of labour. All the parties involved (including employers, employees, and customers) can see the algorithmic system's calculation of delivery distance and time. This helps ensure the efficiency of the delivery system (e.g., dispatching orders to the drivers, managing deliveries, etc.). The app is designed so that customers can track the delivery man on the map, and the employer can see the number of finished orders, delivery time, duration of work time, and customer ratings (Sun 2019: 316-317). Wages are based on the employee's performance (i.e., a minimum wage and a bonus calculated according to the number of orders they deliver per month). It appears that the platform's constant monitoring of the delivery worker's job execution (categorical suspicion), the algorithmic classification of drivers and allocation of privileges according to a worker's performance and customer ratings (social sorting), and the customer's observation of the delivery person's physical movement on the map (surveillance creep) subjects the worker to an overall surveillance that they can hardly escape. In addition, labour platforms that are embedded in several layers of institutional structures cooperate with third-party intermediaries to manage flexible labour, which further fosters new forms of labour precarity. Within this context, delivery workers are treated as independent contractors, whose burden of self-management and risk-absorption is further aggravated by the sense of being readily disposable (Doorn 2020: 147).

In that respect, the algorithmic management that Chinese food delivery platforms use to assign orders and assess a worker's performance does not differ largely from Western food delivery platforms that might (depending on the particular platform) also use a piece-rate model (Doorn 2020: 140), bonus pay, penalising drivers who frequently decline orders, or customer feedback as a quality-control mechanism (Griesbach et al. 2019: 5-7). At the same time, despite similarities in gamified financial incentives, researchers notice that Chinese delivery persons, if compared to their colleagues in New York, face more competition among colleagues (e.g., gamified function of stacking orders, in which drivers need to quickly pick well-paid orders shown on the platform) (Doorn/Chen 2021: 17; 20).

While scholars find that the anticipation and interpretation of platform surveillance and data extraction processes by various stakeholders still needs to be explored (Chan/Kwok 2021: 14), some researchers have enquired into how Western (Griesbach et al. 2019) and Chinese food delivery workers (Sun 2019) experience the algorithmic control over their work. Online surveys and interviews have found that although workers feel subjected to arbitrary authority, they also have a sense of agency (e.g., choice of working time). However, as I argue here, one major difference between Western and Chinese digital laborers is that due to the lack of reciprocal and productive social relationships between employers and employees, Chinese workers have limited means to show their resistance to food delivery platforms' surveillance mechanisms in an organised form. In addition, they might lack the educational background to challenge the power of platform algorithms (i.e., delivery pricing and wage calculation) by building open-source, web-based applications to collect data (on delivery fees) (Doorn 2020: 139; 142). Creating media content appears to be one loophole. The following case study analysing the public discourse of journalists, delivery workers, and customers (here: younger netizens) sheds light on the powerful impact of networked visual images on public attention and reveals culture-specific practices when users engage with media content.

A short video shared by the *NetEase Finance* Weibo account has raised public attention, showing nearby shopkeepers helping the 48-year-old delivery man Liu Jin on January 11, 2021 in Taizhou, Jiangsu Province, after he set himself on fire because he had not been paid his monthly income ("#Jiangsu delivery man" 2021, Fig. 16).

This prompted journalists to investigate the precarious working conditions of this group of employees (Li/Sun 2021), which are traced back to the emergence of "flexible employment online platforms" (e.g., Haohuo App), utilised since 2019 by companies to which the e-commerce takeaway platforms had outsourced the handling of their employment contracts. The subcontracting agreements consider delivery persons as self-employed business owners, which spares the companies from paying social security, overtime hours, or compensation for work-related injuries. The platforms' wage payment system (using the Haohuo app to transfer money to personal Alipay accounts) does not provide a proper remuneration statement from a bank to document the labour relationship between the outsourcing company and the driver. This makes it difficult for workers to be protected by labour arbitration. Delivery workers have attempted to escape the algorithmic governance of platforms that constantly change their bonus policies (e.g., by taking routes other than those suggested by the algorithm, or by establishing groups on social networks like WeChat where they can transfer their orders to each other) (Sun 2019: 319).

Fig. 16: Delivery driver set on fire gets rescued

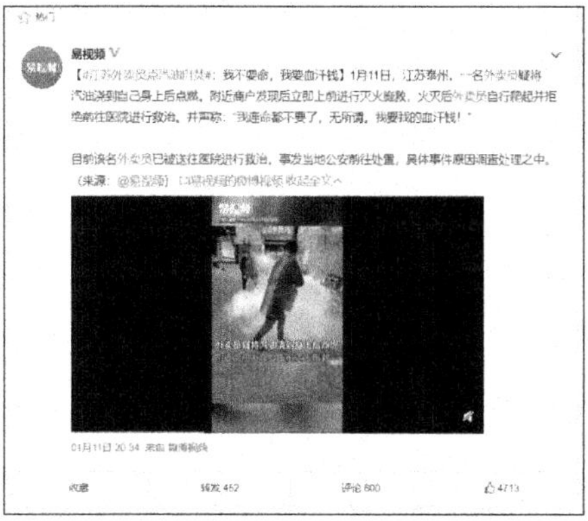

Journalist reports received some attention from the public, with more than 100,000 views on WeChat (Li/Sun 2021), however, it was predominantly single individuals among the group of Chinese workers themselves that drew attention to their plight through internet memes. Memes are image-text-combinations or short videoclips circulated, imitated, and transformed by individual internet users. Memes are a highly visible, important practice in popular and digital culture. Due to their form-related and visual aspects, emotion-related features and their participation and representation patterns, the viral distribution of internet memes has been described as a mirror of processes of crowd psychology (Shifman 2013). Internet memes as short videoclips have recently experienced a transformation due to the emerging social practice of barrage subtitling, which first appeared in Japan and rapidly spread to China with distinctive changes (Nakajima 2019: 99). In barrage subtitling, viewers add a large number of text comments onscreen to videos that follow the timeline of the video, so that viewers have a sense of collectiveness on the video-sharing platform.

One internet meme that was very successful in capturing attention was the so called "Dagongren" ("hard workers") meme, distributed via the popular Chinese video sharing site Bilibili, where three-quarters of users in 2017 were below the age of 25 (Nakajima 2019: 106). This meme criticised the surveillance of delivery workers with tracking tools by platforms, employers and customers (User 'San Lu is poisonous' 2020), and went viral in December 2020. In less than 24 hours, the video "Good morning, Dagongren!" was watched more than 17 million times (Fig. 17), and received 11,815 comments (Fig. 18).

Fig. 17: Internet meme "Good morning, Dagongren!", Fig. 18: 11.815 comments by May 04, 2021

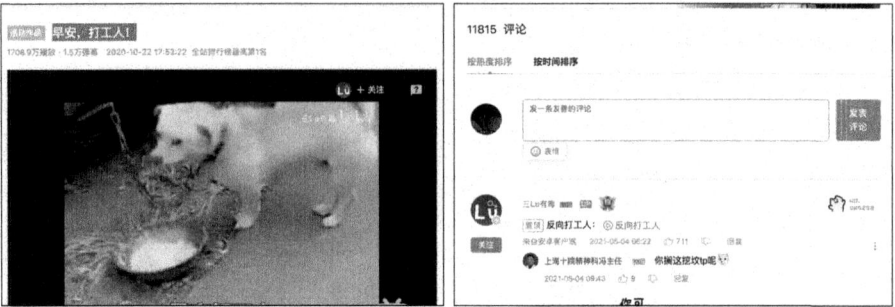

The video shows a barking dog with a voice-over satirically mocking the life of workers. It shouts the following text:

"Good morning, Dagongren! Dagongren has a working spirit. Dagongren are all masters. We want to work quietly and then surprise everyone. We must have faith in our hearts: there is no difficult work, only the brave Dagongren. Has your takeaway order not arrived yet? It's okay, Dagongren is not afraid of anything. It is the princess who depends on others. The Japanese depend on you. The people in the north are from Taipei. People who rely on nen [your] mothers are from Henan. We are the glorious Dagongren on our own. Are you tired? It's alright if you feel tired. Comfort is reserved for the rich. Are you cold? If you feel cold, that's it. Warmth is reserved for those who have cars. Don't be late, because money will be deducted if you are late. Don't dry your tears, because riding an electric bike like this is dangerous. Raise your fist and punch in the air. In order to fight against this world, do not fight for father, do not fight for mother, do not fight for work, do not fight for money. Just desperately be a Dagongren! Try Harder! Dagongren! As long as I work hard enough, the boss will soon be able to live a better life. Come on, Dagongren! As long as I'm good enough! Mankind will move towards a better future. Cheer up! Dagongren! When Dagongren cheers up, tomorrow's sun will no longer exist. And the dazzling light shining in the east is a sign of Dagongren's hard work. Good morning, Dagongren!"

The user speaks for the employees working for delivery services, deconstructing the customer's power to use apps to demand a rush of deliveries and restoring his pride in sentences such as: "Has your takeaway order not arrived yet? It's okay, Dagongren is not afraid of anything". Sentences like "Don't be late, otherwise money will be deducted" refer to the platform company's algorithms' tracking of different categories of driver performance. Sentences like "It is the princess who depends on others", "As long as I work hard enough, the boss will definitely live the life he wants" and "Comfort is reserved for the rich" clearly blame the capital-owning class and deconstruct capitalist ideology.

In a next step, the video was re-edited and uploaded on two other Bilibili user accounts, containing the same content but now displaying 15,000 user comments (barrage, 弹幕) running through the video (Fig. 19).

Fig. 19: Re-edited version "Good night, beaten workers!"

Translation of one user comment running through video (barrage), captured in the screenshot above (Fig. 19): "I cried. Really ruthless. Imprisonment because of a 'wife'. Hit all Dagongren. Are you scolding again? Taiwanese people call this expert out directly. Ha ha ha ha ha ha ha ha. I could kick myself. Henan people feel very upset. The Taiwanese said it was very connotative. Imprisonment because there is no 'wife'. Public execution. People from Henan expressed their displeasure! Proletarians of the world, unite! Brothers, I am here again, in a bad mood, continuing to see Dagongren hhh. San Lu's video. I am really miserable! It hit everyone. Once a day. Watch it again a billion times. This is so true!"

It is not only that the display of users' feedback in edited videos (barrage) creates a new type of image that signals how the video is a trending topic to online audiences. It is also an indicator of a change in everyday practices in East Asian online youth culture. Users are motivated to watch the video again to read through the comments, and users are motivated to comment on the video in the hope that it will be displayed in future edited versions. However, it needs to be pointed out that although everybody can watch videos, only those can comment on them who are registered Bilibili members or who have been invited by current members to become one. Registration is free, but users need to pass a quiz about Japanese anime subculture and about the ways to engage with barrage subtitling to upgrade their level of membership (Nakajima 2019: 106-107). Hence, while user content (barrage in video-based memes) helps extend (passive) users' browsing time and thus plays into the hands of platform operators' growth tactics, the platform seeks to attract more active users by tying exclusive membership to the "privilege" of content production. The emotional gratification that active users get from Bilibili's barrage subtitling practice is the sense of a "sociality of connections", where the main purpose of interaction is based on the formal continuation of online communication, as opposed to clarifying meaning (translation of foreign language video content) in ordinary subtitling (Nakajima 2019: 102).

Two conclusions can be drawn from this case study. First, the barrage subtitling practice demonstrates that platformisation and economic surveillance have redefined digital visual culture by combining a platform's growth tactics (i.e. extending users' browsing time, extraction of user data) with a new aesthetic of short videoclips (users' text comments onscreen to videos, following the time-line of the video) that nourishes the users' sense of collectiveness. Ironically, while criticising surveillance capitalism, workers' memes have stabilised surveillance capitalism by successfully capturing the young audience's attention and prompting them to participate in more platform labour. Second, while platform labour businesses operate in legal grey areas and pose challenges to both the Chinese and Euro-American political systems (Chan/Kwok 2021: 6), Chinese delivery workers are deprived of the means available to their Western colleagues (e.g., workers' strikes, public protest). Instead, they use other means to express their criticism of new forms of labour precarity, and turn to the online sphere (e.g., the video-sharing platform home to China's youth cultures) to generate collective support. It appears that the penetration of China's institutional setting into e-platforms is giving birth to social and cultural online practices so far unseen in the West.

Being torn between promoting management instead of proletariat interests while recognising platform labour as a problem that needs to be regulated, the Chinese government allows workers and young users to collaborate on short video-sharing sites and generate the observed network effects, presumably because it regards the behaviour of both economic actors (i.e., algorithmic categorisation of "dagongren meme" as a trending topic; e-platforms' incentives for users to engage in barrage subtitling) and of users (i.e., criticising not the government, but employers' and customers' exploitation of their labour force with big data analytics) as appropriate.

In the following section, the final case discussed will explore what kind of network effects are considered to promote an "unhealthy" online environment by the state, and so prompt intervention.

5.2 New Input for 'Human Flesh Search': The Role of Government and Platform Patient Data

The process of 'human flesh search' ('人肉搜索') emerged in China twenty years ago; it involves someone disclosing a specific individual's behaviour that allegedly violates certain moral values and socio-cultural norms. The netizen links his or her findings to a particular question or provocative statement, which prompts the formation of an online community to track down a specific individual through a joint effort to harvest more details about the person or about a related event with the goal of revealing the 'truth' and pursuing 'justice' on their own ("Human flesh search" 2021). Recent cases of human flesh search were related to legal and moral aspects or to entertainment (Cheng et al. 2019). For example, in the case of Chinese work safety official Dacai Yang, who was caught in a photograph grinning at the scene of a tragic bus crash in Shaanxi province in 2012, online collaboration of netizens (i.e., digging out images that showed Yang wearing luxury wristwatches) prompted the legal authorities to investigate a potential case of bribery and corruption (Xinhua News Agency 2012). The fact that scholars have identified weak institutionalised trust in China's authoritarian capitalism (Witt/Redding 2012:12) might be one factor that explains this culture-specific type of social online behaviour.

Fig. 20: Wang's original Weibo post; Fig. 21: Wang's original Weibo post including visual trajectory of Zhao

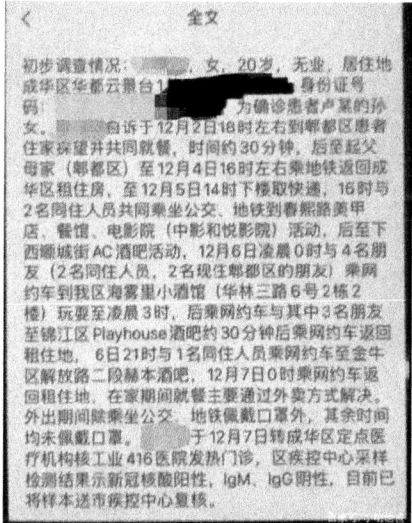 

Platforms have a huge interest in promoting this phenomenon, arranging the posts for human flesh search at the top of their websites, with traditional media spreading these sensational news items and turning them into social events on their social media accounts. In addition, users have become more efficient in exploiting other users' digital traces on social media platforms and visualising them to attract netizens' attention. The Covid-19 epidemic has caused a new twist in the phenomenon of human flesh search because netizens can now 'harness' available personal health data to publicly shame a particular patient who has allegedly violated public measures to control the epidemic. The general digital surveillance and willingness of the Chinese state to share its knowledge – here the provision of data about diagnosed Covid-19 patients – with app users not only differs from other East Asian countries like Singapore, where more targeted techniques for social tagging of the sick ensure the privacy of those in quarantine (Cha 2020: 6-7) but also from the disuse or failed use of smartphone apps in European and U.S. American states for epidemic containment in 2020, as the case of the French contact-tracing app illustrates (Rowe et al. 2020).

Fig. 22: Wang's post shared by users on Baidu Tieba

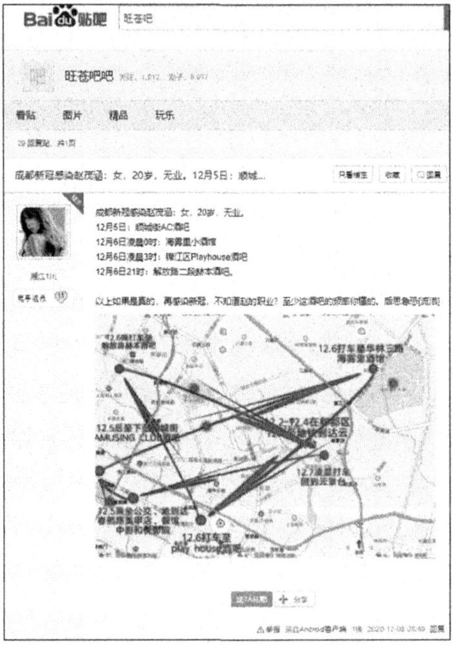

Translation of Wang's post shared by users: "Chengdu Covid-19 infection Zhao Maohan: female, 20 years old, unemployed.
December 5th: AC Bar on Shuncheng Street
At 12am (midnight) on December 6th: Haiwuli Bistro
At 3am on December 6th: Playhouse Bar in Jinjiang District
At 9pm on December 6th: Hepburn Bar on the second section of Jiefang Road.
If the above is true for you too, then you might be infected with Covid-19. You don't know Zhao's occupation? At least you know now how frequently she visited these bars. Worried afterthoughts".

In December 2020, a 20-year-old woman, Zhao Maohan (赵茂涵), living in Chengdu became a hot topic on Weibo overnight. Under the heading of "Chengdu epidemic situation and Zhao Maohan's identity information and activity track", a private 24-year-old male user named Wang had revealed her personal identity and posted an image of her personal location around 23:00 on December 7, 2020, on his Weibo account. Media eagerly reported on the case of human flesh search and published the young man's original posts ("The girl diagnosed with the virus in Chengdu" 2020, Fig. 20-21):

Using the name of the perpetrator "Wang Cang" (旺苍吧) on the Baidu post bar Tieba, users could find and share Wang's posts about Zhao's identity and location history (Wang 2020, Fig. 23):

Wang staged Zhao as a "time bomb", who had deliberately decided to infect others by visiting numerous bars, parks, cinemas, and nail salons for her own amusement within the last 14 days. Other users became engaged in the smear campaign by uploading screenshots of Zhao's social media posts showing photographs of her with friends in a bar (Wang 2020, Fig. 23).

Fig. 23: Photographs showing Zhao with friends in a bar

Hence, the internet mob staged the girl as immoral, and blamed her for causing the return of the epidemic in Chengdu ("I'm Ma Nan" 2020).

Commercial media jumped on the bandwagon ("Zhao Maohan, a girl diagnosed" 2020) and moralised the issue with sensational headlines posted on their social media accounts ("A 20-year-old girl diagnosed" 2020). State media discussed the blurred line between the public's right to know, and the violation of the privacy of user data (Luo/Li 2020), condemned the netizens for revealing a patient's personal information ("The girl diagnosed with the virus in Chengdu" 2020), and presented human flesh search as creating harmful online environments. On its official Weibo account, Chengdu Public Security concluded that Wang had severely violated the privacy rights of user Zhao and thus had to be punished legally ("The girl diagnosed with the virus in Chengdu" 2020).

Neither the journalists nor the Public Security Bureau ever discussed how the government's online publication of personal patient data may have contributed to the emergence of this human flesh search occurrence. Media reports state that it was unclear how Zhao's personal information was leaked ("The girl diagnosed with the virus in Chengdu" 2020). However, for the purpose of containing the epidemic, Chengdu's Health Commission consistently published private information about Covid-19 patients on its website, so this may have spurred Wang's search. Public notification records about the first newly discovered Covid-19 cases in Chengdu from the morning of December 8 (07:47) suggest that the family names of Zhao's grandparents were already disclosed by the Health Commission on December 7:

"Patient 1: Zhao X, female, 20 years old, no fixed occupation, living in Huadu Yunjingtai Community, Cuijiadian, Chenghua District, is the granddaughter of the cases Lu and Zhao in Pidu District confirmed yesterday. Nucleic acid tests were found to be positive and Lu's close contacts were isolated on December 8. After consultation with provincial, municipal and district experts, comprehensive clinics, and after the findings from imaging and laboratory nucleic acid test results, the virus (common type) was confirmed and the patient was transferred to Chengdu Public Health Clinical Medical Center Hospital for isolation and treatment. In the past 14 days, the main places where the patients spent time include: MCC Central Park, Hi Blues Nail Salon, Alley Mala Tang, Haiwuli Small Bar, Playhouse Bar, Hepburn Bar, etc.".

It is likely that Wang came across the details provided by the local Health Commission about Zhao's grandparents (family names, name of residential area and location history), and took these as a starting point to uncover further private information (patient's given name, exact address, and daily activities) in order to identify the people behind the newly confirmed cases in Chengdu. On December 9, Zhao apologised publicly using her Weibo account (User 'Fish balls are not good in Chengdu' 2020).

In summary, the case of the woman from Chengdu illustrates how economic surveillance (i.e., platforms prominently arranging user posts for human flesh search; hashtag grouping of comments) interacts with state surveillance (publication of patient data for epidemic containment) by stimulating a culture-specific social online behaviour through which netizens use a victim's own social media posts to map out the victim's movements, capture audience attention (the girl from Chengdu as a hot topic on Weibo) and motivate other users to become engaged in the smear campaign. Hence, the government's new approach to handling the epidemic (i.e., disseminating real-time data) has provided human flesh search-communities with a new dataset. This example also illustrates how two social implications of social media surveillance - categorical suspicion in the form of state and platform monitoring of smart phone users' activities to control the spread of an epidemic and users' exposure of private lives (surveillance creep) - fatefully 'enrich' each other when netizens engage in human flesh search for Covid-19 patients. The radical indifference of authoritarian states towards the privacy protection of patient data - or, to put it differently, the willingness of authoritarian states to publicly share their knowledge - can accelerate existing forms of problematic online behaviour.

6. Conclusion

Against the background of the theoretical model of social media surveillance, the case studies highlight that some similar societal implications of surveillance capitalism (categorical suspicion, social sorting, surveillance creep) are at stake in both authoritarian and Western democratic states. However, China's institutional setting (i.e., economic, governmental, infrastructural) penetrates e-platforms, and we can observe different effects on users' online behaviour regarding the social use of images on platforms, and users' interaction with visual images and their networkedness. For example, the two case studies in the Infrastructure section suggest that Chinese delivery workers, in collaboration with young Chinese netizens, show their resistance to social sorting in platform labour in different ways (video-based internet memes and their reediting with the barrage subtitling practice) to their Western colleagues (worker strikes). Similarly, Chinese private users engage in types of online behaviour (human flesh search) unseen in the West because the implementation of categorical suspicion for the sake of epidemic control by both the Chinese state and platforms provides Chinese users with access to patient data that Western users do not have due to data privacy protection laws. Furthermore, this culture-specific social online behaviour is fostered by the interaction of economic and state surveillance.

The case studies outlined in the Practice section exemplify how the Chinese government grants economic actors (platforms, brands, celebrities) freedom to commodify user content creation and to mobilise a great mass of people to become entrepreneurs in the digital economy. At the same time, we observe how politically sensitive words are automatically filtered out (categorical suspicion). This state-commerce relationship impacts content production on these platforms and distinguishes Chinese platformisation from its Western counterpart. In the Governance section, the case of the online celebrity Zhang Dayi illustrates that when social media platforms (Weibo) and e-commerce platforms (Alibaba) enact algorithmic censorship of content considered to be a threat to their business, users quickly notice their action due to surveillance creep being in place. Coming up with their own censorship rules suggests a radical indifference to Party rule and thus triggers intervention from China's Cyber Administration (restriction of online business activities).

Hence, the diverse logics of marketisation and economic surveillance (which combine user, platform and state perspectives), interact with different forms of social, political and lateral surveillance and lead to culture-specific social practices of online behaviour. The observed surveillance mechanisms go beyond the concept of surveillance capitalism, so that any analysis of China's internet economy and the online behaviour of its economic and social actors must be embedded into a wider context of political economies and state regulations.

Acknowledgements

I would like to thank my student research assistants, Wushuang Yu and Fujiali, who helped me collect the empirical data discussed in the case studies, and the anonymous reviewers for their valuable comments and suggestions during the revision process.

7. References

7.1 Primary Literature

Anhui Women's Federation (2021): "Creatively Advertising or Insulting Women? Netizens Were Angry, and Purcotton Apologised Twice!" January 9 (https://baijiahao.baidu.com/s?id=1688408457851481944&wfr=spider&for=pc) [Original source in Chinese: "广告创意还是侮辱女性？网友怒了，全棉时代两次道歉！" 安徽妇联].

Brain Instructor (2020): "What Is the Origin of and Story behind 'Versailles Literature' That Has Gone Viral Online?" November 10 (https://baijiahao.baidu.com/s?id=1682986712162606922&wfr=spider&for=pc [Original source in Chinese: 脑洞指导员. "火遍全网的"凡尔赛文学"到底是什么梗？" 百度].

Chengdu Municipal Health Commission (2020): "There are 3 New Confirmed Cases of New Coronary Pneumonia in Our City, All of Which Are Related to the Cases in Pidu District Confirmed Yesterday." Website of Chengdu Municipal Health Commission, December 08 (http://cdwjw.chengdu.gov.cn/cdwjw/gzdt/2020-12/08/content_731e717981644fda8790da24d5d126c8.shtml) [Original source in Chinese: 成都市卫健委. "我市新增3例新冠肺炎确诊病例，均系昨日郫都区确诊病例的关联病例". 成都市卫健委].

China Women's Daily (2021). "#Response: Backfiring Advertisement# ('Creativity' Is Not an Excuse for Abdicating from Responsibility) Recently, #Purcotton# Released a Backfiring Advertisement Titled 'When You Go Home Late at Night and You Are Followed by a Man in Black, What Method Will You Use to Get Rid of Him?' Triggered a Vibrant Discussion among Netizens". Weibo account of *China Women's Daily*, January 8 (https://share.api.weibo.cn/share/235307059.html?weibo_id=4591119284830606) [Original source in Chinese: "#全棉时代回应反转广告#（'创意'不是开脱责任的挡箭牌）近日，#全棉时代#发布的反转广告 '深夜回家遇黑衣人尾随，你会用什么方法摆脱"引发网友热议'." 微博账号: 中国妇女报, 微博].

#Donghuahua# (2021). "99,399 Million Readings and 7827 Comments." Weibo (https://m.weibo.cn/search?containerid=100103type%3D1%26q%3D%23%E8%91%A3%E8%8A%B1%E8%8A%B1%23) [Original source in Chinese: #董花花# 微博话题. "阅读9939.9万 讨论7827." 微博].

"Dongyuan Boiled Wine. The Country Has Stepped Up Information Censorship, and Sina Weibo Was Interviewed. The Reaction of Netizens Was Surprising." Weibo, January 28, 2018 (https://www.sohu.com/a/219459320_100100890) [Original source in Chinese: "东原煮酒。国家加大信息审查力度, 新浪微博被约谈, 网友的反应让人惊讶。微博]

Financial Community Network (2021). "Hot Search on Scolding! PurCotton's Advertisement Is Accused of Insulting Women. The Company's Response: It's Creative Advertisement." Tencent.com, January 8 (https://new.qq.com/omn/20210108/20210108A067XZ00.html) [Original source in Chinese: 金融界网. "骂上热搜! 全棉时代广告被指侮辱女性 公司回应称为广告创意." 腾讯网].

"Good Night, Beaten Workers! 5,394 Million Views, Barrage: 3558, Top 5 in the Ranking." Bilibili, October 27, 2020 (video length 01:17) (https://www.bilibili.com/video/BV1Fi4y177he/?spm_id_from=autoNext) [Original source in Chinese: "活动作品晚安, 被打工人! 539.4万播放, 3558弹幕, 全站排行榜最高第5名"].

"Hard Currency: 5 Core Rules of Kuaishou Live Streaming." Yibang Power Network, August 15, 2019 (https://www.niuxuan.cn/redian/51950.html) [Original source in Chinese: "硬通货: 快手直播带货的5个核心法则.亿邦动力网].

Hello New Life (2020): "Why Is Versailles Literature So Popular? Are Women Scolded for Writing Versailles Literature?" Tencent News, November 20 (https://view.inews.qq.com/a/20201120A0DH2M00) [Original source in Chinese: 你好新生活. "凡尔赛文学为何会火? 女性写凡尔赛就被骂?" 腾讯新闻].

"How to Approach Weibo's Frantic Deletion of Huahua Dong Huahua's Post About Zhang Dayi?" Zhihu (Question and answer forum), April 2020 (https://www.zhihu.com/question/389039128) [Original source in Chinese: 话题讨论: "如何看待微博疯狂删除 花花董花花 喊话张大奕的帖子?"].

Huahuadonghuahua. Weibo account, April 2021 (https://share.api.weibo.cn/share/234263997.html?weibo_id=4617372927787418) [Original source in Chinese: 花花董花花. 微博账号].

"I'm Ma Nan. The King of Virus May Appear in Chengdu. The 20-year-Old Girl Who Accompanies Customers to Bars Has Been Tested Positively and Still Ran All over These Places without a Mask." Weibo, December 8, 2020 (https://card.weibo.com/article/m/show/id/2309404579882750312600) [Original source in Chinese: "我是马男.成都或出现毒王, 20岁陪酒女孩确诊, 不戴口罩跑遍了这些地方." 微博头条文章].

"#Jiangsu Delivery Man Set Himself on Fire with Gasoline#: 'I Don't Want My Life, I Want My Hard-Earned Money.'" Weibo account of NetEase Finance, NetEase Wangyi video, January 11, 2021 (video length: 00:37 seconds) (https://weibo.com/1974561081/JCIEPtsIl?sudaref=cn.bing.com&type=comment) [Original source in Chinese: "#江苏外卖员点汽油自焚#: '我不要命, 我要血汗钱'." 网易财经 (来自 微博视频号), 易视频, 网易视频].

Li, Xiulian/Sun, Yidan (2021): "A Delivery Mhttps://mp.weixin.qq.com/s/KsGC-qGvoI7nmfbxRgsyOaAan Sets Himself on Fire to Ask for a Salary of 4.000

yuan. How to Protect the Rights and Interests of Delivery Staff." WeChat, reposted from Sanlian Life Weekly, February 03 () [Original source in Chinese: 李秀莲 /孙一丹. 李秀莲 /孙一丹. "外卖员自焚讨薪, 想要回4000块为什么那么难." 原创 李秀莉 三联生活周刊].

Little Milk Ball (2020): "'Little Milk Ball Versailles Open Class.' Number of Views: 100.000, barrage: 614." Bilibili, May 9 (https://www.bilibili.com/video/av838098912/) [Original source in Chinese: 小奶球. "小奶球 凡尔赛公开课". 10.0万播放, 614弹幕. Bilibili].

Luo, Yidan/Li, Weijia (2020): "Behind the Information Leakage of the Confirmed Girl in Chengdu: How to Reconcile the Public's Right to Know and the Protection of Personal Privacy?" In: Xinjingbao (Beijing News), official social media account of Xinjingbao, December 11 (https://baijiahao.baidu.com/s?id=1685770548182147179&wfr=spider&for=pc) [Original source in Chinese: 罗亦丹 /李薇佳. "成都确诊女孩信息泄露背后: 公众知情权和个人隐私保护如何调和?" 新京报, 新京报社官方帐号].

Meng Qiqi (2020). Weibo post by @Meng Qiqi77, Nov. 2 and Nov. 7, 2020 [@蒙淇淇77, 微博], quoted after "Why Has 'Versailles Literature' Become a Trending Topic?" In: Jiemian News, November 9, 2020 (https://www.sohu.com/a/430696123_313745) [Original source in Chinese: "凡尔赛文学"冲上热搜是怎么回事?" 界面新闻, 搜狐网].

Pan, Yiling (2017): "Top Web Celebrity Zhang Dayi Reveals the Key to Her Business Success". In: Jing Daily. The Business of Luxury in China, July 19 (https://jingdaily.com/uncovering-business-secrets-chinas-top-web-celebrity-zhang-dayi/).

Purcotton (2021): "Apology." Weibo account 'Purcotton cotton era', January 8 (https://share.api.weibo.cn/share/235305670.html?weibo_id=4591129855793443) [Original source in Chinese: Purcotton全棉时代. "致歉." 微博账号: Purcotton全棉时代].

"Purcotton Apologises for 'Advertisement Alleged to Insulting Women': The Video Was an Advertising Creative and Only Served to Highlight the Cleaning Function of the Product". In: Beijing Commercial Daily, January 08, 2021 (https://www.163.com/dy/article/FVR4B0U40519DFFO.html) [Original source in Chinese: 全棉时代致歉'广告涉嫌侮辱女性'一事: 视频为广告创意, 仅作为突出商品的清洁功能. 北京商报].

Shandong Finance and Economics Report-Economic Herald (2020). "Tmall President Jiang Fan and Cargo Internet Celebrity Zhang Dayi Were Watched by Everyone. Ali's Public Relations Reaction Was like This." In: Taishan Finance, April 20 (http://f.sdnews.com.cn/news/a/1538.html) [Original source in Chinese: 山东财经报道—经济导报. "天猫总裁蒋凡与带货网红张大奕"被围观", 阿里公关的反应是这样的." 泰山财经].

Su, Qi/Meng, Yana/Wei, Jia (2020): "Internet Celebrity Zhang Dayi Was Scolded at, Why Did Weibo Quickly 'Delete Posts, Ban and Remove hot searches'?" In: Burning Finance, April 18 (https://baijiahao.baidu.com/s?id=1664273220065

234150&wfr=spider&for=pc) [Original source in Chinese: 苏琦 /孟亚娜/ 魏佳: "网红张大奕被隔空喊话, 微博为何迅速'删帖禁言撤热搜'?" 燃财经].

"The Advertisement for Makeup-Remover Was Accused of Insulting Women, and Purcotton Apologised: It Was Just to Highlight the Product's Cleaning Function. It Has Been Removed from the Shelves." Qianzhan website, January 08, 2021 (https://www.163.com/dy/article/FVRBBBEC051480KF.html) [Original source in Chinese: "卸妆广告被指侮辱女性, 全棉时代道歉:已下架, 只为突出商品清洁功能." 前瞻网].

"The Girl Diagnosed with the Virus in Chengdu Whose Private Information Was Publicly Exposed: The Man Who Leaked Her Information Was Punished. The Real-Name System Will Become a Trend." In: Investigation Factory, December 10, 2020 (https://baijiahao.baidu.com/s?id=1685686672774761636&wfr=spider&for=pc) [Original source in Chinese: "成都确诊女孩遭信息泄露, 泄露信息男子被处罚, 实名制将是趋势." 调研工厂].

"The 20-Year-Old Diagnosed Girl in Chengdu Is Indeed Working as a Hostess. Are Girls Working as a Hostess in Bars Serious Girls?" Weibo headline article, Xintian Story, December 9, 2020 (https://card.weibo.com/article/m/show/id/2309404580212439646540) [Original source in Chinese: "心天物语. 成都20岁确诊女孩确为酒吧气氛组工作, 酒吧气氛组女生是正经女生吗?" 微博头条文章].

User 'Calabash Baby' (2020). "Dong Huahua and Zhang Dayi Are Both Hot Topics! Who Will Buy Hot Searches for Them Now?" Douban Group, April 27 (https://www.douban.com/group/topic/173236120/) [Original source in Chinese: 葫芦娃. "董花花和张大奕都上热搜 了! 现在谁会给她们买热搜啊?" 豆瓣小组].

User 'Caribbean Big Bubble' (2020). "@Meng Qiqi 77 That's Amazing, You Deleted My Comment and Blocked Me." Weibo, December 15 (https://share.api.weibo.cn/share/235254355.html?weibo_id=4582491820655671) [Original source in Chinese: 加勒比大泡泡. "#蒙淇淇77# 牛逼死了, 删评论还拉黑". 微博].

User 'Fish balls are not good in Chengdu' (2020). "Hello Everyone, I Am the Chengdu Girl Who Was Diagnosed with New Corona Pneumonia. I Apologise to the Citizens of Chengdu Here." Weibo account of Zhao, December 9, 2020 (https://share.api.weibo.cn/share/234241241.html?weibo_id=4580203651671914) [Original source in Chinese: User '鱼丸不好成都'. "大家好, 我是确诊新冠肺炎的那个成都女孩, 我在这里向成都市民致歉". 赵茂涵的微博账号].

User 'Han Xiaofan' (2020). "I Saw Zhang Dayi and Dong Huahua's Posts Constantly Being Deleted. People Who Want to Know More Are So Worried about It." Weibo account of user Han Xiaofan. April 17 (https://share.api.weibo.cn/share/234265485.html?weibo_id=4494733567205550) [Original source in Chinese: 晗小饭. "亲眼看见张大奕董花花的帖子不断被删 吃瓜群众好着急". 微博账号: 晗小饭. 微博].

User 'handsome and witty lyc classmate' (2020). "#Huahuadonghuahua#Amazing Amazing. This Entry Clearly Shows That Other Users Had Re-posted More than a Dozen of Weibo Comments. Hence, Many Weibo Comments Were Deleted. This Demonstrates the Power of the Capital." Weibo account, April 17 (https://share.api.weibo.cn/share/234265356.html?weibo_id=4494736926475048) [Original source in Chinese: 帅气又不失机智的lyc同学. "#花花董花花#牛批牛批. 这个词条明明别人更新了十几条微博. 还是被删了好几个. 只能说 资本牛批". 微博账号: 帅气又不失机智的lyc同学. 微博].

User 'Iceberg Fire' (2020). "Damn, Meng Qiqi's Layout Is Too Small. That's It, You Blocked Me @Mengqiqi 77." Weibo, December 15 (https://share.api.weibo.cn/share/235254355.html?weibo_id=4582491820655671) [Original source in Chinese: 冰山大火. "妈的 蒙淇淇的格局也太小了吧 这就给我拉黑了@蒙淇淇77." 微博].

User 'Max English name is too short, not allowed' (2020). "#Meng Qiqi 77# Said That I Will Be Your Loyal Fan. I Will See You Pretending to Be, and I Will Step on the Snow Every Day to See You. I Am Really Sad Today." Weibo, December 15 (https://share.api.weibo.cn/share/235254604.html?weibo_id=4582527120186116) [Original source in Chinese: Max英文名太短要求不得. "#蒙淇淇77# 说好了当你的忠实粉丝, 看你装逼 再天天踏雪去你, 今天真的伤心了." 微博].

User 'San Lu is poisonous' (2020). "Good Morning, Dagongren! 17,089 Million Views, 15,000 Barrage, Comments." Bilibili account of user 'San Lu is poisonous', October 22 (https://www.bilibili.com/video/BV1Mt4y1e7JY?p=1&share_medium=iphone&share_plat=ios&share_source=COPY&share_tag=s_i&timestamp=1608268806&unique_k=WTVvEu) [Original source in Chinese: 三Lu有毒. "早安, 打工人! 1708.9万播放 · 1.5万弹幕." b站账号: 三Lu有毒].

User 'Zheng went to buy shoes' (2021). "Dong Huahua Deleted All Her Husband's Weibo, Suspected to Be Divorced: Did Zhang Dayi Really Win?" Baidu, January 3 (https://baijiahao.baidu.com/s?id=1687873229323702357&wfr=spider&for=pc) [Original source in Chinese: 郑人去买履. "董花花删除老公所有微博, 疑似离婚: 张大奕真的赢了吗?" 百度].

Wang Cang (2020). "Chengdu Covid-19 Infection Zhao Maohan: Female, 20 Years Old, Unemployed. December 5: Shuncheng Street." Baidu Post Bar, December 8 (https://tieba.baidu.com/p/7137116345) [Original source in Chinese: 旺苍吧吧. "成都新冠感染赵茂涵: 女, 20岁, 无业. 顺城街".百度贴吧].

Xiaoxiang Morning News's official hundred accounts (2020). "Sina Weibo Responded By Being Interviewed." In: Xiaoxiang Morning News, June 11 (https://baijiahao.baidu.com/s?id=1669165617281835720&wfr=spider&for=pc) [Original source in Chinese: 潇湘晨报官方百家号. "新浪微博回应被约谈." 潇湘晨报].

Xianliaogezhu (2021). "Shenzhen Dagongren, With a Monthly Salary of Five Thousand." In: Yidian Information, July 14 (http://www.yidianzixun.com/

article/oVo9GSoo/amp) [Original source in Chinese: 闲聊阁主. "深圳打工仔, 月薪五千." 一点资讯].

"Zhao Maohan, a Girl Diagnosed with the Virus in Chengdu, Was Searched Online: She Is a 'Little Princess' in a Nightclub, Alive." Zhituoluo website, December 9, 2020 (http://www.tl6.net/redian/8563.html) [Original source in Chinese: "成都确诊女孩赵茂涵被人肉: 她是夜店"小公主, 活". 指陀螺第一门户网站].

Zui, Yin Zhichao/Wen, Jiaxin (2020). "'Versailles Literature' Award." In: Eastern Broadcasting Station, Social media account, November 15 (https://www.sohu.com/a/432095178_120068346) [Original source in Chinese: 尹志超/温嘉欣. "'凡尔赛文学'大赏. 东区广播站, 搜狐].

7.2 Secondary Literature

Barbrook, Richard/Cameron, Andy (1996): "The Californian Ideology." In: Science as Culture 6/1, pp. 1-16.

Byung-Chul Han (2017): Psychopolitics. Neoliberalism and New Technologies of Power, London, New York: Verso.

Cha, Victor (2020): "Asia's Covid-19 Lessons for the West: Public Goods, Privacy, and Social Tagging." In: The Washington Quarterly 43/2, pp. 1-18.

Chan, Ngai Keung/Kwok, Chi (2021): "The Politics of Platform Power in Surveillance Capitalism: A Comparative Case Study of Ride-Hailing Platforms in China and the United States." In: Global Media and China 0/0, pp. 1-20.

Cheng, Suang Heng/Lin, Zhijie/Xu, Xiaoying/Zhang, Ying/Zhao, Yixuan (2019): "Human Flesh Search: What Did We Find?" In: Information & Management 56/4, pp. 476-492.

Creeber, Glen (2013): Small Screen Aesthetics: From TV to the Internet, London: British Film Institute, Palgrave Macmillan.

deLisle, Jacques/Goldstein, Avery/Yang, Guobin (2016): "Introduction". In: Jacque de Lisle/Avery Goldstein/Guobin Yang (eds.), The Internet, Social Media, and a Changing China, Philadelphia: University of Pennsylvania Press, pp. 1-27.

de Kloet, Jeroen/Poell, Thomas/Zeng, Guohua/Chow, Yiu Fai (2019): "The Platformisation of Chinese Society: Infrastructure, Governance, and Practice." In: Chinese Journal of Communication 12/3, pp. 249-256.

Doorn, Niels van/Chen, Julie Yujie (2021): "Odds Stacked against Workers: Datafied Gamification on Chinese and American Food Delivery Platforms." In: Socio-Economic Review 00/0, pp. 1-23 (Doi: 10.1093/ser/mwab028).

Doorn, Niels van (2020): "At What Price? Labour Politics and Calculative Power Struggles in On-Demand Food Delivery." In: Work Organisation, Labour & Globalisation 14/1, pp. 136-149.

Fuchs, Christian (2020). "Towards a Critical Theory of Communication as Renewal and Update of Marxist Humanism in the Age of Digital Capitalism." In: Journal for the Theory of Social Behaviour, pp. 1–22 (DOI: 10.1111/jtsb.12247).

Fuchs, Christian (2017): Soziale Medien und kritische Theorie. Eine Einführung, München: UVK Verlag.

Fuchs, Christian (2016): "Baidu, Weibo and Renren: The Global Political Economy of Social Media in China." In: Asian Journal of Communication 26/1, pp. 14-41.

Fuchs, Christian/Trottier, Daniel (2015): "Towards a theoretical model of social media surveillance in contemporary society." In: Communications: The European Journal of Communication Research 40/1, pp. 113-135.

Griesbach, Kathleen/Reich, Adam/Elliott-Negri, Luke/Milkman, Ruth (2019): "Algorithmic Control in Platform Food Delivery Work." In: Socius: Sociological Research for a Dynamic World 5, pp. 1-15 (DOI: 10.1177/2378023119870041).

"Hangzhou Ruhan Holdings Co., Ltd.", Baidu Encyclopedia, July 19, 2021 (https://baike.baidu.com/item/%E6%9D%AD%E5%B7%9E%E5%A6%82%E6%B6%B5%E6%8E%A7%E8%82%A1%E8%82%A1%E4%BB%BD%E6%9C%89%E9%99%90%E5%85%AC%E5%8F%B8/20570694?fr=aladdin) [Original source in Chinese: 杭州如涵控股股份有限公司。百度百科].

Hangzhou Ruhan Holdings Co., Ltd., Official Website, July 19, 2021 (https://www.ruhnn.com/) [Original source in Chinese: 杭州如涵控股股份有限公司官网].

Helmond, Anne (2015): "The Platformisation of the Web: Making Web Data Platform Ready." In: Social media + Society (July-December 2015), pp. 1-11 (DOI: 10.1177/2056305115603080).

Ho, Petula Sik Ying/Jackson, Stevi (2021): "Locating Sexual Politics and Gendered Lives: East Asian Perspectives." In: Journal of Gender Studies 30/5, pp. 503-511 (https://doi.org/10.1080/09589236.2021.1930179).

Hong, Yu (2017): Networking China: The Digital Transformation of the Chinese Economy, Champaign, Illinois: University of Illinois Press.

Hou, Holly Lixian (2015): "On Fire in Weibo. Feminist Online Activism in China." In: Economic and Political Weekly 50/17, pp. 79-85 (https://www.jstor.org/stable/24481829).

"Human flesh search", Baidu Encyclopedia, June 28, 2021 (https://baike.baidu.com/item/%E4%BA%BA%E8%82%89%E6%90%9C%E7%B4%A2/9698961) [Original source in Chinese: 人肉搜索", 百度百科].

Jiang, Ying (2012): Cyber-Nationalism in China. Challenging Western Media Portrayals of Internet Censorship in China, Adelaide: University of Adelaide Press.

Li, Baoshan (2014): "Upholding the Marxist View of the News Media". In: Qiushi Journal. Organ of the Central Committee of the Communist Party of China 6/1 (Jan. 2014), uploaded online on February 8, 2014 (http://english.qstheory.cn/magazine/201401/201402/t20140208_318982.htm).

Lin, Jian/deKloet, Jeroen (2019): "Platformisation of the Unlikely Creative Class: Kuaishou and the Chinese Digital Cultural Production." In: Social Media + Society (Oct.-Dec. 2019), pp. 1-12 (DOI: 10.1177/2056305119883430).

MacKenzie, Adrian/Munster, Anna (2019): "Platform Seeing: Image Ensembles and Their Invisualities." In: Theory, Culture & Society 36/5, pp. 3-22 (DOI: 10.1177/0263276419847508).

"MCN", Baidu Encyclopedia, July 19, 2021 (https://baike.baidu.com/item/MCN/3551331?fr=aladdin) [Original source in Chinese: "MCN", 百度百科].

Mühlhoff, Rainer (2018): "Digitale Entmündigung und User Experience Design. Wie digitale Geräte uns nudgen, tracken und zur Unwissenheit erziehen." In: Leviathan 46/4, pp. 551-574 (DOI: 10.5771/0340-0425-2018-4-551).

Nakajima, Seio (2019): "The Sociability of Millennials in Cyberspace: A Comparative Analysis of Barrage Subtitling in Nico Nico Douga and Bilibili." In: Vanessa Frangville/Gwennaël Gaffric (eds.), China's youth cultures and collective spaces: Creativity, sociality, identity and resistance, Abingdon, Oxon and New York: Routledge, pp. 98-115.

Nigunigu (2021): "How to Get on the List of Trending Topics? What Are the Underlying Rules for Lists of Frequently Searched Words?" In: Zhihu (Question and answer forum), June 23, 2021 (https://zhuanlan.zhihu.com/p/47509110) [Original source in Chinese: 腻咕腻咕. "怎么上热搜？上热搜的规则是什么？". 知乎].

Qin, Bei/Stromberg, David/Wu, Yanhui (2016): "The Political Economy of Social Media in China." Conference paper, pp. 1-23 (https://conference.nber.org/confer/2015/CEfi5/Qin_Wu_Stromberg.pdf).

Reuter, Ora John/Szakonyi, David (2013): "Online Social Media and Political Awareness in Authoritarian Regimes." In: British Journal of Political Science 45/1 (print publication 2015, online publication 2013), pp. 29-51.

Rowe, Frantz/Ngwenyama, Ojelanki/Richet, Jean-Loup (2020): "Contact-Tracing Apps and Alienation in the Age of Covid-19." In: European Journal of Information Systems 29/5, pp. 545-562.

Sallai, Dorottya/Schnyder, Gerhard (2019): "What is 'Authoritarian' about Authoritarian Capitalism? The Dual Erosion of the Private-Public Divide in State-Dominated Business Systems." In: Business and Society, pp. 1-52 (electronic copy downloaded from: https://ssrn.com/abstract=3373637).

Shifman, Limor (2013): "Memes in a Digital World: Reconciling with a Conceptual Troublemaker". In: Journal of Computer-Mediated Communication 18, pp. 362-377.

Srnicek, Nick (2017): Platform Capitalism, Cambridge, Malden, M.A.: Polity books.

Sun, Ping (2019): "Your Order, Their Labour: An Exploration of Algorithms and Labouring on Food Delivery Platforms in China." In: Chinese Journal of Communication 12/3, pp. 308-323 (https://doi.org/10.1080/17544750.2019.1583676).

"The State Cyberspace Administration of China Issued the 'Ten Rules for Interviews' to Promote the Standardisation and Proceduralisation of Interviews." China Netwcom, April 28, 2015 (http://www.cac.gov.cn/2015-04/28/c_1115112469.htm) [Original source in Chinese: "国家网信办发布'约谈十条' 推动约谈工作规范化、程序化."中国网信网].

Tu, Weiming (2002): "Implications of the Rise of 'Confucian' East Asia." In: Shmuel N. Eisenstadt (ed.), Multiple Modernities, New Brunswick: Transaction, pp. 195-218.

Xinhua News Agency (2012): "Netizens Keep an Eye on Officials." August 31 (http://www.china.org.cn/china/2012-08/31/content_26396325.htm).

Van Dijck, José (2014): "Datafication, Dataism and Dataveillance: Big Data between Scientific Paradigm and Ideology." In: Surveillance & Society 12/2, pp. 197-208.

"Versailles Literature". Baidu Encyclopedia (accessed June 2021). URL: https://baike.baidu.com/item/%E5%87%A1%E5%B0%94%E8%B5%9B%E6%96%87%E5%AD%A6/54290433?fr=aladdin [Original source in Chinese:"凡尔赛文学". 百度百科].

Witt, Michael A. / Redding, Gordon (2012). "China: Authoritarian Capitalism". Faculty & Research Working Paper, INSEAD, The Business School for the World, 1-21. Downloaded from the Social Science Research Network electronic library at: URL: http://ssrn.com/abstract=2171651.

Zeng, Jing/Chan, Chung-hong Chan/Schäfer, Mike S. (2020): "Contested Chinese Dreams of AI? Public Discourse about Artificial Intelligence on WeChat and People's Daily Online." In: Information, Communication & Society, pp. 1-22 (https://doi.org/10.1080/1369118X.2020.1776372).

Zhao, Yuezhi (2007): "After Mobile Phones, What? Re-embedding the Social in China's 'Digital Revolution'". In: International Journal of Communication 1, pp. 92-120.

Zuboff, Shoshana (2019): The Age of Surveillance Capitalism: The Fight for a Human Future at the New Frontier of Power, London: Profile Books (Kindle version).

List of images

Fig. 1: Two screenshots taken from advertisement from video version in: China Women's Daily (2021). "#Response: backfiring advertisement# ('Creativity' is not an excuse for abdicating from responsibility). Recently, #Purcotton# released a backfiring advertisement titled 'When you go home late at night and you are followed by a man in black, what method will you use to get rid of him?' triggered a vibrant discussion among netizens". Weibo account of *China Women's Daily*, Weibo, January 08, 2021 15:39. URL: https://share.api.weibo.cn/share/235307059.html?weibo_id=4591119284830606 [Original source in Chinese: "#全棉时代回应反转广告# ('创意'不是开脱责任的挡箭牌) 近日，#全棉时代#发布的反转广告 '深夜回家遇黑衣人尾随，你会用什么方法摆脱"引发网友热议'。". 微博账号：中国妇女报, 微博].

Fig. 2: Financial community network. "Hot search on scolding! PurCotton's advertisement is accused of insulting women. The company's response: It's creative advertisement". *Tencent.com*, January 8, 2021. URL: https://new.qq.com/omn/20210108/20210108A067XZ00.html [Original source in Chinese: 金融界网。"骂上热搜！全棉时代广告被指侮辱女性 公司回应称为广告创意"。腾讯网].

Fig. 3: Financial community network. "Hot search on scolding! PurCotton's advertisement is accused of insulting women. The company's response: It's creative advertisement". *Tencent.com*, January 8, 2021. URL: https://new.qq.com/omn/20210108/20210108A067XZ00.html [Original source in Chinese: 金融界网。"骂上热搜！全棉时代广告被指侮辱女性 公司回应称为广告创意"。腾讯网].

Fig. 4: China Women's Daily (2021). "#Response: backfiring advertisement# ('Creativity' is not an excuse for abdicating from responsibility). Recently, #Purcotton# released a backfiring advertisement titled 'When you go home late at night and you are followed by a man in black, what method will you use to get rid of him?' triggered a vibrant discussion among netizens". Weibo account of *China Women's Daily*, Weibo, January 08, 2021 15:39. URL: https://share.api.weibo.cn/share/235307059.html?weibo_id=4591119284830606 [Original source in Chinese: "#全棉时代回应反转广告# 【'创意'不是开脱责任的挡箭牌】近日,#全棉时代#发布的反转广告 '深夜回家遇黑衣人尾随,你会用什么方法摆脱'引发网友热议。". 微博账号：中国妇女报, 微博].

Fig. 5: "Hard currency: 5 core rules of Kuaishou live streaming". *Yibang Power Network*, August 15, 2019. URL: https://www.niuxuan.cn/redian/51950.html [Original source in Chinese: 硬通货：快手直播带货的5个核心法则。2019-08-15。亿邦动力网].

Fig. 6: Source: "Hard currency: 5 core rules of Kuaishou live streaming". *Yibang Power Network*, August 15, 2019. URL: https://www.niuxuan.cn/redian/51950.html [Original source in Chinese: 硬通货：快手直播带货的5个核心法则。2019-08-15。亿邦动力网].

Fig. 7: Little milk ball. "'Little milk ball Versailles open class'. Number of views: 100.000, barrage: 614". *Bilibili*, May 09, 2020, 20:37. URL: https://www.bilibili.com/video/av838098912/ [Original source in Chinese: 小奶球。"小奶球 凡尔赛公开课"。10.0万播放,614弹幕. Bilibili].

Fig. 8: Meng Qiqi (2020). Two Weibo posts by @Meng Qiqi77 on Nov. 2 and Nov. 7, 2020 [@蒙淇淇77, 微博], quoted after "Why has 'Versailles Literature' become a trending topic?". *Jiemian News*, Sohu.com., November 9, 2020. URL: https://www.sohu.com/a/430696123_313745 [Original source in Chinese: "凡尔赛文学"冲上热搜是怎么回事?". 界面新闻, 搜狐网].

Fig. 9: Cannot be found anymore (URL deleted)

Fig. 10: User 'Max English name is too short, not allowed'. "I can only laugh at you! You really make me sad". *Weibo*, December 15, 2020, 22:37. URL: https://share.api.weibo.cn/share/235254604.html?weibo_id=4582527120186116 [Original source in Chinese: Max英文名太短要求不得. "#蒙淇淇77# 说好了当你的忠实粉丝，看你装逼，再天天踏雪你，今天真的伤心了。微博].

Fig. 11: User 'Iceberg Fire' (2020). "Damn, Meng Qiqi's layout is too small. That's it, you blocked me @Mengqiqi77". *Weibo*, December 15, 2020, 20:24. URL: https://share.api.weibo.cn/share/235254355.html?weibo_id=4582491820655671 [Original source in Chinese: 冰山大火. "妈 蒙淇淇的格局也太小了吧 这就给我拉黑了@蒙淇淇77". 微博].

Fig. 12.: User 'Caribbean Big Bubble' (2020). "@Meng Qiqi 77 That's amazing, you deleted my comment and blocked me". *Weibo*, December 15, 2020 20:17. URL: https://share.api.weibo.cn/share/235254355.html?weibo_id=4582491820655671 [Original source in Chinese: 加勒比大泡泡. "#蒙淇淇77# 牛逼死了，删评论还拉黑". 微博].

Fig. 13: Screenshot of two posts on Donghuahua's Weibo account [(@花花董花花] from April 17, 2020, quoted after: Su Qi, Meng Yana (authors), Wei Jia (editor). "Internet celebrity Zhang Dayi was scolded at, why did Weibo quickly 'delete posts, ban and remove hot searches'"? *Burning Finance*. April 18, 2020. URL: https://baijiahao.baidu.com/s?id=1664273220065234150&wfr=spider&for=pc [Original source in Chinese: 苏琦 孟亚娜 (作者), 魏佳 (编辑). "网红张大奕被隔空喊话，微博为何迅速'删帖禁言撤热搜'"？燃].

Fig. 14: Screenshot of 4 user comments posted on Weibo
- 1st and 2nd user comment has meanwhile be deleted (URL cannot be found anymore)
- 3rd user comment: User 'Han Xiaofan' (2020). "I saw Zhang Dayi and Dong Huahua's posts constantly being deleted. People who want to know more are so worried about it". Weibo account of user Han Xiaofan. *Weibo*, April 17, 2020. URL: https://share.api.weibo.cn/share/234265485.html?weibo_id=4494733567205550 [Original source in Chinese: 晗小饭. "亲眼看见张大奕董花花的帖子不断被删 吃瓜群众好着急". 微博账号：晗小饭. 微博].
- 4th user comment: User 'handsome and witty lyc classmate'. "#Huahuadonghuahua#Amazing Amazing. "This entry clearly shows that other users had re-posted more than a dozen of Weibo comments. Hence, many Weibo comments were deleted. This demonstrates the power of the capital". Weibo account. Weibo, April 17, 2020. URL: https://share.api.weibo.cn/share/234265356.html?weibo_id=4494736926475048 [Original

source in Chinese: 帅气又不失机智的lyc同学. "#花花董花花#牛批牛批. 这个词条明明别人更新了十几条微博. 还是被删了好几个. 只能说 资本牛批". 微博账号: 帅气又不失机智的lyc同学。微博].

Fig. 15: Su Qi, Meng Yana (authors), Wei Jia (editor). "Internet celebrity Zhang Dayi was scolded at, why did Weibo quickly 'delete posts, ban and remove hot searches'"? *Burning Finance*. April 18, 2020. URL: https://baijiahao.baidu.com/s?id=1664273220065234150&wfr=spider&for=pc [Original source in Chinese: 苏琦 孟亚娜 (作者), 魏佳 (编辑)。"网红张大奕被隔空喊话, 微博为何迅速'删帖 禁言撤热搜'"? 燃财经].

Fig. 16: "#Jiangsu delivery man set himself on fire with gasoline#: 'I don't want my life, I want my hard-earned money'". Weibo account of *NetEase Finance*, NetEase Wangyi video, January 11, 2021, 20:37, length: 00:37 seconds. URL: https://weibo.com/1974561081/JCIEPtsIl?sudaref=cn.bing.com&type=comment [Original source in Chinese: "#江苏外卖员点汽油自焚#: '我不要命, 我要血汗钱'". 网易财经 (来自 微博视频号), 易视频, 网易视频]

Fig. 17: Li Xiulian, Sun Yidan (2021a). "A delivery man sets himself on fire to ask for a salary of 4,000 yuan. How to protect the rights and interests of delivery staff". Official Weibo account of *Sanlian Life Weekly*, February 3, 2021. URL: https://s.weibo.com/weibo?q=%23%E5%A4%96%E5%8D%96%E5%91%98%E5%9B%A04000%E5%85%83%E8%AE%A8%E8%96%AA%E8%87%AA%E7%84%9A%23 Original source in Chinese: 李秀莲, 孙一丹. "外卖员自焚讨薪, 想要回4000块为什么那么难". 三联生活周刊

Fig. 18: User 'San Lu is poisonous'. "Good morning, Dagongren! 17.089 million views, 15.000 barrage, comments". *Bilibili* account of user 'San Lu is poisonous', Oct. 22, 2020. URL: https://www.bilibili.com/video/BV1Mt4y1e7JY?p=1&share_medium=iphone&share_plat=ios&share_source=COPY&share_tag=s_i&timestamp=1608268806&unique_k=WTVvEu [Original source in Chinese: 三Lu有毒. "早安, 打工人！1708.9万播放 · 1.5万弹幕". b站账号: 三Lu有毒].

Fig. 19: User 'San Lu is poisonous'. "Good morning, Dagongren! 17.089 million views, 15.000 barrage, comments". *Bilibili* account of user 'San Lu is poisonous', Oct. 22, 2020. URL: https://www.bilibili.com/video/BV1Mt4y1e7JY?p=1&share_medium=iphone&share_plat=ios&share_source=COPY&share_tag=s_i&timestamp=1608268806&unique_k=WTVvEu [Original source in Chinese: 三Lu有毒. "早安, 打工人！1708.9万播放 · 1.5万弹幕". b站账号: 三Lu有毒].

Fig. 20: "Good night, beaten workers! 5.394 million views, barrage: 3558, Top 5 in the ranking". *Bilibili*, October 27, 2020 (video length 01:17). URL: https://www.bilibili.com/video/BV1Fi4y177he/?spm_id_from=autoNext [Original source in

Chinese: "活动作品晚安, 被打工人！539.4万播放, 3558弹幕, 全站排行榜最高第5名].

Fig. 21: Screenshot from Wang's original posts, quoted after: "The girl diagnosed with the virus in Chengdu whose private information was publicly exposed: the man who leaked her information was punished. The real-name system will become trend". *Investigation Factory*, December 10, 2020. https://baijiahao.baidu.com/s?id=1685686672774761636&wfr=spider&for=pc [Original source in Chinese: 成都确诊女孩遭信息泄露, 泄露信息男子被处罚, 实名制将是趋势.调研工厂.

Fig. 22: Screenshot from Wang's original posts, quoted after: "The girl diagnosed with the virus in Chengdu whose private information was publicly exposed: the man who leaked her information was punished. The real-name system will become trend". *Investigation Factory*, December 10, 2020. https://baijiahao.baidu.com/s?id=1685686672774761636&wfr=spider&for=pc [Original source in Chinese: 成都确诊女孩遭信息泄露, 泄露信息男子被处罚, 实名制将是趋势.调研工厂.

Fig. 23: Wang Cang (2020). "Chengdu Covid-19 infection Zhao Maohan: female, 20 years old, unemployed. December 5: Shuncheng Street". *Baidu Post Bar*, December 8, 2020. URL: https://tieba.baidu.com/p/7137116345 [Original source in Chinese: 旺苍吧吧。"成都新冠感染赵茂涵：女, 20岁, 无业. 顺城街".百度贴吧].

Fig. 24: User comments to post by Wang, see: Wang Cang (2020). "Chengdu Covid-19 infection Zhao Maohan: female, 20 years old, unemployed. December 5: Shuncheng Street". *Baidu Post Bar*, December 8, 2020. URL: https://tieba.baidu.com/p/7137116345 [Original source in Chinese: 旺苍吧吧。"成都新冠感染赵茂涵：女, 20岁, 无业. 顺城街".百度贴吧].

Fig. 25: "The girl diagnosed with the virus in Chengdu whose private information was publicly exposed: the man who leaked her information was punished. The real-name system will become trend". *Investigation Factory*, December 10, 2020. https://baijiahao.baidu.com/s?id=1685686672774761636&wfr=spider&for=pc [Original source in Chinese: 成都确诊女孩遭信息泄露, 泄露信息男子被处罚, 实名制将是趋势.调研工厂.

Black Squares and Gucci
Networked Images and the (In)Visibility of Surveillance

Sascha Hosters and Silke Roesler-Keilholz

Abstract

This paper seeks to investigate the (invisible) effects of networked images by introducing their rhizomatic structure in the intersecting spheres of fashion and social media. By juxtaposing different modes of visual campaigns with socio-political and economic incentives, the authors aim to expose a spectrum of visualisations and user behaviour that reflects on the underlying platform dynamics at play in the framework of surveillance capitalism. At one extreme, there is #theshowmustbepaused a.k.a. #blackouttuesday – a social awareness campaign that began in response to the killing of George Floyd and effectively blacked out Instagram for one day on June 2nd, 2020 –; and at the other, there is Gucci, the Italian luxury brand, which posted its own statement on the same day and has established a unique cosmos of kaleidoscopic images with innovative (online) campaigns. As such, this unique event functions as a watershed moment, not only for analysis of the ambiguity and immediacy by which images are shared online, but also for exposing the underlying structure of Instagram's advertising and engagement model. Whereas on its own, the "black square" was born of a socio-political moment of crisis and developed an unintended effect of deletion – the juxtaposition with Gucci's advertising campaigns stands as a paradigm for the commercial appropriation of internet (sub)culture in surveillance capitalism.

Keywords

Networked Images; Fashion; Social Media; Social Awareness Campaign; Internet Subcultures

Blackout Tuesday

If you have an Instagram account and opened it on June 2nd of 2020, something peculiar happened. With the exception of some individual friends or sponsored advertising posts, a flood of black squares erased all visual content from the feed of the popular social network. Despite the controversy the campaign caused and independently of whether it was successful in its initial intended purpose, what could be observed on the platform was significant for understanding the dynamics of the *Attention Economy* (Franck 2019) in *The Age of Surveillance Capitalism* (Zuboff 2019). Kicked off by two marketing professionals in the US music industry in the wake of the killing of George Floyd, #theshowmustbepaused hoped to raise awareness for social justice, the exploitation of black artists in the music business and the ongoing police brutality against black people in the United States, which had reached yet another climax in the already turbulent election year 2020. But as it turned out, this was just the beginning of a long tumultuous summer besides the raging Covid-19 pandemic. The initial Instagram post, which originally included words and a call to action (in white letters on a black square background – see image 1), quickly developed a life of its own. Shortly after posting, it went viral as an image of a black square without text, mostly accompanied by the hashtags #blackouttuesday and #blacklivesmatter.[1] The black square thereby reproduced itself in opaque and rhizomatic ways. Behind the veil of Instagram's powerful individualised algorithms, the direction of the campaign evolved in interplay with between content guidelines, user reach, engagement and modulation, which was further influenced by the infusion of advertising money by hundreds of brands

---

1   The full statement reads: "#TheShowMustBePaused. In response to the murders of George Floyd, Breonna Taylor, Ahmaud Arbury and countless other Black citizens at the hands of police, #theshowmustbepaused is an initiative created by two Black women in music in observance of the long-standing racism and inequality that exists from the boardroom to the boulevard. We will not continue to conduct business as usual without regard for Black lives. Tuesday, June 2nd is meant to intentionally disrupt the work week. Monday suggests a long weekend, and we can't wait until Friday for change. It is a day to take a beat for an honest, reflective, and productive conversation about what actions we need to collectively take to support the Black community. The music industry is a multi-billion-dollar industry. An industry that has profited predominantly from Black art. Our mission is to hold the industry at large, including major corporations + their partners who benefit from the efforts, struggles and successes of Black people accountable. To that end, it is the obligation of these entities to protect and empower the Black communities that have made them disproportionately wealthy in ways that are measurable and transparent. This is not just a 24-hour initiative. We are and will be in this fight for the long haul. A plan of action will be announced. We are tired and can't change things alone. In the meantime, to our Black friends and family: please take the time for you for you and your mental health. To our allies, the time is now to have difficult conversations with family, friends, and colleagues. Please follow @pausetheshow on Twitter and @theshowmusbepaused on Instagram for updates and information. Signed Jamila Thomas and Brianna Agyemang." @theshowmustbepaused on Instagram: "#theshowmustbepaused", accessed August 7, 2021, https://www.instagram.com/p/CA4S2c3nPRE/.

that jumped on the bandwagon with their own appropriated statements and logos (Hanlon 2021: 84).

Fig. 1: Screenshot of the #theshowmustbepaused statement as posted on instagram on June 2nd, 2020. (Url: https://www.instagram.com/p/CA4S2c3nPRE/)

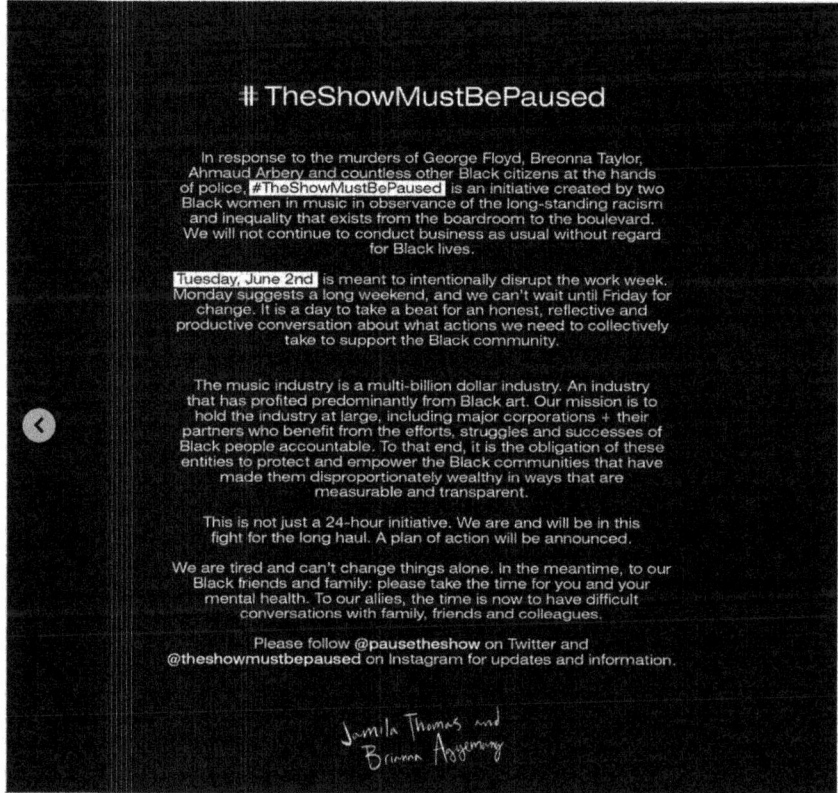

By transforming and therefore unintentionally occupying the #blacklivesmatter hashtags, this moment delivers a case study of (un)intended platform performance and appropriation that is symptomatic for how networked images disseminate in the attention economy under the all-seeing regime of social media platforms. Over the day, the image of the black square spread all over the world like an uncontrolled wildfire, giving new life to a symbol of abstraction that is well-known in art history, as we will show in the following. But besides laying bare the advertising and therefore the surveillance model of the social network by reducing its content to nothing other than sponsored content, it was the disruptive potential of collective online action born from an abstraction of images, which (trans)formed a worldwide call to action that was remarkable: people from Los Angeles to Atlanta, to New York and Berlin and even Teheran, posted the black square in solidarity with the cause and even took it to the streets in the days that followed (Coscarelli 2020; Culver 2020). Spanning the globe, a network of solidarity connected people with each other and enabled a feedback loop between the analogue and digital world that exposes networked images' inherent power of user modulation with visible impact on- and offline. Hashtags established themselves as symbols of these connections. They have a variety of functions in social networks online. In most instances they function as guideposts by labelling all tagged content and therefore making it searchable/findable (this can range from trending topics to locations to colours and food); or they are used to make a statement that may be associated with a cause or a call to action (such as #blacklivesmatter, #fridaysforfuture etc.). In the context discussed here, unfortunately the infectious peer pressure did not just raise awareness for the cause, but also harmed the actual #blacklivesmatter protesters on the streets (cf. Mihalcik 2020; Willingham 2020). Because activists and protesters had been using the associated hashtags (#blacklivesmatter, #blm etc.) to label image and video content in order to visibly document what was going on in real time during the protests, the flood of black squares sur-veilled (in the literal sense of the word as "cover") and blacked out their means of communication (Hanlon 2021: 85) (see fig.2). Widely shared videos of demonstrations and violent encounters of protestors with the police on the streets were replaced by black squares. This led multiple activist-influencers to call for an end to using #blacklivesmatter hashtags in combination with the black square as a symbol of solidarity on the same day (Hanlon 2021: 86). To what extent these networked images can be understood as the foundations of mutual observation, intervention and control and thus as a moment of surveillance is apparent in this context.

Fig. 2: Screenshot of Musicians' Instagram accounts taken from New York Times Article Coscarelli 2020: #BlackoutTuesday: A Music Industry Protest Becomes A Social Media

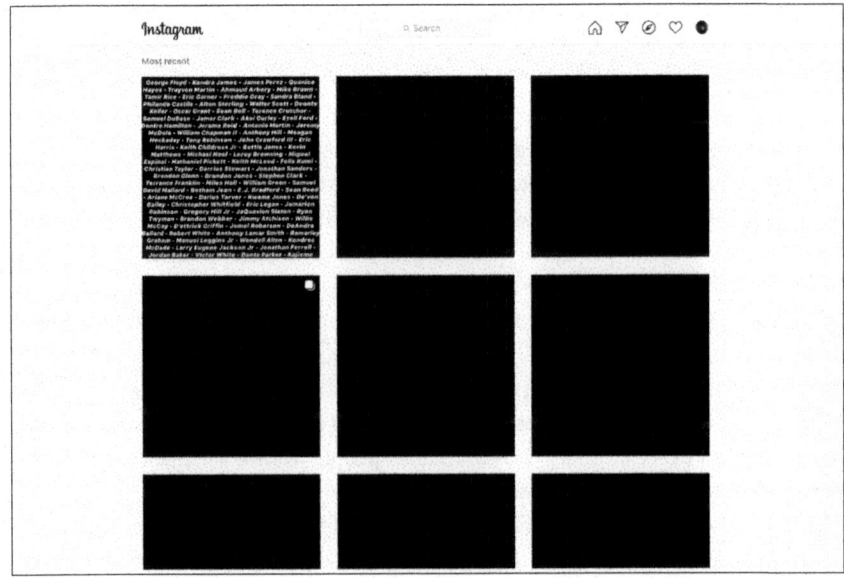

Networked Images as Rhizomes

That the 2020 Black Square campaign at the heart of this discussion originated from two black female social media marketing professionals in their twenties is remarkable in this context. By 2021, we must have come to terms with the fact that life in virtual spheres is as consequential as reality itself. Networked images are the basis and grammar of our reality today. To be exposed to them means to be exposed to the world and to be affected by them, not just emotionally; they also decisively influence our actions (e.g., by reposting or recreating previously seen content or demonstrating in the streets). The rhizome seems to be the most fitting thought pattern for the analysis of the diverse units at play in this regard. The point of rhizomatic thinking lies in the fact that it can be understood as the indication of an object as well as it being reflected on a meta level. In 1977, Gilles Deleuze and Felix Guattari drew on the rhizome in their seminal work *A Thousand Plateaus. Capitalism and Schizophrenia* as a metaphor for a postmodern/post-structuralist model of epistemic organisation of knowledge as well as a tool to describe the world more appropriately (Deleuze/Guattari 1987: 5). The term, which has been borrowed from the botanical definition for root networks in plants, is intended to replace the older hierarchically organised and previously dominant model of the tree as a new paradigm of thinking. It anticipated the operating mode and the technological structure of the emerging internet (Baran 1964; Berners-Lee 1990; Bunz 2009). Models based on trees, as they are represented in classic encyclopaedias and libraries, for instance, are structured in hierarchical and dialectic ways: every element is exclusively placed in a singular organisation pattern, which is related to a higher level and can give precedence to one or multiple elements. Deleuze and Guattari lament the limited epistemological capabilities of the hierarchical model that is based on dichotomies, because of its rigidity and limitation in regard to potential changes in perspectives – thus it lacks the needed adaptability which is more appropriate for their (and our) current times. They introduce the rhizomatic network structures of plants as an alternative metaphor that can assimilate towards a model of multiple interwoven figures of thought. The authors describe the characteristics of the rhizome as follows: the first and second distinguishing feature are the "principles of connection and heterogeneity: any point of a rhizome can be connected to anything other and must be" (ibid.: 8). Various (semantic) areas relate to each other. The third feature marks the "principle of multiplicity: it is only when the multiple is effectively treated as a substantive, multiplicity, that it ceases to have any relation to the One as subject or object, natural or spiritual reality, image and world" (ibid.: 8). In addition to this characteristic, Deleuze and Guattari add as a fourth feature the "principle of asignifying rupture: [...] A rhizome may be broken, shattered at a given spot, but it will start up again on one of its old lines, or new lines" (ibid.: 10). Breaks and ruptures therefore don't signify finalities; furthermore, they are inherently productive and stand for the beginning of something new. The characteristics five and six are defined as the "principles of cartography and decalcomania" (ibid.: 13). Rhizomes are not obliged to any structural or generative model. They are not aware of any genetical axes or deep structures. Rhizomes are interwoven multi root systems which cannot be understood in dichotomies. What we want to highlight in this context is that the most diverse facts of the matter at hand can be related to each other. By recognising and defining the "heterogeneity" of rhizomatic structures, something new is created. Rhizomatic thinking signifies the liberation of defined structures of power, and thus, a multitude of perspectives and approaches can be connected freely. The rhizome has been used widely and early on as a metaphor for internet discourse; nevertheless, its anti-hierarchical structure as well as the inherent urge to create new meaning and connections resonates with the evolution of the black square in off-and online contexts.

Appropriation & Surveillance

Whether the black square was an act of conscious appropriation is irrelevant. But as an abstract and easily reproducible "poor image" it became a virally shared common practice that works in the logic of "poor images" and "meme culture" that Hito Steyerl described in her essay "In Defense of the Poor Image" in 2009. Even though Steyerl is concerned with the low-resolution aesthetic of reproduced visual media artefacts – which the black square abstracts even further by turning the last remnants of visual representation into a black void – we want to suggest that the distribution and potential for subversive disruption Steyerl is discussing is also applicable in this context. As opposed to the high-definition images we are exposed to by professional multimedia productions in film, TV and increasingly online; the abstracted "poor image" lives (or used to live) on the fringes of the web as the epitome of bootleg culture. As a copy of copies and ripped content, it suffers a loss of quality through multiple careless conversions into various data formats; by being reformatted, overwritten, and widely shared over whatever online channels or physical data carriers available at the time (cf. Steyerl 2009: 1). In that sense Steyerl reads the "poor image" as a kind of disruptive opportunity that is worth pursuing as an alternative means of connection. It lies beyond the saturated multimedia mainstream run by advertising and corporate interests:

The circulation of poor images creates a circuit, which fulfills the original ambitions of militant and (some) essayistic and experimental cinema – to create an alternative economy of images, an imperfect cinema existing inside as well as beyond and under commercial media streams. (Steyerl 2009: 7)

To what extent the black square of 2020 is caught in a tension between the disruptive potential of abstracted images and commercially produced hyperreal HD images in the context of surveillance capitalism lies at the heart of this analysis.

Fig. 3-5: Sample of brand statements featuring adopted slogans on black square backgrounds on Instagram and Twitter by Toyota USA, L'Oreal, BMW USA (Screenshots taken from Hanlon 2021: 89, 90, 92)

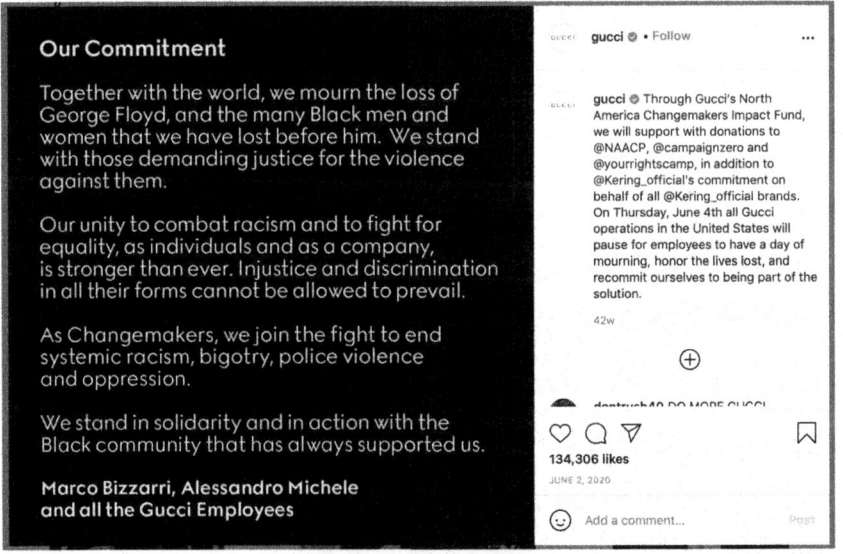

Fig. 6: Gucci Statement on Instagram on June 2nd, 2020. (Url: https://www.instagram.com/p/CA87e99iJz9/)

As a moment of silence that uniquely "blacked out" Instagram for one day, June 2nd became a minimised blueprint for what seemed to develop into the prevalent modus operandi for the distribution of images (and ideas) on the social network today. Political, social, and cultural narratives are recycled in engagement-driven interactive feedback loops between users and marketing professionals that range between consumer motivation and social subversion. While most users got rid of the original text of #theshowmustbepaused in favour of the abstraction of the black square only as a presumed sign of solidarity, companies and brands used the opportunity to issue their own statements in relation to the ongoing events, and in most cases they decided to add written statements either on top or below in the caption. Hanlon acutely observes in this context that "every statement issued by a brand in support of Black Lives Matter or racial equality acts as an advertisement for that brand" and further,

> due to the structure of social media posts and the brand tendency to make their brand name or logo their profile picture on social media channels, virtually every brand statement in social media includes that brand's distinctive brand assets. If a brand posts on Twitter that it stands for justice and equality and will fight to make a better world, its logo will appear next to that statement. (Hanlon 2021: 89-90)

Public social crises sparking trending conversations or controversies therefore present a free opportunity for brands to amplify their image with branded content/statements. This does not go unnoticed among activists and often sparks criticism for brands as accusations of "woke washing"[2] emerge (Sobande 2019: Vredenburg 2020). From a branding perspective, whether they follow up on their statements or not becomes secondary, as some form of attention – good or bad – has been generated regardless. To name some examples in this context, brands like Toyota, BMW and L'Oréal published their own statements on black squares, which can be defined somewhere between a statement of solidarity and a slogan promoting their brand. In that sense, this moment created a potential new genre in advertising that could be understood as a *crisis opportunity* (see fig. 3-5). The pressure to position themselves quickly in these moments of crisis seems to be even higher in industries with raised public exposure such as the entertainment and fashion industries. Economically interlinked by way of celebrity and glamour culture, they tend to amplify each other's messages rhizomatically, leading to more engagement via influencers and so-called cultural pioneers (cf. Later & Fohr Influencer Marketing Report 2021). Among the many luxury fashion brands, Gucci also posted a black square statement on June 2nd (see fig. 6). Though it was released through its Instagram channel and therefore includes its logo, the statement on the black square itself is not branded and is marked as "our commitment". Compared to the other examples, Gucci seemed to have chosen a middle way without adding additional branding or logos, expressing solidarity and commitment "signed" with the

---

2 Similarly to "green washing" or "white washing", "woke washing" refers to blanket statements of brands that express solidarity on their social media channels online without following up with concrete actions in the context of popular activist themes such as environmental protection and social justice issues.

CEO's and creative director's actual names, representative of all the company's employees. Whether the commitment was sincere and is truly adopted remains to be seen, but opting against the opportunity for a branded black square image with the potential to be re-shared as so many other companies did, could be seen as a sign of sincerity in the context of this moment of solidarity and silence. Or maybe it is just another ingenious marketing trick that makes Gucci seem more unique, for that matter. Either way, when taking a closer look at the commitments and campaigns of the Italian luxury brand in the years since Alessandro Michele's arrival as creative director, the company seemed to have undergone a renaissance that revitalised the brand as a trendsetter in design, presentation, marketing, and sales. In the transition from 2019 to 2021, Gucci made a conscious effort towards more transparency in processes of production, presentation and distribution that can be traced throughout their published content (cf. Hosters, Roesler 2021/1: 2). As such, Gucci is particularly interesting in how it positions itself at the forefront, not just of disrupting the fashion industry – for instance by taking the pandemic as a chance to re-invent its organisational structures and pressures – but also with their innovative use of new media technologies, social and virtual platforms, and forays into the gaming sector. The diverse content Gucci presents on all kind of different online channels is another example of the interrelated functionality of networked images in rhizomatic formations. They enable different points of entry to the Gucci Fashion and media universe, and whether this happens on YouTube, Snapchat, TikTok, Instagram, the Gucci app or the print edition of Vogue is irrelevant, as the familiarity and coherence across the channels is perfectly adjusted to each other. On the flip side, underlying these efforts is a dependency on the algorithmic social networks where they are published. In that regard the appropriation of crisis moments by the retail sector functions as a heightened moment of surveillance capitalism, as it perpetuates a social media dynamic that is triggered by advertisers and networks and calls to act through its networked images.

As June 2nd passed, the (visual) silence of the black square was replaced quickly by "business as usual" with an added political and activist twist. Footage of violent demonstrations and clashes with the police, toppling statues, burning cars and buildings dominated the social networks and news cycles for the following weeks and months. The neologism "doom-scrolling" was invented to describe the daily activity millions of people had been engaged in since the ongoing lockdowns had started. The addictive potential of spectacular (and violent) content might have been a blessing in disguise for the tech companies and news networks, which were profiting from skyrocketing engagement and TV rates.[3] On the side of the consumer/user, though, reports on the addictive potential as well as the detrimental

---

3   The fashion and online retail industry could make up for their assumed losses in the first half of 2020 with record breaking profits in the second half of 2020 and first quarter of 2021 (Cf. Kering, LVMH Reports 2021).

social and psychological effects of social media use became increasingly common (cf. Beller 2006; Hills 2009). Additionally, greater polarisation and alienation have been analysed in diverse societies across the globe (Post 2019; Esteban/Ray 1994).

Following Shoshana Zuboff's remarks, we are not just giving up our privacy by using "free" products online, but we are also dealing with a new economic paradigm of *surveillance capitalism*. Because the use of online platforms is so convenient but also inextricably linked to our computers, devices and the internet at the same time, the tech providers are all-pervasive and relentless in their pursuit of new data. This data – which Zuboff defines as *behavioural surplus* – is used by the big players in Silicon Valley (e.g., Google, Facebook) to generate profits by selling it to the highest bidding advertisers (Zuboff 2019: 63-97). Aided by complex algorithms and artificial intelligence, the goal of so-called big tech companies and their social media platforms changed from collecting behavioural data to improve their products to predicting and influencing users' (and potential customers') desires with uncanny precision. Subjected to the power of free markets and its venture capitalist investors, Silicon Valley went through a decisive paradigm shift that established an unprecedented business model, which revolves around and is founded on the exploitation and collection of user data to establish a seemingly irreversible market dominance. The question is, have we already reached the point of no return? The so-called "surveillance assets" which are a decisive part of the overarching system of surveillance capitalism are able to manipulate the customer's actions to the point of directing them to desired locations (see Zuboff's discussion of Pokemon Go). Correspondingly, Zuboff states:

Big data [...] is not a technology or an inevitable technology effect. It is not an autonomous process [...]. It originates in the social, and it is there that we must find it and know it. [...] I explore the proposition that big data is above all the foundational component in a deeply intentional and highly consequential new logic of accumulation that I call surveillance capitalism. (Zuboff 2015: 75)

In this regard, surveillance capitalism is understood as a new form of information capitalism "to predict and modify human behaviour as a means to produce revenue and market control" (ibid.: 75). This results in influencing human behaviour with clear intentions of exploitation and profiteering (that the big tech companies like to cloak in a veil of positive image campaigns). She continues:

Data about the behaviours of bodies, minds, and things take their place in a universal real-time dynamic index of smart objects within an infinite global domain of wired things. This new phenomenon produces the possibility of modifying the behaviours of persons and things for profit and control. (ibid.: 85)

Sounding fatalistic, Zuboff concludes: "In the logic of surveillance capitalism there are no individuals, only the world-spanning organism and all the tiniest elements within it" (ibid.: 85). We would like to suggest the hypothesis that the described processes and explorations of surveillance capitalism are based on rhizomatic structures as well, as at the same time, they are only able to function by way of these structures. Additionally, the rhizome as a metaphor can help to make the seemingly invisible surveillance structures at work in these networks visible and tangible.

Zuboff's argumentation falls in line with Gilles Deleuze's concept of "control societies", "which are in the process of replacing disciplinary societies" (Deleuze 1922: 139). Following Foucault, control societies initiated "the organisation of spaces of vast enclosure", as well as the nowadays familiar feeling of never being finished with anything (ibid.: 139-140). Because societies of control operate with computers that enable the mutation of capitalism to that of a "higher-order production" and success is determined by taking control of the market by any means necessary, "corruption thereby gains a new power" (ibid.: 141). Deleuze distinguishes control from discipline, which used to be of long duration and discontinuous. Control, on the other hand, is short-term focused, continuous and has a rapid rate of turnover, and in that sense is more adequate to the short attention spans that communication on social media networks seems to result in. "Man is no longer man enclosed, but man in debt" (ibid.: 141). Deleuze forecasts a modulation of behaviour, Zuboff diagnoses it. And while we analyse it, the free markets continue to exploit data to modify and influence user behaviour, resulting in sales of luxury fashion (and other products) at new all-time highs – paradoxically in a time of a global pandemic in which the physical social interactions have been steadily pushed into virtual realms.

The abstraction of the black square as a blank canvas enabled it to become a symbol for social justice because that was as much dependent on timing and context as on the social network it was distributed on. The symbol of the black square transformed through viral reproduction and distribution techniques independently of its original source, and thereby managed to transcend isolated social media filter bubbles. While this also led to the commercial appropriation of the symbol by brands (in obvious ways as has been shown with L'Oréal or Gucci), or pressure for cultural institutions to position themselves in response, it also reached diverse populations across the world and so resulted in concrete action on- and offline, demanding real change and consequences in response. We can understand the phenomena of the black square in 2020 as an anomaly and a chance for active intervention on behalf of the users inside of the framework of surveillance capitalism, in which every like, share, comment etc, is stored, analysed, evaluated, and sold again. But as the initial campaign itself is positioned somewhere between marketing campaign and viral performance, the power of the black square's symbolism escaped easy definitions. It created a 21st century example of the power of abstraction and rhizomatic swarm dissemination. It not only informed public opinion and emotions but also triggered public action in an age in which the excess of imagery and virtual meetings had become the norm.

2020 was not the first time a "black square" had been used for disruptive purposes. A closer look at the trajectory of its symbolism and (art) history shows that it has transformed its (non) meaning time and time again, and thus was able to create new canvases for projections more representative of their respective time and contexts. What can be learned from this history of semantic change? To what extent do art history and (fashion) media studies intersect at the threshold of platform surveillance capitalism and (new) modes of representation that spark social action by way of abstraction?

(In)visible Layers: The Evolution of the Black Square

At first glance, Kasimir Malevich's *Black Square* has nothing to do with either fashion, social media or black lives. The painting was first shown at "The Last Futuristic Exhibition of Paintings 0,10" in St. Petersburg in 1915 and counts as one of the foundational pieces of "suprematism" – an art movement that decisively rejected any mimetic representation of nature or reality by embracing abstraction in the depiction of basic geometric forms such as squares, circles or lines, and reducing the colour palette to gradients of black and white (Malevich 7 – The Non-Objective World) (see fig. 7). (It is perhaps a foreboding that the black square seems to take the position of a surveillance camera in the top corner of the room in the exhibition view. It overlooks the space and the other exhibits). By rejecting the representative practices of the preceding art movements (which decisively influenced their own training), Malevich, Rodchenko (the Russian avant-garde as a whole) as well as Wassily Kandinsky and Hilma af Klint independently in Sweden made the case to embrace radical abstraction at the turn of the 20th century, which paved the way for "modern art" as we know it. In the introduction of Malevich's manifesto of suprematism "Die gegenstandslose Welt" (Eng. "The Non-Objective World")[4], contributor and Bauhaus architect Ludwig Hilberheimer describes Malevich's motivation as though "he insisted that art and the feelings which generate it are more basic and meaningful than religious beliefs and political conceptions" (Malevich 1959: 7). Art had to be purified from any institutional influence to free its full potential. In Malevich's own words, he defines suprematism as "the supremacy of pure feeling in creative art" and does away with "Academic naturalism, the naturalism of the Impressionists, Cézanne's, Cubism, etc." – and thereby radically rejects their dialectic methods and any form of representational objectivity in artworks in favour of the Suprematist method. In this modus, "the appropriate means of representation is always the one which gives fullest possible expression to feeling as such and which ignores the familiar appearance of objects" (ibid.: 67). By way of erasing objectivity for the ultimate

---

4   The original German version was published by Bauhaus in 1928.

subjective experience, Malevich finds refuge in the image of the "desert in which nothing can be perceived but feeling" thus transforming "the art of the past which stood, at least ostensibly, in the service of religion and the state," towards "new life in the pure (unapplied) art of *Suprematism,* which will build up a new world – the world of feeling" (ibid.: 68).

Fig. 7: Paintings by Kasimir Malevich on view in "0,10: The Last Futurist Exhibition of Pictures." Saint Petersburg. December 1915-January 1916. Black Square is in the top corner. (Screenshot taken from Tupitsyn 2019, Url: https://post.moma.org/the-subject-of-nonobjective-art/)

The networked images shared on social media today are also playing with feelings and emotions with the intention of influencing our perceptions and actions. In both examples of black squares, old and new, we are confronted with variations of deletion and overwriting. Appearing to be unrelated due to the sheer difference of time and the media technologies used, a closer look exposes several analogous layers. Not too long ago in 2015, new x-ray imaging technologies enabled researchers to uncover the underlying traces of two previous paintings and written words under Malevich's black square, adding mystery to his artwork by enabling speculation about the "racist" nature behind the overpainted remark.[5] In this case new media

---

5   Researchers uncovered two other suprematist paintings as well as the inscription "negroes fighting in a cave, during the night" in Cyrillic underneath the layers of black and white that form Malevich's famous black square. Art historians pointed to another artwork by the French poet and humourist Alphonse Allais and his close

imaging technologies enabled us to make visible what was probably never intended to be visible. Today, on the other hand, new image distribution technologies cloak their underlying structures in a flood of endlessly (re)produced visual content, to the extent that the obvious becomes invisible. In either case, the abstraction of the square enables a paradoxical state of interpretation that disconnects and therefore can differ greatly from the originators' original motivation and intention. The image thus becomes alive and develops a dynamic life of its own that is independent of its creator, ready to create new semantic meaning in relationship with the viewer, whose interpretation is dependent on context, place, time and as a result, their subjective experience. This applied back in 1884 and 1913 as it does now in 2021. In 1913, Malevich felt the urge to clarify his original motivation in order to correct what he understood as a mis-perception in the public's reaction after the exhibition:

The black square on the white field was the first form in which non-objective feeling came to be expressed. The square = feeling, the white field = the void beyond this feeling. [...] Yet the public saw in the non-objectivity of the representation the demise of art and failed to grasp the evident fact that feeling had here assumed external form. (ibid.: 76)

The rupture between original intention in public (art) practice and public perception as well as the act of overwriting establishes another analogy to the black square of 2020. Where the transformation in Malevich's square happened at the hands of the artist and can be understood as an internal dialogue with a previous painting, the original Instagram post of the #theshowmustbepaused campaign was drowned out by the swarm dissemination and brand appropriation in public view. The performative speed and platform dynamic of viral social media posts can decouple from its original almost instantly. In her essay "In defense of the poor image", Steyerl concludes in this context:

The poor image is no longer about the real thing - the originary original. Instead, it is about its own real conditions of existence: about swarm circulation, digital dispersion, fractured and flexible temporalities. It is about defiance and appropriation just as it is about conformism and exploitation. In short: it is about reality. (Steyerl 2009: 9)

friend Paul Bilhaud that features the same written allusion in relation to a black rectangle. Allais published a series of proto-abstract colour rectangles with "humorous" captions for an April fool's edition book in 1884. Particularly the white and black ones stand out in this context. Whereas the caption under the white rectangle reads "Première communion de jeunes filles chlorotiques par un temps de neige" (Eng.: First Communion of Anaemic Young Girls in the Snow) the black one is entitled "Combat de nègres dans une cave, pendant la nuit" (Negroes fighting in a cave, during the night.") (cf. Neuendorf 2015).

Adding to the ambiguities in the distribution and perception of "poor images", Steyerl expands on this point in the context of evolving documentary practices (such as the phone video recordings of violent clashes during the protests) and observes in "A Language of Practice":

However, documentary expressions are not only a possible arena for public debate. Their production creates material arrangements which organize things and humans in ever shifting combinations throughout dispersed geographical locations. They connect humans and machines, images and sounds, hard drives, and desires. As common practices or as shared operational procedures, they anticipate alternate forms of social composition. To work on these conditions means to work on reality today. (Steyerl 2008: 149)

Steyerl reminds us that taking the redundant and disconnecting factor of producing and looking at networked images on social media into consideration, helps us not just to understand them as an undeniable part of reality but furthermore as an opportunity for it to be potentially reorganised. According to Zuboff, this can just happen on a level of immense scale and engagement on the part of the public. In this context, we want to understand the *black square 2020* as such an opportunity. As a blueprint for the type of social media activism that could potentially lead us into a more democratic future from the bottom up, as opposed to being exploited for raw data by systems of surveillance that determine 21st century means of production and distribution.

Fig. 8: Illustration of Alphonse Allais - "Combat de nègres dans une cave, pendant la nuit." (Url: https://www.wikiart.org/en/alphonse-allais/negroes-fighting-in-a-tunnel-by-night)

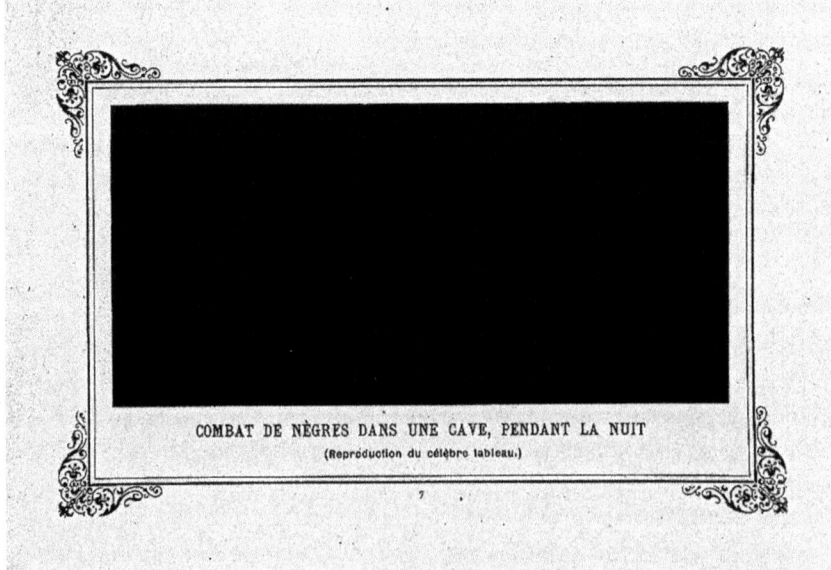

The rejection of objectivity in favour of the subjective experience that Malevich mentions also sounds familiar one century later. When trust is eroding in traditional democratic pillars such as the government, science, the free press, and in religious and cultural/educational institutions throughout western democracies – we must ask ourselves if Malevich's vision of inventing a new world of feeling (and affect) has infected reality in the information age in ways he could not have imagined during his time. Recent studies vehemently tie affective actions to the rise of the internet and its reorganisation through so called big tech monopolies. They find resonance in the "big five" media conglomerates of Hollywood in the 20th century – with the exception that today's players invented a completely new business model, which does not just generate its profits from and for entertainment purposes but to a much greater extent from the surveillance and behaviour prediction/modulation of its users. As unregulated capitalism knows just one way forward – the way of increasing profits – it is questionable to what extent the said companies will rein in their hunger for siphoning off precious data in order to grow more. We must start asking the question more seriously: Are we serving technology, or is technology serving us?

In the fashion world, the recursive influence between online/youth and meme culture and its traditional luxury houses became abundantly clear in the last decade. Under consistent pressure to (re)invent itself due to the tight deadlines of the annual fashion calendar and its seasons, the fashion industry has been at the forefront of creating and/or appropriating youth trends and experiments with new media technologies such as VR/AR. Consequentially, the question who is influencing whom is becoming relevant for the fashion world as well. One option to make the seemingly invisible surveillance structures of the networked images online visible is the metaphor of the rhizome. Although the crux of the matter might be that "surveillance capitalism" as suggested by Zuboff functions so effectively precisely *because* of its opaque design. Gucci presents itself paradoxically as down to earth in this context. Inherently exclusive due to the high cost of its luxury products, but simultaneously relatable and almost pure in its dedication to fashion as an art form. The DNA of the brand seems to be becoming visible increasingly in their latest campaigns, but this sudden transparency also works as just another form of manipulation fuelling consumer desires. It could well be another sophisticated branding mirage that covers up a range of semantic meaning behind its colourful layers, similarly to Malevich's square.

Analogous to the political and social disruptions shaking the US and the world in 2020, the Russian avant-gardists produced their most influential work in the early 20th century in a period in which it was extremely difficult to remain nonpartisan. Political polarisation in the public sphere was the norm at that time as well, and the urge to take sides in an increasingly ideological conflict echoes into the present. The goal of the Russian avant-garde "to achieve unmediated creations that would replace any form of 'prostituted art'" in order for artists to "pursue their own revolutions against artistic and conventions and restrictive institutions" can be applied in a like manner to the contemporary situation (cf. Tupitsyn 2019). Whereas the art of the late 19th century and the beginning of the 20th century was "prostituted" through the influence of the church and the state, today's "art" – or rather its "content" – is prostituted through the influence of brand advertising, of corporate and financial interests that determine not just our means of production but also public perception and social interaction. Without doubt, Malevich was heavily influenced by the media technologies that were emerging at the beginning of the 20th century. His suprematist composition #78 "expressing the feeling of wireless telegraphy" anticipated the idea of wireless internet even in 1915 (see fig.9). As such, Malevich succeeded in reinventing the old medium of painting by way of abstraction, making the invisible wireless transmissions of the new media technologies visible. With futuristic x-ray imaging technology becoming reality a century later, we managed to see through Malevich's square and its layers of black and white, uncovering discourses that remind us as much of our troubled history as of our diverse and common humanity.

Fig. 9: Screenshot of "Suprematist composition expressing the feeling of wireless telegraphy." 1915. Taken from Malevich 1959: 83.)

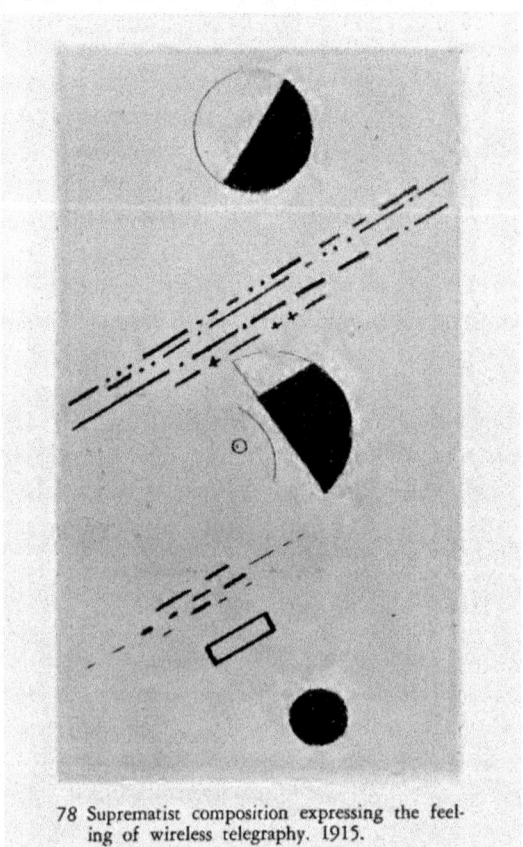

78 Suprematist composition expressing the feeling of wireless telegraphy. 1915.

In Conclusion...

The online evolution of the black square in 2020 can be understood as a unique moment in (social) media history, born out of a moment of social crisis nested somewhere between a marketing campaign and a collective art-activist performance. Through the campaign's independent far-reaching impact on- and offline as well as the transformation of the Instagram feed that followed over the day, social, cultural, and commercial interests picked up on some of its elements, leading to different outcomes. Hijacking hashtags became a weapon as a result, and an awareness of contemporary issues of social justice and inequality found their way into the public discourse. To what extent these issues will be addressed to spark positive change or have been utilised in the platform dynamics of surveillance capitalism remains to be seen. By zooming in on the distribution and reproduction patterns of networked images such as the black square, their rhizomatic structure becomes visible in the way that they transcend pre-defined algorithmic bubbles and independently spread to the furthest reaching corners of the network. The speed and performative pressure of how networked images operate online could be revealed as well. The addictive and speedy quality of convenience in social media networks seems to be more powerful than critical engagement. In that regard, the most spectacular and extreme perspectives tend to be amplified without sufficient contextualisation or critical distance. The black square 2020 campaign and its paradoxical deletion of #blacklivesmatter content make us aware that networked images adhere to arbitrary rules of platform mechanics that can twist and disrupt in unintended ways. Even though Black Lives Matter is as much a social media movement as it is a social justice movement that operates internationally today, the black square and its story of appropriation also stands as a paradigmatic example of the exploitation of a moment of social crisis by commercial interests within the framework of surveillance capitalism. Paradoxically, genuine expressions of solidarity exist next to brand appropriations of the same theme on social media today. The on- and offline impact of the black square campaign and the disruptive power of its uncontrolled viral dissemination shows us that the power of the masses has a real impact when it is coordinated towards a common cause. We should start to use it more often.

References

Andersson, Victoria/Jandér, Louise (2016): "Social Media, Insta-Culture and The Reinvention of Fashion Week." (http://hb.diva-por- tal.org/smash/get/diva2:941385/FULLTEXT01.pdf).

Baran, Paul (1964): On Distributed Communications: I. Introduction to Distributed Communications Networks Memorandum RM-3420-PR, Santa Monica.

Baudrillard, Jean (1991): Der Symbolische Tausch und der Tod, München: Matthes & Seitz.

Berners-Lee, Tim/Gailliau, Robert (1990): WorldWideWeb: Proposal for a Hypertext Project. (http://www.w3.org/Proposal.html).

Bronfen, Elisabeth (2004): "Recycling von Gewalt und Gesetzlosigkeit." In: Prinzler, Helmut & Jatho, Gabriele (eds.). New Hollywood 1967-1976. Trouble in Wonderland, Berlin: Bertz, pp. 15-32.

Bruni, Frank (2018): "Alessandro Michele, Fashion"s Modern Mastermind." In: New York Times Magazine (https://www.nytimes.com/2018/10/15/t-magazine/alessandro-michele-gucci-interview.html).

Bunz, Mercedes (2009): Die Geschichte des Internet. Vom Speicher zum Verteiler, Berlin.

Coscarelli, Joe (2020): "#BlackoutTuesday: A Music Industry Protest Becomes A Social Media Moment." In: The New York Times. (https://www.nytimes.com/2020/06/02/arts/music/what-blackout-tuesday.html)

Chrisman-Campbell, Kimberly (2016): "Is This the End for Fashion Week? Traditional, Seasonal Fashion Shows are Exhausting, Expensive, and Increasingly Irrelevant – and Many Designers are Opting Out." In: The Atlantic (https://www.theatlantic.com/entertainment/archive/2016/02/the-end-of-the-runway/461862/).

Coscarelli, Joe (2020): "#BlackoutTuesday: A Music Industry Protest Becomes a Social Media Moment." In: The New York Times (https://www.nytimes.com/2020/06/02/arts/music/what-blackout-tuesday.html).

Culver, Jordan (2020): "Say his Name! George Floyd!": Nationwide Protests Continue on 'Blackout Tuesday' in Chicago, Miami, Phoenix, across US." In: USA Today (https://www.usatoday.com/story/news/nation/2020/06/02/george-floyd-blackout-tuesday-protests-us/3128699001/).

Esteban, Joan-Maria; Ray, Debraj (1994): "On the Measurement of Polarization." In: Econometrica 62/4 (https://doi.org/10.2307/2951734).

Franck, Georg (2019): "The Economy of Attention." In: Journal of Sociology 55/1, pp. 8-19.

Deleuze, Gilles (1972): "Postscript on the Societies of Control". In: Szeman, Imre/Kaposy, Timothy (eds.) (2010), Cultural Theory: An Anthology, Malden, MA: Wiley-Blackwell, pp. 139-142.

Deleuze, Gilles; Guattari, Félix (1987): A Thousand Plateaus. Capitalism and Schizophrenia. London: Continuum.

Hanlon, Paul (2021): "Manufacturing Redemption: An Analysis of Brand Responses to the Killing of George Floyd." MA-Thesis. Ontario: Queen's University

Hilberheimer, Ludwig (1959): "Introduction." In: Malevich, Kasimir, The Non-Objective World. Chicago: Paul Theobald and Company.

Hills, Matt (2009): Participatory Culture: Mobility, Interactivity and Identity. In: Creeber, Glen/Martin, Ryoston (eds.), Digital Cultures: Understanding New Media. New York: McGraw Hill, pp. 107-121.

Hosters, Sascha; Roesler-Keilholz, Silke (2021): "Fashion Media Studies." In: Kommunikation. Medien 13 (https://eplus.uni-salzburg.at/JKM/periodical/titleinfo/6199615)

Hosters, Sascha; Roesler-Keilholz, Silke (2020): "Of course a horse... Oder: Von Mode, Pferden und anderen Sehnsüchten im Sommer der Pandemie." In: Mitteilungen des Regensburger Verbunds für Werbeforschung – RVW 8/2020, pp. 5-13 (https://epub.uni-regensburg.de/50903/1/Mitteilungen_RVW_8-2020.pdf).

"Later & Fohr Influencer Marketing Report: The Selling Power of Influencers", 2021 (https://get.later.com/influencer-marketing-report-selling-power/).

Malevich, Kasimir (1959): The Non-Objective World. Chicago: Paul Theobald and Company.

Mihalcik, Carrie (2020): "Blackout Tuesday's Flood of Black Squares May Be Silencing #Blacklivesmatter Hashtag and Protesters." In: Cnet (https://www.cnet.com/news/blackout-tuesdays-flood-of-black-squares-may-be-silencing-blacklivesmatter-hashtag-and-protesters/).

Neuendorf, Henri (2015): "X-Ray Analysis Gives Shocking New Insights into Kazimir Malevich's "Black Square"." In: Artnet News (https://news.artnet.com/art-world/kizimir-malevich-black-square-363368).

Post, Senja (2018): "Polarizing Communication as Media Effects on Antagonists. Understanding Communication in Conflicts in Digital Media Societies." In: Communication Theory 29/2, pp. 213-235 (https://doi.org/10.1093/ct/qty022).

Steyerl, Hito (2009): "In Defense of the Poor Image." In: e-flux journal #10 (http://worker01.e-flux.com/pdf/article_94.pdf).

Steyerl, Hito (2008): "A Language of Practice." In: Stallabrass, Julian (ed.), Documentary: Documents of Contemporary Art, London: Whitechapel, pp.145-151.

Sobande, Francesca (2020): "Woke-Washing: 'Intersectional' Femvertising and Branding 'Woke' Bravery." In: European Journal of Marketing 54/11, pp. 2723-2745. (https://doi.org/10.1108/EJM-02-2019-0134).

"The Hollywood Antitrust Case: aka The Paramount Anti-Trust Case," 2005 (http://www.cobbles.com/simpp_archive/1film_antitrust.htm).

Tupitsyn, Margarita (2019): "The Subject of Nonobjective Art." (https://post.moma.org/the-subject-of-nonobjective-art/).

Willingham, AJ (2020): Why Posting a Black Image with the „Black Lives Matter" Hashtag Could Be Doing More Harm Than Good. In: CNN. Online (https://www.cnn.com/2020/06/02/us/blackout-tuesday-black-lives-matter-instagram-trnd/index.html).

Vredenburg, Jessica/Kapitan, Sommer/Spry, Amanda et al. (2020): "Brands Taking a Stand: Authentic Brand Activism or Woke Washing?" In:

Journal of Public Policy & Marketing 39/4, pp. 440-460 (https://doi.org/10.1177/0743915620947359).

Zuboff, Shoshana (2015): "Big Other: Surveillance Capitalism and the Prospects of an Information Civilization." In: Journal of Information Technology 30, pp. 75-89.

Zuboff, Shoshana (2018): The Age of Surveillance Capitalism. New York: Public Affairs.

Automating Platform Spectators
Algorithmic Montage and Affective Scroll in TikTok

Alexandra Anikina

Abstract

Algorithmic automation of visual culture opens an interesting discussion of the negotiation of agency and circulation of affect between the user and the network. On audiovisual platforms, the algorithmic procedure is looped into the demands of attention economy, keeping the user watching. Taking TikTok as the main case study due to its compelling assemblage of surveillance tactics tailored to techno-embodied modes of spectatorship, this paper questions how platforms renegotiate the user-spectators' agency and produce new modes of watching and experiencing images. I investigate algorithmic montage and affective scroll as TikTok's key attention capture and instrumentalisation devices, built into the lacunae of behavioural opportunity and capitalising on the affective drive of the moving image flow. I argue that users should be seen as user-spectators whose agency undergoes a double negotiation, as users who can interact with the platform and as spectators who are subjected to specific modes of attention capture; their agential dis/empowerment is, therefore, contingent and framed by the specific epistemic and aesthetic affordances of the platform governmentality. Considering the role of algorithmic montage and affective scroll leads to new insights in how algorithmic surveillance simultaneously participates in the aesthetic and temporal figuration of platform spectatorship and conditions the tactics of resistance to the algorithmic logic.

Keywords

TikTok; Algorithmic Montage; Affective Scroll; User-Spectatorship; Agency

Algorithmic automation of visual culture opens an interesting discussion of the negotiation of agency and circulation of affect between the user and the network. Machinic epistemologies of pattern-finding and predictive analytics are inserted into the cultural production, delegating the decision-making to algorithms (Parisi 2017). The phone becomes a "biopolitical screen" (Väliaho 2014) that depends on data collection to produce a data shadow of its spectators. In audiovisual platforms, this data shadow, in turn, informs the sequences of algorithmic montage and the temporalities of scrolling through the image feeds, forming unique assemblages of experience and affect and posing new questions regarding how spectatorship is formed on platforms.

Algorithmic automation allows social media networks based exclusively on audiovisual communication to thrive by exploiting the audiovisual automatism, scrolling and autoplay functions built into the interface. TikTok presents a particularly compelling case for investigation because of how successful it appears to be in capturing the user-spectator's attention. Like many other platforms, TikTok hides the extent of data collection that it relies upon within the language of user agreement terms. Surveillance is reformulated as a personalisation service for the customer and is built into the platform-specific regimes of showing and watching, that regulate to which images, for how long, and in connection with which other images the users' gaze is directed.

This paper focuses on how the algorithmic procedure behind the images shapes the modes of attention capture and spectatorial agency. As algorithmic montage produces a mode of capture through the videos unfolding on the screen, it performs as an affective drive of neoliberal technoculture. As the users try to uncover the algorithmic logic and engage in creating and promoting specific types of content that could compete with the algorithm itself, it opens up a consideration of their agential dis/empowerment within the network. However, while these agential acts are more visible, attention should be paid to how the affective scroll shapes the experience of watching. Looped into attention economy, the affective scroll and algorithmic montage produce new angles for considering the circulation of affect in the media ecologies formed by human users and platforms.

How can we approach a mode of spectatorship organised around a data shadow of the viewer? How can we think about the networked images' representation and its procedural infrastructure in relation to the experience of watching? How is the participants' agency framed by the platform? What temporalities and affects does the platform enact, and how are these embedded in the loops of attention economy? In this paper, I will consider these questions using the case of TikTok and its specific production of spectators through the use of algorithmic montage and affective scroll. Considering the role of algorithmic automation in the "affective scroll" leads to new insights into how algorithmic surveillance simultaneously participates in the figuration of data spectatorship and in the tactics of resistance to the algorithmic logic behind the interface.

Digital Subject – Digital Spectator?

Recent discussions in critical digital theory, media studies and visual culture have reflected the changing status of images in the context of their proliferation, accumulation and analysis by contemporary audiovisual platforms. The proliferation of images on platforms and their infrastructural effects and affects have been described as the mass image (Cubitt 2017, 2021), networked image (Rubinstein and Sluis 2008; Cox et al. 2021), platform seeing (Munster/MacKenzie 2019) and photography off the scale (Dvořák/Parikka 2021). These terms and approaches pay attention to infrastructures, the computational architectures and networks that underlie the contemporary media landscape and define the presences, scales and speeds of the image production, distribution and circulation. They also underline the changes in perception and in new relationships that the human subject builds with the images in her network, pointing out the difficulty of speaking about the image structures that have a complicated relationship with visibility and representation.

Anna Munster and Adrian MacKenzie describe "platform seeing" as a paradigmatic shift in which "collections of images operate within and help form a field of distributed invisuality in which relations between images count more than any indexicality or iconicity of an image" (2019: 18). Like other approaches mentioned above, they underline the difficulty of situating the role of representation in the networked image. The vast datasets of images and their further computational analysis, ordering and operation produce a qualitative change in the sociotechnical make-up of the platform, in the perception of the users, and in the very paradigm of the "visual" as a way of knowing "how to see and observe":

We will argue that image ensembles have a qualitative and material effect on the contouring of the emergent sociotechnicality of both platform "life" and "perception"; that is, at the conjunction of image ensembles and artificial intelligence architectures, devices and hardware, *platform seeing* transpires as a new mode of invisual perception. (ibid.: 6)

They further underline that platform seeing "is not simply 'machine vision'… but a making operative of the visual by platforms themselves" (ibid.). Platform seeing comes with a complicated dynamic of visibility and invisibility, in which addressing the mechanics of a proprietary algorithm is largely impossible. As Munster and McKenzie point out, the operativity of the platforms "cannot be seen by an observing 'subject' but rather is enacted via observation events distributed throughout and across devices, hardware, human agents and artificial networked architectures such as deep learning networks" (2019: 5). The editors of this issue aptly note that the images become "calm" and "silent" as part of invisible architectures behind the screen frame. Platform seeing means considering the operativity of platforms like YouTube, Snapchat, Instagram and others through the events that construct different scales of attraction and duration, different methods of keeping the user watching, and different ways of compiling the flows of moving images. By striving to capture the milliseconds, seconds and minutes of attention, each platform projects its own audiovisual space with precise choices for automation, perception and attention – a specific affective assemblage of architectures behind representation. With surveillance tactics serving as an affective engine of TikTok image feeds but remaining obscured by the proprietary nature of the algorithms, the investigation of the platform's infrastructure, design and interface remains the way to analyse the algorithm without access to its actual mechanics and acknowledging it as a methodological difficulty.

While not unique in the exploitation of its users' attention, TikTok presents a particularly interesting case for addressing the forms of agency and spectatorship emerging between the algorithmically enhanced montage and the human audience. The videos on TikTok serve as data fodder for the algorithm. The user is always already a user-spectator, inhabiting a particular relationship with the image and its infrastructure. The role of surveillance in the construction of the image feed, as well as the temporality and internal operation of the space of moving images sorted and organised by algorithms into feeds and flows seem to be crucial points in discussing this relationship. Investigating this platform within the framework of an encounter between a user-spectator and an apparatus or an assemblage – as a bodily and spatial arrangement that involves the interaction of viewers with moving images and each other through a technical artefact – opens up the visible aspects of the algorithm for questioning.

Could one speak in terms of "spectator" and "spectatorship" to describe what takes place between the user and TikTok? After all, the act of viewing does not take place in the cinema, nor does it follow the established narratives, production pipelines and temporalities. The contemporary studies of digital media take different stances on using the term spectatorship. Anne Friedberg insists that the computer users are not viewers or spectators because of the interactivity in their relationship with the screens (2010). Michele White in her work on internet spectatorship (2006) uses the term to highlight the visual space of the internet as an apparatus of control, but also to complicate the relationship that the users have with the screens. She aptly notes that in the researchers' interpretations, "visual and textual representations of Internet activity and empowerment displace the more static processes of Internet looking and reading" (2006: 10), and that the act of "spectating" remains in the background in relation to more interactive forms.

It is hard to deny that platforms, be it laptop-bound streaming websites or transitory mobile social media feeds, produce specific – technically, socially and culturally arranged – modes of watching. In these modes of viewing, the user-spectator is bound not only to the algorithmic governance – through the algorithmic procedures – but also to the "governance" of the image, expressed as aesthetisation of these flows of data and as affective capture of attention. To understand this means to speak about user-spectators as digital subjects inhabiting both the aesthetic and the algorithmic field.

Olga Goriunova points out that platforms tend to create a "digital subject", understood as "an abstracted position, a performance, constructed persona from data, profiles and other records and aggregates" (Goriunova 2019: 126). Digital subjects are not exactly the individuals that they refer to but rather separate entities constructed at a distance. For TikTok, this translates to the subject's interests, habits, labour and leisure regimes, level of interaction and feedback, and macro- and microtemporalities of watching. The hashtag becomes both a node of individual connection and an indication that somewhere within the underlying statistical models not only the video, but also its viewer is marked as belonging to a particular viewing public. Furthermore, Katrina Sluis, speaking about photographs shared on social media networks, suggests that not only "human spectatorship is increasingly accounted for as 'clickthroughs', 'conversion rates', and 'traffic'" (2020: 122), but that also "the computer is an increasingly important spectator of photography" (2020: 114), meaning that for the users who produce images, there is a consideration of the algorithm itself as a potential judge making decisions on their sharing and proliferation.

The choices that TikTok user-spectators make regarding the durations of engagement, allowances of attention span, reactions and interactions constitute easily definable courses of action that they might take *as users*. The remit of these gestures is often approached in terms of self-expression, participation, engagement and, most interestingly, as "slacktivism" in relation to political action.[1] However, their presence on the platform *as spectators* is less clear and is more dependent on the affordances of the platform. The meticulous procedural and infrastructural creation of fragmented publics through the use of hashtags, metadata and algorithms in TikTok reveals the extent of the management of digital subjects, but it does not exactly describe *what it means* to be part of these virtual publics. The fragmentation (in the sense of individualisation of each personal feed) makes hashtags, subscriptions and live viewer counts into levers of control, and organises many individualised spectatorship bubbles that form the media ecology of the platform.

In this sense, the negotiation of agential positions between the user-spectators and the platform appears as another crucial research problem with different scales, taking into account the platform, other user-spectators, the algorithm and the images. It is interesting, therefore, to consider the agency of user-spectators as not completely controlled, but framed by the specific epistemic and aesthetic affordances of the platform. Antoinette Rouvroy's work highlights exactly this contingent character of the governance of such digital subjects, data shadows constructed at a distance:

The only "subject" algorithmic governmentality needs is a unique, supra-individual, constantly reconfigured "statistical body" made of the infra-individual digital traces of impersonal, disparate, heterogeneous, dividualized facets of daily life and interactions. This infra- and supra- individual statistical body carries a kind of "memory of the future" whereas the strategy of algorithmic governmentality consists in either ensuring or preventing its actualization. (Rouvroy 2012: 11)

---

1   See Chapter 2 in Dennis (2019) for a comprehensive review of these debates.

Such "memories of the future" acquire a particular urgency as images (or, rather, as images moved by algorithms). The case for understanding spectatorship as part of the platform's affective drive calls for a better understanding of its constituent parts: design and interface elements, algorithmic montage model and its continuous revision and operation, but also for a particular way in which the user-spectators engage with the platform, the conditions of the attention capture mechanisms, the dynamics of watching, the limits of the platform's control, and the user's creative and critical agency.

Thus, in order to see the dynamics of watching, seeing and experiencing between individual feeds, trans-individual hashtag clouds and statistical models of attention capture and retention, we need a theory that resists the naturalisation of platforms as neutral sites of communication, self-expression or public forums that facilitate political debate, and instead questions the users' agency and interaction with automated image infrastructure. The platform needs to be interrogated with a view to establishing how exactly the images factor in the processes of agential dis/empowerment and how the interpretation of images as productive representations (messages, reactions) might obscure the co-optation of attention and affect, hidden in the underlying procedure.

The Spectator Surveilled

Underlying the affective scroll, there are mechanisms of surveillance, masked as a personalisation service. Commercially motivated surveillance guarantees the smooth operation of the flow of images that translate the user-spectators' attention into revenue. In doing this, it operates within legal and technological limits of data collection, which are constantly probed and adapted as the company strives to keep the balance between profitability and avoidance of reputational risks.

TikTok was released in 2016 as the international version of the social media platform Douyin, owned by the Chinese company ByteDance. In marketing reports TikTok is commonly presented as a promising arena: a new platform aimed at a younger audience and particularly successful in securing their attention for longer than other platforms. In 2021, it counted 689 million monthly users, having experienced growth from 5 to 18 per cent of global internet users who use TikTok between 2018 and 2020 (Iqbal 2021). The often-cited reason for this growth is the assumption that TikTok's algorithm relies on careful analysis and orchestration of its spectatorships: how and to whom to show each uploaded video. In many social marketing reports, this competitive feature is described, from the producer's side, as "test-driving" the popularity of a video on a smaller audience before promoting it to a higher visibility trench or dropping it; and from the spectator's side, it is said that the delivery of the videos is tailored to these sample audiences, based on the analysis of their preferences and watching behaviour. TikTok's press release from 2020 helpfully outlines an additional aspect:

While a video is likely to receive more views if posted by an account that has more followers, by virtue of that account having built up a larger follower base, neither follower count nor whether the account has had previous high-performing videos are direct factors in the recommendation system. (TikTok 2020)

This ensures that the priority in the final montage lies with the specific linkages identified between the videos and the users' interests, producing a more diversified and rhizomatic system than the recommendation algorithms that put priority on the competitive performance of the users.

TikTok's Privacy Policy is one of the few official sources of information that feed the speculative investigations and reverse engineerings of the algorithm. The US version, updated on June 2, 2021, contains a paragraph on "Image and Audio Information" in the section describing the data that TikTok collects automatically. It states that the app

may collect information about the images and audio that are a part of your User Content, such as identifying the objects and scenery that appear, the existence and location within an image of face and body features and attributes, the nature of the audio, and the text of the words spoken in your User Content. We may collect this information to enable special video effects, for content moderation, for demographic classification, for content and ad recommendations, and for other non-personally-identifying operations. We may collect biometric identifiers and biometric information as defined under US laws, such as faceprints and voiceprints, from your User Content. Where required by law, we will seek any required permissions from you prior to any such collection. (ByteDance 2021a)

In the version written "for the EEA, United Kingdom or Switzerland", this section is absent. The data collection related to images and audio is defined, more modestly, within the general content: "We may collect information about the images and audio that are a part of your User Content, such as identifying the objects and scenery that appear, the existence and location within an image of face and body features and attributes, the nature of the audio, and the text of the words spoken in your User Content" (ByteDance 2021b). For those jurisdictions outside of these zones, 15 additional versions of the Privacy Policy are provided, each using a significantly less detailed description of data collection.

The differences between the versions reveal how ByteDance navigates various legal terrains, using the localised versions of the user agreement as trial incursions into what the users will allow the platform to collect. Where the legislation has not been developed enough to regulate which types of data can or cannot be collected and how, the Privacy Policy simply omits the details. The amendments to the European policy were also likely impacted by the charges against TikTok's data collection strategies. In 2020 the former Children's Commissioner for England Anne Longfield (2020) brought a lawsuit against TikTok and its parent company ByteDance "for illegally collecting millions of children's private information in the

UK and Europe and sharing it with unknown third parties for profit", including biometric information. In 2021, the European Consumer Organisation (BEUC) issued a complaint against TikTok on misleading the consumers on the types of data collected and on the data processing practices in their user agreement (BEUC 2021).

TikTok's algorithm, like other platforms' recommendation systems, operates in a grey legislative zone, the safe haven of algorithmic governance in the last decade. ByteDance rolls out new functionalities to test them not only on the userbase but also in the legislative space in which the local versions of the platform operate. This is noticeable not only in the user agreements but also in the changes made to the system following journalistic investigations into algorithmic censorship of topics potentially deemed troublesome by the company: content related to protests, LGBTQ and disability communities, "controversial" political questions – in other words, the content that the company classifies as risky for commercial interests (Reuter/Köver 2019; Reuter 2021). In the documentation provided in one of these investigations, the comparison between two different versions of internal tagging of such topics as "Risks" and, later, "General" (Reuter/Köver 2019) is telling: where censorship becomes unprofitable, it can be rearranged in a way that satisfies the user base. This is also reflected by the recent discussions of "shadowbanning", a covert censorship tactic by which certain posts are not deleted from the platform but are simply not shown to the users (Rauchberg 2022; Savolainen 2022; Peterson-Salahuddin 2022). As Jessica Sage Rauchberg points out, "shadowbans are not random: they reflect networks of oppression and marginalization that circulate in offline cultural discourses" (2022: 197), so the scale and the extent of the bans is constantly balanced between the users' engagement and public critique in such a way that ensures the platform's profitability.

Recently, TikTok also began to offer auto-caption and text-to-speech options in select countries. Given the visual nature of the platform, these features are advertised as a part of accessibility and inclusivity efforts (Hind 2021). Auto-caption significantly widens the metadata associated with each video and the potential semantic correlations between them. Acknowledging the closeness of the commercial media landscape and surveillance, as Nick Dyer-Witherford and Svitlana Matviyenko (2019) suggest, this becomes another example of tactical data collection presented as a service.

The algorithm, therefore, presents a particular type of surveillance, tailored to the efficiencies of the attention economy. It produces a model that "makes sense" of the audiovisual information, as the affective scroll must guarantee continuous attention. At the same time, it accumulates an archive that can be cross-referenced, analysed and continuously modelled into a better algorithm. Here, I return to Rouvroy, addressing such models of algorithmic correlation as a type of governmentality that does not directly confront the subjects, but only deals with their data shadows:

...unlike "visible", "scopic" surveillance generating "norms" which remain, broadly, intelligible to individuals, and available for them to compare and attune their behaviours, algorithmic governmentality carefully avoids any direct confrontation with and impact on flesh and blood persons. [...] What matters is the possibility to link any trivial information or data left behind or voluntarily disclosed by individuals with other data gathered in heterogeneous contexts and establish statistically meaningful correlations. (Rouvroy 2012: 11-12)

The user-facing side of the algorithm, therefore, presents a visualisation that only makes "sense" to the underlying infrastructure. It combines algorithmic decisions on what becomes relevant to the spectator at any given point with the algorithmic decisions and settings that define the more specific durations and modalities of the images, following the work on natural language processing, computer vision and data mining developed at ByteDance AI Lab (ByteDance 2018).

Affective Scroll

If, as Yves Citton suggests, "attention is becoming the hegemonic form of capital" (2014: 89, my translation), then the (algorithmic) socio-technical design of TikTok is looped into considerations of attention economy. Unlike the cinematic spectatorship of the 1970s, firmly situated in the darkness of the cinematic theatre, platform spectatorship is built into the lacunae of behavioural opportunity, into the mobile screens and the ebbs and flows of hyper-connected and distorted labour-leisure distinctions. Jonathan Crary aptly points out that free time in 24/7 capitalism "is far too valuable not to be leveraged with plural sources of solicitation and choices that maximize possibilities of monetization and that allow the continuous accumulation of information about the user" (2013: 53). At the launch, the videos in the TikTok feed lasted from 15 to 60 seconds. Having secured the userbase, TikTok has expanded its temporal allowances: in 2021, the upper limit was extended to 3 minutes, and in 2022 – to 10 minutes.

TikTok's architecture is organised not just around the attentive gaze, but also around swiping and tapping gestures. A swipe down assures the scroll; a swipe up returns to the previous video or refreshes the whole feed if it's done on the first video seen. A swipe down within a live stream transfers to another live stream. A side swipe to the right opens up the profile of the user who posted the video with links to other videos they have produced.

Like many other social media feeds, TikTok produces a kind of sliding visuality – one scrolls and scrolls, the thumb matches the rhythm of the gaze. The hypnotism of this movement, and the ease with which the user can fall into a "rabbit hole" of videos only to emerge minutes, if not hours, later, calls for closer investigation. It becomes important to distinguish analysis of the image *flow* itself from analysis of images on TikTok as individual representations, or even as a database of moving images and sounds.

The image flow prioritises attention capture. While human attention is grabbed by specific representations, from the point of view of the algorithmic infrastructure, the representation is only significant for the platform insomuch as it acts as a conduit and a trap for human attention. The image flow, then, appears as one of the levers of cognitive-behavioural governance, as a paradigm of "user experience-oriented" design – promising a seamless experience reconciling the micro-temporalities of networks and human perceptual apparatus, and tailored to recognise the needs of the users before they are even consciously expressed (Dieter/Gauthier 2019).

The works of Tiziana Terranova on network culture and Jodi Dean on communicative capitalism provide interesting insights for understanding the information space in which affect operates. Tiziana Terranova, referencing information theory, underlines that information rarely exists as an isolated message: it is always surrounded by other signals from which it needs to be extricated. Contemporary information flows need to be considered not just as strings of messages with a potential to be interpreted, but also as affective noise that has its own influence on perception outside of the realm of representation: "images are not so much decoded for meaning as consumed, that is absorbed and relayed" (Terranova 2004: 140). The images act as affective conduits, but they also disguise the operations that sort and remix them into a continuous temporal feed. The networked images "are not representations, but types of bioweapons" within the information ecology (Terranova 2004: 141), which capture the attentive gaze and its intensities.

Jodi Dean points out that in communicative capitalism, the "extras" of communication constitute their own kind of affect, no less powerful for being incidental:

The additive dimension of communication for its own sake designates an excess. This excess isn't a new meaning or perspective. It doesn't refer to new content. It is rather the intensity accrued from the repetition, the excitement or thrill of more. In the reflexive doubling of communication, the enjoyment attached to communication for its own sake displaces intention, content, and meaning. (2010: 39)

The question of affective scroll on TikTok is constituted by the embodied technological experience of the users and the particular modes of engagement that the feed is asking for. The feed is temporal: the modes of engaging, ranging from attentive to distracted looking, scrolling or even listening, all suggest a modulation of intensities, meaning that what TikTok offers to the user-spectator is also a particular modulation of temporalities in which the body can participate.

In TikTok's socio-technical design, the affective scroll interfaces the body with the gaze. The modulation and fluctuations of mediatic intensities constitute a powerful tool for keeping the users occupied with the platform. While some platforms such as YouTube include an option for the moving image content to play automatically, TikTok feed requires the user to swipe the video down in order to proceed to the next one. Jonathan Beller points out that "bodies must be trained to interface with affect machines through the overcoming of certain physical encumbrances", that film "turns movement into thoughts and feelings, or, more generally, affect" (2006: 95). Almost as a direct illustration of such "training", TikTok creates a particular mode of visual automatism: a cybernetic feedback loop between the algorithm, the user's attention and the user's thumb which feeds into the soothing array of moving images.

The affective scroll, therefore, becomes a key attention capture device that makes human faculties part of the platform's assemblage. Following Beller's thinking on the cinematic mode of production, the instrumentalisation of attention is part of "media's capitalization of the aesthetic faculties and imaginary practices of the viewers" (2006: 14). The instrumentalised forms of attention capture take advantage of smaller-than-small temporalities to "plug into" the existing routines of labour and leisure. In this sense, the automatism of human participants becomes a crucial part of platform spectatorship. Maeder and Wentz (2014) point out the similarity between the digital "seriality" of web interfaces that allows progression from one video to another seamlessly, and the televisual "flow" of browsing through television channels. Using YouTube as an example, they write that "as a cultural technique, browsing through YouTube might by now have become as intuitive as writing letters or zapping through TV channels" (2014: 133). If one considers the habituated bodily movement as a part of the technological assemblage, the user-spectator cannot be considered simply passive or active; the habituated aspects of the act of watching form a set of affordances that are as significant as those of the platform.

TikTok presents a particular case of automatism grounded in anticipation and in avoiding interruption. The cognitive assemblage of TikTok's temporality is discussed as anticipatory: following the behavioural principle of random reinforcement (Albright 2019: 328-329), the next video is always associated with a potential dopamine reward (Albright: 2020). Not all interactions with TikTok's interface, therefore, can be considered as enabling the users' agency by default. Some gestures, such as transitions between the feeds, the profiles and the messaging screen, sending messages and creating videos, can be seen as "navigational gestures" (Verhoeff/Cooley 2014) that underline the user-spectators' choice in where to direct the movement. However, the gesture needed to sustain the uninterrupted flow of images – a continuous swiping down – becomes automatised in itself, a movement *prescribed* by the platform. Within the feed and its affective scroll, the potential to navigate is foregone in favour of automatising the user-spectator's body to provide the kinetic energy to sustain the flow of images: part of an engine, rather than a steering wheel. This is an intentional choice on the part of the platform: the auto scroll is not included even as an option, and the #autoscroll hashtag reveals that many users are requesting the implementation of this function, wondering about its absence and sharing the names of third-party applications that allow them to do that.

Furthermore, interfacial gestures also become part of data collection: the TikTok user-spectator's body is thoroughly implicated in the data shadow: the data transmitted by and collected from the device includes "IP address, user agent, mobile carrier, time zone settings, identifiers for advertising purposes, model of your device, the device system, network type, device IDs, your screen resolution and operating system, app and file names and types, keystroke patterns or rhythms, battery state, audio settings and connected audio devices" (ByteDance 2021a).

The flow of the affective scroll, therefore, has to be understood as a balancing act between the agency of the spectators and the affordances of the platform. It also, crucially, has to be considered within and in relation to other temporalities that the body embraces, as an unconscious labour of keeping the flow of images uninterrupted. Noting that "to look is to labour" (2018: 24), Pasi Väliaho writes:

To put it bluntly, while we watch a film, zap between channels, lurk online, we do not simply "pay" attention; rather, we sell, unknowingly perhaps, our powers of paying attention to the industry in exchange (in most cases) of pleasure. (ibid.: 25)

Acknowledging the affective power of the scroll does not mean reducing the complex assemblage to a Pavlovian response that the platform elicits from the user. Rather, it means dismantling the game of algorithmic behaviourism through the investigation of its visible devices – interfacial clues, durations, intensities and rhythms – in order to approach more closely to the temporalities and networks of our attention spans, and of the unconscious labour we contribute to the contemporary platform's visuality.

Algorithmic Montage

First-person view: I open TikTok. The first video that I see is an ad hashtagged as a dancing challenge for a brand. For the first three seconds, the interface is not visible, apart from the "Skip ad" button. After the video has repeated a couple of times, the app suggests two more buttons: "Join this hashtag" and "Replay". I tap outside of both buttons to proceed to the two feeds: "Following" and "For you". The latter produces the following sequence on my small screen: a live concert; an animation of a singing cookie that is making cookies; an ad from an arthouse movie platform; a video from a language-learning channel, which is the first that seems to be directly related to my likes; a figure skater doing a beautiful trick on the ice rink; a live stream of a man speaking to an animal puppet on his hand. As I pause on the live stream, the puppet reverses the camera to show the number of spectators on its computer increase in real-time. The puppet thanks the audience in Mr Bean's voice.

Throughout the previous sections I have attempted to trace the visible outlines of the invisible computational model that defines what is shown to the user-spectators. One level down from this, there is another imagination: that of smaller, fleeting, accidental unfoldings of this algorithm into specific sequences of images on the user-spectators' screens. If one were to record them or even imagine them lying on the editing table, these sequences could suggest further speculations on the data shadows of their owners. How are we defined, as user-spectators, by what we watch?

In the earlier discussion of digital culture in the late 1990s and the 2000s, the term "montage" appeared in the discussions of new media as one of the functions of the old media meant to be subsumed or remediated by the new (Manovich 2001; Bolter/Grusin 2000). Other early approaches saw it in the light of the hypertextuality of digital culture and its capacity to fragment and remix content, drawing on various literary and cinematic traditions that attended to montage as a creative or political tool (see, for example, Druckrey 1994). In TikTok, montage appears to be accomplished by algorithmic personalisation. The personalised level of algorithmic montage – the individual selection of videos and different short videos and microgenres – creates further questions. One of the leaks of TikTok's official documentation (Smith 2021) suggests that "retention" and "time spent" are the two guiding metrics in selecting which videos to choose. In the imaginary montage sequence laid out on the editing table, the specifics of the user-spectator's data shadow become clearer. As journalistic investigations show, the TikTok algorithm is prone to creating "rabbit holes" of content based on one particular interest, independent of whether the content is positive or potentially harmful. Assisted by the watching bots, the Wall Street Journal visual investigation (WSJ Staff 2021) suggests a scenario of a bot "viewer" who pays particular attention to content related to depressive states. TikTok's official response states that the experiment is not representative of the normal viewer's diverse interests; the experiment shows, however, that eventually the potential for the spectator to see videos different from her interests becomes slim.

The architecture of the algorithm and its rhizomatic connections, based on the analytics of user surveillance, constitutes what I would call a poetic-affective drive of audiovisual platforms, an instrument for the capture and instrumentalisation of what makes the digital subject into a spectator as well. In 1953, American avant-garde filmmaker Maya Deren participated in a symposium "Poetry and the Film", organised by Cinema 16. In her contribution, she outlined a vision for "vertical montage". She suggested a reading of poetry as "vertical", as opposed to the "horizontally" unfolding dramatic development of a narrative. Poetry, for her, "is a 'vertical' investigation of a situation, in that it probes the ramifications of the moment, and is concerned with its qualities and its depth", and it is "concerned not with what is occurring, but with what it feels like, or what it means" (Deren 1963: 174).

She expanded this notion to include cinema: for her, a poetic film containing this kind of vertical montage must be short, since it is difficult to maintain such intensity. She describes the difference between horizontal narrative development and vertical poetic development in the following way:

> ... it isn't that one action leads to another action (this is what I would call a "horizontal" development), but they are brought to a center, gathered up, and collected by the fact that they all refer to a common emotion, although the incidents themselves may be quite disparate. Whereas, in what is called a "horizontal" development, the logic is a logic of actions. In a "vertical" development, it is a logic of a central emotion or idea which attracts to itself even disparate images which contain that central core which they have in common. (Deren 1963: 178)

The poetic approach to film images seems like an apt description for the forms of algorithmic montage occurring on TikTok. The algorithmic set of correlations between videos is perfectly arranged; each consecutive hashtag acts as a form of poetic organisation, unfolds into a new story, forming a structural relationship only existing in the current moment; and within each hashtag, a new hashtag can be found and activated. Without an endpoint, algorithmic montage has a temporality that is characterised by a sliding sense of continuity, rather than by a linear progression. The procedure itself becomes the main attraction; not so much for the sake of the images, but rather for the *promise* of them and for the specific temporality of the affective scroll.

Contingent Agencies, Contingent Publics

The TikTok spectators who engage in producing their own content and invent new microgenres engage with both other users *and* with the algorithm, the construction of which is contingent on data collection. The procedural algorithm is therefore generative and formed of human and non-human participants. It is also self-directing; it has limits and affordances set within procedures, and it is actualised as a live flow. Returning to the idea of the distance at which the "digital subject" is constructed, it is often the awareness of this distance that can produce affective tension and, potentially, a critical or creative response from the user. In other words, the *users'* agency (as engagement with and knowledge of algorithms) makes up part of the mechanisms of the algorithmic montage and the affective scroll; which, in turn, has consequences for them as *spectators*. Even more importantly, their agency is shaped by their perceptions of themselves as spectators and creators – and, therefore, as part of the watching public.

Antoinette Rouvroy points out that agency can be conceived in epistemic terms as a possibility for critical and reflexive capabilities, which, under the conditions of algorithmic governance are disregarded "in favour of computational, preemptive, context- and behaviour-sensitive management of risks and opportunities" (Rouvroy 2012: 2). She defines critique, following Foucault, as "a practice that suspends judgment and an opportunity to practice new values, precisely on the basis of that suspension" (Foucault 1990). If the algorithmic infrastructure of TikTok provides an efficient, real-time, operational epistemic environment, one that renders the correlations gleaned from data collection and analysis immediately actionable, what kind of space is there left to shape an alternative epistemic approach through images? There are three considerations to this question.

First of all, it is necessary to consider the fact that the user-spectators of TikTok actively compete with the algorithm itself by trying to uncover its logic and creating specific types of content that would be successful, by their estimation, within the current algorithmic model. The hashtags that the users attach to their videos reveal this knowledge as a separate microgenre. #algorithmexplained, #algorithmeposed, #algortihmhacks and #tiktokalgorithm feature suggestions on how to beat the algorithm at its own game. #algorithmupdate and #newalgorithm present the users' analyses and suggestions on the updates. Similar to the way game developers sustain the player base's interest with regular updates and prompt the creation of content by the users, TikTok incidentally (or strategically) leaks the details of the algorithm's operations (see Smith (2021) for an example of a leak, and Cotter (2019) for a reframing of users' engagement with visibility as "play").

Users' attitudes towards algorithmic recommendation systems have been recently discussed as algorithmic "folk theories", pointing out that the users' preconceptions, beliefs and assumptions about the algorithm are important factors in their life on the platform. Taina Bucher describes this as "algorithmic imaginaries" – "what algorithms are, what they should be, how they function, and what these imaginations, in turn, make possible" (2018: 157). She argues that the imaginations of algorithms can be as socially and culturally significant as their immediate functionality and operation. Investigations drawing on folk theories' approach to TikTok or Douyin underline that such imaginaries bear weight in the users' thinking about identity (Karizat et al. 2021) and authenticity (Barta/Andalibi 2021), and even turn into specific tactics and methods that the users employ to "audit" algorithms for harmful behaviour (DeVos et al 2022).

This also introduces an interesting consequence of seeing the TikTok users as user-*spectators*. The platform can be approached as a space with a specific sense of techno-embodied temporality, to which the user-spectators can retreat from their own pressures and anxieties. But it can also be seen as a form of experiencing moving images that is affective, malleable, under constant revision, and modifiable in dialogue with the non-human part of the assemblage. The time spent (or wasted) on a platform is not only a resource of attention economy, but also an indication of when and why the user-spectator has stepped in and out of the image *flow* as a particular mode of engaging with images.

In the absence of access to the specific choices behind each video, the methodology of the "imaginary editing table" can become an important intermediary between the research questions, users' assumptions about how the algorithm works and the actual sequence of videos on the screen. The concrete sequences of algorithmic montage reveal what TikTok prescribes to be visible or not, turning the "threat of invisibility" into a mechanism of control (Bucher 2018: 84). Even if awareness of the algorithmic procedure is high, the instruments that the users have are scarce in relation to limiting the visibility of certain content and in relation to guiding the spread of suggested videos.

Secondly, the consideration of hashtag spectatorship appears not as a monolithic apparatus, but rather as a multiplicity of fragmented publics, at the same time connected and dispersed. I have considered the algorithmic montage as a flow of intensities; these intensities can also include the feeling of participation in social life. The presence of markers such as likes, comments and view counts create an imaginary of a watching public (which is, in fact, also fragmented and individualised for each user like a targeted advertisement). This multitude of imaginaries of the filter bubble spectatorship produces, at the same time, real connections, but also a virtual community that, unlike the "recursive publics" of coders (Kelty 2005) and other communities relying on collective tool-making, lacks powerful instruments for collective action. Therefore, while the degrees of politicisation of TikTok user-spectators remain debatable, the spectatorship itself becomes reframed both as an imaginary and as a networked and refracted public, the extent of whose agency often expresses itself in sharing the instruments of algorithmic literacy with each other (Abidin 2021). These are not only users who are aware of the algorithm, but also those who are aware that their participation on the platform constitutes a kind of labour, either as content producers or as the attention-paying public.

Finally, the dynamics of representation and procedurality within TikTok's algorithmic montage also play an important epistemic role. Videos as singular representations, while interpretable by users, only remain significant for the platform in terms of the metrics of their attractive performance. The procedural underlining that assembles and moves these images into algorithmic constellations, reveals the underlying commercial interests of the platform, and limits rather than enables the participants' choices for a meaningful (dis)engagement with the flows of images. As Jodi Dean suggests, "decomposition and recombination appear more as aspects of our capture in affective networks than as tactics of resistance" (Dean 2010: 29).

Within the renegotiations of agency on the platform, the algorithm itself constitutes a point of awareness for the user base. Images act as passage points for social relations; image flows are organised according to the actually existing desires for social connection, acknowledgment, exchange or pleasure. At the same time, the images also enact their own affect through algorithmic temporalities, logics and rhythms. In other words, besides the relationships of users to other users, the platform strategically enables a relationship to the image itself and to the algorithm underlying it – and it is in this domain that the capture of affect and co-optation of various social energies and desires takes place.

Conclusion

The image is capitalism's hiding place; algorithmic operations exist unseen behind images. Focusing on how the algorithmic procedure behind images shapes the regimes of watching, I looked at algorithmic montage and affective scroll as two entry points into attention capture and spectatorial agency. The algorithmic montage is a visible expression of commercial surveillance – data collection tactics that the platform relies on to produce data shadows of the spectators as digital subjects. The platform *user* (a word implying that the users can *use* the platform as they want), is also a *user-spectator*, whose agency and engagement with the platform are shaped by contingent imaginaries and continuously updated instruments of algorithmic governmentality. In this assemblage, the affective scroll serves as a temporal device, a poetic-affective drive of the moving image flow, which is appropriated to fuel neoliberal socio-technics. The scroll ensures the capture of affect and the seamless transition between attention time and the platform's revenue. Finally, the scroll is also shaped around the imaginaries of the publics that aid the co-optation of various acts by the user-spectator (production of images, reactions to other users, self-expressions) into the loop of the attention economy, where they feed back into the construction of digital subjects and fragmented spectatorships.

Bibliography

Abidin, Crystal (2021): "From 'Networked Publics' to 'Refracted Publics': A Companion Framework for Researching 'Below the Radar' Studies." In: *Social Media + Society* 7 (1), pp. 1-13.

Albright, Julie M (2019): *Left to Their Own Devices: How Digital Natives Are Reshaping the American Dream*, New York: Prometheus Books.

Albright, Julie (2020): "Is TikTok Digital Crack Cocaine? Speaking with Dr. Julie Albright, Author of Left To Their Own Devices Interview by John Koetsier", January 16, 2020 (https://johnkoetsier.com/is-tiktok-digital-crack-cocaine-speaking-with-dr-julie-albright-author-of-left-to-their-own-devices/).

Barta, Kristen, and Nazanin Andalibi (2021): "Constructing Authenticity on TikTok: Social Norms and Social Support on the 'Fun' Platform". *Proceedings of the ACM on Human-Computer Interaction* 5 (CSCW2), pp. 1-29.

Beller, Jonathan (2006): *The Cinematic Mode of Production: Attention Economy and the Society of the Spectacle*, New Hampshire: University Press of New England.

BEUC (2021): "TikTok without Filters", BEUC The European Consumer Organisation (https://www.beuc.eu/tiktok#theaction).

Bolter, J. David, and Richard Grusin (2000): *Remediation: Understanding New Media*, Cambridge, MA; London: MIT Press.

Bucher, Taina (2018): *If...Then: Algorithmic Power and Politics*, Oxford: Oxford University Press.

ByteDance (2018): "ByteDance AI Lab – Research Areas", ByteDance AI Lab, (https://ailab.bytedance.com/research).

ByteDance (2021a): "Privacy Policy U.S. | TikTok", 2 June 2021 (https://www.tiktok.com/legal/privacy-policy-us?lang=en).

ByteDance (2021b): "Privacy Policy EEA/UK/CH | TikTok", 5 October 2021 (https://www.tiktok.com/legal/privacy-policy-eea?lang=en).

Citton, Yves (2014): *Pour une écologie de l'attention*, Paris: Seuil.

Cotter, Kelley (2019): "Playing the Visibility Game: How Digital Influencers and Algorithms Negotiate Influence on Instagram." In: *New Media & Society* 21 (4), pp. 895–913.

Cox, Geoff, Annet Dekker, Andrew Dewdney, Katrina Sluis (2021): "Affordances of the Networked Image." In: *The Nordic Journal of Aesthetics* 30 (61-62), pp. 40–45.

Crary, Jonathan (2013): *24/7: Late Capitalism and the Ends of Sleep*, London: Verso Books.

Cubitt, Sean (2017): "The Uncertainty of the Mass Image: Logistics and Behaviours." In: *Digital Creativity* 28 (4), pp. 265–78.

Cubitt, Sean (2021): "Mass Image, Anthropocene Image, Image Commons." In Tomás Dvořák and Jussi Parikka (eds.), *Photography Off the Scale*, Edinburgh: Edinburgh University Press, pp. 25–40.

Dean, Jodi (2010): "Affective Networks." In: *MediaTropes* 2 (2), pp. 19–44.

Dennis, James (2019): *Beyond Slacktivism*, Springer International Publishing.

Deren, Maya. (2000 [1963]): "Poetry and the Film: A Symposium with Maya Deren, Arthur Miller, Dylan Thomas, Parker Tyler. Chairman Willard Maas. Organized by Amos Vogel." In: P. Adams Sitney (ed.), *Film Culture Reader*, New York: Cooper Square Press, pp. 171–86.

DeVos, Alicia, Aditi Dhabalia, Hong Shen, Kenneth Holstein, and Motahhare Eslami (2022): "Toward User-Driven Algorithm Auditing: Investigating Users' Strategies for Uncovering Harmful Algorithmic Behavior." In: *CHI Conference on Human Factors in Computing Systems*, (https://doi.org/10.1145/3491102.3517441).

Dieter, Michael, and David Gauthier (2019): "On the Politics of Chrono-Design: Capture, Time and the Interface." In: *Theory, Culture & Society* 36 (2), pp. 61–87.

Druckrey, Timothy (1994): "From Dada to Digital: Montage in The Twentieth Century." In: *Aperture* Summer, pp. 4–7.

Dvořák, Tomás, and Jussi Parikka, eds. (2021): *Photography Off the Scale*, Edinburgh: Edinburgh University Press.

Dyer-Witheford, Nick, and Svitlana Matviyenko (2019): *Cyberwar and Revolution: Digital Subterfuge in Global Capitalism*, U of Minnesota Press.

Foucault, Michel (1990): "Qu'est-Ce Que La Critique?" In: *Bulletin de La Société Française de Philosophie* 84 (2), pp. 35–63.

Friedberg, Anne (2010): "The End of Cinema: Multimedia and Technological Change." In: Marc Furstenau (ed.), *The Film Theory Reader: Debates and Arguments*, Routledge, pp. 438–52.

Goriunova, Olga (2019): "The Digital Subject: People as Data as Persons." In: *Theory, Culture & Society* 36 (6), pp. 125–45.

Hind, Stephanie (2021): "Introducing Auto Captions | TikTok", April 6, 2021 (https://newsroom.tiktok.com/en-us/introducing-auto-captions).

Iqbal, Mansoor (2021): "TikTok Revenue and Usage Statistics (2021)", Business of Apps, April 8, 2021 (https://www.businessofapps.com/data/tik-tok-statistics/).

Karizat, Nadia, Dan Delmonaco, Motahhare Eslami, and Nazanin Andalibi (2021): "Algorithmic Folk Theories and Identity: How TikTok Users Co-Produce Knowledge of Identity and Engage in Algorithmic Resistance." In: *Proc. ACM Hum.-Comput. Interact.*, 305, 5 (CSCW2), pp. 1–44.

Kelty, Christopher (2005): "Geeks, Social Imaginaries, and Recursive Publics." In: *Cultural Anthropology: Journal of the Society for Cultural Anthropology* 20 (2), pp. 185–214.

Longfield, Anne (2020): "TikTok Data Claim UK", (https://tiktokdataclaim.uk/).

MacKenzie, Adrian, and Anna Munster (2019): "Platform Seeing: Image Ensembles and Their Invisualities.". In: *Theory, Culture & Society* 36 (5), pp. 3–22.

Maeder, Dominik, and Daniela Wentz (2014): "Digital Seriality as Structure and Process." In: *Eludamos. Journal for Computer Game Culture* 8 (1), pp. 129–49.

Manovich, Lev (2001): *The Language of New Media*, Cambridge, MA; London: MIT Press.

Parisi, Luciana (2017): "Reprogramming Decisionism." In: *E-Flux*, no. 85 (October) (https://www.e-flux.com/journal/85/155472/reprogramming-decisionism/).

Peterson-Salahuddin, Chelsea (2022): "'Pose': Examining Moments of 'Digital' Dark Sousveillance on TikTok." In: *New Media & Society*, April.

Rauchberg, Jessica Sage (2022): "#Shadowbanned: Queer, Trans, and Disabled Creator Responses to Algorithmic Oppression on TikTok." In: Paromita Pain (ed.), *LGBTQ Digital Cultures*, Routledge, pp.196-209.

Reuter, Markus, and Chris Köver (2019): "TikTok: Cheerfulness and Censorship", November 23, 2019 (https://netzpolitik.org/2019/cheerfulness-and-censorship/).

Reuter, Markus (2021): "Insider Reports on Censorship Techniques at ByteDance", February 20, 2021 (https://netzpolitik.org/2021/tiktok-insider-berichtet-ueber-zensurtechniken-bei-bytedance/).

Rouvroy, Antoinette (2012): "The End (s) of Critique: Data Behaviourism versus Due Process." In: Mireille Hildebrandt and Ekatarina De Vries (eds.), *Privacy, Due Process and the Computational Turn*, Routledge, pp. 157–82.

Rubinstein, Daniel, and Katrina Sluis (2008): "A Life More Photographic." In: *Photographies* 1 (1), pp. 9–28.

Savolainen, Laura (2022): "The Shadow Banning Controversy: Perceived Governance and Algorithmic Folklore." In: *Media Culture & Society*, March.

Sluis, Katrina (2020): "Beyond Representation? The Database-driven Image and the Non-Human Spectator." In: Stephen Bull (ed.), *A Companion to Photography*, Hoboken, NJ: Wiley, pp. 113–29.

Smith, Ben (2021): "How TikTok Reads Your Mind", *The New York Times*, December 6, 2021 (https://www.nytimes.com/2021/12/05/business/media/tiktok-algorithm.html).

Terranova, Tiziana (2004): *Network Culture: Politics for the Information Age*, London: Pluto Press.

TikTok (2020): "How TikTok Recommends Videos #ForYou." June 18, 2020 (https://newsroom.tiktok.com/en-us/how-tiktok-recommends-videos-for-you/).

Väliaho, Pasi (2014): *Biopolitical Screens: Image, Power, and the Neoliberal Brain*, Cambridge, MA; London: MIT Press.

Väliaho, Pasi (2018): "The Brain's Labour." In: Hunter Vaughan and Tom Conley (eds.), *The Anthem Handbook of Screen Theory*, London: Anthem Press, pp. 13-31.

Verhoeff, Nanna, and Heidi Rae Cooley (2014): "The Navigational Gesture: Traces and Tracings at the Mobile Touchscreen Interface." In: *NECSUS. European Journal of Media Studies* 3 (1), pp. 111–28.

White, Michele (2006): *The Body and the Screen: Theories of Internet Spectatorship*, MIT Press.

WSJ Staff (2021): "Inside TikTok's Algorithm: A WSJ Video Investigation", *Wall Street Journal*, July 21, 2021 (https://www.wsj.com/articles/tiktok-algorithm-video-investigation-11626877477).

Datafication
and Operative Images

Seeing Like a Border
Biometrics and the Operational Image

Mark Andrejevic, Volcic Zala

Abstract

This article considers the role played by automated vision in transforming bodies into "operational images" that enable the expansion of borders into enclosures – and the multiplication of these enclosures. In this respect, we seek to expand on Chris Rumford's (2011) invitation to consider what it might mean to "see like a border" (67). We argue that the iconic character of the image – as representation – is collapsed into its operational character by the automated sensing system, and then go on to consider the traces of the visual that remain in the context of such 'images'. We then consider the modality of governance that operates in the register of the operational image – one in which physical space becomes deformable at the granular, individual level, along the lines envisioned by Deleuze in his discussion of societies of control (Deleuze 2017). The resulting form of governance might be described, drawing on the work of Michel Foucault, as the deployment of a granular form of biopower – one that requires the milieu, or environment, to become deformable and customisable. This, of course, is the mode of power and control anticipated by those who seek to develop and capture the terrains of augmented and virtual reality – or, in more recent terminology, the realm of the "metaverse".

Keywords

Biometrics, Surveillance, Borders, Operational Image, Biopower, Automation

Introduction

In the wake of the COVID-19 pandemic, the International Air Transport Association (IATA) announced its development of a travel pass that would enable international verification of air passengers' vaccination status. The association's so-called 'One ID' would link to pertinent information about travellers, including, where relevant, COVID-19 test results and recovery status (Baratti 2021). It would also link to travel credentials, including passengers' passports and electronic tickets, creating what the Association described as a "one-stop shop to securely and conveniently let you verify that you meet COVID-19 health requirements for your journey" (Baratti 2021). In order to facilitate the transmission of the growing number of credentials needed to travel in the pandemic era, IATA proposes to link all relevant information stored by the 'One ID' system to a biometric token – the most 'seamless' one being facial recognition, because it can operate at a distance. As its promotional material suggests, once established, the 'One ID' system would be developed to be 'interoperable' with international commercial and public infrastructures: "In order to make this vision a reality we need to agree on global standards for a digital identity that can be trusted and recognized by the industry and governments" (IATA 2021).

The promise of interoperability envisions what amounts to a globally legible unique ID that could operate across the multiplying borders, boundaries and checkpoints associated with attempts to manage circulation during (and perhaps beyond) the pandemic. The experience of many countries during the pandemic has been a dramatic increase in technologies of control and the resulting 'friction' associated with requirements to quarantine or self-quarantine, to check-in to any location visited outside the home, and to provide proof of vaccine status and test results. Crossing borders and boundaries became less of an exceptional process and more of an ongoing one. A simple shopping trip might mean checking into half a dozen different locations, and repeatedly displaying one's vaccine status via a digital or hard copy passport. Varying levels of enforcement created a potentially porous system, in many cases dependent on human labour power to verify that check-in restrictions were being followed and to verify the eligibility of individuals to enter particular spaces.

The biometric solution proposed by the IATA presents itself as a generalisable one because the check-in process is, fundamentally, a process of em-bordering: of constructing and navigating a proliferating set of borders. Checking in to a café or a movie theatre might seem, at least according to governmental logics, a lower stakes security issue than crossing an international border. But the threat of the pandemic ups the stakes for a growing range of boundary controls. Potentially, the virus is a matter of life and death – and simultaneously a security risk (because of the potential of further contagion and the resulting need for added restrictions with their consequent economic and societal consequences). Thus, it is perhaps not surprising that the initiative for boundary management might build on tools for border control – not least because of the relative success of biometric technology at many international borders in verifying traveller identity. The deployment of this technology has passed largely without pushback, in part because of the realised promise to reduce lengthy waiting times and to make the border control process seemingly less onerous.

The success of facial recognition technology at the border builds on the role played by the photographic image in the history of identification papers more generally (e.g., Browne 2015; Robertson 2010). The image provides a link between possession and identity – it offers assurance that the holder of a credential is in legitimate possession of that credential. The result is what might be described as an ongoing attempt to ground identity in bodily features and traces, from physical descriptions to DNA scans. However, the ability to engage in efficient, real time verification of credentials envisioned by the IATA – and thus, indirectly, the management of the proliferating borders and boundaries associated with pandemic management – relies on automated forms of identification that can take place at a distance. In this respect, the affordance of the image – as information that can be detected and processed 'touchlessly' – is embraced by schemes like the 'One ID' program. As borders and checkpoints multiply, the displacement of human vision by machine vision takes place in the name of speed, efficiency, and accuracy. The IATA claims in its promotional literature, for example, that "the future of aviation is biometric" (IATA 2021).

If this is indeed the case, the same might be said of the future of boundary management more generally. The result of collapsing credentials into bodies so they can be read passively, at a distance, is effectively to envision a world in which we carry the boundary with us wherever we go, so that it can be asserted at will by those with access to the sensors and the database. In this respect the boundary becomes something more like an en-framing enclosure – not a two-dimensional line to cross, but a space within which, at any point, a checkpoint can be inserted and enforced. Taken to the limit, the border might never be fully "crossed" as a punctual event, but experienced more as an ongoing process of bordering. This is the fantasy, for example, of the US alt-right activist Charles Johnson, who reportedly wanted to use Clearview AI's facial recognition app, "to identify every illegal alien in the country" (in O'Brien 2020). In the world envisioned by Johnson, authorities – and perhaps anyone with access to a smart phone – could constantly monitor the faces around them to determine who might match a database of people known to have illegally crossed the border. The border would then coincide with the threshold of automated visibility. It would be imposed by those with access to the monitoring technology, and experienced by those who carry the border on the surface of their bodies. Louise Amoore (2006) anticipates this outcome in her work on border technology in the wake of post-9/11 surveillance strategies: "the biometric border signals ... a significant turn to scientific and managerial techniques in governing the mobility of bodies; and an extension of biopower such that the body, in effect, becomes the carrier of the border as it is inscribed with multiple encoded boundaries of access" (2006, 347-8). During the pandemic, these boundaries continued to multiply, accelerating the push toward the use of automated technology to verify credentials and secure circulation.

This article considers the role played by automated vision in transforming bodies into "operational images" that enable the expansion of borders into enclosures – and the simultaneous multiplication of these enclosures. In this respect, we seek to expand on Chris Rumford's invitation (in Johnson et al. 2011) to consider what it might mean to "see like a border" (67). We argue that the iconic character of the image is collapsed into its operational character by automated sensing systems, and then consider what traces of the visual remain in the context of such 'images'. We analyse the modality of governance that operates in the register of the operational image – one in which physical space becomes modulate-able at the granular, individual level, along the lines envisioned by Deleuze in his discussion of societies of control (Deleuze 2017). The resulting form of governance might be described, drawing on the work of Michel Foucault, as the exercise of a granular form of biopower – one that requires the milieu, or environment, to become malleable and customisable. This, of course, is the mode of power and control anticipated by those who seek to develop and capture the terrains of augmented and virtual reality – the goal of the so-called "metaverse". For Mark Zuckerberg, the "metaverse" refers to a world in which enhanced graphics and sensors make it possible to create virtual spaces for interaction and communication that provide an engaging sense of co-presence at a distance (Zuckerman, 2021).

Embodying the Border

It was only in the late 19th century that nation states gained control over the "legitimate means of movement" (Torpey 2018, 4). The timing was in part the result of the need to create the "elaborate bureaucracies and technologies that only gradually came into existence" (8) – a process accelerated by the development of photography as a means of linking a document to the physical person. However, as Simone Browne's (2015) history of racialised surveillance in the US notes, prior to the state monopoly on the regulation of circulation, private entities and individuals developed early versions of passports to police the movement of slaves. The passes carried by slaves who had been given permission to leave the plantation often carried identifying descriptions to ensure that the bearer was not a runaway. As Browne puts it, "The slave pass system relied on the notion that the slave could be known through a written identification document" (2015, 52).

This use of physical description characterised early passports – again as an attempt to link the document to its bearer. Craig Robertson notes in his history of the US passport that by the late 18th century, "The introduction of physical descriptors on passports transformed the passport into a document that sought to establish the 'unambiguous identity' of the bearer; that is, it pushed the passport in the direction of a modern identification document" (2010, 65). The use of such descriptors became necessary for travel beyond the reach of communities in which individuals were known and recognised – not just for traveling to another country. In some parts of Europe in the early 19th century, an early version of a passport could be required for journeys as short as eight miles from home (Robertson, 2010).

There were obvious challenges with the attempt to arrive at a physical description that would uniquely identify the bearer. Despite bureaucratic attempts to standardise written portrayals, "the description could not be guaranteed to abstract an individual's physical appearance into a document so it could always be seen as an accurate resemblance by all those who looked at the document and the bearer" (Robertson, 2010: 72). By the early 20th century, in response to tighter regulations on travel during World War I, a photograph became a required identificatory element in passports, as it "was considered to produce a 'truthful' image that could be used to reliably link a person to a passport and thus accurately establish an individual's identity" (81). The shift to mechanical reproduction evinced a faith in the objectivity of the camera – as well as the level of detail it provided – over the subjectivity and selectivity of written descriptions (Roberston, 2010). However, verification of legitimate possession still relied upon the perceptions of a third party – the official charged with assessing whether the image matched the person.

When the visual image fails, the result can be a further turn to the body, as Browne (2012) demonstrates in her discussion of the case of Suaad Hagi Mohamud. Mohamud, A Somali-born Canadian, found herself stranded in Kenya after a trip from her home in Toronto when officials questioned her identity and refused to let her board a flight home because, "her lips looked different than those in her four-year-old passport photo" (2012, 78). The Canadian government confiscated her passport, giving Mohamud two weeks to find a way to prove her identity. The eventual outcome hinged on a DNA test that proved her genetic link her to her Canadian-born son. When the visual image proved indeterminate from the perspective of the authorities, her only recourse was a further appeal to bodily identification.

One result, perhaps unsurprisingly, was the use of Mohamud's case to argue for DNA-encoded passports (Browne, 2012). The challenge, of course, is that until a system for instant, remote DNA testing is developed, relying on DNA verification is likely to obstruct circulation rather than to facilitate it. Attempts to increase the efficacy of border identification at a moment when borders continue to expand and multiply thus tend, increasingly, toward reliance upon automated vision – with the qualification that the character of the image itself changes to become readable by machines rather than humans. In the sense invoked by Harun Farocki, the image becomes not the symbolic representation of an object for another human being (such as the border control officer tasked with comparing Suaad Mohamud's photo to her face), but "part of an operation" (2004, 17). Machine readability is not necessarily confined to the human visual register: the data image not only reduces facial features to digital templates, it can also combine these templates with images captured by infrared systems (body temperature, for example) and laser (cardiac signature). If there is always a gap between sign and referent, image and body, the promise of automated biometrics is to eliminate it as far as possible by dispensing with the representational function of the image.

The Migration of the Border

The response to the COVID-19 global pandemic reinforced a tendency identified by recent border studies toward the expansion and proliferation of borders: "Borders are not only provisional, but also rather proliferating precisely through their contingent nature and the shift in resources and enforcement practices to offshore and interior locales" (Mountz in Johnson et al. 2011, 65). Using this formulation, Mountz is responding to US laws that allow for citizenship checks at any location within 100 miles of the border – dramatically expanding the space within which border control can take place. Amoore describes a similar transformation with respect to the use of RFID-equipped smart cards that enable the tracking of non-citizens' "whereabouts within the US" (Amoore 2006, 343). These technologies anticipate the proliferation of checkpoints, borders, and boundaries resulting from pandemic restrictions.

In Australia, for example, state borders took on renewed relevance during the pandemic, when state governments blocked interstate travel and started to militarise border crossings. Undocumented entrants to Queensland from New South Wales, for example, could be fined and 'deported' back to their state of origin. Border passes were issued to essential workers who needed to cross state lines, and checkpoints established at highway border crossings. These were not limited to state lines but were also established at the perimeter of cities like Melbourne, whose residents were restricted from traveling to regional Victoria. Within the city, residents were confined to a 5km radius, which could be enforced at any time by police checking IDs or pulling over cars whose registration plates linked to addresses from another part of town. Such developments recapitulate Mountz' description of the effects of the migration of the border, which, "increasingly crops up in unlikely places – the laundromat, the grocery store, the bus station" (in Johnson et al. 2011, 65). They also recall the European travel passes of the 19th century required for travel beyond one's local community. The "border" in question was a malleable one that could be reconfigured and imposed as needed.

In the wake of the pandemic, checkpoints requiring credentials multiplied across the spectrum of available spaces, from the local swimming pool to the workplace to the art museum. In this respect, as Chris Rumford puts it, "Borders are no longer seen only as lines on a map but as spaces in their own right (as in the idea of 'borderlands') and as processes; in short, there has been a shift from borders to bordering (or rebordering, on some accounts)" ((in Johnson et al. 2011, 67). Amoore, Marmura, and Salter (2008) make a similar point in their discussion of biometric borders: "The smart border is a diffuse one physically extending both beyond and inside its geopolitical location and involving a multiplicity of sites for the surveillance of movement" (2008, 99).

The purpose of such borders is not so much to limit circulation but to secure it. The pandemic highlighted the point made by Salter in his work on immigration and visa control that, from the perspective of state authority, mobility represents, "the constant condition of threat" (2006). When the movement of people through space poses a risk, the response is to saturate space with technologies of control. Amoore argues that mobility becomes the function of borders: "No longer strictly a matter of disciplinary practices that stop, prohibit, enclose, delimit or proscribe, the work of the contemporary border is conducted in and through movement itself" (in Johnson et al. 2011, 64). Our analysis links this observation to Rumford's description of all that lies within the border as a borderland – a territory subject to ongoing forms of control anywhere within its confines and not simply at the edges. In practice, the result is the multiplication of the very boundaries that technologies for "seamless" transit seek to streamline.

A regime of credentials for local travel may have been manageable at the human level in the 18th century, when an eight-mile trip was a significant journey, but under contemporary conditions, it would be unenforceable without automated tracking and enforcement. By the same token, check-in stations at every shop, venue, restaurant, café, and office building impose new forms of 'friction' on public circulation. Without a ready means of responding efficiently to the escalating need to verify status and credentials, circulation is impeded. The increasingly granular control of people's movements associated with the pandemic response – but also with emerging strategies for customising and stratifying shared space (through the creation of 'VIP' experiences in sports venues and casinos, for example) set the stage for an automated, biometric solution. If sensors can link captured data to individual bodies with a high degree of reliability, both control and circulation can be enhanced simultaneously – or at least that is the marketing strategy deployed by the industry (e.g., Hutchins & Andrejevic 2021). The result is a self-stimulating cycle of data collection and control. More checkpoints mean more data about individual patterns of movement and behaviour, which, in turn, feed into strategies for managing circulation more effectively. The data can be used to identify risks (such as threatening behavioural patterns) and leverage opportunity (for targeted marketing). The result, as Amoore suggests, is that, "emergent forms of bordering seek to reconcile security with mobility and sovereignty with economy" (in Johnson et al. 2011, 64).

One familiar analogy for the proliferation of borders, boundaries, and checkpoints is, unsurprisingly, the ongoing enclosure of online space. With the platformisation and appification of the online world – as well as corporate control over proprietary software – various virtual checkpoints have multiplied to the point that the average user with online access has somewhere around 100 passwords (Rowe, 2021). The surveillance-based economic model of the online economy relies on detailed monitoring and tracking of online activity, and thus on techniques for unique identification and verification. Thus, a world in which we have to check in to all the physical spaces we visit is already anticipated by the forms of gatekeeping and access control that take place online. Using our phone to check in to the supermarket or a movie theatre amounts to a physical-world echo of having to login to Amazon.com or Netflix. In the world envisioned by the "One

ID" system – and other systems of biometric identification – checkpoints in the physical world could perform some of the same functions as online ones: allowing us to pay, for example, based on our verified identity (without having to produce cash or swipe a card).

This connection to the online surveillance economy is perhaps telling, insofar as the migration, multiplication, and expansion of borders relies in no small part on offloading bordering practices onto the private sector (Amoore 2006). In this respect, the invocation of the pre-history of passports is apt: the government may have instituted a monopoly on the legitimate control of mobility (Salter, 2006), but it is coming to enlist a growing range of private technologies for monitoring and tracking circulation, originally developed for commercial use. In the pandemic context, for example, private vendors manage QR-code check-in systems in some locales, and large tech companies assist governments in developing and managing contact tracing systems. Pandemic restrictions also resulted in offloading the responsibility of monitoring customer check-in and vaccine status to private establishments. By the same token, IATA's 'One ID' may have been developed to enforce nation-state border controls, but it is designed to be inter-operable with the proprietary systems that retail outlets and other businesses use to verify vaccine status – and, presumably, other personal details. If such a system does indeed successfully flow out from the international border system to increasingly local checkpoints in shopping malls and workplaces, the next logical step would be for commercial outlets to link it to bank accounts and credit cards to facilitate "seamless commerce". The development of such systems will need to be closely monitored to ensure they protect what remains of people's control over their personal information.

"Seeing Like A Border"

If bordering processes are coming to permeate spaces rather than simply surround or enclose them, then they become, "key to understanding networked connectivity" (Rumford, in Johnson et al. 2011, 68). Rather than treating the life of the nation or society as what takes place "within its borders", the bordering process needs to be approached as "constitutive" of social and political life (ibid.). The verification process, then, is not limited to the issues of defining citizenship or national belonging but has to do with the ways in which the ongoing processes of border control come to permeate social, economic, and political interactions. Such an approach requires a much more comprehensive intervention than is envisioned in this article, but it provides a background for considering the deployment of automated images in managing the ongoing circulation of flows within border-permeated space.

This section takes the question posed by Rumford literally: how do borders *see* under the conditions of their electromagnetic proliferation? Perhaps the defining feature of this type of border vision is automation. As in the case of the online world, proliferating boundaries, selective access, and the channelling of circulation threatens to outstrip unaided human capabilities. As in other spheres of production and circulation, the promise of automated information processing is to enable more efficient use of existing resources and infrastructures. Thus, IATA promotes the prospect of automated biometric response as a means of managing growth and the increased amount of information that needs to be collected about passengers: "In order for future generations to fly sustainably, we need to rethink broad sections of the industry itself, developing infrastructure and new processes that can cope with future demand without relying on ever bigger airports... IATA's 'One Id' allows for a paperless airport experience using a single secure biometric travel token such as face, fingerprint, or iris scan for all travel processes" (2021). Building on systems that are currently familiar to many travellers, the Association's promotional video portrays a system that uses facial recognition technology as a means of facilitating seamless verification – no need for physical contact or overly involved data capture processes: passengers simply walk by a camera that manages an automated gate.

The biometric approach relies on the capture of an image – although one that is automatically converted into digital, machine readable code that can be compared with a stored template. The array of points used to create a face print does not necessarily rely on conventional camera technology – it can also be produced using infrared and laser technology. In other words, the human-readable image disappears into the automated system – and the comparison that takes place is distinct from human forms of recognition. As Rebecca Uliasz (2020) puts it, "as images of faces are amassed in digital form, the face recedes from our sight" (2020, 3). There is no question of matching an image to a referent, but rather of generating a probability based on the fit between two digital templates. Hoelzl and Marie (2021) describe this shift as the replacement of the paradigm of the image by the "dynamic relation between data and data that is the foundation of the algorithmic paradigm of the image" (233). This relation is a mutable, probabilistic one that is "subject to database updates, connection speed, screen resolution and navigational options provided by the software" (234). The output of such systems has little to do with what we call recognition (despite the terminology) – it simply couples digital data with an automated, probabilistic response: access is permitted or denied, risk is assessed and reported, an outcome of some sort results.

The artist Trevor Paglen, who has done extensive work on machine vision and automated image classification, has described the disappearance of the image in terms of its operationalisation. In doing so, he builds on Farocki's (2004) description of "operative images", arguing that automated systems have reached the point of being able to dispense with human readable representations: "There's really no point. Meat-eyes are far too inefficient to see what's going on anyway. Nowadays operational images are overwhelmingly invisible, even as they're ubiquitous and sculpting physical reality in ever more dramatic ways" (Paglen 2014). Such systems no longer need to rely on apparatuses that reproduce the optical logic of human vision. Nor are they limited to input in the visual register or spectrum. A composite digital biometric image could, for example, combine a faceprint with a voice print, a gait print, and/or a cardiac signature – all of which can be collected remotely and passively.

Multi-modal biometrics are designed to increase accuracy – an ongoing concern, given the potentially high stakes of biometric identification as a border technology and reports of issues with bias, accuracy and the potential for fraud. From the perspective of the border's gaze, there is no need for the image to be uniquely visual. Pantenburg (2016) argues, for example, that "the operational image is a key player in today's replacement of the eye" (55). For him, "On this level, it would no longer be justified to speak of images, since the visual presentation of the data [to the extent that it even exists] is a mere epiphenomenon of processes of calculation" (57). Nevertheless, the process of seeing "like a border" retains attributes of visuality insofar as it relies on remote, high-speed, directed sensing. Touchlessness has become a priority in the pandemic era, but even prior to concerns of contagion, it was framed as a means of reducing "friction" while also enabling passive and covert forms of data collection.

Automated biometric classification based on operational images facilitates the border's function as a spatial sorting mechanism, and it does so under conditions of multiple, overlapping boundaries with proliferating sorting criteria. To operate effectively, such systems must be able to scan crowds and identify their component individuals in real time. The biometric "token" becomes a form of metadata that collapses a body into an identity and thus into the range of available stored information about that identity ("is there a vaccine record, a test record, indication of diagnosis and recovery, a visa, a verified citizenship document, etc."). This data, in turn, enters into a series of responses, including the reconfiguration of physical space: authorities may be notified (if, for example, quarantine borders have been transgressed), gates may close or open, turnstiles may direct passengers to different queues, elevators may stop at particular floors. Machinic forms of identification feed into the automated production and reconfiguration of physical space.

This is the model of control anticipated by Gilles Deleuze – with reference to Felix Guattari – in his short description of "societies of control": "Felix Guattari has imagined a city where one would be able to leave one's apartment, one's street, one's neighborhood, thanks to one's (dividual) electronic card that raises a given barrier; but the card could just as easily be rejected on a given day or between certain hours; what counts is not the barrier but the computer that tracks each person's position-licit or illicit -and effects a universal modulation" (1992, p. 7). The difference, of course, is that the card is replaced by one's body, distilled into a machine-readable biometric template. This shift directly inscribes credentials onto bodies and the credentials consequently shift from representing what one possesses (ticket, ID card, etc.) to what one *is* – as captured and defined by the biometric sensor.

Granular Governance: The Deployment of Biometric Biopower

Automated biometric images, then, enable new ways of sorting, regulating, and governing individuals as they move through spaces imbued with capabilities of identification, verification, and inference. The latter category derives from the para-identificatory information that can be read off the body: surface body temperature, facial expression, pulse rate, and pattern of movement, for example. Biometrics can directly capture information about body function and activity – beyond the print or template used for unique identification. In other words, the mutable character of the sensor-generated data image enables it to participate in a proliferating array of operations. Inferences can be made about medical conditions, stress level, emotions and even intent. Biometric identifiers can be used to uniquely identify the movements of individuals throughout the course of the day, enabling inferences based on patterns of activity (do these deviate from the usual activity of a particular individual? do they reproduce patterns of activity that, in the past, have been correlated with risk, threat, or opportunity?). Biometrics makes the relationship between identity and space legible in ways that recall the tracking capability of online spaces. With this connection in mind, the remainder of this section considers how the operational link between the individual and the corresponding surrounding space lends itself to an enhanced form of biopower that operates simultaneously at the level of the individual and the population. Drawing on Foucault's references to "environmental" forms of governance, we argue that the operationalisation of identification and verification reduces the role of subjectification in governance and control. The result is an emphasis on pre-emption rather than deterrence and on comprehensive rather than symbolic monitoring and surveillance.

Automated governance of the movement and circulation of individuals relies on the proliferation of spaces that are both monitored and, to some degree, malleable. Characteristic of remote, automated recognition and monitoring is the introduction of digitally facilitated individuation into strategies for biopolitical control. In the pandemic context, for example, the goal is to couple techniques for managing risk at the population level – including, for example, routine disinfection, social distancing, and mask wearing – with increasingly individuated forms of identification, monitoring, and tracking. This means developing sensors to determine whether, for example, individuals are wearing masks – and automated checkpoints to prevent entry if they are not. More generally, biometric inference could be used to create and track proliferating categories of risk and opportunity: particular patterns of movement or elevated stress levels (measured, for example, by the remote tracking of cardiac activity or changes in surface body temperature) might be correlated with malicious intent. Other patterns might be of use to advertisers, public health authorities, and so on. The enclosures that facilitate information collection and dynamic sorting can exist in overlapping relations with one another or can be embedded within each other. Their proliferation enables higher resolution forms of sorting and control – enacting a dynamic version of what Michel Foucault describes as governance via the environment or the *milieu*.

In his work on biopower, Foucault (2003, 2007, 2008) distinguishes between disciplinary and populational regimes of governance. The former, exercised upon the individual, he describes as an "anatomo-politics" (2003: 43) concerned with the individual-as-body – a discrete, bounded unit. It manifests in the regulation of bodily movements and dispositions: regimens of drilling, exercising, and training. At the populational level, by contrast, the focus is on overall statistical regularities. Intervention in the biopolitical register takes place at the environmental and regulatory level: draining swamps, imposing hygiene guidelines, instituting health insurance systems, developing and maintaining sewage and ventilation infrastructures, and so on. The target is overall populational characteristics, rather than particular individuals: birth rates, morbidity and mortality, and so on. These two forms of governance are distinguished by the ways in which they configure their objects: "Both technologies are obviously technologies of the body, but one is a technology in which the body is individualized as an organism endowed with capacities, while the other is a technology in which bodies are replaced by general biological processes" (2003: 249). Foucault notes that the two levels complement one another (2003): "the two sets of mechanisms – one disciplinary and the other regulatory – do not exist at the same level. Which means of course that they are not mutually exclusive and can be articulated with each other" (2003, 250).

The development of automated sorting infrastructures that rely on passive sensor systems results in a reconfiguration of the relationship between discipline and biopower. If discipline relies on the internalisation of norms in order to regulate individual bodies, automated forms of control do not. Individual bodies can be regulated externally through customised intervention by the environment. Spaces can be reconfigured in real time to sort individuals based on detailed biometric information by reading the surface of their bodies at a distance.

Such systems address what might be described as the threat of symbolic inefficiency in the disciplinary register. As Foucault's (2012) work on disciplinary power makes clear, discipline relies on the symbolic power of the monitoring apparatus – rather than on its comprehensiveness or accuracy. The central tower in the panopticon prison – or, in contemporary terms, the surveillance camera in the shopping mall – gain their efficacy through their public display (as in the case of the familiar sign reminding customers to "smile – you're on camera"). The smooth functioning of disciplinary power thus draws on processes whereby the symbolic injunction is internalised: "I see that I'm being watched so I better behave according to the rules". If, as Gordon (2002) notes in her work on the role of visibility in Foucault, power can be exercised subjectlessly (that is, it does not need to manifest itself in the form of a 'bearer' of power), it nonetheless requires a subject to act upon – since it takes hold precisely through processes of subjectification.

In his original formulation of the Panopticon, Jeremy Bentham (2011) described the symbolic power of the spectacle of surveillance as a marvel of efficiency. An entire prison might be controlled by the mere spectacle of a watchtower once the inmates are properly conditioned – that is, once they become disciplined subjects. By contrast, automated, environmental governance addresses the prospect of the failure of the internalisation of disciplinary imperatives – that is, the failure of subjectification. It responds to the prospect that the spectacle of surveillance may not result in the adoption of "correct" behavior. For example, rather than relying on a well-disciplined population to follow prescribed hygiene regimens, automated checkpoints simply block access to people who are not wearing masks, or who are wearing them incorrectly.

Thus, automated intervention offers to make up for the potential or anticipated failure of disciplinary subjectification. In so doing, however, it marks a shift in the politics of control away from causal logics of prevention and toward active forms of detection, intervention, and pre-emption. If disciplinary control relies on the efficiency of subjectification to achieve its ends through the conscious modification of behaviour, environmentality operates according to a logic of externality. It seeks to channel behaviour in ways that lie beyond conscious control and to intervene in real time when such attempts fail. This type of control is much weightier, in terms of infrastructure and resources, than panopticism, whose goal was to render actual surveillance superfluous.

By contrast, the version of automated control that takes the form of environmental modulation and response relies on the widespread deployment of automated sensing and surveillance infrastructures in conjunction with customisable physical and virtual spaces. This model is a familiar one in the tech sector, which is increasingly preoccupied with "smartening" space in both its virtual and physical forms. Emerging models of augmented and virtual reality envision precisely the combination of surveillance and automated response that characterise what we have been describing as environmental forms of governance. The goal is to capture as comprehensive a data image as possible – ideally one that would allow the redoubling of both individuals (as avatars) and environments (as virtual, smart, or augmented spaces). Writing about the future of augmented reality, Kevin Kelly, the founding editor of *Wired* magazine, anticipates the future importance of the totalised image: the construction of reality's "digital twin": "To recreate a map that is as big as the globe – in 3D, no less – you need to photograph all places and things from every possible angle, all the time, which means you need to have a planet full of cameras that are always on" (2019).

The digital ingestion of the physical world, in its entirety, renders it operational: the world itself becomes caught up in a sequence of automated actions. Taken to this extreme, of course, such a vision is incoherent and logically impossible (every camera would need another camera to watch it). However, as the ongoing development of virtual reality and augmented reality tools suggest, this process of comprehensive data capture remains the ideal-typical form of the ultimate platform to which digital control aspires.

The politics of control at work in such fantasies dispenses entirely with the familiar components of Enlightenment-style democracy, including that of the informed, reflexive subject (increasingly the target of theoretical critiques, perhaps uncoincidentally). Operational governance relies upon strategies for channeling behaviour and response in real time, and is thus aligned with recently fashionable theories of "nudge" and "mechanism design" in economic theory (see, for example, Thaler & Sunstein, 2009 and Viljoen et al., 2021). These approaches rely on the imposition of structured conditions for directing individuals according to priorities that are non-transparent to them. In many cases, such forms of governance depend on the real-time adjustment of individual choice conditions – a process facilitated by automated forms of environmentality. Such examples are becoming increasingly routine: refrigerator cooler displays in shops that adjust what customers see in response to their inferred age, gender, and other characteristics captured by smart cameras; custom messages superimposed upon augmented reality displays, and so on. The form of governance envisioned by customisable environments is neither control through coercion nor the internalisation of disciplinary imperatives and priorities. Rather, it is a form of automated behaviourism.

In this regard, the promise of the biometric, operational image is to construct a granular process of social sorting. In the biopolitical schema, environmental governance takes place at the level of the population. In his lectures on biopolitics, Foucault suggests that governance at the environmental level can take place without the standardisation and homogeneity of disciplinary control. When introducing the concept of environmentality, he discerns, "a massive withdrawal with regard to the normative-disciplinary system" in which "discipline-normalisation" is displaced by interventions that modify, "the terms of the game, not the players' mentality" (2008, 261-262). We might put it this way: environmental level governance does not require the standardisation or routinisation of behaviour – or even thought – as long as changes in the "rules of the game" result in an overall population-level effect.

When viewed in the context of environmental governance, the alleged capabilities of automated recognition bypass what Salter (2006) describes as the agentic moment in the subject's capitulation to power – the need to provide an account of oneself, or even to state one's name in response to the border patrol officer, who, once equipped with an automated recognition system, no longer needs to ask. This is an important short-circuit because, in Salter's term, it forecloses the space of resistance on the part of subjects who are deprived of the choice to provide an account of themselves. This account is, rather, generated automatically, in the form of the operational image. The subjective process of internalisation is displaced by the promise of pure externalisation – of turning the individual inside-out by reading all that needs to be known off the surface. If, in Salter's (2006) account, "at the border the document is compared to the body which is compared to the story" [of the traveler]" (181), all three are collapsed into the biometric profile by the operational image. The goal is to eliminate the need to rely on the subject's potentially deceptive account along with any possible slippage between document and carrier.

Relatedly, in the context of automated biometrics, the distinction between individual monitoring – associated with the labour-intensive process of discipline – and environmental modification breaks down with the advent of mass identification and targeted response. Consider the distinction between smart and "dumb" cameras. When every street corner is equipped with a CCTV camera, disciplinary logics still prevail. Because there is no way for everyone to be watched all the time, uncertainty is mobilised as a force maximiser whereby the camera functions as a reminder to behave. By contrast, when cameras are endowed with the ability to recognise, record, and process everyone and everything in their field of vision, there is no longer any need to rely on the symbolic efficacy of surveillance, since actual intervention can take place automatically. The goal is no longer to have to rely on the subject's compliance. Biometric enclosures thus enable what might be described as a continuous process of "embordering" – at any given moment within their monitored embrace, a change in individual status can be detected and acted upon. Perhaps someone did not comply with self-isolation requirements and is circulating in public while symptomatic. In a space equipped with biometric sensors, a rise in surface body temperature could trigger a response – whether in the form of an automated notification, a blocked entrance, or a notification to authorities.

Consider the example of a convenience store in Tacoma, Washington, which received international media attention for pilot-testing a facial recognition system designed to automatically lock its doors to prospective customers whose faces appear in a database of "known robbers and shoplifters" (Hellmann 2019). A system like this in a foyer could detect an individual with recorded symptoms, or someone whose pattern of movement or behaviour correlated with threat indicators. The obverse of risk is opportunity: similar systems could detect someone motivated to make a purchase, place a bet, or require a service.

A World Wide Web of Borders

Automated biometric monitoring envisions the multiplication of borders on a scale that starts to approach that of the digital enclosures of the online world. In the physical world commercial spaces, for example, cannot exert the same kind of control they do online. We can, for the moment, enter shops, theatres or concert venues without being uniquely identified. Online, we are recognised automatically when we log into our shopping, viewing, or listening accounts. Even before we log in, we can be uniquely identified by our browsing activity and other tracking systems (even the idiosyncrasies of our keyboard and mouse use can serve as a unique biometric identifier). The deployment of biometric sensors offers to render identities and movements in physical space legible in an analogous fashion. We carry our metadata with us in the form of our faces, our gaits, our fingerprints and cardiac signatures. These, along with the pattern of our movements and behaviour, constitute the images generated for biometric sensors that link our identity to the customisation of physical space. These are not images for public display but are data portraits that enter into chains of operations reconfiguring the space through which we move. The passport photo may itself become obsolete once the machine becomes responsible for confirming one's identity. The disappearance of the representational image coincides with the ubiquity of its operational, biometric counterpart. The COVID-19 pandemic contributed to the proliferation of checkpoints and the data that can be collected at them. However, in so doing, it did not mark an exception to contemporary monitoring practices so much as the intensification of their ongoing development. We can anticipate that some of these checkpoints will eventually fall by the wayside, but the logics they represent are likely to endure, and the pressure to succumb to the biometric solution will only increase.

References

Amoore, L. (2006): Biometric borders: Governing mobilities in the war on terror. In: *Political geography*, 25/3, pp. 336-351. https://doi.org/10.1016/j.polgeo.2006.02.001.

Amoore, L./Marmura, S./Salter, M. B. (2008): Smart borders and mobilities: Spaces, zones, enclosures. In: *Surveillance & Society*, 5/2. https://doi.org/10.24908/ss.v5i2.3429.

Baratti, L. (2021): What Role Will Facial Recognition Tech Play in Post-Pandemic Travel? In: *Travel Pulse*. Retrieved from https://www.travelpulse.com/news/travel-technology/what-role-will-facial-recognition-tech-play-in-post-pandemic-travel.html).

Bentham, J. (2011). *The Panopticon Writings*, edited by M. Bozovic. London, UK: Verso.

Browne, S. (2012): Race and surveillance. *Routledge handbook of surveillance studies*, 72-79.

Browne, S. (2015): *Dark Matters: On the Surveillance of Blackness*. Durham: Duke University Press.

Deleuze, G. (2017): *Postscript on the Societies of Control*, pp. 35-39. Routledge.

Farocki, H. (2004): Phantom Images. 29. *Public: New Localities*, pp. 12-22.

Foucault, Michel. (2003): *"Society Must Be Defended"*. In: Lectures at the Collège de France, 1975-1976, translated by David Macey. New York: Picador.

Foucault, Michel. (2007): *Security, Territory, Population*. In: Lectures at the Collège de France, 1977-78, translated by Graham Burchell. New York: Palgrave Macmillan.

Foucault, Michel. (2008): *The Birth of Biopolitics*. In: Lectures at the Collège de France, 1978-1979, translated by Graham Burchell. New York: Palgrave Macmillan.

Foucault, M. (2012). *Discipline and Punish: The Birth of the Prison*. London, UK: Vintage.

French, M./Eric. M. (2013): Public Health Intelligence and the Detection of Potential Pandemics. In: *Sociology of Health & Illness* 35/2, pp. 174-187. https://doi.org/10.1111/j.1467-9566.2012.01536.x.

Hutchins, B., & Andrejevic, M. (2021): Olympian surveillance: Sports stadiums and the normalisation of biometric monitoring. *International Journal of Communication*, 15, pp. 2-20.

Hellmann, M. (2019): "When Convenience Meets Surveillance: AI at the Corner Store." In: *The Star Online*, Retrieved from https://www.thestar.com.my/tech/tech-news/2019/07/06/when-convenience-meets-surveillance-ai-at-the-corner-store/#I3PrWJyeg8oPgP2P.99.

Hoelzl, I., & Marie, R. (2021): The Martian Image (On Earth). In *The Palgrave Handbook of Image Studies* Palgrave Macmillan, Cham, pp. 233-246.

IATA (2021): One ID. In: *International Air Transport Association*, Retrieved from https://www.iata.org/en/programs/passenger/one-id/.

Johnson, C./Jones, R./Paasi, A./Amoore, L./Mountz, A./Salter, M./Rumford, C. (2011): Interventions on rethinking 'the border' in border studies. In: *Political Geography*, 30/2, pp. 61-69. https://doi.org/10.1016/j.polgeo.2011.01.002.

Kelly, K. (2019) "AR Will Spark the Next Big Tech Platform—Call It Mirrorworld." Wired, 12 February. https://www.wired.com/story/mirrorworld-ar-next-big-tech-platform/.

O'Brien, L. (2020): The Far-Right Helped Create The World's Most Powerful Facial Recognition Technology. In: *HuffPost*, Retrieved from https://www.huffpost.com/entry/clearview-ai-facial-recognition-alt-right_n_5e7d028bc5b6cb08a92a5c48?6p8.

Paglen, T. (2014): Operational Images. *E-Flux*, no. 59. Retrieved from http://www.eflux.com/journal/59/61130/operational-images/.

Pantenburg, V. (2016): *Working images: Harun Farocki and the operational image*. In: *Image operations*. Manchester: Manchester University Press.

Robertson, C. (2010): *The passport in America: The history of a document*. Oxford: Oxford University Press.

Torpey, J. C. (2018): *The invention of the passport: Surveillance, citizenship and the state*. Cambridge: Cambridge University Press.

Thaler, R. H., & Sunstein, C. R. (2009). *Nudge : Improving Decisions about Health, Wealth and Happiness*. London: Penguin Books.

Uliasz, R. (2020): Seeing like an algorithm: operative images and emergent subjects. In: *AI & Society*, pp. 1-9. https://doi.org/10.1007/s00146-020-01067-y.

Viljoen, S., Goldenfein, J., & McGuigan, L. (2021). Design choices: Mechanism design and platform capitalism. *Big Data & Society, 8*(2), 1-13, 20539517211034312.

Zuckerman, E. (2021) Hey, Facebook, I Made a Metaverse 27 Years Ago. *The Atlantic*, October 30. Retrieved from: https://www.theatlantic.com/technology/archive/2021/10/facebook-metaverse-was-always-terrible/620546/.

Doing Google Maps
Everyday Use and the Image of Space in a Surveillance Capitalism Centrepiece

Peter Gentzel, Jeffrey Wimmer, Ruben Schlagowski

Abstract:

The article focuses on the app Google Maps. In structural terms, Google Maps is committed to the production logic of platform or surveillance capitalism, insofar as the collected user data are utilised both to maintain Google Maps as a "cartographic infrastructure" (Plantin 2018) and to predict and manipulate behaviour (Zuboff 2019). On the other hand, Google Maps presents an "image of the world" that, as a product of platform capitalism, also conveys specific notions that we depict by using the concepts of "networked images" or "operational images" (Farocki 2004; Rubinstein & Sluis 2008).

First, we traced the development of Google Maps and classified it using cartographic principles and criteria. Building on that, we performed two empirical studies. In a first step, we highlight findings on the everyday usage practices of Google Maps. In a second step, we characterise city maps produced by residents of a medium-sized city in Germany using an app developed by us. The project thus sheds light on the appropriation aspect of Google Maps and, by exploring the microlevel of individual usage practices, knowledge, and skills, provides an empirical contribution that is comparatively rare in the context of platform studies. Developing a map application furthermore enables us to show that the selection of knowledge and its spatial anchoring – the "image of the world"– follows a different logic when certain individuals create a map for specific locations (e.g., multimodal routes to "hidden culture").

Keywords

Datafication, Digital Cartography, Google Maps, Mapping App, Surveillance Capitalism

1. Introduction: Surveillance Capitalism, Platform Cartography and Networked Images

This special issue aims to bring together theoretical and analytical studies of networked images with platform and surveillance capitalism studies. This objective is based on at least two assumptions: First, that an image carries specific meaning for people's actions and knowledge, and that this meaning needs to be found outside the image, for instance, in the way it is used in everyday life, in the transmission of knowledge, or in the cultivation of specific aesthetic strategies. Second, in the age of platform and surveillance capitalism, a distinct genre of images, the networked images, has emerged, and unfolds meaning in everyday life that is related to the platform logic. Consequently, the connection between the analysis of a specific production regime (platform and surveillance capitalism) and the products thereof (networked images) cannot be exhausted in a description of the aesthetics and contents of images. It must focus on the usage practices, the production, use and modulation of the image. At the latest since the work of Stuart Hall (1997), the polysemy of texts and discourses (both written and visual) has been part of the consensus body of knowledge in communication and media studies. That means our analysis cannot rely on mere inference (from content to meaning), i.e., the description of media artefacts, disregarding their appropriation practices. This is why we have designed our empirical study to combine observation, enquiry and a participatory approach.

The subject of our contribution is maps, which transport images of the world, knowledge of and about spaces, make them publicly accessible, and, in turn, through their appropriation (e.g., navigation, orientation, annotation), influence actors' construction of space (Lefebvre 1991). Maps thus literally convey worldviews, i.e., representations of the world in which we live that always emphasise certain aspects of this world while neglecting others. Thus, maps may or may not contain nation-state boundaries, place different continents at the centre, depict certain regions larger than others, or may or may not use symbols to show certain points of interest and colours to represent topographical features. Compared to the vast majority of other public communication media, maps seem to have a robust evidential power. Compared to journalistic texts or social media debates, maps may or may not always be up-to-date or show the wrong area, but they do not contain opinions; they do not manipulate us. Cartographic analyses have of course shown that this attribution of objectivity and neutrality is not true, but from an everyday use perspective, maps are considered to be objective, contributing to a feeling of security and information (see chapter 3). Presumably, the comparatively constant imagery over centuries (usage of symbols, arrangement schemes, scaling logic, etc.) and the partly mathematical, rule-governed production process (the map projection) explain to a certain degree why people usually regard maps as valid and objective.

Our contribution analyses what is probably the most widely used map in human history, which has achieved a *"structural* dominance in the maps sector" (McQuire 2019: 155, emphasis added): Google Maps. According to the thesis formulated at the beginning of this paper, we focus on the one hand on the production, i.e., the technical and economic functioning of Google Maps, and on the other hand on the product – the map in the sense of an image of the world that is routinely used in everyday life.

The relevance and critical potential of our argumentation result from the combination of (1) analytical concepts of platform and surveillance capitalism with descriptions of networked (and operational) images and (2) insights and findings on digital maps as mobile communication media. From a theoretical and empirical point of view, this is accompanied by the challenge of combining macro-analytical approaches that seek to conceptualise production logic and products theoretically with the analysis of (media) routines and the everyday practices of individual users on the micro-level.

As outlined above, we refer to both "platform capitalism" and "surveillance capitalism", which are two slightly different concepts. The former focusses on a business model based on data, while the latter refers to an economic system. Platform capitalism, accordingly, is more related to action strategies, policies, and technical designs, whereas surveillance capitalism aims at the overarching operating principle of monitoring human experience by means of generating and processing behavioural data for the purpose of predicting and manipulating actions. From that merely structure-oriented (macro) perspective, Google Maps seems to be a centrepiece of contemporary surveillance capitalism. Shoshana Zuboff describes the techno-economic construction of Google's Maps, Earth, and Streetview apps as two intertwined circuits of data collection, filtering, and exploitation: in the first step, data that is consciously produced and provided (e.g., map editions, ratings) as well as more unconsciously produced data (e.g., geo-referenced usage, browsing history) are used (cf. van Dijk 2013) to improve the product (e.g., real-time traffic flow display, accurate and up-to-date topographic information). In a second step, this data is used to measure, predict, and manipulate user behaviour for the purposes of advertising, to stimulate acts of consumption and influence choices (Zuboff 2019: 128-175).

For Jean-Christophe Plantin, Google Maps represents the central infrastructure for geographical knowledge that operates as a "cartographic platform" (2018: 490). Critical potential emerges from this characterisation when we consider essential findings of platform research, for example, the constantly asserted yet false promise of neutrality (Gillespie 2010). However, it is not only users and their accounts to whom platform operators grant different rights, but also bodies of knowledge that are either privileged or discriminated. Tarleton Gillespie defines precisely this decision-making power over content and knowledge as "[...] the central commodity platforms sell meant to draw users in and keep them on the platform, in exchange for advertising and personal data" (2018: 41). Both findings, the double data collection and exploitation circuit of surveillance capitalism and the central commodity of platforms, evoke a parallel increase in participation and closure or re-centralisation of spatial knowledge (Plantin 2018: 489). It means that the quantity and quality of data collection and filtration make Google Maps a "knowledge infrastructure" (Plantin et al. 2018) that is maintained and simultaneously monopolised through everyday use of the app. Thus, while the production of spatial knowledge qua Google Maps use is no longer in the hands of single powerful actors, it is operated by all app users. At the same time, however, spatial knowledge and spatial images in the form of maps are selected by corporation decisions (platform operators) and their algorithmic execution, and consequently monopolised – simply because of the generic linkage of use and maintenance of the infrastructure.

We found instructive points of reference for an analysis of the Google map as an "image of space" in the context of studies of "networked images" (Rubinstein/Sluis 2008). The term refers to the digital transformation of images as visual products of photography or film. It also points to fundamental changes in image production and usage practices due to their technical and communicative integration into the present convergent, data-driven, and commercialised communication culture of the internet. For the production, dissemination and use of photographs – in a sense, the photographic culture –, it is possible to observe a transformation "from an individual to a communal activity", from a "print-oriented to a transmission-oriented, screen-based experience" (Rubinstein/Sluis 2008: 9). Another congruent finding is one relating to the homogenisation of knowledge and practices: On the one hand, photographic images are becoming far more performative through editing, tagging, remixing, and sharing practices; on the other hand, the surveillance-capitalist processing logic of these image data is accompanied by a clear canonisation of image cultures, as can be observed, for example, in the relatively uniform categories and motifs of stock photo archives. Of course, individually created, shared, and mixed photos are not identical to images of space, but the aforementioned practices and actions, and the effects thereof on the variety of aesthetics and knowledge presentation are a common characteristic. Building on Harun Farocki's notion of "operational images" (2004; Pantenburg 2017), Thomas Elsaesser's discussion of technical images (Elsaesser/Alberto 2014; Elsaesser 2017) is interesting at this point. According to his reading of Farocki, the central feature of the digital image in its algorithmic environment may not be representation (of reality) but operation. Thus, operation as the essence of the data-driven, capitalist-oriented visual regime not only leads to a different way of dealing with images, i.e., clicking instead of seeing, but also "promotes seeing as registering and controlling over seeing as recognizing and understanding" (Elsaesser 2017: 222). Consequently, the operation of platform capitalism images, which has always been scripted or "editorialized" already (Elsaesser/Alberto 2014) is not a solely aesthetic quality but also an instruction for action and a perception pattern. From an intensely culturally pessimistic point of view, those operational images tend to work as a "life manual" and "placebo for a more active, productive and interpersonal engagement with the world" (Elsaesser 2017: 224).

Both research perspectives are highly relevant because, in combination, they allow us to understand the interplay between cartography as a platform (production) and the map as a networked and operative image of the world (product). In particular, the interrelationship between participation and closure, ubiquity and canonisation, inscription/editorialising and usage directs our analysis to a combination of "questions of knowledge" (What image of the world does Google Maps present?) and "questions of usage" (How exactly does the image "network" and "operate" in everyday life?). As outlined above, both platform studies and studies concerning the imagery of "networked and operational images" base their arguments on changing practices of using media technologies or communicative attributions of meaning. Empirically, however, this micro level of everyday use is comparatively underexposed – as it is in cartography studies as well (e.g., Farman 2010: 884). There are not many studies that answer questions like: How do people use Google Maps in everyday life? What do they know about Google Maps' working principles and how their app use contributes to maintaining the "knowledge infrastructure"? Does this knowledge motivate users to use other mapping apps, or do other factors stimulate alternative forms of use? How can the "image of the world" of Google Maps be characterised? What spatial information do people select when mapping their hometown?

We will first trace the evolution of Google Maps into a "cartographic infrastructure" and explore the Google map as an "image of the world". That primarily descriptive argumentation draws selectively on geographical and cartographic studies to illustrate the implications of this new "cartographic regime" through its historical situatedness. We then present our empirical findings on the use of Google Maps in everyday life. Building on this, we present our second empirical study, the editing of a city map by inhabitants of that city. To this end, we developed our own alternative mapping app. We will discuss the body of knowledge, information, and imagery that people selected and enacted to map their hometown. Finally, we summarise our empirical results.

2. Becoming Infrastructure: Google Maps and "Cartography as Platform"

The administrator and owner of Google Maps is the private technology company Google/ Alphabet – probably the most dominant actor in surveillance or platform capitalism alongside Facebook and Amazon (Zuboff 2019; Srnicek 2017). Reliable usage figures are difficult to find. It is estimated that between 1 and 2 billion people use Google Maps every month; the mobile app, which has been available since 2007 (the year the iPhone launched), topped the download charts for mobile apps for several years (McQuire 2019: 152-153; Ström 2020: 6). The figures show clearly that Google had already become the largest and most influential map producer in the world (history) in 2006 (within two years of the development of Google Maps). As mentioned above, some studies assign to Google Maps the status of an infrastructure in the present, which means that without Google Maps, routines of space appropriation, orientation, navigation and information would collapse. The basis for the status of infrastructure is the reciprocal linkage of usage practices and production processes, i.e., the construction of the Google map takes place in surveillance capitalism according to the model of "cartography as platform" (Plantin 2018). The principle of this model can be summarised as follows: Based on proprietary software and interfaces (APIs), georeferenced data of different scales (from individual end-users, companies and organisations, states) are collected and analysed by and for Google. In a first step, this serves to optimise its product; in a second step, it serves to optimise behaviour monitoring, prediction, and manipulation (e.g., "nudging", Yeung 2017). Zuboff's foundational conceptualisation of surveillance capitalism (2019) focuses on the epistemological, social, cultural, and power implications of this financially driven cycle of data collection, filtration, and use. In terms of practices, the production and presentation of spatial knowledge to optimise the product by usage data can be understood as infrastructural work. The Google map is updated and maintained qua use, and the spatial knowledge derived from that vast amount of georeferenced data is monopolised (Plantin et al. 2018; Plantin 2018). This "participatory strategy" (McQuire 2019: 152) is emblematic of platform capitalism in general, and Google Maps specifically. In terms of structure, the core of this strategy is linking one's product with other applications (and thus operations). APIs are, in a sense, the technical bridge between Google Maps and the commercial internet. Furthermore, we are now interested in how this bridge is designed and constituted symbolically and communicatively, in terms of map content and map actions. From a platform capitalistic point of view, it seems only rational to include as much georeferenced information as possible (including location-based ratings and comments, links to other sites) in the map, the image of space, to make Google Maps the starting point for other internet-based practices.

2.1 The Development of Google Maps in the Context of the Digitisation of Media and Cartography

Google's corporate policy was redefined in 2002, a change which encompassed the rejection of principles such as freedom from advertising and privileging of high-value knowledge, which meant, for Sergey Brin and Larry Page, first and foremost secured, scientific knowledge stocks (1998). Google bought key technologies, knowledge and actors in the field of digital map production in 2004. Among others, they acquired the start-ups "Where2Technologies", "Keyhole", and "ZipDash" and hired the CEOs of those companies, Brian McClendon, Lars and Jens Rasmussen and Mark Grady (Gannes 2009; Glasze 2015: 33-34; McQuire

2019: 151-152; Ström 2020: 8). Immediately after the launch of the iPhone in 2007 and the subsequent widespread social adoption of smartphones, Google developed the Ground Truth project in 2008 (Plantin 2018). Ground Truth refers to the base maps of Google Maps, which were continuously updated, enhanced, and maintained by collecting heterogeneous and diversely scaled data streams from a wide variety of actors (states, companies, users) (McQuire 2019). This data is collected via sensors, GPS, GIS, and the geoweb (as a set of georeferenced data) through proprietary software (APIs) and then processed according to surveillance or platform capitalist principles. The goal of manual and algorithmic data processing is to target users, to animate them, technically and symbolically, to expand their usage practices quantitatively and qualitatively. Accordingly, individual parts of Google Maps are customized (e.g., based on previously searched destinations, products, actors on the internet) to highlight places that are most likely to interest users and are associated with purchase actions (Luque-Ayala/Neves 2019: 459; McQuire 2019: 154-156). The extension of use is ensured by means of the interweaving of Google Maps with the infrastructure of the commercial internet – in both directions: On the one hand, according to the logic and goal of surveillance and platform capitalism, it also captures those data about internet-based activities that occur before, after, and outside of app use. On the other hand, the potential of digital data is exploited by linking the mapped, visualised georeferenced data with further information and services outside the digital map. Consequently, the mapped spatial knowledge is not limited to topographic information or politically defined areas, but potentially encompasses the entire range of digital data (e.g., appropriately tagged homepages, reviews, photos, posts, tweets) and makes this information accessible via the map itself. In short, "the commercial-consumer orientation of Google Maps [...] fits their advertising-driven revenue model" (McQuire 2019: 158).

The significance and consequences of this development of Google Maps into a "cartographic infrastructure" can be clarified if one positions it in relation to traditional forms of selecting and processing spatial knowledge and understands it in the context of the transformation of maps into digital "geomedial action spaces" (Abend/Harvey 2017). Regarding the concepts of networked and operational images, we thus pursue a twofold strategy: First, we consider the selection processes in the creation of maps, i.e., we ask which content is privileged and which is excluded (or what kind of world Google Maps stages). Next, we look at maps as part of media practices in everyday life to draw conclusions about how they are used. To recognise substantial changes, we will also historically classify the production process and the mediality of maps.

2.1.1 Knowledge of Space

A comprehensive analysis of socially disseminated and culturally transmitted knowledge of space would need also to consider numerous actors, institutions, practices, standardisation achievements, and technologies. This would include, for example, the verification and canonisation of geographic knowledge, the recognition of maps by state institutions, or the teaching of knowledge stocks and competencies for the "correct" reading of maps in schools. In the following, we limit our observation to the question of which actors and selection processes traditionally permeate cartographic practice. The argument aims to outline more clearly the changing power of selection and design for maps as images of space. We have already presented the main findings for "cartography as platform": Spatial knowledge is subject to a new tension between "participation and closure" (Plantin 2018) or, to use the words of cultural geographer Georg Glasze, the "universalization of geoinformation" is juxtaposed with new forms of "fragmentation" (2015: 36).

Traditionally, the production of maps was incumbent upon cartographers who, based on available knowledge (e.g., about continents, sea routes, or through celestial observation), mathematical principles (e.g., triangulation, scales, and coordinate systems), technical artefacts (e.g., sextants, photography), and ideas (e.g., Ptolemaic worldview, religious worldview, power relations), transferred location-bound phenomena or facts into symbols and arranged them on a surface. The production of these images of space is thus subject to mathematical principles, questions of power, and the worldviews of the cartographers and their clients themselves.

Mathematical aspects, which were also processed mathematically, include, for example, generalisations such as the conversion of three-dimensional space into a two-dimensional surface using correction factors and coordinate systems, or the rule-governed reduction of distances to scale. In this sense, cartography is a scientific discipline and a specific mathematical technique, accompanied by a correspondingly scientific concept of objectivity and a claim to truth. Through the historically oriented work of cartographer Brian Harley (1989, among others), critical cartography has gained prominence since the 1970s (Glasze 2015), making social scientific categories such as interests and power relevant. Harley's work focuses less on map projection than on the (conscious or unconscious) selection of information. Compared to the mathematical reduction of size, this content reduction, the selection of information is much less transparent and subject to many more heterogeneous factors (e.g., resources, religious or political interests). Drawing on the work of Foucault, Derrida, and Barthes, Harley consequently conceives of maps as texts that refer to (external) power structures and are instruments of power enforcement: "Behind most cartographers, there is a patron; in innumerable instances, the makers of cartographic texts were responding to external needs. Power is also exercised with cartography" (1989: 12).

Specific images of the world manifest themselves in maps; for example, the choice of centre and periphery is significant. This becomes obvious when comparing world maps that show either the European, the American or the Asian continent at the centre. The historical perspective is also telling. For example, the centre of the world was defined religiously for a long time, which is why Mecca or Jerusalem was positioned at the centre of the map (Ström 2020). Probably the most prominent example here is the Mercator map, initially designed for maritime voyages, which represents the geopolitical supremacy of Europe in colonial times by placing Europe at the centre and depicting its area in comparison to Africa, for instance, as far larger than would be the case using purely mathematical generalisations to faithfully reduce all continents to scale (Harpold 1999; Wood/ Fels 2008; Farman 2010). Another striking example relating to the representation and exercise of geopolitical power through maps is the global location of the prime meridian at the site of the Royal Observatory in Greenwich in 1721 (Ström 2020). However, (geopolitical) power is exercised through maps not only on a global scale through centre and periphery or size ratios, but also for nation-state identity politics, by means of the use of symbols. In Germany, for example, there is still no official symbol for non-Christian buildings such as mosques or synagogues (Glasze 2015: 31).

This listing of mathematical-technical and power-based selection processes for spatial knowledge is only a tiny sketch illustrating which processes, actors, and types of power (religious, economic, military) critical cartography has made visible for analogue maps. After the following remarks on maps as "media of space", we will take a closer look at some selection principles of the Google map.

2.1.2 Media of Space

The selection and arrangement of spatial knowledge, the image of space, is also significantly influenced by the materiality of the data (digital or analogue) and the medium. Here, too, it is worth looking to the past: while the first maps took the form of clay tablets, papyrus scrolls, woodcuts, and copperplate engravings, the development of printing technology (lithography, typography; offset printing) had a considerable influence on the shape of maps. Analogue maps have arranged symbols in the plane since the 19th century and are logocentric in design. Map texts are thus largely stable: a relationship between centre and periphery cannot be changed, the selected sections and applied boundaries are fixed within a given set of prearranged items of information. The analogue map is a fixed format end product of cartographic efforts and decisions. In other words, it is a linear medium that leaves users very little room for change.

This changed fundamentally during the process of digitisation. Communication and media studies mean or associate the term digitisation with changes such as the mobilisation and miniaturisation of media technologies, technical, economic, format-related, social, and cultural convergence, datafication, and related processes of fragmentation of the public sphere (including the echo chamber effect and filter bubbles). Consequently, if maps are understood as media, they are also affected by these processes. It is beyond the scope of this article to discuss all of them, and so we will focus instead on a few examples.

Pablo Abend and Francis Harvey refer to digital maps as "geomedial action spaces" (2017), aiming to describe the transformation of maps from a final product of cartographic work to an unfinished, continuously changeable medial action space. This means that digital maps are no longer unchangeable, linear, logocentric arrangements of symbols on a surface that users may or may not consume. Digital maps are not the same for every user and offer multiple possibilities for interaction and manipulation: They are constructed egocentrically, i.e., the respective user is at the centre of the map (in two ways: on the one hand, the location of the smartphone forms the central point of the mobile map, and on the other hand, map contents are potentially adapted to user behaviour). Their contents are multimodal and -medial and thus no longer limited to static, temporally unchangeable symbols, lines and numbers. They are not limited in their area to the dimensions of wood or printing paper, which is why the represented space does not have to be reduced and cut out in a generalised way. With digital displays and touchscreens, it is up to the user to choose which section of the map is displayed, to change the scaling, to select from different contents or to feed in their own contents. The digital map often does not stand alone, but is networked with further services and data streams, which in turn affect the individually displayed map information in real-time (e.g. traffic flow). Finally, there are no specific maps anymore that have to be acquired, folded, and transported. Digital maps can be used as part of the mobile digital media ensemble at any time, in any place, and for any georeferenced multimodal information and activities for any location in the world (Farman 2010; Abend/Harvey 2017; Lammes 2017; Shapiro 2018; Luque-Ayala/Neves 2019; Palipane 2019; Ström 2020).

2.2 Google Maps as Knowledge and Media of Space

This short historical excursion has shown that (both analogue and digital) map production is necessarily linked to selection processes. Spatial knowledge and images of the world in the form of maps were and continue to be dependent on power relations, technical potentials and restrictions. Against this background, what can now be said about the spatial knowledge of Google Maps, Google's image of the world?

Some aspects of the Google map are critical from a "classical" cartographic perspective. For example, some national borders are not consensual and are mapped on the Google map in a way that favours one party, as in the case of Taiwan and Tibet (Farman 2010: 878), and currently also Crimea. Furthermore, the dominance of the English language leads to signatures and labels that do not correspond to the locally embedded cultural practice of designation (e.g., other names, written symbols, iconic signs). That means people who are not skilled in English (or another dominant world language) may have problems decoding Google Maps. In addition, it is fundamentally true that highly datafied spaces are shown much more accurately and, in more detail, with more app functionality – in short, they have a "better" cartographic infrastructure than spaces about which and in which somewhat less data is produced. In the age of cartography as platform, it is basically true that spaces in which more people use mobile digital media more frequently are privileged, i.e., at the very least they are represented in greater detail.

As discussed earlier, data is not neutral; its collection and processing follow a specific capitalist logic. Data filtering by one of the most powerful protagonists of surveillance and platform capitalism leads to a digital mapping of public space that not only privileges economic actors and content but also continuously adapts the map text to individual usage patterns of internet-based applications and programs. In this respect, Google Maps depicts all places on earth, but what it shows is potentially different for each user and ultimately serves to sell products and services.

Due to the dependency on location, individual zoom, processed digital usage data, availability and topicality of local data, no uniform selection and arrangement of spatial knowledge can be analysed. Obviously, in the networked image of public space, economic content is highly important. The signatures for retailers, restaurants or tourist attractions vary in colour, not in size – in city centres, for example, the signatures of fast-food stores are (depending on the zoom) just as large as those of the marketplace, city hall or cathedral. Moreover, the categories of location-based "discovery" – as a feature to stimulate app and further internet use – are overwhelmingly associated with forms of consumption (e.g., restaurants, clubs, shows, shopping), with the time of day and reviews of products and services factoring in alongside location (McQuire 2019: 156; Ström 2020: 9). The findings of a study by Timothy Erik Ström also point to an economic contour of centre-periphery arrangement: for example, the centre of major Western cities, accessed via a stationary desktop computer, is often found in economically prosperous areas such as banking centres (2020: 9).

However, the fact that power, and thus the selection and arrangement of spatial knowledge in the Google map, is defined by consumption can be impressively demonstrated beyond Western consumer landscapes. Luque-Ayala and Neves accompanied Google initiatives that aimed to generate specific georeferenced data ("points of interest") for places that had hardly been data-fitted so far and to integrate them into the Google map. Based on observations and interviews of corresponding initiatives in Brazilian favelas, they conclude that Google is working on the commercialisation of public space and the commodification of spatial perception:

"First, it [Google Maps] provides a general sense of place and orientation. Second, it offers a targeted form of spatial knowledge around business transactions and/or forms of consumption. And third, it enables the incorporation of business locations and sites of consumption within an emerging and calculative sense of place. [Google's mapping projects are] never meant to be the calculability of communities as a whole, nor of their deficiencies, complexities and aspirations, but of their economic flows and businesses." (Luque-Ayala/Neves 2019: 460, 467)

3. Case Studies: Use of Google Maps and Producing an Alternative Map

Our argumentation thus far has shown the extent to which Google Maps can be understood as a centrepiece of surveillance capitalism and has discussed the functioning of "cartography as platform". We went on to deal with the selection mechanisms for the acquisition of spatial knowledge on Google Maps and have worked out how far the image of the world of Google Maps is based on economic power.

In the following, we aim to analyse the everyday usage practices of Google Maps empirically. On the one hand, we focus on exploring the significance of and knowledge about the functioning of Google Maps as a cartographic infrastructure. Second, we elicit conditions for the use of alternative digital maps. In this step, we attempt to create alternative cartographies of space that are not guided by economic principles. For this purpose, we used a participatory approach to develop a mapping app and asked residents to map characteristics of their hometown that are important to them.

3.1 The Seamless Embedding of Google Maps in Everyday Life

For this part of our study, an attempt was made to compile a sample that was as diverse and comprehensive as possible in terms of social circles, in line with theoretical sampling. In addition to balanced gender and age distribution, subdivisions were made for occupation, leisure activities, media/technology affinity and use of mapping apps. The final sample consisted of 20 media users, with the youngest participant being 17 and the oldest 56 years old.

Qualitative guided interviews were conducted for the data collection. The advantage of this method is that the predetermined catalogue of questions offers the interviewer an orientation as to what contents are of interest for the study. At the same time, it leaves enough room to react flexibly to the answers from the respective interviewee and to ask specific questions. Thus, all given topics are dealt with and the interviewees' individual particularities are sufficiently documented. The guideline was divided into several thematic blocks, but the questions could be moved flexibly depending on the flow of the conversation. In order to gain an understanding of why participants use mapping apps in general and Google Maps in particular, in other words, to understand what a cartographic infrastructure means in everyday life, the topics related to the selection, reception and appropriation of mapping apps were, among others: Awareness of mapping apps, access and download behaviour, use of features, quality assessment, navigation, inclusion in media repertoire. The second part concerned the ways in which the use of smart mapping apps affects the recipient. Here, the perception of the city and the knowledge and attitude towards datafication processes and the "power" of platforms like Google were explored. Three processes which display the seamless social embeddedness of Google Maps in everyday life will be presented in following sections.

3.1.1 Reaching a Destination without Effort and in a Planned Manner

In general, the interviews show that users have very strong trust in Google Maps mostly because of the practical value of the app in everyday life. "I actually rely on the app, especially when I need to get somewhere quickly, because I think it will pick out the fastest route" (Anka). The routes suggested by Google Maps are predominantly perceived as very appropriate and are frequently used because, from the users' point of view, they provide a lot of information that helps with planning their everyday life. For most, it represents a safe and reliable way of planning that also takes little time. Very often, people report using Google Maps in advance to look at a route or a place:

"Um, yes, I just drove to Augsburg last week and I knew that a main road was closed, and so I didn't really know how else to get there because it wasn't passable. That's why I looked at the route before the journey. And I also used Google Maps to navigate in the car while I was driving" (Lena).

Users greatly appreciate the fact that the app not only provides routes, but a lot of other information that makes planning easier or provides assistance for direct use. For example, changes such as road closures or traffic jams can be displayed, and alternative means of transport and costs for these are included:

"What I find very good is that after [...] I can see on Google Maps how I can get there by public transport, as well as estimate the distance on foot or the approximate cost of taxis, or even see what the distance is by car, etc. I can really compare how I would get there by car with other means of transport. I can really compare how I can get there best and fastest" (Tanja).

In addition to information on traffic situations, information on places is also highly valued. For example, Google Maps provides information about opening hours or tells the user what to expect in advance through reviews and pictures.

"If I'm driving long distances that I haven't driven often or at all, and I want to know when I have to leave in order to arrive at a certain time. Or if I don't know when the shops, pubs, whatever, are open. That's what Google Maps says" (Kowalski).

"You simply have a different personal experience, and you can also find out what other people think about a place and how they rate it. For example, an opinion about a bar. Then I can draw on other people's experiences and learn more than just the name of the bar. And it's not fake – it's from normal users, real guests, real visitors. You can rely on that a little bit" (Lena).

What is particularly positive for the interviewees is that time details for routes are calculated in advance:

"It's quick. Which is a time saver, of course. It's practical and easy. You just indicate where you want to go, then the destination address and it immediately suggests how to drive or walk and even suggests different routes. It's just convenient" (Maria).

Thus, the app gives the respondents the feeling that they are provided first and foremost with a route, but also with a great deal of important additional information around the actual route. This provides a sense of security and control for users that is not questioned further. The structural interweaving of Google Maps with the commercial internet is appreciated by its users in terms of security and control of information, which is used to optimise navigation practices.

Regarding the platform status and its inherent communicative power, we only found critical comments in three interviews, such as this prototypical remark:

"Yes. I find it a bit problematic in general, that they [the destinations] are already dependent on how much the respective company pays Google, that they appear first now, for example, or appear from a zoom level that is further out, and so on. So maybe that would be the only thing that goes more in the direction of marketing. Instead of me really benefiting from it. But on another level, which is not necessarily relevant for me as a user, it's a bit problematic that you, as the owner of a business, are actually so dependent on being placed on Google Maps, because so many people use it to find the nearest hairdresser or fishmonger or whatever. So maybe that's a point of criticism, that Google doesn't have enough competition or that it's actually the most important map tool, with the economic effects" (Markus).

3.1.2 Individual Customisation and Active Participation as a Requirement

Although the interviewees are consistently positive about the fact that the app takes over many tasks, it is still important to them to be able to participate actively or at least to have the feeling of being able to do so. For example, respondents state that they would like to be able to choose their own favourites from the routes presented and adapt them additionally to their own needs, such as the choice of means of transport:

"I definitely look at them, the suggestions. And I usually take the one that I find the easiest, because with some of them you have to turn off five times more or whatever. But I don't look at whether it's two km more or less, I look at what's easiest to ride, or when cycling, which routes I find appealing in terms of the landscape and the surroundings" (Lorena).

The app is rated negatively if it is not sufficiently adapted to the user's individual situation. For example, the location cannot be correctly identified (Anka) or no further settings, such as an adjustment to the vehicle can be made:

"But now, we specifically search for travel with our motorhome... we would like the possibility [...] that it would then ultimately find a suitable route or road for me on the basis of this. Just like you find in classic navigation devices in motorhomes that are specially designed for that" (Mareike).

This goes hand in hand with the positive assessment of the filter functions in the Hidden Culture app (see next section), which allows users to determine for themselves what is displayed on maps: "I like it. Yes, because you can choose the topics that really interest you" (Anka).

In terms of participation and individualisation, the option in Google Maps of creating one's own route and saving favourite places is very much appreciated. This gives users the opportunity to have a say in which places are found on the app and to participate actively in its design:

"So even on Google I've written a lot of reviews, I also like to add pictures and do it in detail. And if I like the app and I'm on the road there myself, of course I'd like to send detailed reviews to maybe bring others closer. Clearly, or also to share my own experiences" (Roland).

It should be noted here that the respondents consider uploading their own content to be good in principle, but mostly too complicated or time-consuming: "Yes, I could imagine creating places. [...] [B]ut when so many people contribute at the same time, it can be very good, but also very messy [...]" (Lorena). For our participatory mapping app, co-creation remains a very important aspect, the implementation of which needs to be further developed (see next section). We could not observe any explicit critical reflections about the usage of further (viz. unconscious) internet browsing, georeferenced data by Google to maintain the cartographic infrastructure or observe behaviour in space.

3.1.3 More than the Obvious as Wishful Thinking

For the interviewees, a mapping app should not only show the most obvious things; they also hope to gain additional knowledge, so called added value, or the possibility to see new places that they would not have found without the app. "Especially on a nice summer evening, walking through the city to see a little bit of something. So NOT (!) according to the motto 'the way is the goal', clearly" (Roland). The interviewees particularly like the discovery function in the app we developed, because they were familiar with it from Google Maps. This is seen not only as a positive way to get to know strange places better, but also as a way to find new things in their own city:

"I often notice when I'm out with friends and want to have a coffee. Then we often say, 'hm where are we going' and actually there are a thousand cafés in Regensburg. But still, I'm always overwhelmed by where to go, and I always go to the same ones. That's why I think it wouldn't be so bad to get a bit of inspiration or something, just as a kind of motivation. Just try something new, especially if they upload pictures or audio content or something. If you can listen in, oh what kind of music is playing or what are the people like? I think that would be really cool. So, I can already imagine that, yes" (Nadine).

Here, too, the co-creative aspect of mapping and navigation apps is expressed, because the possibility of uploading one's own places means that, in addition to the obvious places, "insider tips" (Roland) can also be entered and explored. The users' collective knowledge can thus be used to look beyond the obvious. The possibility of adding one's own knowledge and pictures to the specific places also makes it possible to explore this more deeply.

"There will always be people who know their way around a city better and know other, less well-known corners. They know insider tips or places that have just opened. Or even if they are more hidden. That I wouldn't find as a non-local. And that's practical when others can draw your attention to them" (Lena).

The creation of routes in our participatory mapping app also contributes to this. It makes it possible to visit places selected by other users. The interview participants particularly like the fact that places are suggested to them that they would not have come across without the app and that they can also facilitate this experience for other users:

"It's my birthplace. I might know some corners or know a few more things that could perhaps be shared or I would like to be shared with a lot of others. And because of that, or just a little bit, yes, share your own view through it" (Maria).

"Or with special things that you don't really discover. For example, other restaurants or bars or hostels or something that you wouldn't have seen right away. I can totally imagine that I would use that. I would definitely follow the routes in order to get to know something new" (Lena).

Users don't just expect a map that shows places or routes from one point to another, they want to be actively involved in what's happening, they want to be able to contribute to the design of the maps themselves, and through this co-creation they expect to receive not just the obvious, but also insider tips and additional information.

3.1.4 The (Un)conscious Centrality of Google Maps in Users' Everyday Life

The findings outlined above can be condensed into several contiguous processes and associated theses. Firstly, Google Maps manages to economise and rationalise the spatial and urban experience without the business model behind it really being perceived, understood and evaluated by its users. By doing so, Google Maps has been able to monopolise this domain of everyday life. Every respondent without exception preferred and/or used Google Maps as their default mapping app. Additional mapping apps are only downloaded if they fit better to hobbies like hiking, camping or motorbike riding. This suggests that other mapping apps are more likely to be influential when the surroundings are not well known but are essential to everyday activities. Specific practices exist in the use of Google Maps such as ratings/lists as well as route generation. These are the two features that are most used by all users, regardless of lifestyle and socio-demographics. Goal-oriented navigation is on the rise, while strolling is becoming less common, even though most respondents express a desire for (exclusive) "surprises" and "insider tips". Google Maps successfully integrates the medium of the map into a whole media world, even dominating it, because it works in combination with other interactive applications (e.g., rating, localisation). The possibility to participate in and through Google Maps is considered important by the users when asked, but participation is not known in all its analytical and normative dimensions, and not really exercised in everyday usage of Google Maps. Although the vast majority of respondents can be classified as passive users, the possibility to create their own content seems to be of relevance. This is most likely due to the fact that almost all respondents state that they rely on reviews from other Google Maps users for everyday decision-making situations, such as choosing a restaurant or leisure activities. Even though Google Maps already offers some ways to engage and interact with others, this lacks a certain personal touch. Although it is possible to give ratings and thus publicly express one's opinion, a more individual and self-determined form of participation is missing.

3.2 Alternative Mapping of Spaces

In the second step of our study, we build on the diverse notions and overall appreciation of *active* participation, which implies the intentional definition, selection and production of spatial knowledge. Thus, we developed an alternative map for the city centre of Augsburg, a medium-sized city in Germany, by utilising that participatory approach (detailed presentation: digista.de). As described, due to its status as infrastructure i.e., the widespread and deeply interwoven use of Google Maps in everyday practices, it is not possible to simply think and design an alternative image of space. Following the basic assumptions of a connection between production regime and product, we designed the production process as participatory. The main differences to many other forms of digital cartography, the production of the Google map and the dominant logic of the digitisation of urban spaces (Hollands 2008; Kitchin 2014; Söderström et al. 2014; Rabari/Storper 2015) can be summarised by three dimensions: 1) producing knowledge, not correlating data; 2) starting with the people and the place, not with technology (McFarlane/Söderström 2017), and 3) leaving out the data-driven capture of behaviour and opinions in the form of ratings and lists. Following principle 3, for example, we do not use data on our server for personalised recommendations or advertising. Further, we only use direct feedback channels for the improvement and maintenance of our app.

We asked a total of 20 students from Augsburg to create an image of the city space. The knowledge presented was not generated by merging existing digital data and traces but was produced by city residents and referenced at concrete locations. As inspiration material, we presented Bruno Latour and Emilie Hermant's Webopera "Paris: invisible city" (1998) to the study participants and gave them time to explore it both individually and in groups. Afterwards, groups discussed how the basic idea of mapping local knowledge and practices instead of mapping the city "at a glance" could be implemented in the context of our study. In joint discussions, five subjects finally emerged: 1) hidden culture, 2) history, 3) religion, 4) water, and 5) sounds. Each topic is deeply interwoven with the city's history or present. Augsburg played a significant role, for instance, in negotiating the religious peace between Protestants and Catholics in the 16th century, and the city's water management system was added to the UNESCO World Heritage List in 2019. The four groups then developed a concept for mapping this knowledge. In the process, a strategy crystallised that all four groups used: Important local places were identified and linked thematically. In contrast to the production of the Google map and the dominant form of digitisation of cities, no existing geo-referenced data were linked, specific behaviour patterns were not evaluated, and the urban space was not understood as a 'platform' with structures that can be technically mapped utilising data correlation. However, local people generated knowledge based on locally relevant topics.

In order to make this content accessible, we developed a mapping app that enables the integration of multimodal content (photos, videos, texts, sounds) into the map on site and allows these local points to be linked through the construction of routes. Thus, the substantial local knowledge was not presented on the basis of individual places (geo-referenced data points) but via thematic routes connecting places. Initially, five routes were available (actually many more), which can be used to explore and assimilate the urban space in a theme-oriented way. As a digital, mobile map, it features the characteristics described above (ego-centred; scroll and zoom function; designability based on other media content) but is not linked to the infrastructure of the commercial internet, and the content production does not follow a data-driven logic.

We used the Ionic framework for cross-platform frontend development (https://ionicframe-work.com) with (the opensource) leaflet (https://leafletjs.com)

and the Openstreetmap API (https://www.openstreetmap.org) for the basic map functions. For routing between georeferenced content, we used the Graphhopper routing API (https://www.graph-hopper.com). All georeferenced data that users create is stored in a MySQL database, which can be accessed using a custom REST API that we developed. Of course, our digital map app has several features (such as zooming and editing) that we mentioned above in the context of digitising map media (chapter 2). Unlike Google Maps, however, our map is not interwoven with the commercial internet by construction, i.e., georeferenced information (or augmentations) must be deliberately created and added to the base map (Openstreetmap). Thus, it is up to the user to decide which information is tied to which places and in what way (photo, text, video). By linking them to thematic routes, we were able to ensure that in addition to singular "points of interest", characteristic features of Augsburg's urban space were also mapped.

We will now present the thematic route "hidden culture" as an example of place-based content. The individual local "points of interest" include street music and street art and thus combine classic tourist attractions (like places where classical musicians play, public museums, opera houses and concert halls) with local art in public space. In doing so, those points of interest also include somewhat less powerful actors (street musicians, sprayers) and link somewhat less frequented urban places.

Fig. 1: App screenshots of the topic selection page (left), a short description of a locative media object "Schwabenwand" in the map after selection (middle) and the details page for the same object containing various images (right).

Fig. 2: The details page for "Schwabenwand" scrolled further down, showing both a text and a video (left), multiple points for the route "hidden culture" (middle) and the corresponding navigation instructions (right).

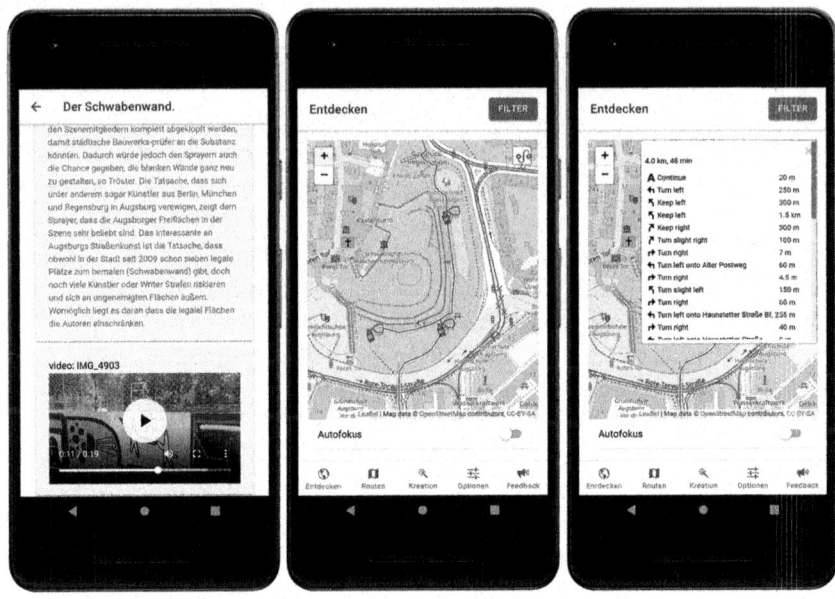

Figures 1 and 2 illustrate the app's structure: First, users can choose from one of the five topically framed roudescribed above and view the individual locations. In our example, the route "hidden culture" and the point of interest "Schwabenwand" are selected. For "Schwabenwand", a specific description and a video are available. Spraying graffiti is permitted on the "Schwabenwand" in Augsburg. The linked video shows how such graffiti is created. The middle part of Figure 2 shows the "hidden culture" route, which connects the different points of interest thematically and geographically, e.g., places in the city centre where street musicians usually stand, and contains links to video recordings of their performances.

Figure 3 shows a designed object that was tagged with the question "Is this street art?" If one takes a closer look at the individual points on the route, it is also noticeable that graffiti in the city centre is much more political but with a less depictive or pictorial design. In contrast, the graffiti on the Schwabenwand, which is a little further away from the city centre, is aesthetically more elaborate but less political. The explanation is simple: in the city centre, spraying is a criminal act. On the Schwabenwand, it is welcome. The local security policy, therefore, has an impact on the design and form of (political) street art: political messages are preferably sprayed at highly frequented locations with a minimum investment of resources, while artworks with little by way of provocative political messaging are elaborately designed over a more extended period.

Fig. 3: A selected locative media object that lies on the route "hidden culture" (left) and detail pages for two objects on that route, showing street art on feeder pillars (middle, right).

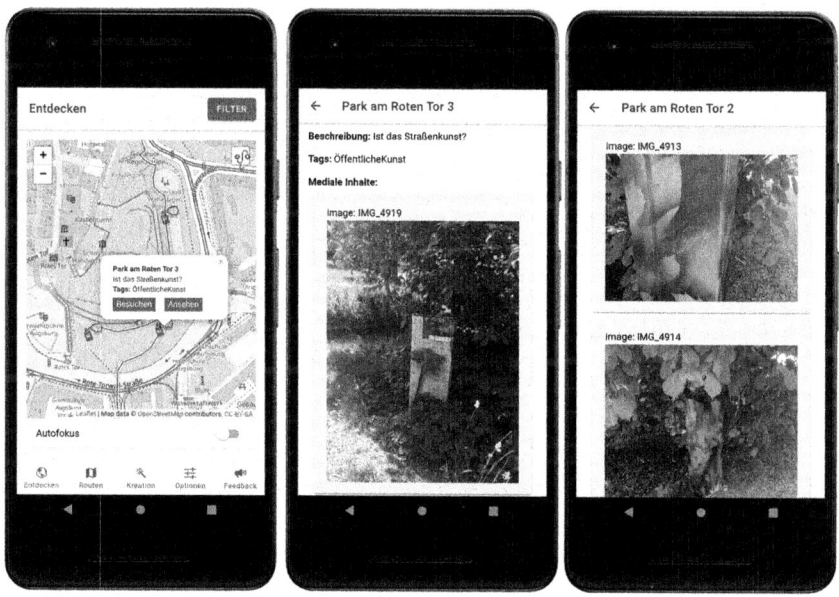

We have chosen this example because it clarifies that (urban) spaces are always also political and artistic spaces for the citizens – and that the corresponding user is linked to local factors that can also be represented in maps (and analysed through them). Due to the massive restrictions on the use of public space during the Coronavirus pandemic in 2020 and 2021, we were not able to create other thematic routes. Our next step is the curated creation of routes by different citizens of the city. This could be used specifically to allow less privileged actors, such as the homeless and migrants, or less tech-savvy people such as pensioners, to map "their" city as well. In that way, we want to exercise "power through maps" to make the complexity of urban spaces visible – and to create alternatives to the commercially oriented cartography of Google Maps.

4. Conclusion

The starting point of this paper was the assumption that the production process of maps influences the product, the image of the world and the knowledge of space that maps present. We have described this connection for Google Maps as a structural centrepiece of surveillance capitalism and cartographic infrastructure. As such, Google Maps is firmly linked to the commercial internet and is subject to data-driven filtering processes. Google represents a map of the world that consists of organised, tagged and structured georeferenced data, which are filtered and designed according to the principles of surveillance and platform capitalism. Findings from cartography-focused studies suggest that in historical comparison Google Maps preserves a consumption-oriented image of space. The conceptions of networked and operational images show additionally that we can understand digital images in the commercial internet only through their modes of use ("clicking instead of seeing") rather than through their aesthetics or the quality of their representation of reality.

Our empirical studies thus targeted two dimensions: map content as an image of space and everyday uses of Google Maps. First, we explored the practices and routines related to Google Maps. Unsurprisingly, it emerged that Google Maps, as a mobile app on smartphones, is firmly integrated into people's digital media ensemble, used to navigate urban spaces without disruption and as quickly as possible. Moreover, the features of the networked image of space have infiltrated expectations and routines. Google Maps is no longer used only as a "map", but also to find out further information (including opening hours, available goods, prices), reviews of products and ratings of services.

In the second part of our study, we wanted to create alternative images of space. To this end, we developed a map app and asked residents to portray their living space on a digital map. For this participatory mapping approach, characteristic local knowledge and shared interests must be prioritized over data- or technology-driven concepts. In other words, the map content needs to be deliberately selected and produced. We further defined that knowledge of space by linking singular "points of interest" to form specific routes. These routes offer understandings of space and stage worldviews in the map that focus on cultural practices, artistic design and civil protest in public space – a substantially different approach from the mostly consumer-oriented content shown in Google Maps.

5. References

Abend, Pablo/Harvey, Francis (2017): "Maps as Geomedial Action Spaces: Considering the Shift from Logocentric to Egocentric Engagements." In: GeoJournal 82, pp. 171-183.

Bittner, Christian/Michel, Boris (2013): "Das Dekonstruieren der web2.0 Karte. Vorschläge zur Analyse dynamischer und interaktiver Karten multipler und diffuser Autorenschaften." In Cryl, Inga/Nehrdich, Tobias/Vogler, Robert (eds.), geo@web. Medium, Räumlichkeit und geographische Bildung, Wiesbaden: VS, pp. 111-126.

Brin, Sergey/Page, Lawrence (1998): "The Anatomy of a Large Scale Hypertextual Web Engine." In: Computer Networks and ISDN Systems 30 (1-7), pp. 107-117.

Caquard, Sebastien (2014): "Cartography II: Collective Cartographies in the Social Media Era." In: Progress in Human Geography 38/1, pp. 141-150.

Cochrane Logan/Corbett Jon (2018): "Participatory Mapping." In: Servaes J. (ed): Handbook of Communication for Development and Social Change, Singapore: Springer, pp 1-9.

Crampton, Jeremy W. (2008): "Keyhole, Google Earth, and 3D Worlds: An Interview with Avi Bar-Zeev." In: Cartographica 43/2, pp. 85-93.

Dodge Martin (2017): "Cartography I: Mapping Deeply, Mapping the Past." In: Progress in Human Geography, 41/1, pp. 89-98.

Dolata, Ulrich (2018): "Internetkonzerne: Konzentration, Konkurrenz, Macht." In Dolata Ulrich/Schrape, Jan-Felix (eds.): Kollektivität und Macht im Internet. Soziale Bewegungen – Open Source Communities – Internetkonzerne, Wiesbaden: Springer VS, pp. 101-130.

du Gay, Paul et al. (1997): Doing Cultural Studies: The Story of the Sony Walkman, London: Sage.

Elsaesser, Thomas/Alberro, Alexander (2014): "Farocki: A Frame for the No Longer Visible." In: e-flux Journal 59, https://www.e-flux.com/journal/59/61111/farocki-a-frame-for-the-no-longer-visible-thomas-elsaesser-in-conversation-with-alexander-alberro/

Elsaesser, Thomas (2017): "Simulation and the Labour of Invisibility: Harun Farocki's Life Manuals." In: Animation: An Interdisciplinary Journal 12/3, pp. 214-229.

European Environment Agency: Data and Maps. https://www.eea.europa.eu/data-and-maps

Farman, Jason (2010): "Mapping the Digital Empire: Google Earth and the Process of Postmodern Cartography." In: New Media & Society 12/6, pp. 869-888.

Farman, Jason (2011): Mobile Interface Theory, Routledge: NY.

Farocki, Harun (2004): "Phantom Images." In: Public 29 (New Localities), pp. 12-22.

Gannes, Liz (2015): "Ten Years of Google Maps, from Slashdot to Ground Truth." In: Vox: Recode. (https://www.recode.net/2015/2/8/11558788/ten-years-of-google-maps-from-slashdot-to-ground-truth)

Gillespie, Tarleton (2010): "The Politics of 'Platforms'." In: New Media & Society 12/3, pp. 347-364.

Gillespie, Tarleton (2018): Custodians of the Internet: Platforms, Content Moderation, and the Hidden Decisions that Shape Social Media, New Haven: Yale University Press.

Glasze, Georg (2015): "Neue Kartografien, neue Geografien: Weltbilder im Digitalen Zeitalter." In: APUZ, Themenheft Weltbilder 65/41, pp. 29-37.

Goodchild, Michael F. (2007): "Citizens as Sensors. The World of Volunteered Geography." In: GeoJournal 69/4, pp. 211-221.

Hall, Stuart (1997): "The Work of Representation." In: Stuart Hall (ed.): Representation. Cultural Representations and Signifying Practices, London: Sage, pp. 15-61.

Harley, Brian (1989): "Deconstructing the Map." In: Cartographica 26/2, pp. 1-20.

Harpold, Terry (1999): "Dark Continents: A Critique of Metageographies." In: Postmodern Culture 9/2, pp. 1-37.

Hollands, Robert (2008): "Will the Real Smart City Please Stand Up?" In: City 3/12, pp. 303-320.

Johnson, Richard (1986): "What is Cultural Studies Anyway?" In: Social Text 16, pp. 38-80.

Kitchin, Rob (2014): "The Real-Time City? Big Data and Smart Urbanism." In: GeoJournal 79, pp. 1-14.

Lammes, Sybille (2017): "Digital Mapping Interfaces: From Immutable Mobiles to Mutable Images." In: New Media & Society 19/7, pp. 1019-1033.

Latour, Bruno/Hermant, Emilie (1998): Paris: Invisible City, http://www.bruno-latour.fr/virtual/PARIS-INVISIBLE-GB.pdf

Lefebvre, Henri (1991): The Production of Space, Oxford: Basil Blackwell.

Luque-Ayala, Andres/Neves Maia, Flavia (2019): "Digital Territories: Google Maps as a Political Technique in the Re-Making of Urban Informality." In: Environment and Planning D: Society and Space, 37/3, pp. 449-467.

McFarlane, Colin/Söderström, Ola (2017): "On Alternative Smart Cities." In: City 3-4/21, pp. 312-328.

McQuire, Scott (2019): "One Map to Rule Them All? Google Maps as Digital Technical Object." In: Communication and the Public 4/2, pp. 150-165.

Nold, Christian (ed.) (2009): Emotional Cartography: Technologies of the Self, London: Softhook.

Obaid, Mohammad/Kurdyukova, Ekaterina/André, Elisabeth (2012): "City Pulse: Supporting Going-out Activities with a Context-aware Urban Display." In: Advances in Computer Entertainment, pp. 529-532.

Palipane, Kelum (2019): "Multimodal Mapping — a Methodological Framework." In: The Journal of Architecture 24/1, pp. 91-113.

Pantenburg, Volker (2017): "Working Images. Harun Farocki and the Operational Image." In: Eder, Jens/Klonk, Charlotte (eds.): Image Operations. Visual Media and Political Conflict, Manchester: Manchester University Press, pp. 49-61.

Plantin, Jean-Christophe (2018): "Google Maps as Cartographic Infrastructure: From Participatory Mapmaking to Database Maintenance." In: International Journal of Communication 12, pp. 489-506.

Plantin, Jean-Christophe, et al. (2018): "Infrastructure Studies Meet Platform Studies in the Age of Google and Facebook." In: New Media & Society 20/1, pp. 293-310.

Rabari, Chirag/Storper, Michael (2015): "The Digital Skin of Cities: Urban Theory and Research in the Age of the Sensored and Metered City, Ubiquitous Computing and Big Data." In: Cambridge Journal of Regions, Economy and Society 8, pp. 27-42.

Rubinstein, Daniel/Sluis, Katrina (2008): "A Life More Photographic." In: Photographies 1/1, pp. 9-28.

Ryan, Brent D. (2011): "Reading Through a Plan." In: Journal of the American Planning Association 77/4, pp. 309-327.

Schulz-Schaeffer, Ingo/Lettkemann, Eric (2018): "Lokative Medien: Inklusion und Exklusion in öffentlichen Räumen." (TUTS - Working Papers, 1-2018). Technische Universität Berlin, Fak. VI Planen, Bauen, Umwelt, Institut für Soziologie, Fachgebiet Technik- und Innovationssoziologie.

Shapiro, Aaron (2018): "Street-level: Google Street View's Abstraction by Datafication." In: New Media & Society 20/3, pp. 1201-1219.

Söderström, Ola/Paasche, Till/Klauser, Franciso (2014): "Smart Cities as Corporate Storytelling." In: City 3/18, pp. 307-320.

Srincek, Nick (2017): Platform Capitalism, Cambridge: Polity Press.

Ström, Timothy Erik (2020): "Journey to the Centre of the World: Google Maps and the Abstraction of cybernetic capitalism." In: Cultural Geographies, pp. 1-19.

van Dijck, José (2013): "'You Have One Identity': Performing the Self on Facebook and LinkedIn." In: Media, Culture & Society 35/2, pp. 199-215.

Wood, Denis (1992): "How Maps Work." In: Cartographica 29/3-4, pp. 66-74.

Wood, Denis/Fels, John (2008): "The Natures of Maps. Cartographic Constructions of the Natural World." In: Cartographica 43/3, pp. 189-202.

Yeung, Karen (2017): "'Hypernudge': Big Data as a Mode of Regulation by Design." In: Information, Communication & Society 20/1, pp. 118-136.

Zook, Matthew/Graham, Mark (2007): "The Creative Reconstruction of the Internet: Google and the Privatization of Cyberspace and DigiPlace." In: Geoforum 38/6, pp. 1322-1343.

Zuboff, Shoshana (2019): The Age of Surveillance Capitalism: The Fight for a Human Future at the New Frontier of Power, New York: PublicAffairs.

Frameworks and APIs

Ionic: https://ionicframework.com
Leaflet: https://leafletjs.com
Openstreetmap: https://www.openstreetmap.org/
GraphHopper: https://www.graphhopper.com/

The Invisualities of Capture in Amazon's Logistical Operations

Armin Beverungen

Abstract

This paper explores the status of visuality in surveillance capitalism by considering its role in the management of Amazon's logistical operations. Whereas Amazon is often portrayed as being at the forefront of developments in surveillance associated with face recognition technologies, a focus on its logistical operations highlights the more mundane role of the barcode scan. The barcode is considered a calm image, central to the operation of capture in the warehouse and beyond. Logistics is here marked by invisualities, wherein visuality is operationalised to optimise logistical flows of data, things and people, rather than geared towards visual forms of surveillance. These invisualities mean that power is exercised primarily through the scan as capture, with power characterised as operational and environmental. Recent developments in logistics towards augmented video surveillance and its associated networked images must also be assessed in the context of this mode of power and its economy.

Keywords

Logistics, Barcode, Amazon, Operational Images, Environmentality

Amazon Between Barcode and Face Scan

In a paper published in the *Whole Earth Review* a few months after the 9/11 attacks, entitled "Your face is not a bar code", the computer scientist and humanities scholar Phil Agre (2001) put forward a strong plea for the prohibition of face recognition technologies. A key part of his argument was that it is false to assume that faces are already barcodes: whereas barcodes are machine readable and unique identifiers, faces are much harder to read and to remember for people, and are often mistaken for one another. Effectively, however, what face recognition technologies may achieve is that faces could be treated much like barcodes. As they become machine-readable, images of faces become networked and computable, and thus "easily communicated, compared, stored, and associated with other information" (Agre 2001: 76). Agre's comparison of barcodes and faces highlights the importance of focusing on the specificity of media technologies of capture and surveillance. Whereas barcodes are logistical media for capture widely in use today, face recognition technologies constitute the current high-water mark of surveillance. Are we moving towards the future warned against by Agre, where the face is effectively becoming a barcode, and the barcode scan is being replaced by face recognition? This paper will explore this question in relation to Amazon's logistics, which operate between the barcode and face scan.

Amazon is often portrayed as a surveillance capitalist, one that makes surveillance convenient, intimate and embracing. West considers Amazon to be providing "surveillance-as-a-service", both through "selling products and services consumers can use to conduct surveillance on their own domestic spaces", and by offering surveillance "as a key ingredient for providing personalised goods and services" (2019: 29). The twin technologies at the centre of Amazon's consumer technologies for surveillance are Ring and Alexa. The Ring Always Home Cam, the latest iteration of Amazon's smart home security devices, is a flying indoor security camera that can be directed to fly around and deliver images of indoor space to one's mobile phone. In the promotional video it is used to chase a burglar out of the house.[1] Alexa is Amazon's voice assistant, which can be accessed through many of its devices, most notably the different Echo smart devices Amazon sells for smart homes. What makes Amazon's offers special, according to West, is that "Amazon's tools and techniques of surveillance create tremendous intimacy between consumer and brand – achieved through the sensations of being seen, heard, and known" (ibid.: 31). Munn similarly notes that the Echo can be conceived as an "'architecture of embrace' – a computational zone running in an intimate domestic space" focused on gathering as much information as possible (2018: 94).[2]

In addition to voice recognition, object and face recognition technologies have gained importance in these offers for Amazon's consumers. Rekognition, a product that is part of its Web Services division, is Amazon's deep learning tool that allows its user to "identify objects, people, text, scenes, and activities in images and videos" and "provides highly accurate facial analysis and facial search capabilities" – or so Amazon claims.[3] Rekognition is at work in recent Echo Show devices equipped with Visual ID, which recognises faces both to unlock

---

1   See https://youtu.be/i2jFN_QEcS4.
2   For the sake of clarity of argument in relation to Amazon's logistics, I am leaving out discussions of how Amazon's surveillance technologies also trade in architectures of fear, for example in the way Rekognition has been deployed by U.S. Immigration and Customs Enforcement (Weise 2021), or in the way its Ring technologies "produce fear and paranoia of the racialized Other" (Bridges 2021: 830) when used by police accused of racial profiling. Needless to say, this blurring between state and corporate surveillance (Bridges 2021: 838) also complicates the characterisation of Amazon as a surveillance capitalist (Zuboff 2019: 268).
3   See https://aws.amazon.com/rekognition (accessed 12.08.2021).

devices and to rotate screens to orient towards users' faces. Amazon Astro, the "household robot for home monitoring" introduced in late 2021 and available to select consumers only, similarly relies on object and face recognition to orient itself in space and to address its users.[4] Rekognition is also deployed in Amazon Go stores, and has recently been put in place in other stores such as Starbucks (Lyons 2021). Huberman suggests that Amazon Go stores, equipped with "high ceilings to accommodate the cameras and sensors that are used to meticulously track the movements of merchandise and shoppers", promise convenience in that they make checkouts and their accompanying queues redundant, since tracked goods can be billed automatically (2021: 339). This convenience for Huberman operates "as an ideology that is central to Amazon's abilities to exploit the behavioral surplus of its customers and legitimate new forms of capital accumulation and extraction" (ibid.: 337).

A shift from a focus on the consumers of Amazon's surveillance products to the labour involved in delivering these products (and the convenience associated with them) highlights how surveillance for workers is less embracing and intimate, and more insidious and unpleasant. Whether in the warehouse or in last mile delivery, workers are usually understood to be "subject to a system of total surveillance" (Delfanti 2021b: 68). In the following, by exploring the role of visuality in the management of Amazon's logistical operations in the fulfilment centre in particular, I want to partially contest these accounts. What I will demonstrate is that the kinds of advanced face recognition technologies and their associated networked images have not been established in these warehouses. Rather, what comes to the fore is a more mundane technology: that of the barcode scan. While also implicated in surveillance, I suggest that the barcode scan can be understood more productively as partaking in capture and in a mode of power characterised by environmentality and operationalism, rather than panopticism. Furthermore, Amazon's logistical operations are marked by invisualities produced by calm images such as the barcode, with visuality operationalised for optimising the flows of data, things and people, rather than for visual forms of surveillance. The economy of this mode of power and its invisualities must also be considered when accounting for the ways in which face recognition technologies and augmented video surveillance more broadly are being put to work in logistical operations. Finally, the contrast between how consumers and workers are subjected to these technologies highlights the shifting politics of technology and their distribution between these spheres.

In proceeding, and taking a cue from Agre that the specificity of media technologies of surveillance must be accounted for, I draw on logistical media theory (Hockenberry et al. 2021) to highlight the role of logistical media such as barcode scanners, but also of architecture, in the operations of power in Amazon's

---

4   See https://youtu.be/sj1t3msy8dc.

fulfilment centres. LeCavalier, in his account of Walmart's architecture of fulfilment, notes that there, "architecture's role as a tool has expanded significantly as it operates at different scales to orchestrate desire fulfilment, control territories, discipline bodies, and catalyse cultural growth" (2016: 25; on architecture as media, cf. Kamleithner et al. 2015). We can also expect to find other media of organisation (cf. Beverungen et al. 2019) in Amazon's fulfilment centres, media which, optical or not, serve logistics. Peters has suggested that digital media in particular "traffic [...] in organization, power, and calculation", "serve [...] as logistical devices of tracking and orientation", and their innovations are to be found in "the structures of everyday life and the organization of power" (Peters 2015: 7; on logistical media, cf. Rossiter 2016). What logistical media are to be found in the "continuously computed environments" (Thrift 2008: 95) of logistics at Amazon?

Architecture of Flows and Logistical Media of Capture[5]

The architecture of Amazon's fulfilment centres, whether these were purpose built or not, is extremely reductive – standardised, pre-engineered and prefabricated (Lyster 2016: 156). Not much more than a big shell, the large warehouses contain different areas for the storage of different sized goods in different shelving systems (for stowing and picking by humans, forklifts, or robots), areas for the reception of goods as well as their packing and delivery, plenty of conveyor belts connecting these areas, and of course amenities for labour. There are only few levels, with shelving for robots or human pickers and stowers, usually across three levels, and for bulk items on one level with high ceilings, with conveyor belts higher up and sometimes half levels or balconies stretching across the sides. There are only as many walls as necessary, with many open spaces occupied by machines (e.g., for packing or labelling), conveyor belts, shelves and work stations. The architectural shell of the building is pierced with docking stations for trucks, for delivery and reception of goods, emphasising the way these fulfilment centres are part of wider logistical networks. Architecture becomes infrastructural here, with the building's shell "merely a necessary provision to keep the vast material handling system protected from the elements", which "only obscures the more active process of connecting one interior to another" (LeCavalier 2016: 26, 96). "It's not that architecture has disappeared", Lyster notes: "rather, it has been synthesised into a flow field, such that conduit (flow) and node (space) merge into a single seamless artifact" (2016: 158).

Several hundred people work in fulfilment centres at any one time, and the architecture and material arrangement of the space are geared towards them

---

5   Observations and analysis in this and subsequent sections is informed by two site visits to Amazon fulfilment centres in Germany, interviews with trade union representatives at Amazon, and the newspaper reports and academic literature cited.

fulfilling their role in logistical operations. There are turnstiles at the entrance that can be opened using chip cards, stairs, body scanners at the entrance (to prevent theft), many marked paths, a canteen, toilets, stairs and doors. On the work floor of the fulfilment centre itself, there are a wide variety of stations for receivers, who receive goods, for packers, who pack shipments, and, in the case of fulfilment centres with robots, also stations near the robot zones for stowers, who put goods on shelves, and pickers, who take them off again. The work stations are integrated into the logistical flows via conveyor belts, which move the ubiquitous totes in which goods travel before they are finally packaged for delivery. Stations are equipped with screens, buttons and scanners, in order to both give directions to workers and to track the movement of goods. Those not working at stations, such as stowers and pickers who walk around to store and retrieve goods from shelving, are equipped with handheld scanners which, via screens and sounds, give directions and equally enable goods to be scanned in order to be tracked.

The fulfilment centre as an environment, then, is teeming with logistical media, both fixed and mobile. As Lyster notes with regards to logistical operations more broadly: "Mechanical devices and their digital prosthetics – trackers, codes, responders, and scanners – are collapsed into a synthesised systemic interface" (2016: 156). Here in Amazon's fulfilment centres, it is the logistical media – the scanners, the buttons and the totes – which constitute an interface for the algorithmic system that manages logistical flows and logistical labour. And there is one operation that is central: barcode scanning. All goods, and all containers for goods – the totes, the shelves and the packages – are marked with individual barcodes. And as soon as goods change their place of storage – that is, are put into the tote by a receiver, put onto a shelf by a stower, put back into a tote by a picker, packed by a packer – both the goods and the containers are scanned. Since Amazon wants to track individual goods, all of them are equipped with an individual barcode, rather than the more standard Universal Product Code (UPC) more widely in use (cf. LeCavalier 2016: 63-75 for a history of the barcode). Here, the barcode as a logistical medium acts as a translator, "to translate physical objects into information to be managed", and as one of many "coupling technologies that facilitate the internal compatibility within logistical systems" (LeCavalier 2018: 105).

It is Agre's concept of capture (1994) that explicates this operation of the scan. For Agre, capture originally stems from "the elaborate representational schemes of industrial time and motion studies" (ibid.: 108) such as those of Frederick W. Taylor and Lilian and Frank Gilbreth. Key to the computational operation of capture are two aspects: the capture of data by computer systems and their sensors, and the representational schemes that allow certain processes or semantics to be mapped in the computer system (ibid.: 106). Capture points to a particular operation of power: it is not only a matter of monitoring or recording activity, but equally a matter of imposing the representational schemes as grammars of action (ibid.: 109-110). This is also the case when, in Amazon's fulfilment centres, the handheld scanners or workstations not only record activity by a scan or the push of a button, but give directions to workers. The scanning of individual barcodes generates all the data essential for tracking goods in the warehouse that the algorithmic control system relies on. The data also suffices to manage and assess labour, to prompt team leaders to check on workers, e.g., when their scanning is interrupted or their breaks are taking too long – recorded as "time-off-task". It also allows for all sorts of amalgamated statistics and calculations on performance and productivity. This evaluation and assessment of work on the basis of data generated by scans is the central way in which labour is managed in the warehouse (Delfanti 2021a).

As Kanngieser notes with reference to the use of RFID technologies in logistics, what "is at stake here is an equivocation of agency between workers and the objects they are required to move along the supply chain" (2013: 599). It is through the scanning of objects that the activities of workers are tracked, and this equivocation is far from accidental. Rather, it demonstrates how the scan integrates the management of labour into Amazon's logistical operations. It also points to the economy of this power. As Elmer has reminded us, Foucault insists on the way that "disciplinary mechanisms lie at the heart of the political economy" (Elmer 2012: 25), so that forms of power must coincide with political economic logics, as discipline did for a long time with industrial capitalism. Referring to Deleuze's reading of Foucault and his notion of "control societies" as well (Deleuze 1992), Elmer notes that what comes into view is a "self-governing machine that not only subtly coerces subjects into docile states, but also integrates such subjects into the machinations of wider economies, including the circulation of information and objects" (2012: 27). It is the economy of the scan with its dual function of tracking objects and people which makes it so economical: it becomes key to the circulation of goods in logistics while it enables power to be exercised over workers. What role does visuality play in this economy of power?

Invisualities and Operational Images

The architecture of Amazon's fulfilment centres, then, as well as the spatial arrangement of the different areas for receiving, storing, retrieving, packing and sending goods, is designed so as to optimise logistical flows, rather than surveillance. Consider the layout and arrangement of spaces within the fulfilment centre. Amazon has carried out many zoning studies to optimise "the tricky relationship between time and space in the warehouse" (Lyster 2016: 95). The results of these studies are visible today, for example, in "fast picking zones", where very popular products are stored *en masse* on pallets near stations, or in "batches", where popular products are available for picking at multiple points in the warehouse (ibid.). The movement of bodies around these spaces is part of these studies, with the aim to optimise the movements of bodies rather than make them visible, that is, to reduce the length of the tracks pickers have to follow to pick goods for delivery, speeding up delivery times. Amazon's zoning studies may be reminiscent of the time and motion studies of Taylor and the Gilbreths, which sought to optimise work design and ergonomics for productivity. Yet while their focus, as well as the media of the stopwatch and the camera they deployed, were primarily directed at the human body and its sequential movements (cf. Pias 2017: 32-49; Gregg 2018: 34-40), Amazon's studies on space utilisation are concerned with optimised sequences and arrangements between people and logistical media in space.

Even if the spatial arrangements of architecture and logistical media in the fulfilment centre are not specifically designed for visual surveillance, they are nonetheless amenable to it. There are still a lot of open spaces on the shop floor; the work stations are equipped functionally but not, for example, to reduce visual or acoustic interference; and in particular, team leaders moving around the shop floor can easily visually supervise their team members, and when prompted by the algorithmic system, intervene in their work. Union organisers also report that in some fulfilment centres, there are balconies which do not seem to serve a purpose other than granting managers a bird's eye view of the shop floor. There are also accounts of operations managers who, during busy times such as Prime Day or the busy period prior to Christmas, walk up and down alleys under the roof usually reserved for maintenance – very visibly, in order to let workers know that they are being watched.[6] Yet, contrary to what US-based reports suggest (e.g., Hanley/Hubbard 2020), in fulfilment centres in Germany there is no CCTV surveillance except at the perimeters of the site, and no other ways in which augmented video technologies such as face recognition come into play.[7] In this sense, it would seem the operation of capture executed with the barcode scan is complemented by rather anachronistic forms of human visual surveillance reminiscent of the panopticon (Foucault 1977: 195-228).

Yet where the primary role of visuality in the fulfilment centre comes to the fore lies in the barcode scan itself. Barcodes can be considered what Farocki calls "operational images", that is, "images made by machines for other machines" (Paglen 2014: 1). The advent of operational images, as Paglen recounts, means that "human eyes were becoming anachronistic", with "machines and images starting to 'do' things in the world" and thereby inaugurating a "new visual regime" (ibid.). Veel (2012) suggests that operational images or what she refers to as "calm imaging" is a key feature of ubiquitous computing, and is associated with broader media technological reconfigurations of sensing and attention (cf. Hansen 2012). The barcode is a rather simple example of these calm, operational images, insofar as its informational content is rather limited and fixed, in contrast to examples such as images from drone surveillance or retail motion trackers (Paglen 2014:

---

6   These two aspects were reported to me during interviews with union representatives at fulfillment centres in Germany in 2017.

7   There is, however, the accusation of illegal, automated surveillance also said to include cameras, brought up by a coalition of Amazon employees, trade unionists, lawyers, and civil rights activists as part of the Amazon Workers Against Surveillance coalition. See https://organizeawas.de/en/ (accessed 12.08.2021).

1), where image data potentially yields more patterns than can be algorithmically extracted (Rothöhler 2018: 38). In that way barcodes offer little propensity for further surveillance beyond the immediate recording of the scan itself as it reflects how labour moves things – its economy is exhausted yet effective.

We are thus dealing with the invisualities of Amazon's logistical operations in the fulfilment centre. Invisualities, for MacKenzie and Munster, refers to the operationalisation of images, wherein "observation operates in and through the image but is not *of* the order of the visual" (2019: 6; cf. Azar et al. 2021). As Rothöhler observes with regards to the operationalisation of images in automation: "We are thus surrounded not only by computing machines that can do without human input, but also by image machines that do not value images" (2018: 37). Yet Amazon's fufilment centres are not fully automated (Delfanti/Frey 2021), and the invisualities are complemented by focused kinds of visualities, namely visualisations of the data generated through capture. As Wright notes, visualisations "imply that not all computational processes can be fully automated and left to run themselves", and that human decisions or actions are still called for (2008: 79). So, the screens of handheld scanners or those installed at workstations order workers to complete certain tasks prescribed by the grammars of action inscribed in the warehouse management system. Supervisors sit at mobile workstations staring at screens with various visualisations of performance data for humans and machines, calling for optimisation. In the reception area of the fulfilment centre, screens attached to walls inform workers of their centre's key performance indicators in competition with others, calling for more competition. These visualisations, based on practices of depicting and modelling data, produce particular forms of attention (cf. Halpern 2014: 21-7).

Where automation is more advanced, namely in those fulfilment centres with robots carrying shelves, which effectively make storage mobile, and where "instead of machine buildings populated with robot-like humans" we see a "machine landscape of building-like robots" (LeCavalier 2019: 53), the invisualities of Amazon's logistical operations come to the fore yet more sharply. Several hundred of the robots would be moving around thousands of shelves in flat-surfaced and fenced "human exclusion zones" (LeCavalier 2019), receiving orders through an auction system, and only meeting human workers at the work stations set up at the edges of the fenced area, which humans enter only for repair and maintenance tasks. LeCavalier describes how inhumane (and invisual) these zones are: "the bots only need a small light to scan the codes on the floor. As a result, the human exclusion zone is dark. Dark and quiet. It is large enough that the rows of racks receding in the distance, when viewed from the outside, disappear into the blackness beyond" (ibid.: 54). Since robots orient themselves in space by scanning QR-codes on the floors via infrared scanners, and include other sensors to detect other robots, human operators or other obstacles such as goods that have fallen off shelves (Wurman et al. 2007), little lighting is required. These human exclusion zones are equally zones of invisuality.

Surveillance between Panopticism and Operationalism

The invisualities of Amazon's logistical operations in the fulfilment centre point to a very specific way in which surveillance operates there. It is far less embracing and intimate than Amazon's surveillance technologies for consumers, with logistical media in the fulfilment centre attached less to workers' bodies, being less intimate with them, interacting through quite simple, standard logistical interfaces of buttons and screens. This insight runs somewhat contrary to accounts of Amazon as a leading example of a "despotic", "digital Taylorism" (Staab/Nachtwey 2016; Altenried 2019). According to these accounts, one might have expected more insidious logistical media at work, allowing labour processes to be monitored and evaluated even more meticulously. For example, Moore and Robinson suggest that Amazon monitors workers via "wearable" and "arm-mounted terminals" (2016: 2779). Yet the scanners do not attach to the body in the way quantified self technologies such as Amazon's fitness and health band Amazon Halo do: the handheld scanners merely scan barcodes; they do not collect bodily information or track specific body movements. In that sense they are less invasive than quantified self technologies.

What is striking, nonetheless, in accounts of control in Amazon's fulfilment centres, is how control is experienced as practically total (cf. Beverungen 2021: 12). This is often understood to be an effect of surveillance. Delfanti, for examples, notes that "in the warehouse, workers are subject to a system of total surveillance" (2021b: 68), and Ajunwa et al. cite Amazon as an example of "limitless worker surveillance" (2017: 744). The account here corroborates these positions insofar as the operation of capture through the barcode scan can be considered the technical basis for such surveillance. For a long time, scholars of surveillance have associated these kinds of computation with surveillance, at least since Clarke's coining of the term "dataveillance" (1988). The sense of total control afforded by surveillance and capture is exacerbated by the one-sided opacities actively operationalised in performance management. The performance of individual workers is evaluated on the basis of a single performance indicator, which in itself is opaque and hardly comprehensible, and cannot even be reconstructed by trade unions from various productivity indicators.[8] Delfanti characterises this as "augmented despotism" (2021a: 48-51), effectively a technologically mediated form of arbitrary authority, where managerial decisions that could be transparent are hidden behind opaque machinery.

At the same time, the account here contradicts other accounts on surveillance at Amazon, with regards to both the logistical media at work and the forms of power associated with surveillance. In particular, this is the case for accounts which conceive of power as panoptic. Despite longstanding critiques in scholar-

---

8   This was reported to me by a trade unionist during an interview in 2019.

ship on surveillance of the panoptic frame of analysis and attempts to characterise post-panoptic forms of power (e.g., Boyne 2000; Elmer 2012), the frame of the "electronic panopticon" (Chen 2017) or more recently the "algorithmic panopticon" (Woodcock 2020) is applied in particular to an analysis of power in platform labour. With regards to Amazon, Manokha has forcefully claimed that a move "towards absolute panopticism" can be discerned for workers under digital surveillance, in that "the three main assumptions behind the panopticon" – the omnipresence of the manager, universal visibility, and the presumption of constant surveillance – "are now increasingly fulfilled" (2020: 547). In a similar vein, Delfanti argues, with reference to Foucault, that "Amazon is developing and deploying digital technology that extends and deepens Bentham's panopticon further: [...] workers are constantly watched, recorded, their labour measured, and their activities monitored" (2021b: 69).

It may be a moot point to note that the scan, as an operation of capture on which the algorithmic management of labour in Amazon's fulfilment centres relies, is not "constant" but rather discontinuous. While Delfanti refers to the report by Hanley and Hubbard (2020) mentioned above and mentions a set of other examples of (visual) surveillance, the suggestion that these add up to 'total surveillance' does not account for the US-centricity of the report, nor does it fully explain how visual surveillance relates to the barcode scan. Where Manokha does note that "if workplace surveillance was previously [...] limited to supervisors' eyes, it is now continuous" (2020: 541), he opens an opportunity to reflect on the logistical media of surveillance replacing the line of sight. However, this opportunity is thwarted by insisting on the metaphor of the gaze, when he writes that "with modern means of surveillance, the supervisor is always 'looking', even when not physically present" (ibid.). The argument here is that these nuances matter, insofar as an account of surveillance requires a careful consideration of its economy and its limits. For example, it might be easy to get rid of CCTV cameras, but much harder to get rid of the barcode scan that is so entangled with logistical operations. A political response would thus need to focus less on privacy, as e.g., Zuboff (2019) does, and more on what Rossiter calls the "politics of parameters" (2016: 71-72), which challenges the kinds of parameters through which computational systems record, represent and govern human behaviour.

A focus on the invisualities of logistical operations here highlights two things in particular. On the one hand, it demonstrates the limited way in which the barcode as a rather simple kind of calm image can be repurposed for more elaborate forms of augmented surveillance, particularly in contrast to other calm images operative in augmented video surveillance, which provide such opportunities. On the other hand, attention to the specific ways in which calm imaging works complicates the story of transparent surveillance. The longstanding association of computing with the transparency required for surveillance is remarkable in itself, since it relies on a forgetting of the processes of capture and the generative aspects of computing in constructing representations of the world (Chun

2005; Agre 1997). This is exacerbated with the invisualities described above, since when machines "see", seeing "is no longer centred, singular or indexical of truth or reality, as it was mistakenly thought to be [...], but takes on new distributed and contradictory forms" (Azar et al. 2021: 1095). In particular, "seeing" is neither primarily about humans, nor for humans, so knowing is decoupled from seeing (ibid.: 1098); the coincidence of machine seeing and managerial knowing cannot be assumed. This insight also puts into question the three central premises of the panoptic analysis: the omnipresence of the manager, universal visibility and the presumption of constant surveillance.

The analysis above also – on the other hand – suggests a different analytic of power in contrast to the panoptic. Power here appears as environmental and operational: the invisualities of logistical operations point to the ways in which fulfilment centres become "continuously computed environments" (Thrift 2008: 95). Power here is environmental in the sense that the fulfilment centre as environment becomes programmable, via a paraphernalia of logistical media. Andrejevic points out how sensory monitoring and data-driven control rely on the modulation of environments: "to treat [them] as a flexible, programmable context, analogous to that of virtual reality" (2020: 18). Power here is operational in the way it is coincident with the logistical operations as described above, with capture at the centre of these operations, and in the way this "operationalism" relies on automated responses (ibid.). With reference to Foucault's notion of environmental power (see also Massumi 2009; Gabrys 2016), Hörl notes: "here it is not 'surveillance' but 'capture' that serves as the fundamental concept of Environmentality, whose basic problem consists in capturing and controlling, in managing and modulating behavior, affects, relationships, intensities, and forces." (Hörl 2018: 162). Power moves further away from panoptic and disciplinary logics in modulating human behaviour, beyond the prompts that scanners and screens provide. This power "does not need to tame the wilderness of facts and behaviours; neither does it aim at producing docile subjects"; instead, the subject of this power is a "statistical body", which allows for the establishment of "statistically meaningful correlations" (Rouvroy 2013: 157) to predict and modulate behaviour.

That is not to say that there are no other forms of power at play in Amazon's fulfilment centres, or that the panoptic frame of analysis is wholly exhausted. Amazon complements capture with what remains of the disciplinary effects of surveillance, as sketched above; a lot of competition between precarious workers, teams and different fulfilment centres, to induce more self-discipline; elements of cultural management such as its ubiquitous leadership principles; and even aspects of gamification (cf. Beverungen 2022). As the sociologist Ulrich Bröckling has noted, "making humans governable always uses more than one register" (2017: 194). Yet the focus on economy suggests that these other forms of power are less essential for Amazon's logistical operations, more supplementary to the key operation of capture and its associated invisualities and forms of environmental power. It also explains why face recognition or quantified self technologies are currently seldom in use in the fulfilment centre: it is the economy of the barcode scan that explains why it has persisted despite the way these newer technologies have been hyped and have been ascribed a promise of yet more total surveillance and control.

Beyond the Barcode

How to make sense, then, of the discrepancies between the accounts of Amazon as a surveillance capitalist and a supplier of surveillance-as-a-service, and the account of the rather mundane centrality of the barcode scan for Amazon's logistical operations in the fulfilment centre? One way is to consider the situation a reversal of Winner's discussions of the politics of artefacts, where he noted: "That 'democracy stops at the factory gates' was taken as a fact of life that had nothing to do with the practice of political freedom" (1980: 133). The assumption was that if there was a way to make technology democratic, it would have to be outside places such as Amazon fulfilment centres. The point that Zuboff's work on surveillance capitalism (2019) makes so forcefully is that the kind of instrumentarian power that Amazon and other surveillance capitalists deploy deprives us of our freedom as consumers – Zuboff's attention is on consumers, not workers. So, the counterintuitive argument here is that at least there seem to be constraints in place in the workplace – even at Amazon, more so outside the US, in Europe – which constrain the use of some of the more invasive, total forms of control such as those associated with face recognition technologies, which can be made use of more fully in relation to consumers.

The constraints on the use of these technologies in the workplace – imposed for example by strong trade unions and by regulations on technologies at work – condition the economy of power, thereby contributing to the economy of the barcode scan, and constraining the use of more advanced technologies of capture. However, the COVID-19 pandemic has lefts its mark here as well, at least in the US, and there are suggestions, partly taken up by Delfanti (2021b: 70) and others, that augmented video surveillance is making inroads into fulfilment centres. During the summer of 2020, Amazon introduced "distance assistants" in its fulfilment centres in the US, which were meant to ensure social distancing during the Covid-19 pandemic (Vincent 2020). These were based on augmented video surveillance, which would track workers and measure the distance between bodies. While focused on bodily movements, much like more traditional forms of panoptic surveillance, they also operated and intervened automatically, and thus reproduced the operational, environmental mode of power explored above. They could potentially, if they remain, be repurposed for more elaborate forms of visual surveillance and more minute tracking of bodily movements.

Beyond the fulfilment centre, Amazon experiments more freely with more advanced surveillance technologies – and perhaps sees more of a need to do so, considering the environments in which last mile delivery workers in particular operate, which must be modulated in ways different from the fulfilment centre. Hockenberry suggest that the cultural concept of "cellularity" (2022: 265) is central to programming labour on the last mile through mobile phones. These devices, which are also cameras and image processing machines, bring with them their own operational images, including the barcodes found in the fulfilment centre, but also satellite images or the pictures workers need to take of delivered parcels where "the system does not intend for the consumer to see the worker, the worker need not see the consumer. It is the camera – the system – that sees" (Hockenberry 2022: 273). In early 2021, it was also reported that, in the US, Amazon was deploying AI-powered cameras called Driveri to monitor delivery van drivers (Di Stefano 2021; Delfanti 2021b: 71), which – supposedly for safety – track activities both on the road and around the van as well as the drivers themselves. The instructional video explains in detail the kinds of analytics the system promises, for example, with regards to attention and distraction, road rage and theft. Insofar as the system – developed by a company called Netradyne – connects these calm images to various platforms for machine learning and adds them to operational databases, the system would contribute to kinds of "platform seeing" (MacKenzie/Munster 2019) way beyond what occurs with barcodes in fulfilment centres, and therefore also opens up avenues for quite different modes of surveillance.

Consumers are equally at the behest of Amazon's experiments in modulating environments through logistical media such as the Echo and Ring devices explored in the introduction. Hill suggests that the ubiquity of Amazon's platform creates an unconscious consumption, as we virtually inhabit an omnipresent marketplace: Amazon's platform, as a "central nervous system", hides behind a wide variety of interfaces (2020: 525). Hill describes how the various Alexa voice-controlled devices, such as the Echo devices or Fire tablets, exemplify the disappearance of habitual media and "a process of withholding from awareness what ought to be at the centre of our attention" (ibid.: 524). Bridges similarly suggests that Amazon's devices constitute a kind of "urban camouflage" of its infrastructure and thus an "infrastructural obfuscation" (2021). These effects concern not just those consumers buying the gadgets who consequently become subject to Amazon's behaviour modulation, but also those who may pass the Ring devices pointing towards public spaces, making passers-by subject to "racialized algorithmic sorting" and "data violence" (Bridges 2021: 832). This concern is certainly not alleviated by Amazon Sidewalk, a kind of mesh established between Amazon devices, further networking both these devices and their invisualities.

These cases from the last mile and the home suggest that, beyond the fulfilment centre, a different economy of power reigns, one where the operations of capture are not associated only with the comparatively simple calm images of the barcode, but where Amazon experiments rather freely with object and face recognition technologies that extend and exacerbate the environmental and operational power at play. These technologies produce more elaborate invisualities and forms of "platform seeing" (MacKenzie/Munster 2019), which offer potential for surveillance. The spectre of control certainly looms large here, considering Veel's warning, with reference to the kinds of calm images circulating in technologies of face recognition and neuromarketing, that these technologies "highlight how difficult it is to determine when calmness capsizes in control" (2012: 126). Yet, considering the account offered here of the economy and mode of power associated with the invisualities of Amazon's logistical operations, suggestions that these kinds of arrangements of devices constitute a kind of "surveillant assemblage" (Haggerty/Ericson 2000), which potentially provide total surveillance, may be premature when the limited experimental status of many of these technologies is also considered.

A more fundamental shift in the invisualities of Amazon's logistical operations materialises, however, in the Amazon Go stores mentioned above. While they are currently only operating experimentally in the UK and USA, they are spaces that eliminate the requirement for last mile delivery, as customers come to Amazon to pick up their goods. In Amazon Go stores, customers check-in with their NFC-enabled smartphones, and there is no need for a check-out, as picked-up goods are traced not via scanning or RFID chips but via augmented video cameras, and are automatically charged to the customers' Amazon accounts. Here, the barcode is potentially replaced by other logistical media: "deep learning algorithms, sensors and cameras in the ceiling control the selection, placement and replacement of all the goods, rendering obsolete the iconic barcode" (Lyster 2019: 102). In this way, the central operation of the scan is potentially replaced by augmented video surveillance and object recognition technologies. Here, the continuity of logistical operations become apparent, as Amazon moves further into the heart of cities and as customers are reimagined as picking agents: "Amazon makes little distinction between a customer in a shop or picking agent working at their fulfillment centers. In fact, it stresses the similarities between the two: both locate items from an inventory" (Stewart 2018). Being caught, never mind whether as workers or consumers, in these modulated environments, perhaps augmented video surveillance and its associated networked images may slowly precipitate a further shift in the economies of power and the invisualities of Amazon's logistical operations.

The author would like to thank Ilia Antenucci, Maja-Lee Voigt and Daniela Wentz for comments on earlier versions of this paper.

References

Agre, Philip (2001): "Your Face Is Not a Bar Code." In: Whole Earth Review 106/ Winter, pp. 74-7.

Agre, Philip (1994): "Surveillance and Capture: Two Models of Privacy." In: The Information Society 10/2, pp. 101-27.

Agre, Philip (1997): "Beyond the Mirror World: Privacy and the Representational Practices of Computing." In: Philip Agre/Marc Rotenberg (eds.), Technology and Privacy: The New Landscape, Cambridge, MA: MIT Press, pp. 29-61.

Ajunwa, Ifeoma/Crawford, Kate/Schultz, Jason (2017): "Limitless Worker Surveillance." In: California Law Review 105/3, pp. 735-76.

Altenried, Moritz (2019): "On the Last Mile: Logistical Urbanism and the Transformation of Labour." In: Work Organisation, Labour & Globalisation 13/1, pp. 114-29.

Andrejevic, Mark (2020): Automated Media, New York, NY: Routledge.

Azar, Mitra/Cox, Geoff/Impett, Leonardo (2021): "Introduction: Ways of Machine Seeing." In: AI & SOCIETY 36/4, pp. 1093-1104.

Beverungen, Armin (2021): "Remote Control: Algorithmic Management of Circulation at Amazon." In: Marcus Burkhardt/Mary Shnayien/Katja Grashöfer (eds.), Explorations in Digital Cultures, Lüneburg: meson press, online first.

Beverungen, Armin (2022): „Automatisiertes Verhalten: Regierungskünste Bei Amazon." In: Georg Toepfer/Sophie Gräfe (eds.), Wissensgeschichte des Verhaltens. Interdisziplinäre Perspektiven, Berlin: DeGruyter, forthcoming.

Beverungen, Armin/Beyes, Timon/Conrad, Lisa (2019): "The Organizational Powers of (Digital) Media." In: Organization 26/5, pp. 621-35.

Boyne, Roy (2000): "Post-Panopticism." In: Economy and Society 29/2, pp. 285-307.

Bridges, Lauren (2021): "Infrastructural Obfuscation: Unpacking the Carceral Logics of the Ring Surveillant Assemblage." In: Information, Communication & Society 24/6, pp. 830-849.

Bröckling, Ulrich (2017): Gute Hirten Führen Sanft: Über Menschenregierungskünste, Berlin: Suhrkamp.

Chen, Julie Yujie (2017): "Technologies of Control, Communication, and Calculation: Taxi Drivers' Labour in the Platform Economy." In: Phoebe V. Moore/Martin Upchurch/Xanthe Whittaker (eds.), Humans and Machines at Work: Monitoring, Surveillance and Automation in Contemporary Capitalism, New York, NY: Springer, pp. 231-252.

Chun, Wendy H.K. (2005): "On Software, or the Persistence of Visual Knowledge." In: Grey Room 18, pp. 26-51.

Clarke, Roger (1988): "Information Technology and Dataveillance." In: Communications of the ACM 31/5, pp. 498-512.

Deleuze, Gilles (1992): "Postscript on the Societies of Control." In: October 5, pp. 3-7.

Delfanti, Alessandro (2021a): "Machinic Dispossession and Augmented Despotism: Digital Work in an Amazon Warehouse." In: New Media & Society 23/1, pp. 39-55.

Delfanti, Alessandro (2021b): The Warehouse: Workers and Robots at Amazon, London: Pluto Press.

Delfanti, Alessandro/Frey, Bronwyn (2021): "Humanly Extended Automation or the Future of Work Seen through Amazon Patents." In: Science, Technology, & Human Values 46/3, pp. 655-82.

Elmer, Greg (2012): "Panopticon – Discipline – Control." In: Kirstie Ball/Kevin D. Haggerty/David Lyon (eds.), Routledge Handbook of Surveillance Studies, Abingdon and New York, NY: Routledge, pp. 21-9.

Foucault, Michel (1977): Discipline and Punish: The Birth of the Prison, trans. A. Sheridan, New York: Vintage.

Gabrys, Jennifer (2016): Program Earth: Environmental Sensing Technology and the Making of a Computational Planet, Minneapolis: University of Minnesota Press.

Gregg, Melissa (2018): Counterproductive: Time Management in the Knowledge Economy, Durham: Duke University Press.

Haggerty, Kevin D./Ericson, Richard V. (2000): "The Surveillant Assemblage." In: The British Journal of Sociology 51/4, pp. 605-22.

Halpern, Orit (2014): Beautiful Data: A History of Vision and Reason since 1945, Durham: Duke University Press.

Hanley, Daniel A./Hubbard, Sally (2020): Eyes Everywhere: Amazon's Surveillance Infrastructure and Revitalizing Worker Power, Washington D.C.: Open Market Institute.

Hansen, Mark B. N. (2012): "Ubiquitous Sensation: Toward an Atmospheric, Collective, and Microtemporal Model of Media." In: Ulrik Ekman (ed.), Throughout: Art and Culture Emerging with Ubiquitous Computing, Cambridge: MIT Press, pp. 63-88.

Hill, David W. (2020): "The Injuries of Platform Logistics." In: Media, Culture & Society 42/4, pp. 521-36.

Hockenberry, Matthew (2022): "Cellular Capitalism: Life and Labor at the End of the Digital Supply Chain." In: Mark Graham/Fabian Ferrari (eds.), Digital Work in the Planetary Market, Cambridge: The MIT Press, pp. 263-80.

Hockenberry, Matthew/Starosielski, Nicole/Zieger, Susan (eds.) (2021): Assembly Codes: The Logistics of Media, Durham: Duke University Press.

Hörl, Erich (2018): "The Environmentalitarian Situation." Trans. N. F. Schott. In: Cultural Politics 14/2, pp. 153-73.

Huberman, Jenny (2021): "Amazon Go, Surveillance Capitalism, and the Ideology of Convenience." In: Economic Anthropology 8/2, pp. 337-49.

Kamleithner, Christa/Meyer, Roland/Weber, Julia (2015): „Medien / Architekturen. Einleitung in den Schwerpunkt." In: Zeitschrift für Medienwissenschaft 12/1, pp. 10-18.

Kanngieser, Anja (2013): „Tracking and Tracing: Geographies of Logistical Governance and Labouring Bodies." In: Environment and Planning D 31/4, pp. 594-610.

LeCavalier, Jesse (2016): The Rule of Logistics: Walmart and the Architecture of Fulfillment, Minneapolis and London: University of Minnesota Press.

LeCavalier, Jesse (2018): "New Interfaces in the Automated Landscapes of Logistics." In: FOOTPRINT 23, pp. 105-14.

LeCavalier, Jesse (2019): "Human Exclusion Zones: Logistics and New Machine Landscapes." In: Architectural Design 89/1, pp. 48-55.

Lyons, Kim (2021): "New Starbucks Pickup Store in NYC Uses Amazon Go Cashierless Technology." In: The Verge, November 18 (https://www.theverge.com/2021/11/18/22789116/starbucks-pickup-store-amazon-go-cashierless-technology).

Lyster, Clare (2016): Learning from Logistics: How Networks Change Our Cities, Basel: Birkhäuser.

Lyster, Clare (2019): "Disciplinary Hybrids: Retail Landscapes of the Post-Human City." In: Architectural Design 89/1, pp. 100-5.

MacKenzie, Adrian/Munster, Anna (2019): "Platform Seeing: Image Ensembles and Their Invisualities." In: Theory, Culture & Society 36/5, pp. 3-22.

Manokha, Ivan (2020): "The Implications of Digital Employee Monitoring and People Analytics for Power Relations in the Workplace." In: Surveillance & Society 18/4, pp. 540-54.

Massumi, Brian (2009): "National Enterprise Emergency: Steps Toward an Ecology of Powers." In: Theory, Culture & Society 26/6, pp. 153-85.

Moore, Phoebe V./Robinson, Andrew (2016): "The Quantified Self: What Counts in the Neoliberal Workplace." In: New Media & Society 18/11, pp. 2774-2792.

Munn, Luke (2018): Ferocious Logics: Unmaking the Algorithm, Lüneburg: meson press.

Paglen, Trevor (2014): "Operational Images." In: E-Flux 59/November, pp. 1-3.

Peters, John D. (2015): The Marvelous Clouds: Toward a Philosophy of Elemental Media, Chicago: University of Chicago Press.

Pias, Claus (2017): Computer Game Worlds, Zurich: Diaphanes.

Rossiter, Ned (2016): Software, Infrastructure, Labor: A Media Theory of Logistical Nightmares, New York: Routledge Taylor & Francis Group.

Rothöhler, Simon (2018): "Calm Images." In: MERKUR 72/833, pp. 32-42.

Rothöhler, Simon (2021): "Calm Images: The Invisible Visual Culture of Digital Image Distribution." In: Olga Moskatova (ed.), Images on the Move: Materiality – Networks – Formats, Bielefeld: transcript, pp. 73-86.

Rouvroy, Antoinette (2013): "The End(s) of Critique: Data Behaviourism versus Due Process." In: Mirellie Hildebrandt/Katja de Vries (eds.), Privacy, Due Process and the Computational Turn: The Philosophy of Law Meets the Philosophy of Technology, London: Routledge, pp. 143-67.

Staab, Philip/Nachtwey, Oliver (2016): "Market and Labour Control in Digital Capitalism." In: TripleC: Communication, Capitalism & Critique 14/2, pp. 457-474.

Stewart, Matthew (2018): "Amazon Urbanism: Patents and The Totalizing World of Big Tech Futures." In: Failed Architecture, May 23 (https://failedarchitecture.com/amazon-urbanism-patents-and-the-totalizing-world-of-big-tech-futures/).

Thrift, Nigel (2008): Non-Representational Theory: Space, Politics, Affect, Abingdon: Routledge.

Veel, Kristin (2012): "Calm Imaging: The Conquest of Overload and the Conditions of Attention." In: Ulrik Ekman (ed.), Throughout: Art and Culture Emerging with Ubiquitous Computing, Cambridge, MA: MIT Press, pp. 119-32.

Vincent, James (2020, October 1): "Amazon's Palm Reading Starts at the Grocery Store, but It Could Be so Much Bigger." In: The Verge, October 1 (https://www.theverge.com/2020/10/1/21496673/amazon-one-palm-reading-vein-recognition-payments-identity-verification).

Weise, Karen (2021): "Amazon Indefinitely Extends a Moratorium on the Police Use of Its Facial Recognition Software." In: The New York Times, May 18 (https://www.nytimes.com/2021/05/18/business/amazon-police-facial-recognition.html).

West, Emily (2019): "Amazon: Surveillance as a Service." In: Surveillance & Society 17/1/2, pp. 27-33.

Winner, Langdon (1980): "Do Artifacts Have Politics?" In: Daedalus 109/1, pp. 121-36.

Woodcock, Jamie (2020): "The Algorithmic Panopticon at Deliveroo: Measurement, Precarity, and the Illusion of Control." In: ephemera: Theory & Politics in Organization 20/3, pp. 67-95.

Wurman, Peter R. et al. (2007): "System and Method for Maneuvering a Mobile Drive Unit." December 20 (https://patents.google.com/patent/US20070290040A1/en?oq=US20070290040A1).

Zuboff, Shoshana (2019): The Age of Surveillance Capitalism: The Fight for a Human Future at the New Frontier of Power, New York: PublicAffairs.

Automated Vision

Apple Memories and Automated Memory-Making

The Networked Image Inside the iPhone Chip

Gabriel Pereira

Abstract

In 2016, for the first time Apple introduced what it called "advanced computer vision" to organise and curate users' images. The key selling point for Apple Memories was that all computation would happen inside the user's device, relying on the privacy afforded by Apple's widely used smartphone, the iPhone. This article offers a case study of Apple Memories and its automated memory-making, focusing on three dimensions: the vision of Apple Memories; how this vision gets infrastructured through the A11 Bionic chip; and how Apple Memories engages users in automated memory-making. This analysis raises important questions regarding privacy and surveillance capitalism as, even if operating on-device, Apple Memories still relies on the datafication of the personal archive via the automation of image analysis (computer vision) and personalisation. Building upon Mackenzie and Munster's (2019) notion of "platform seeing", I argue that control over the networked image today goes beyond data brokering for behavioural analysis and advertising. Apple Memories' framing of computer vision as an intimate, always-on and personal way of remembering is part of a wider goal of exploiting personal data to bolster user engagement, generate even more data, and ultimately accumulate infrastructural power across Apple's "walled garden" digital ecosystem.

Keywords

Surveillance Capitalism, Infrastructure, Computer Vision, Networked Image, Platform Vision

Apple Memories and Automated Memory-Making: The Networked Image Inside the iPhone Chip

In 2016, for the first time Apple introduced what it called "advanced computer vision" (Federighi 2016) to organise and curate users' images. This move marked a shift from the company's previous focus on creating easier ways for users to sort through their own content. The new application, Apple Memories, "automatically creates curated collections of your most meaningful photos and videos" through a colossal "11 billion computations per photo" (Federighi 2016). The timing of this announcement was conspicuous, as just a year earlier a similar application had been released: Google Photos, a cross-platform app that automatically organises images uploaded to Google's cloud service. What was particularly new about Apple Memories, and what became its key selling point, was that all computation would happen inside the user's device, relying on the privacy afforded by Apple's widely used smartphone, the iPhone.

Before the digital era, personal archives were primarily composed of laminated pictures, cassette tapes, letters and other memorabilia that were stored and shared mostly in the private sphere. Digitisation transformed these archives into digital objects, accessed and managed through software and networks (van Dijck 2007). Images and videos became data: shared through platforms as well as "analysed and remapped to new contexts via algorithms" (Rubinstein/Sluis 2008: 21). Apple Memories continues this history by bringing computer vision analysis and personalised recommendations to remediate images and videos into "Memories": automatically curated and labelled collections one can export as videos or just save for future appreciation. As the algorithm operates on the iPhone itself, the promise is that the simpler past of personal archives organised as carefully-kept boxes can be revived, as opposed to other companies' reliance on the ethereal "cloud".

Just a year before the launch of Apple Memories, the term "surveillance capitalism" was proposed by scholar Shoshana Zuboff. Zuboff used this term to address the "institutionalizing practices and operational assumptions of Google Inc." (2015: 75) and other large Internet-based firms, particularly in how they extract and collect data to predict future user behaviour for advertisement targeting. As she further develops in her 2018 book, surveillance capitalism does not only seek to know people's behaviour well enough to predict their next steps, it also aims at modifying behaviour. This, she argues, puts individual autonomy, what she terms "the right to the future tense" (Zuboff 2018: 329), under threat. Zuboff's arguments, though subject to criticism from some scholars (cf. Doctorow 2020; Morozov 2019; Sadowski/Ongweso Jr 2020), have found much resonance in scholarship, popular media (e.g., Orlowski's *The Social Dilemma*, 2020) and the wider public debate, particularly in discussions around personal data privacy and the political economy of digital capitalism.

Although very critical of Google and Facebook, Zuboff is quite lenient on Apple, even arguing that the company "has so far drawn a line, pledging to abstain from many of the practices that I locate in the surveillance capitalist regime" (2018: 23). Indeed, already in 2014, Apple's CEO Tim Cook declared the company's intentions on privacy by saying: "Our business is not based on having information about you. You're not our product" (Wakabayashi 2014). As the company's business model relies on selling hardware products and services, not advertisements, Cook's argument is that Apple and its privacy-oriented applications such as

Apple Memories are the antidote to Google and Facebook's surveillance capitalist practices.

However, even if operating on-device and in a privacy-preserving manner, Apple Memories still relies on the datafication of the personal archive via the automation of image analysis (computer vision) and personalisation. As I argue through this article, control of the networked image today goes beyond buying and selling data for behavioural analysis and advertising. Building upon Mackenzie and Munster's (2019) notion of "platform seeing", my argument is that the infrastructures of machine seeing are important means for the consolidation of platform power. To engage in this issue, this article offers a case study of Apple Memories and its automated memory-making. It focuses on three dimensions: 1) the vision of Apple Memories; 2) how this vision gets infrastructured through the iPhone hardware (the A11 Bionic chip), and 3) how Apple Memories engages users in automated memory-making. By bridging these facets, I discuss the consequences Apple Memories raises for notions of privacy and surveillance capitalism, making the suggestion to think instead of platform and infrastructural power.

This article is framed on a methodological sensitivity to both the "algorithmic imaginary" (Bucher 2017: 31) proposed by Apple, and how it is transformed into materiality – the iPhone's chip as well as the app's interface and affordances. Aligning with previous scholarship that avoids the "immaterial trope" (Blanchette 2011: 1043), this strategy of engagement opens "a space to examine how objects and object properties frame cultural practice" (Dourish 2017: 47; Parks 2015). Algorithmic formations are thus not only technical, but sociotechnical – formed by intricate relations between software, hardware, institutions, people and other non-human actors (Seaver 2017; Amoore 2020).

I begin this article by reviewing previous literature on the relations between memory-making, networked images and computer vision. Then, I move on to three analytical sections. The first engages in a critical discourse analysis of the vision behind Apple Memories, particularly how it is marketed as an experience by its developers. The materials analysed are Apple's rhetoric on the Memories feature during its conferences for software developers, WWDC (2016 to 2018). The second analytical section focuses on the A11 Bionic chip and its "infrastructural politics" (Parks/Starosielski 2015), engaging with Apple's presentation of it (iPhone X unveil and press materials describing the chip) as well as its particular architecture.[1] The third analytical section offers a brief reflection on the actual user experience of the application. Though not discussed in depth here, this finding originates from a broader systematic analysis of Apple Memories' interface and affordances (Bucher/Helmond 2017), which followed the walkthrough method

---

1   To understand the emerging dynamics of chip architecture, I consulted hardware design books and conducted two expert interviews with chip design researchers.

proposed by Light, Burgess and Duguay (2018).[2] Finally, in the discussion section, I argue how Apple Memories' shift of computer vision and personalisation to the intimacy and proximity of the smartphone entails important questions about platform and infrastructural power.

Memory-Making in the Age of the Networked Image

Technology and memory-making have always been interconnected. As described by philosopher Bernard Stiegler (2010), embodied memory-making (i.e. what we recollect or remember as we go through the world) has always related to different forms of technical exteriorisation. These exteriorisations have moved through different kinds of objects, records and traces in the history of humanity – from cave drawings to photographs. What is particularly recent, though, is the digitisation of memory-making. José van Dijck suggests thinking about this digital shift as mediated memory-making: "the activities and objects we produce and appropriate by means of media technologies for creating and re-creating a sense of past, present, and future of ourselves in relation to others" (2007: 21). Digitisation, she argues, comes with decisive consequences and "is likely to affect our very concepts of memory and remembering" (ibid.: 50).

This article is concerned with the important role that images and videos play in our mediated memory-making today. The Internet and its networked character have undoubtedly brought seismic changes to the "production, distribution, consumption and storage of images" (Rubinstein/Sluis 2008: 9). We not only produce an enormous number of images every day, but also constantly share them through social media platforms and other networks (cf. Leaver et al., 2020). These images have led to new photographic practices, connected to "a more alive, immediate and often transitory practice/form", one that is often an "immediate, rather fleeting display of one's discovery of the small and mundane" (Murray 2008: 151). Beyond the content of these images, a key shift is how photos are now born-digital "data pieces" that afford automated organisation and classification (Mackenzie/Munster 2019). As images become data, they are now "influenced by computational processing, algorithmic query, automation, and dynamism, not to mention social conditions, user expectations, technology dependencies, storage requirements, and a host of other characteristics of how we create and use technology" (Bailey 2013). Throughout this article, I refer to the networked image as this recent paradigm of image relations marked by networked and datafied condi-

---

2 As part of the larger project from which this article stems, I employed and further analysed the app using the tools of "step-by-step observation and documentation of an app's screens, features, and flows of activity", as suggested by Light, Burgess and Duguay (2018: 882).

tions, which is intricately tied to the emergence and popularisation of the smartphone as a sensing technology (McCosker/Wilken 2020).

The networked image's "information overload" (Seaver 2019) has led companies to offer services for curating and remixing our images for us. Among others, Apple Memories and Google Photos have become popular products, with features to automatically cut through the clutter of our personal archives using personalised algorithms. This shift towards "automated memory-making" (Pereira 2019; Jacobsen/Beer 2021) embeds an algorithmic and predictive logic into how we remember and forget. In these applications, the archive is no longer a static collection of images, but formed of relational elements in a computerised network, where the algorithm "autonomously [classifies] and [ranks] people's past content to produce and deliver these ready-packaged 'memories'" (Jacobsen/Beer 2021: 22). A crucial driving assumption that enables this shift to automation is that the networked image, much like all else in the world, is data: "made of things that fit in stable and distinct categories" (Mackenzie 2015: 433; cf. Jacobsen/Beer 2021: 34-35). That means the system is based on a particular set of assumptions of what images and memories can be, and how much they (supposedly) matter to individuals.

As argued by scholar Benjamin N. Jacobsen, automated memory-making applications such as Apple Memories create "narratives about people's lives in everyday life" (2020a: 1). Through the concept of "algorithmic emplotment", Jacobsen suggests how these narratives are constituted: "data, people, objects, events, and temporalities are variously correlated and woven together, construed into coherent narratives, where causation and intelligibility are given" (ibid.: 13). It is important to foreground how the creation of such algorithmic narratives relies on automated decisions on what to prioritise and make visible (c.f. Amoore 2020; Gillespie 2014). This form of giving power to substitutes that act for us is much akin to what Hito Steyerl (2014) has termed "proxy politics": "Does your camera decide what appears in your photographs? Does it go off when you smile? And will it fire in a next step if you don't?" Algorithms, these "intricate, dynamic arrangements of people and code" (Seaver 2019: 419), affect people as they surface some narratives as opposed to others, shaping the way people interact with their archives by defining what is meaningful (Jacobsen 2020a: 7).

This algorithmic character of automated memory-making is not only present in what images it surfaces, but also in the algorithmic analysis of the images themselves. Computer vision, the algorithms for interpreting images into data, allows for different forms of visual perception, such as scene analysis and object recognition. Although these systems present themselves as efficient and objective, they have been described by critical scholarship as limited "calculative practices", marked by ways of seeing with "human-machine prejudices such as those related to gender and race" (Azar et al. 2021: 1095). In short, applications such as Apple Memories rely on the automated reduction of all the possibilities of what is in an image into "a single human-readable and actionable meaning" (Amoore 2020:

156). This reduction, for example, does not consider each particular image's "context, history, and subtext" (Pereira/Moreschi 2020: 1202).

Finally, automated memory-making also implies a form of "dataveillance", a "continuous surveillance through the use of (meta)data" (van Dijck, 2014). Users give algorithms access to their images to sort through them, most often operating under-the-surface and generating information which is shared inconspicuously with other algorithms, part of what Paglen (2016) called "machine-to-machine seeing". Algorithmically generated information about images may be used to feed memory recommendations in an app, but also for targeted advertisement or other forms of monetisation. It is most often very difficult to note and trace these operations, which explains why much scholarly discussion has focused on how dataveillance operates in "the cloud" (see van Dijck 2014; Myers West 2017). However, this is not the only architecture possible. As will be discussed in this article, the smartphone can also serve as a technology for automated data extraction and analysis.

The Vision of Apple Memories: Emotive and Private Technology

The algorithm is a proxy for automated memory-making in Apple Memories, defining how images and videos are sorted, organised and ranked (cf. Jacobsen/Beer 2021). But how is this relation framed by Apple? I now focus on analysing how Apple's marketing presents its automated memory-making, depicting the algorithm as an emotive technology that can conveniently and efficiently surface the users' affective relations with their networked images. However, this intimacy is only to be trusted due to the way it functions privately and offline ("all on device").

Apple Memories was first presented at WWDC 2016, during a keynote by Apple's senior VP of Software Engineering Craig Federighi. Apple Worldwide Developers Conference (WWDC) is a yearly event held by Apple in San José, California (USA). It is directly targeted towards software developers and has an attendance of around 6,000 people. The conference has existed since 1983, with the main proposition of engaging its developer community in technical and design-focused sessions, hands-on labs and other activities. In the past two decades, Apple began to unveil new hardware, software and operating systems during the conference. The audience, composed mostly of technophiles, is always hungry for the release of new and improved technologies, and Apple capitalises on their presence as a way of both generating buzz on new products and further connecting them to the company's "walled garden" ecosystem.

Touted as "the big news in Photos", the advanced computer vision in Apple Memories was described as a way to analyse users' pictures and videos completely on-device by "taking advantage of the power of the advanced silicon". Federighi (2016) started his presentation by explaining that deep learning would now be used not only to recognise people's faces, but also objects and scenes. He boasted: "we do 11 billion computations per photo to be able to detect things like: there's a horse, there's water, there's a mountain" (ibid.). That, he said, allows for you to search images on device, but "the magic in experiencing your photos isn't just about finding the photo you're looking for, it's about being reminded serendipitously of a memory that would be so special" (ibid.). Behind this serendipity would be the algorithm of Apple Memories, based on a state-of-the-art artificial intelligence that "clusters together photos and relates them based on location, the people involved, the scenes" (ibid.) (see Fig. 1). That was the first time that Apple had announced a shift from empowering users to curate their own images to the implementation of an automated process, whereby an algorithm selects and curates the user's archive into video collages, albums and search results.

Fig. 1: Screenshot from Federighi's 2016 WWDC Keynote: In the image, photos of a trip are clustered together (location, people involved, scenes) in an imaginary tridimensional network.

The most striking aspect of Federighi's presentation of Memories in 2016 is how strongly it proposes this new technology as having an emotive character. I use the word emotive here to signify "arousing intense feeling" (Stark 2019: 120), thus "intensifying affect, feeling, sensation, and even emotion" (ibid.: 121). In this sense, the AI behind Memories is presented as capable of surfacing the underlying affective relations of one's archive by connecting images' metadata (location, time) and content (people, scenes, objects) (see Fig. 1). Federighi's (2016) argument is that we take too many pictures, but "we never go back to actually assemble them into something we'd want to watch". The benefit of the user experience of Apple Memories relies precisely on automating the affective relations of image curation: "we can figure out that you might want to see photos of a highlight reel of the last weekend or the last year and offer those to you at just the right time" (ibid.). What sets these connections apart, in Federighi's words, is that they are the "most relevant to you", "people that are special to you", "the most special photos" or "highlights" (ibid.). The algorithm is described as an emotive technology, with the power of predicting the user's affective memories, of making the invisible emotional connections with the images visible.

The emotive character of Memories is reiterated in Federighi's keynotes during WWDC 2017 and 2018. Incremental features are added: In 2017, the potential to "capture things like activities, like scuba diving [...], anniversaries, these really touching memories of your children growing up, and most importantly, your pets" (Federighi 2017). In WWDC 2018, a tab called "For You" is introduced to the Photos app, where all Memories are collected, but also where the algorithm highlights "a photo that you took on this day in past years" (Federighi 2018). For the 3 years it was discussed on WWDC, the Memories feature was described consistently as the careful traversal of the personal archive to automate the thoughtful, loving look to the past for your convenience ("so you don't have to").

Apple Memories' construction as an emotive actant becomes even more pronounced in the 2017 ad spot entitled "The Archives" (see Figs. 2 and 3). In the ad, we see a bespectacled elderly man as he traverses multi-storied archive rooms, selecting bits and pieces of film and moving photos. A mellow song plays as he cuts the images by hand and watches excerpts on TV screens, putting them together in a film. We then see the grey-haired man's final *oeuvre* as his eyes become watery and a soft tune is played. It shows a moving collage of special moments of a family through time. This video, as we find out, is actually being played on an iPhone that is held by a crying woman. She then presses a button on the iPhone's screen that says "Best of the Year 2016", and we see a light turn on in the man's archival room. He briefly glances at it and goes back into the archive. The texts "Memories", "Movies Made for You on iPhone 7", and "Practically Magic" come onto the screen, as we see the old man walking through the old-school setting of the archive once again.

This ad complements Apple's presentations at WWDC in that it materialises the underlying imaginary proposed by Apple Memories' corporate-speak. The ad's depiction of the archive resonates with its most popular conception: "slightly obsolete and abandoned places where usually the archivist or the caretaker is someone swallowed up in the dusty corridors of bureaucracy, information management, and organisational logic that makes the archive a system" (Ernst 2012: 1). Apple Memories, however, directly breaks with this bureaucratic conception of the archive. As rhetorically represented in the ad, we have a trove of personal data (the archive) that can be automatically edited on the push of a button (instantly, magically) by a loving, well-intentioned algorithm (the old man). Consequently, this experience will generate results that are emotive: the touching, tear-in-the-eye positive surprise of seeing the images serendipitously selected by the algorithm. The ad's depiction of film reels, old editing machines, file cabinets and other paraphernalia also connect the algorithm to old-school memory-making and its family rituals, reminding of a nostalgic past whose emotional overtones the algorithm claims to emulate.

Figs. 2 & 3: Screenshots from the ad spot "The Archives" (2107) presents an elderly man (above), carefully curating images inside of the iPhone. The result is shown in the user's hands (below): "Practically Magic".

It is important to relate this intimacy and emotive character of Apple Memories to its key selling point: the fact that the app operates on-device, as opposed to on the "cloud". This privacy aspect was frequently mentioned in Apple's WWDC keynotes, through constant reaffirmation that Apple "is out of the loop" and "won't see [your] data". In a WWDC 2016 talk show, it was even described by a commentator as a "180-degree different tactic" (Caldwell/Sargent 2016) than that used by Google and Facebook, because images do not need to be transferred outside of the user's personal space, their mobile device. The framing of Memories as an emotive technology relies on this safeguarding of privacy. "The Archives" ad relates to this: the elderly man (algorithm) works alone and carefully to manually curate memories, further sedimenting this notion of secrecy and trust, privacy and nostalgia. This representation of intimacy can be contrasted to the attempt by data centres to project safety through impersonal, "emptied, technified spaces" (Holt/Vonderau 2015: 72).

Memories is framed in Apple's marketing speak as a personalised experience that is unique to the users and their affective relations. I suggest understanding it through its emotive character, how it "intensif[ies] the experience and expression of human feelings" (Stark 2019: 118). The app promises the automation of the emotional relation with the archive, but in a way that is actually caring and intimate. As opposed to the widely disseminated view of the algorithm as a distant, cold calculation or even as a form of uncontrolled data extraction without privacy, Apple Memories symbolises the promise of "Practically Magic". It understands your images and emotions, while operating within the privacy of your phone.

The Infrastructure of Apple Memories: Continuous and Optimised Platform Seeing

The rise of Apple Memories and its vision of emotion and privacy is enabled by a new generation of embedded hardware systems. Looking at this material aspect augments the understanding of the vision behind Apple Memories as well as indicates what lies behind it. I will now turn to how the A11 iPhone chip operates as a visible infrastructure for the private operation of applications like Apple Memories, while also building an infrastructure for "platform seeing" (Mackenzie/Munster 2018).

The story of the A11 Bionic chip goes back a decade before its 2017 launch. In 2008, just one year after the release of the first iPhone, Apple's founder Steve Jobs laid a clear strategy for the future: for the company to differentiate itself, he proposed, "you have to own your own silicon. [...] You have to control and own it" (Stone et al. 2016). He went on to develop a long-term plan: Apple needed to design the chip that would be inside its smartphones. The A4 chip became, in 2010, the first product that originated from the shift to Apple-designed chips.

By 2017, Apple released its thirteenth chip, the A11 Bionic, as part of the unveiling of the iPhone X. It was described as the "most powerful and smartest chip ever in a smartphone" (Pangambam 2017), with Phil Schiller (senior VP of Worldwide Marketing) touting its capabilities: "everything we've seen is powered in iPhone X by the amazing new A11 Bionic chip" (ibid.). Throughout the reveal, the chip was represented as an immense two-dimensional dark square, and each of its new parts was discussed. One key innovation was highlighted in particular: the Neural Engine. Promised as a game-changer, the Neural Engine would embed predictive computing into the chip's architecture itself. Phil Schiller described it as

a specialized hardware built for a specific set of machine learning algorithms. This is another example of the incredible collaboration between the hardware and software teams that's only possible at Apple. The Neural Engine is a state-of-the-art ultrafast processing system that uses the highest density computing ever. It's a dual core design; it can perform over 600 billion operations per second. (ibid.)

Beyond the immense buzz, the Neural Engine (or NPU) can be understood as a hardware accelerator for machine learning functionalities – more specifically, deep learning. Because AI has become such an important part of the computation Apple sees as important in smartphone systems, chip design now dedicates some of the "silicon real state" to do the kinds of computation specific to deep learning (massively parallel operations) (see Mackenzie/Munster 2018: 17). In other words, rather than using the CPU or the GPU for AI, the NPU is designed to do only this specific type of computation, thus optimising speed and battery consumption.

This infrastructuring of prediction in the smartphone can be understood through the emergence of "platform seeing" (Mackenzie/Munster 2019). This concept suggests that a new mode of visuality unfolds from the fact that images today are "not simply quantified, but labelled, formatted and made 'platform-ready'" already through their "persistent processing by everyday devices" (ibid.: 8). Mackenzie & Munster assert that, in contemporary times, images exist within *"ensembles"* (large swaths of image data), a consequence of their "plat-formatting" (ibid.: 15, original emphasis). As such, visual culture is now distributed and invisible, focused much more on operational functions and Big Data ensembles than its historical goal of representation. A crucial element of this shift is its reliance on new hardware, e.g., the A11 Bionic chip, which transforms images into connected data by "the intermediating agency – at once technical, cultural, economic, and political – of the platform as ongoing operations that transform, order and circulate" (ibid.: 9).

As the NPU is embedded into the iPhone, the smartphone becomes a platform for predictive capabilities. The concept of "platform" here goes beyond the everyday understanding of social media platforms such as Facebook, connecting it instead to platform studies' focus on "computing devices" and "software environments" (see e.g., Plantin et al. 2018). Platforms are systems that allow different modular components to be installed on them (e.g., apps), although the control over the affordances and limitations of the system is up to whoever builds and maintains the platform (most often corporations such as Apple or Google) (see Bogost/Montfort 2009). By saying the iPhone becomes a platform for prediction, I am highlighting how prediction becomes infrastructural, an integral part of this platform. As seen in Apple Memories, predictions continually evolve and change based on our inputs. Algorithms experiment with images by attributing different features to them, experimenting in seeing features and patterns across the entire collection (which is why it operates better in hardware that allows for massively parallel operations). In other words, prediction does not mean simply "building a model that predicts, but trying very many predictive models in an algorithmically controlled order" (Mackenzie 2013: 398). This highlights the processuality of Apple Memories: it's always running in the background, exploring different models to understand and relate the image collection. Automated memory-making is not certain or fixed, but a continuous process across the large collection of a user's images.

In line with the "incorporation of platforms into hardware in devices" (Mackenzie/Munster 2019: 5), Apple's chip both centralises image plat-formatting within Apple's control and decentralises how it happens – away from the cloud, into our pocket. The infrastructuring of machine learning seeks not only to make predictive capabilities faster and more responsive to users; it also embeds prediction into the infrastructure so that future features and experiences may rely on it (a "platform"). This suggestion builds upon the connections traced by other scholars (e.g., Plantin et al. 2018; Plantin/Punathambekar 2019), finding that platforms are becoming infrastructural, particularly as they use their control over data and computation to expand and embed themselves "in our daily existence, taking over more and more functions formerly provided by other, less restrictive means" (Plantin et al. 2018: 12).[3]

When looked through this lens of the infrastructuring of platforms, it becomes clear how platform seeing in the device is "a hardware 'hook' for artificial intelligence to insert itself pervasively into everyday life, fostering a ubiquitous, platform-driven consumer-level deep learning" (Mackenzie/Munster 2019: 15). Operations of data extraction such as the computer vision that enables Apple Memories sink deeper into the infrastructure and make datafication a pervasive element of everyday life – with the goal of exploiting the produced data for financial gains, as indicated by both Zuboff (2018) and Couldry and Mejias (2019). Although Apple's marketing may sell the chip as belonging to the user, the chip is actually anything but. The user does not have any direct access to the chip or its capabilities, relying on what Apple (as a platform) allows to run and operate in its integrated hardware-software system. The platform for seeing, a "centrally designed and controlled system" (Plantin et al. 2018), is tightly integrated with the infrastructure of machine seeing.

However, as suggested by Holt and Vonderau, "[i]nfrastructural politics is not just about what is deliberately hidden from sight or is invisible; it is equally about the hypervisibility created around *some* of an infrastructure's component parts, all while most of the relations it engenders and the rationality embodied in its overall system sink deeply in obscurity" (2015: 80, original emphasis). The A11 Bionic chip is not only made a visible infrastructure through its presentation, but also through its performative marketing. The Bionic branding of the chip makes an ambiguous case: On the one hand, the conceptualisation of Bionic is directly

---

3   The concept of "infrastructure" here builds upon definitions by Star and Ruhleder (1996) as well as its extension by other researchers (e.g., Plantin et al. 2018; Plantin/Punathambekar 2019; Parks/Starosielski 2015). In sum, the concept brings attention to how information systems acquire characteristics of ubiquity, reliability and durability. The concept of infrastructure thus complexifies digital culture through understanding the sociotechnical networks that give information systems support, though they often fade into the woodwork and become banal.

related to the Neural Engine, which itself is named after neural networks and their supposed inspiration on the "McCulloch-Pitts model of the neurone" (Mackenzie 2017: 46). This use of nomenclature related to the human brain connects it with the idea that the machine itself can learn, think and understand things like a human (i.e. an emotive technology). On the other hand, the Bionic branding also implies the user becoming bionic, augmenting themselves with the "the power of the advanced silicon" (Federighi 2016) and the functionalities it enables (e.g., automated memory-making).

In the above analysis of the A11 Bionic chip, we can see the "infrastructural politics" (Parks/Starosielski 2015) of the chip: it is hidden from sight, embedding platform seeing and its predictive capabilities into our devices, while also being hypervisible and mystified. The NPU's increase of the speed and power-efficiency of predictions turns the iPhone into an infrastructure for continuous experimentation with large image collections and their connections.

The Affordances of Apple Memories: Locking the User in a Predictive Regime

The vision of Apple Memories is one of affective and emotional surfacing of connections between images, which may be understood within the wider goal to tightly integrate platform seeing into a device's hardware. But how does Apple Memories work in practice? What are the affordances and constraints it offers the user?

Upon setting up the iPhone, the Photos app (within which Memories resides) is installed and set up by default. It is also directly connected to Apple's iCloud, which serves as the most seamless way to backup photos to "the cloud". The Memories functionality automatically creates image collections and recommendations – be it through themes (e.g., "Dining", "One Year Ago"), faces recognised across the photos and places or categories (e.g., "Lakes", "Animals"). Memories can be seen as such collections or exported as a "'Memory movie', in which different related 'memories' are added to a slideshow, which can be customised by the user in terms of 'mood' (music and editing style), 'length' (short, medium, or long) and 'personalisation' (add or delete specific photos)" (Jacobsen 2020a: 7).

There is no way of opting out of the automated analysis of Photos and Apple Memories. There are only two options for influencing how such image analysis and curation work: a toggle for whether the user wants to be shown "Holiday Events" from their home country, and a button for resetting suggested memories. The sorting and ranking of images happen exclusively through the pre-made categories, which the user can't alter, add to or remove. Additionally, the system uses push notifications ("You Have a New Memory") to nudge the user into connecting with the application.

The affordances of image analysis and recommendation, as described, are all pre-set: not only are the categories pre-defined, but so are the ranking and metrics used to organise the relations between images. For example, Apple Memories creates collections from perceived events, such as "Night out in [City Name]" or "Friday Dinner". Connections may be shaped by features visible to the user, including the image contents, or the picture location metadata. However, there are also opaque interconnections the system does not ever disclose through its interface. According to Apple's Tech Brief (2019), social groups may be identified by "people who often show up in photos together" and "Calendar and Contacts [integrations are used] to understand important personal dates like birthdays and anniversaries". That means the extraction of data and its interrelations are much broader and opaque than what is ever presented to the user via the interface, with key integrations across the iPhone platform.

The user is actually able to create Memories collections by selecting photos, but this is a contrived process that only works within a particular month or day, not through the whole collection. The fact that the system is inflexible and opaque makes handing the personalisation to the machine the path of least resistance, while also inviting the user to the "Practically Magic" sensation advertised by Apple.

Apple Memories offers users the ability to share their memories as a collection of images or an automatically edited video. Moreover, Memories is also shared by default across other Apple products logged into the same account. Featured Photos from Memories are displayed in widgets in the Apple TV and the Apple Watch, for example. The system, however, does not allow the tags produced through the app, or any of the data created through the image analysis it performs to be exported (i.e., there's no interoperability).

As can be seen in this description, Apple Memories' affordances prioritise curation through the system's predictive capabilities. This means a change in the affordances of memory-making for the user: they are invited to work together with the algorithm, with few (and rather laborious) possibilities for manual intervention (cf. Reinis 2019). The algorithmic operations are, by design, made without much influence (or understanding) from the user.

Platform Seeing Beyond Privacy and Surveillance Capitalism

Apple Memories' shift of computer vision and personalised recommendation to the device is framed around notions of emotion and privacy. The iPhone chip, in turn, is positioned as a visible infrastructure, both materially and symbolically indicating the embedding of predictive capabilities within devices. Through such "platform seeing", the whole of the image collection is formatted continuously to platform operations and conditions: "large-scale patterns of associations between features" (Mackenzie/Munster 2019: 18). Finally, Apple Memories' functionality is completely automated, operating under the surface with almost no user involvement or knowledge. The user cannot opt-out, peek into or modify these "invisual cultures" of data extraction, thus being locked into Apple's digital ecosystem.

What are the consequences of Apple Memories and its shift of image analysis and recommendation to the device? In this last section, I will argue that the concern about privacy and surveillance capitalism is insufficient when it comes to the on-device operation of "platform vision". As well described by Sadowski, the focus on privacy and security "elide[s] the systemic issues of inequity and exploitation that are endemic to the contemporary political economy of data" (2019: 9). While extracting and collecting personal data for behavioural analysis and targeted advertisements is a pressing issue, it is not the exclusive way networked images and data extraction matter.

Apple's power relies not on owning user data, but on the monopoly that it has, as a platform, to process this data and transform it into a wider, lucrative "ecosystem". Although Apple Memories promises privacy and not to spy on users, that does not mean users are not a product. Birch et al. (2021) similarly argue that the "power of Big Tech is vested in this process of assetizing users rather than from the 'ownership' of personal data" (13; cf. Zuboff 2018: 94 on the definition of "surveillance assets"). The networked image plays a key role as part of Apple's operation as a powerful platform and infrastructure for the networked image. Through on-device computer vision and personalisation, Apple Memories: 1) creates an always-on service to engage users; 2) generates more and better data about users; and 3) turns prediction into an infrastructure, with many potential future uses. As will be discussed, the value creation through Apple Memories is rather indirect and speculative, rather than the most often discussed elements of selling behavioural user data for advertisers.

The "Stickiness" of Nostalgia

First, the networked image is a rich asset for platform seeing, as it is directly related to our everyday practices of sociality, connection and memory-making. In the case of Apple, the (monopolistic) capacity to control the networked image, as well as the infrastructure of prediction, matters: it gives Apple the power to create a relation with the user by remediating their personal data (i.e. to produce "Memories"). Apple Memories seeks to "enhance product stickiness" (Jacobsen 2020b: 101), getting users involved and engaged within the Apple ecosystem. In this sense, these algorithms may be said to operate "captologically": using the analysis of user behaviour and their images to "elicit more interactions", thus keeping them "hooked" (Seaver 2018: 430). As described by Reinis, Apple Memories is an "attempt to use the affective power of nostalgia to intimately connect users with platforms and reshape subjectivity with ultimately commercial prerogatives" (2019). In sum, Apple Memories deploys its unique control over the predictive infrastructure to both form an emotional relation with the user and hook them as an active participant in the company's ecosystem (cf. Prey/Smit 2018).

More Data

Second, Apple Memories' private operation turns the user into a willing participant in the continuous extraction and analysis of personal data. The notions of intimacy and emotion are key ways to pull the user in. Joey Tyson, Apple's Privacy Engineer, was clear about this when presenting to developers at WWDC 2018. In his words, "privacy-friendly machine learning" allows to build "a relationship of trust with your users", therefore laying "a foundation for better engagement" (Tyson 2018). He proposes that

as users understand why you're collecting data, how it's being used, as you handle that data respectfully and thoughtfully, you're going to get better data, because they're going to be more comfortable using your apps and sharing information, and this builds loyalty over time. (ibid.)

The private operation of Apple Memories, as described by Apple's engineer, helps to get users to allow computer vision to gather and analyse intimate data on a large scale (especially on particularly intimate data). In this sense, privacy is helpful – rather than a deterrent – for platform seeing to take hold, thus increasing user engagement and information collection.

Infrastructuring Prediction, Platforming Vision

Third, and most importantly, Apple Memories is about infrastructuring Apple's platform power. Whoever controls the infrastructure can define the possibilities of how such infrastructure will (and will not) be used for data collection and analysis. The centralisation of power within Apple's "walled garden" means that, although it might not "own" the data, it builds a monopoly over its operationalisation. The focus that has been given to privacy (i.e. protecting against data mining from third-parties) ignores the power that such control over the infrastructure generates (i.e. the power to control the data extraction and analysis, including the connection of images and their categories/ranking). The users do not own the hardware and cannot modify it, or even access the data they have produced.

Apple operates as a "walled garden" platform for this specific reason: it has full control over hardware, software, and services. This arrangement benefits Apple, as it can tightly control all the different facets of user experience for its benefit (e.g., the App Store, of course, but also the seamless analysis of images through its custom-made hardware). Tech critic and scholar Evgeny Morozov similarly argues that "surveillance capitalism" is not the only form of "unequal exchange" and to think so would "ignore all the ways in which Apple regularly pushes its customers around, even preventing them from using third-party repair services" (2019).

In this sense, Apple Memories means Apple taking indirect control of users' image collections, a form of power and value-creation that is speculative and future-oriented. This is different from using this behavioural data to directly inform advertising or improve algorithms. Instead, what it allows is for this data to remain within Apple's "walled garden", where only Apple can decide what to do with it. Although the "walled garden" may be framed as protecting user privacy, it crucially monopolises power to determine how platform seeing operates. Through platform seeing, image collections take on "a different value as future-oriented assets" (Mackenzie/Munster 2019: 10) – as opposed to "the archival logic of social media platforms" (ibid.; see also Zuboff, 2018). Controlling the infrastructure of platform seeing means control over how it (and its data assets) will be used in the future, including for surveillance or commercialisation. Function creep, broadening the data collection and sharing, could happen at any point – be it through changes in the systems' Terms of Service or by including new services and advertising for Apple's products. Data collection in the hands of (monopolistic) platforms with infrastructural power over our devices raises questions we already know the answer to: "There is no reason to assume that a corporation, unless specifically checked from doing so, won't use the personal data it collects or buys in its own interests and against an individual's interests" (Couldry/Mejias 2019: 163).

However, this is not only a concern for a faraway future: there are many signs that surveillant power can take hold in systems engineered for privacy. Metadata mining, which is often considered to be more important than actual content data, is an issue in Apple's operation, particularly because it is "exceedingly difficult to see, study, and analyze" (Cooke 2020). Moreover, techniques such as differential privacy could potentially allow the identification of not a particular individual, but a general population. For example, in discussing COVID-19 contact tracing apps, digital rights scholar Michael Veale (2020) has argued that the issue is not privacy, but "the kind of infrastructural power" that contact tracing apps enable for Apple or Google. That is, although these tools may strive for privacy, their embedding in all devices means "Apple and Google can understand and intervene in the world, while truthfully saying they never saw anybody's personal data" (ibid.).[4]

---

[4] After this article was submitted for review, Apple announced a new functionality to scan users' images and videos being uploaded to iCloud for Child Sexual Abuse Material (CSAM). Instead of conducting such a scan on the cloud servers, which is common, Apple would leverage the computation of users' iPhones (Brodkin 2021). This move was met by criticism and outrage, with experts and organizations pointing out the potential issues of the integration of surveillance on the device. Due to this response, the functionality has been temporarily removed. However, it serves to

By pushing computer vision and predictive personalisation to the user's device, and operating it within a "walled garden" ecosystem, Apple has a monopoly over both platform seeing and its enabling infrastructure. The framing of computer vision as an intimate and personal way of remembering is part of its goal of exploiting personal data to bolster user engagement, more data and the accumulation of platform and infrastructural power within its closed-off digital ecosystem. Apple Memories is, thus, an interesting case of how the networked image today may be enabled by information architectures which, although they may not involve direct value creation through the selling of behavioural data, still rely on data extraction and analysis for the benefit of the platforms which control them.

Conclusion

Apple's shift toward on-device computer vision for automated memory-making may increase user privacy, but it also means the embedding of platform seeing into our devices. Data extraction is now embedded in our always-on smartphones. These extractive operations are framed and sold as emotive and private technologies, but they are actually key ways for infrastructuring predictive capabilities, while also creating services that "hook" users and create more data. Although much scholarship has centred its critique on the surveillant power of the "cloud", I argue that even if operating privately, computer vision allows the problematic consolidation of platform and infrastructural power. This suggests a need to rethink what "surveillance capitalism" means for the networked image: not only a question of data collection for behavioural analysis and ad targeting, but also a way of reaching into and profiting from our personal and intimate memories.

In closing, it is worth mentioning that Apple Memories' control over automated memory-making also raises important issues for our subjectivation. In Apple Memories, the algorithm becomes the curator of what is meaningful enough to be a "memory". Through its suggestions, it helps shape what gets forgotten or remembered, making it difficult to hide from or evade its logic. Following Couldry and Mejias (2019), this emergence of platform seeing could mean a break of human autonomy and the "minimal integrity of the self". Rather than being built around self-determination of individuals, the self is invaded by the automation created by Apple. As suggested by Mark Andrejevic, the "political challenge for the foreseeable future will be contesting the subsumption of subjectivity and judgment to automated media" (2020: 21). The fact that the algorithmic processing is private and operates in our pocket means that their narratives can

> show how the infrastructuring of image recognition by Apple, as discussed in this article, can lead to problematic forms of control and analysis of users' images.

be more tightly interwoven with people's lives. The changes this domestication of prediction may bring to our ways of seeing and remembering images still remain to be discovered – but as I have shown, they will likely be intimately tied to the interests of those with platform and infrastructural power.

References

"The Archives." Apple, September 20, 2017 (https://www.youtube.com/watch?v=OX16DYluC4w).

Amoore, Louise (2020): Cloud Ethics: Algorithms and the Attributes of Ourselves and Others, Durham: Duke University Press.

Andrejevic, Mark (2020): Automated Media, London: Routledge.

Apple (2019): "Photos Tech Brief." (https://www.apple.com/ios/photos/pdf/Photos_Tech_Brief_Sept_2019.pdf).

Azar, Mitra/Cox, Geoff/Impett, Leonardo (2021): "Introduction: Ways of Machine Seeing." In: AI & Society 36, pp. 1093-1104.

Bailey, Jefferson (2013): "Disrespect des Fonds: Rethinking Arrangement and Description in Born-Digital Archives." In: Archive Journal 3 (https://www.archivejournal.net/essays/disrespect-des-fonds-rethinking-arrangement-and-description-in-born-digital-archives/).

Birch, Kean/Cochrane, DT/Ward, Callum (2021): "Data as Asset? The Measurement, Governance, and Valuation of Digital Personal Data by Big Tech." In: Big Data & Society 8/1, pp.1-15.

Blanchette, Jean-François (2011): "A Material History of Bits." In: Journal of the American Society for Information Science and Technology 62/6, pp. 1042-1057.

Brodkin, Jon (2021): "Apple Explains How iPhones Will Scan Photos for Child-Sexual-Abuse Images." Ars Technica, August 8 (https://arstechnica.com/tech-policy/2021/08/apple-explains-how-iphones-will-scan-photos-for-child-sexual-abuse-images/).

Bucher, Taina (2017): "The Algorithmic Imaginary: Exploring the Ordinary Affects of Facebook Algorithms." In: Information, Communication & Society 20/1, pp. 30-44.

Bucher, Taina/Helmond, Anne (2017): "The Affordances of Social Media Platforms." In: Jean Burgess/Alice Marwick/Thomas Poell (eds.), The SAGE Handbook of Social Media, London: Sage, pp. 223-253.

Bogost, Ian/Montfort, Nick (2009): "Platform Studies: Frequently Questioned Answers." In: Proceedings of the Digital Arts and Culture Conference (http://citeseerx.ist.psu.edu/viewdoc/summary?doi=10.1.1.542.9299).

Caldwell, Serenity/Sargent, Mikah (2016): "Full Transcript of the Talk Show at WWDC 2016 with Phil Schiller and Craig Federighi." In: iMore, June 18 (https://www.imore.com/our-full-transcript-talk-show-wwdc-2016-phil-schiller-and-craig-federighi).

Cooke, Thomas N. (2020): "Metadata, Jailbreaking, and the Cybernetic Governmentality of iOS: Or, the Need to Distinguish Digital Privacy from digital privacy." In: Surveillance & Society 18/1, pp. 90-103.

Couldry, Nick/Mejias, Ulises A. (2019): The Costs of Connection: How Data is Colonizing Human Life and Appropriating it for Capitalism, Stanford: Stanford University Press.

Doctorow, Cory (2020): How to Destroy Surveillance Capitalism, New York: Stonesong Digital.

Dourish, Paul (2017): The Stuff of Bits: An Essay on the Materialities of Information, Cambridge: MIT Press.

Ernst, Wolfgang (2012): Digital Memory and the Archive, Minneapolis: University Of Minnesota Press.

Federighi, Craig (2016): "WWDC 2016 Conference Keynote." In: Apple WWDC 2016 (https://developer.apple.com/videos/play/wwdc2016/101/?time=3681).

Federighi, Craig (2017): "WWDC 2017 Conference Keynote." In: Apple WWDC 2017 (https://developer.apple.com/videos/play/wwdc2017/101/?time=3633).

Federighi, Craig (2018): "WWDC 2018 Conference Keynote." In: Apple WWDC 2018 (https://developer.apple.com/videos/play/wwdc2018/101/).

Gillespie, Tarleton (2014): "The Relevance of Algorithms." In: Tarleton Gillespie/Pablo J. Boczkowski/Kirsten A. Foot (eds.), Media Technologies: Essays on Communication, Materiality, and Society, Cambridge, Mass.: MIT Press, pp. 167-193.

Holt, Jennifer/Vonderau, Patrick (2015): "'Where the Internet Lives': Data Centers as Cloud Infrastructure." In: Lisa Parks/Nicole Starosielski (eds.), Signal Traffic: Critical Studies of Media Infrastructures, Champaign: University of Illinois Press, pp.71-93.

Jacobsen, Ben/Beer, David (2021): Social Media and the Automatic Production of Memory: Classification, Ranking and the Sorting of the Past, Bristol: Bristol University Press.

Jacobsen, Benjamin N (2020a): "Algorithms and the Narration of Past Selves." In: Information, Communication & Society, pp. 1-16.

Jacobsen, Benjamin N (2020b): 'You Have a New Memory': Mediated Memories in the Age of Algorithms, University of York.

Light, Ben/Burgess, Jean/Duguay, Stefanie (2018): "The Walkthrough Method: An Approach to the Study of Apps." In: New Media & Society 20/3, pp. 881-900.

Mackenzie, Adrian (2013): "Programming Subjects in the Regime of Anticipation: Software Studies and Subjectivity." In: Subjectivity 6/4, pp. 391-405.

Mackenzie, Adrian (2015): "The Production of Prediction: What Does Machine Learning Want?" In: European Journal of Cultural Studies 18/4-5, pp. 429-445.

Mackenzie, Adrian (2017): Machine Learners: Archaeology of a Data Practice, Cambridge, Mass.: MIT Press.

Mackenzie, Adrian/Munster, Anna (2019): "Platform Seeing: Image Ensembles and Their Invisualities." In: Theory, Culture & Society 36/5, pp. 3-22.

McCosker, Anthony/Wilken, Rowan (2020): Automating Vision, New York: Routledge.

Morozov, Evgeny (2019): "Capitalism's New Clothes." In: The Baffler, February 4 (https://thebaffler.com/latest/capitalisms-new-clothes-morozov).

Murray, Susan (2008): "Digital Images, Photo-Sharing, and Our Shifting Notions of Everyday Aesthetics." In: Journal of Visual Culture 7/2, pp. 147-163.

Myers West, Sarah (2019): "Data Capitalism: Redefining the Logics of Surveillance and Privacy." In: Business & Society 58/1, pp. 20-41.

Paglen, Trevor (2016): "Invisible Images (Your Pictures are Looking at You)." In: The New Inquiry, December 8 (https://thenewinquiry.com/invisible-images-your-pictures-are-looking-at-you/).

Pangambam (2017): "iPhone X September 2017 Event Keynote (Transcript)." The Singju Post, September 15 (https://singjupost.com/apple-ceo-tim-cook-iphone-x-september-2017-event-keynote-transcript/?singlepage=1).

Parks, Lisa (2015): "Stuff You Can Kick: Toward a Theory of Media Infrastructures." In: Patrick Svensson/David Theo Goldberg (eds.), Between Humanities and the Digital, Cambridge, Mass.: MIT Press.

Parks, Lisa/Starosielski, Nicole (eds.) (2015): Signal Traffic: Critical Studies of Media Infrastructures, Urbana: University of Illinois Press.

Pereira, Gabriel (2019): "Apple Memories and Automated Memory-Making: Marketing Speak, Chip-Engineering, and the Politics of Prediction." Selected Papers of #AoIR2019: Proceedings of the 20th International Conference of the Association of Internet Researchers (https://www.gabrielpereira.net/Apple-MemoriesAoIR2019Gabriel.pdf).

Pereira, Gabriel/Moreschi, Bruno (2020): "Ways of Seeing with Computer Vision: Artificial Intelligence and Institutional Critique." In: AI & Society 36, pp. 1201-1223.

Plantin, Jean-Christophe/Lagoze, Carl/Edwards, Paul N./Sandvig, Christian (2018): "Infrastructure Studies Meet Platform Studies in the Age of Google and Facebook." In: New Media & Society 20/1, pp. 293-310.

Plantin, Jean-Christophe/Punathambekar, Aswin (2019): "Digital Media Infrastructures: Pipes, Platforms, and Politics." In: Media, Culture & Society 41/2, pp. 163-174.

Prey, Robert/Smit, Rik (2018): "From Personal to Personalized Memory." In: Zizi Papacharissi (ed.): A Networked Self and Birth, Life, Death, New York: Routledge, pp. 209-223.

Reinis, Sara (2019): "Manufactured Recollection." In: Real Life Magazine, June 10 (https://reallifemag.com/manufactured-recollection/).

Rubinstein, Daniel/Sluis, Katrina (2008): "A Life More Photographic: Mapping the Networked Image." In: Photographies 1/1, pp. 9-28.

Sadowski, Jathan (2019): "When Data is Capital: Datafication, Accumulation, and Extraction" In: Big Data & Society 6/1, pp. 1-12.

Sadowski, Jathan/Ongweso Jr., Edward (2020): "Zuboff is a PSYOP." In: This Machine Kills (https://soundcloud.com/thismachinekillspod/4-zuboff-is-a-psyop).

Seaver, Nick (2017): "Algorithms as Culture: Some Tactics for the Ethnography of Algorithmic Systems." In: Big Data & Society 4/2, pp. 1-12.

Seaver, Nick (2018): "Captivating Algorithms: Recommender Systems as Traps." In: Journal of Material Culture 24/4, pp. 421-436.

Seaver, Nick (2019a): "Knowing Algorithms." In: Janet Vertesi/David Ribes (eds.), DigitalSTS: A Field Guide for Science & Technology Studies, Princeton: Princeton University Press.

Seaver, Nick (2019b): "Preferential Technics and the Cosmology of Overload." Talk at AIAS Music and AI Conference, Aarhus University 2019.

Star, Susan Leigh/Ruhleder, Karen (1996): "Steps Toward an Ecology of Infrastructure: Design and Access for Large Information Spaces." In: Information Systems Research 7/1, pp. 111-134.

Stark, Luke (2019): "Affect and Emotion in digitalSTS." In: Janet Vertesi/David Ribes (eds.), digitalSTS: A Field Guide for Science & Technology Studies, Princeton: Princeton University Press, pp. 117-135.

Steyerl, Hito (2014): "Proxy Politics: Signal and Noise." In: e-flux 60 (https://www.e-flux.com/journal/60/61045/proxy-politics-signal-and-noise/).

Stone, Brad/Satariano, Adam/Ackerman, Gwen. "The Most Important Apple Executive You've Never Heard Of." Bloomberg, February 22 (https://www.bloomberg.com/features/2016-johny-srouji-apple-chief-chipmaker/).

Tyson, Joey (2018): "Better Apps through Better Privacy." In: WWDC 2018 (https://developer.apple.com/videos/play/wwdc2018/718/).

van Dijck, José (2007): Mediated Memories in the Digital Age, Stanford: Stanford University Press.

van Dijck, José (2014): "Datafication, Dataism and Dataveillance: Big Data between Scientific Paradigm and Ideology." In: Surveillance & Society 12/2, pp. 197-208.

Veale, Michael (2020): "Privacy is not the Problem with the Apple-Google Contact-Tracing Toolkit." In: The Guardian, July 1 (http://www.theguardian.com/commentisfree/2020/jul/01/apple-google-contact-tracing-app-tech-giant-digital-rights).

Wakabayashi, Daisuke (2014): "Apple CEO Tim Cook: Your Data Is Not Our Business." In: The Wall Street Journal, September 15 (https://www.wsj.com/articles/BL-DGB-37722).

Zuboff, Shoshana (2015): "Big Other: Surveillance Capitalism and the Prospects of an Information Civilization." In: Journal of Information Technology 30/1, pp. 75-89.
Zuboff, Shoshana (2018): The Age of Surveillance Capitalism, London: Profile Books.

Images of Resistance
Thinking about Computer Vision AI in Surveillance Capitalism through Images of Marielle Franco

Vinicius Ariel Arruda dos Santos, Bruno Moreschi, Amanda Jurno, Didiana Prata, Monique Lemos, Lucas Nunes Sequeira

Abstract

This article examines the ambivalent dynamics of activism in social media and online platforms. Made up of Brazilian researchers from areas such as Communication, Visual Arts and Design, Anthropology, Computer Science and Engineering, our group analysed 213,083 images shared on Instagram that are part of the hashtag #MariellePresente, an online political manifestation that arose in response to the assassination of Brazilian councilwoman Marielle Franco in 2018, an unsolved case. After collecting images with a Python programming language script, we used two Computer Vision/Artificial Intelligence tools to read them (Google Cloud Vision and YOLO Darknet). The results show the capitalistic logics inscribed into these technologies and also shed light on the role played by both online activism and data analysis tools. Thus, the consequences of the shift of political movements online became apparent: by helping activism to find its audience, online platforms simultaneously subject its cause to demands of 21st century digital capitalism (Zuboff 2019; Srnicek 2017; Bruno 2013; Crary 2013; Beiguelman 2020).

Keywords
Marielle Franco; Computer Vision; Activism; Social Media

1. Who Killed Marielle? And Who Ordered the Killing?

Marielle Franco, a Brazilian black lesbian feminist, a member of the City of Rio de Janeiro Council, was murdered during a military intervention in Rio de Janeiro in 2018. She was a human rights activist that focused on political minorities, namely the LGBTQIA+ community and the black population in Rio. Her political battles led her to take the role of rapporteur for an inquiry on military abuse just one month before her assassination. The councilwoman, a member of the opposition left-wing party Socialism and Liberty (PSOL), was sitting inside a car when she and her chauffeur, Anderson Gomes, were fatally wounded by gunshots.

The subsequent protests were massive (BBC 2018), raising the question: "Who killed Marielle?". Indignation mounted on social media (e.g., Facebook, Instagram and Twitter), as images of or about Marielle were posted with the hashtag #MariellePresente (Marielle [is] present). In just a few weeks, her history, her murder and the consequent repercussions turned Marielle into a symbol, as mentions of her name peaked (Fig. 1), reaching 567,000 posts on Twitter 19 hours after the crime (Bastos/Guerra 2018: 2). Investigations made little progress, leading to an uptick in the outrage among those sympathetic to the causes she had supported. Furthermore, the lies of suspects (Corsini 2021), police officers' interference (BBC 2019), and loss of crucial evidence (Franco 2021) created a sense of impunity that persists to this day. New facts linking the assassination to supporters of the current Brazilian president, Jair Bolsonaro (BBC Brazil 2020), raised the suspicion that the delay was a deliberate obstruction of justice, which prompted a change in the rallying call of the protests to: "Who *ordered* the killing of Marielle?".

Fig. 1: Distribution of search requests for "Marielle Franco" on Google – reaching its peak in March 2018. Credits: Google Trends 2021.

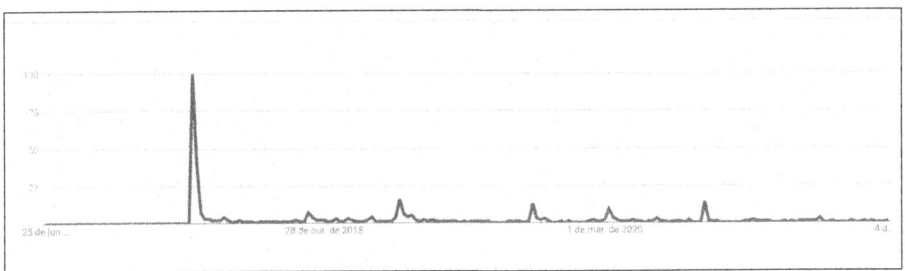

This ongoing research[1] brings together academics from Communication, Visual Arts and Design, Anthropology, Computer Science and Engineering – members of the Group on Artificial Intelligence and Art/C4AI at the University of São Paulo. We tested how Computer Vision (CV) tools treated images posted on Instagram with the hashtag '#MariellePresente', to find out whether Artificial Intelligence (AI) tends to read images according to the logic of consumption and captures the singularities of activist images when they flow through the internet. In this paper,

---

1   This research is related to the Scientific Initiation of Vinicius Ariel, Computer Engineering undergraduate, with Bruno Moreschi's supervision at the Faculty of Architecture and Urbanism of the University of São Paulo, with the support of the PIBIC scholarship CNPq, in the years 2020/2021. It also involved Lucas Nunes Sequeira's PIBIC/CNPq research scholarship, under the supervision of Fabio Gagliardi Cozman. The project began with the investigations carried out by Didiana Prata in her PhD at the same Faculty, whereby she studies the aesthetic of dissent images in social networks, in a visual cultural context.

we draw on the work of authors who study capitalism at the beginning of the 21st century (Bruno 2013; Crary 2013; Srnicek 2017; Zuboff 2019; Beiguelman 2020). We propose to analyse the results obtained with CV tools to better understand the underlying mechanisms that form part of the surveillance capitalism on the web. Thereby, this text adds to others on Marielle's presence on the internet, such as the investigation of image sharing associated with her (Goveia 2018), and a study on the polarization of the case (Ruback/Oliveira 2018).

2. The Images of Marielle

Back in 2018, the posts linked to the hashtag '#MariellePresente' aimed to inform local users of her murder, but soon achieved a national and international impact (Goveia 2018). Unlike other image sharing protests, though, this one continued on social media as the killers' impunity persisted, and the hashtag's meaning became broader. Soon, it started being used as a political demonstration – e.g., in favor of progressive flags –, on posts not related to Marielle, becoming a self-affirmation of being part of a broader online community (Fig. 2).

Fig. 2: Photo posted by a person celebrating New Year's Eve linked with #MariellePresente.
Credits: Instagram user @danimartinsbarros.

The images related to Marielle are part of a digital context characterised by the intense spread of media content – e.g., almost 20 billion images were shared on Instagram in the first half of 2021.[2] This overproduction of politically engaged

---

2   "Internet Live Stats." July 25, 2021 (https://www.internetlivestats.com/).

images and street manifestations has led to them being termed "dissent images" by Didiana Prata (2020), since they mobilise specific activist groups to fight for their rights on social media through a fragmented visual narrative. These images travel fast and infiltrate informational flows in small formats, since they are "poor images", as defined by Steyerl (2009: 7). She argues that they do not seem to be significant when analysed individually, but they manage to be influential when analysed together.

For the purposes of this work, we gathered two sets of images. The first one was originally part of the netart project "Calendário Dissidente", which investigates the flow of dissent images on Instagram. From the over 300,000 images collected for the Calendário, 69.8 percent were labelled with "#MariellePresente". From this set, we chose 83 images related to Marielle that had reached the threshold of 50,000 likes by August 2020, extracted using the Instaloader library (Graf/Koch-Kramer 2016) for the Python programming language. The second set consists of 213,000 images posted on Instagram from January 2019 to August 2020, using the same scraping method.

Fig. 3, Fig. 4: On the left, the most liked Marielle related image on Instagram by the time of our analysis (January, 2019 to August, 2020); on the right, the image with the most total pairs on Google Cloud Vision. Credits: @brunamarquezine (Im.3), @hugogloss (Fig. 4).

Next, we observed how these images were understood by two pre-trained CV tools – Google Cloud Vision and YOLO. Google Cloud Vision[3] (GCV) is a commercial CV tool focused on business analytics; and YOLO Darknet is a non-profit CV tool (Redmon/Farhadi 2018). Those programs were chosen for this initial study due to their simplified usage, having robust pre-trained models, and for being open source. Although methodologically, it would be more appropriate to report on the operability of computer vision algorithms used by online platforms, these are not

3 "Google Cloud Vision." (https://cloud.google.com/vision/).

available for public use. Therefore, we focus on testing GCV's Label Detection and Internet Detection tools, which are both image labelling methods. YOLO conducts a simpler analysis, as a result of being trained with Microsoft COCO (Lin et. al 2014), an image dataset compiled with the intent of recognizing only 91 object types. Based on these CV analyses, we discuss ambivalences that activism faces within the capitalist framework of social media. We finish this initial research paper with an open conclusion on how images of Marielle managed to break through the exclusion of black people in digital contexts.

3. Marielle and Digital Activism's Paradox

As Crawford argues, "classification is an act of power" (2021: 127), since naming, categorising and organising information has always had an intimate relationship with the narratives these powers construct. AI classifications are subjective, as they dictate which categories are attached to a given label, besides the labels that are available to begin with. The problem with all classifications is that they become invisible as they get embedded in infrastructures and in the routine. Therefore, Crawford points out that "we can easily forget that the classifications that are casually chosen to shape a technical system can play a dynamic role in shaping the social and material world" (ibid.: 128). In this research, we start from the premise that AI uses classification to encode power and that it is not a bug – as the AI industry has traditionally claimed – but a part of the mechanisms of knowledge production. Because every dataset and training machine contains a worldview, "the result is a statistical ouroboros: a self-reinforcing discrimination machine that amplifies social inequalities under the guise of technical neutrality" (ibid.: 131).

The pre-trained GCV's Label Detection tool analysis works by reading an image as stand-alone data and labelling it with predefined classifications that Google AI understands as the best fit to what the image shows. By running this tool over our two image sets, we confirmed a consumerist bias: the tendency to classify content as objects of consumption observed in previous studies (Moreschi/Pereira 2020) also applied to our group of images – almost regardless of what they showed. We identified eleven different labels related to "clothing" or "fashion" in general (Fig. 5). Also, we found out that images showing one person – positioned in the middle – were labelled as 'posing' (Fig. 6). Even images that do not depict people fell under this capitalist logic: some of those that include text were labelled as "Advertising" (Fig. 7). We noted that the "mistakes" made by the AI are usually attempts to grasp the context in these images, for example when it implied that Marielle is a singer (Fig. 8 and Fig. 9), and that Carlos Bolsonaro (politician and son of the current president of Brazil, Jair Bolsonaro) is a businessperson (Fig. 10). Besides, Google tended to brand black people as part of entertainment and/or sports contexts, confirming stereotypes already pointed out in previous research studies, both in the specific field of algorithmic studies (Silva 2020: 438) and in other areas such as the History of Art and artistic images (Benedita/Moreschi 2017). This imprecision in defining context may be the reason why Google itself avoids relying too much on 'on-image-information' for search queries[7].

Despite also detecting bags and other fashion accessories (Fig. 12), YOLO tends to be less 'subjective' in its labelling because its labels are only object-related. Although bias is also present in the list of objects it is trained to recognise, it tends to be more assertive than GCV. As we discuss below, these results say little about Marielle, let alone about the online movement that emerged after her death. Instead, they reveal how these online images are read and inserted into a capitalism-centred context (Mueller 2021).

Fig. 5: Labelling focused on fashion and physical appearance ('Beauty', 'Fashion model', 'Dress', 'Street fashion' and 'Fashion design'). The favela context was not recognised by Google AI (GCV). Credits: @adrianalima.

Fig. 6: Other people are also read from a consumer perspective. The 'Black lives matter' (in Portuguese) is not considered by GCV. Credits: @icaro.

Images of Resistance   235

Fig. 7: The message disseminated by thousands of people and two important hashtags presented in the image are classified as 'Logo' and 'Brand' by GCV.

Fig. 8 and Fig. 9: GCV also often reads Marielle as someone who is singing, labelling images with 'Music Artist', 'Talent Show' and 'Performing Arts'. This did not happen so often with images of white people in a similar position. Credits: @fatimabernardes.

Fig. 10: The image's headline informs us that Carlos Bolsonaro (in the picture) is being investigated for his participation in Marielle's death. GCV reads it as 'Businessperson'. Credits: @midianinja.

Fig. 11: The image of black people protesting at Marielle's death was labelled as 'Fun' and 'Smile' by Google's AI (GCV), softening the political content. Credits: @icaro.

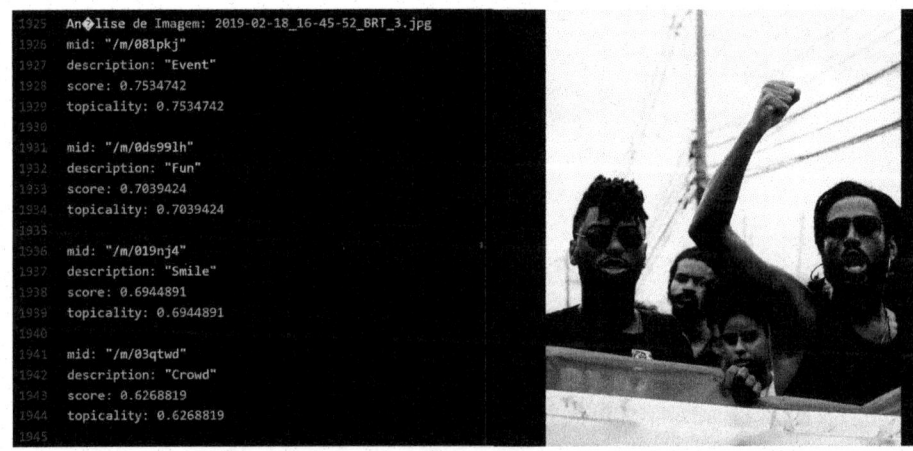

Fig. 12: Unlike GCV, YOLO tends to be more direct in its labelling, even though it also reads fashion and consumer accessories. Credits: @icaro.

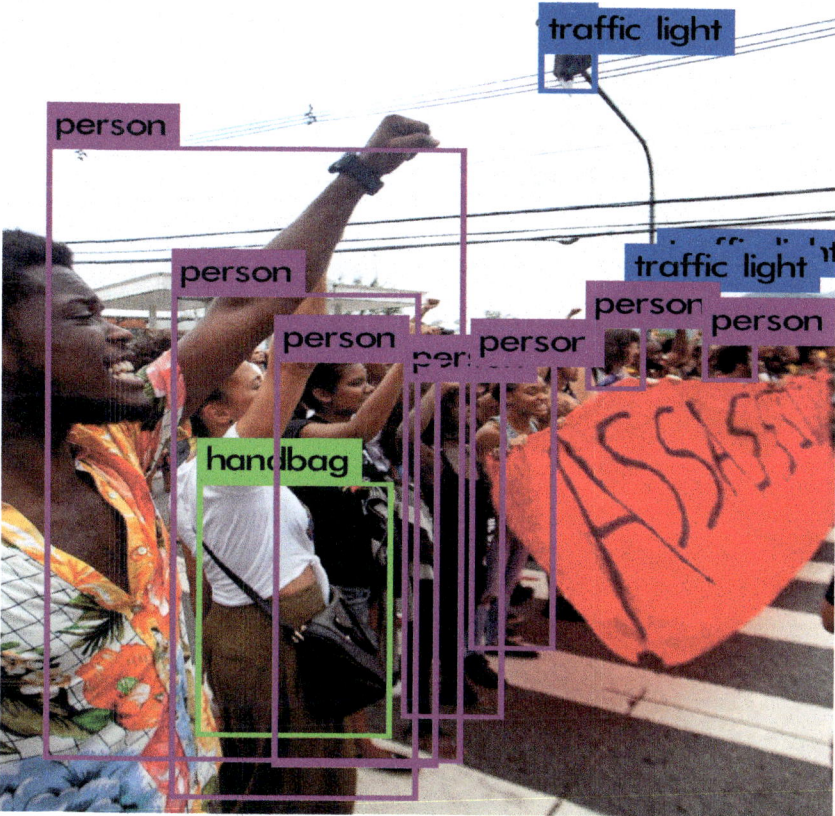

Another Google's CV tool, Internet Detection, also demonstrates how images tagged with "#MariellePresente" might circulate online, instead of just discussing how the "raw" information of the image might be understood. By searching these images and information about the web pages they appear on, this tool is able to identify Marielle individually as herself (Fig. 13), and also to grasp the context that is not present in the images, such as her political party (Fig. 14) or nationality (Fig. 15). Some of the classification labels would even suggest a glimpse of opinion in defence of Marielle, probably extracted from the web: the "Brazilian Police Militias" label (Fig. 16) implies the participation of the police in the crime; and *"Quem matou? Quem Mandou Matar?"* (Who killed [her]? Who ordered the killing?) (Fig. 17), one of the few that were shown in Portuguese, reinforces that the assassins are yet to be found. Summarising, the outcomes suggest that tools like GCV are able to identify the "community" that an image belongs to by following its track on the web (and other metadata available) rather than by looking at its contents – a relationship more visible when iterating the tool through images that have contextual meaning, as is the case with activists' images.

Fig. 13: Marielle's image by GCV's Internet Detection, recognizing her and the context surrounding her death. Credits: @caiapitanga.

Fig. 14: One of the images of Marielle tagged with the name of her party. Results in Portuguese are rare: we are dealing with a tool that reads the world from the hegemonic English language, even when analysing images unrelated to North American contexts. Credits: @criolomc.

One of our main intentions in surveying CV tools is to go beyond discussing the specific problematics they create and replicate, and to understand these results in the broader context of contemporary surveillance capitalism. In her book on surveillance capitalism, Zuboff (2019: 97) states how technology companies gather data from their users' behaviour and sell advertisers the opportunity to use targeted ads on consumers most susceptible to carrying out a purchase. As a result, companies now compete for all possible aspects of daily life connected – and yet to be connected – to the internet, and also build online platforms that encourage interaction between users, advertisers and service providers (Srnicek 2019: 31). Keeping users engaged in their services and preserving these digital communities, such as the one created by "#MariellePresente", the platforms need to understand the users' affinities, including political views. Therefore, context-sensitive tools capable of tracking images are a powerful resource for feeding communities content that they are more likely to interact with (Oremus 2016), thus generating data in the form of behaviour surplus (Zuboff 2019: 430), while also creating a sense of personal belonging (Gwendolyn 2013: 403).

Fig. 15: GCV labelled an image of Marielle with 'Afro-Brazilians'. This is one of the few times Google AI offered a result in Portuguese: 'favela'.

Fig. 16: Image of Rio's 2019 Carnival, when Marielle's widow, Mônica Benicio, used the scene to protest at Marielle's death. It was tagged by GCV as 'Brazilian police militias' – implying some coherent complaints of police interference. Credits: @midianinja.

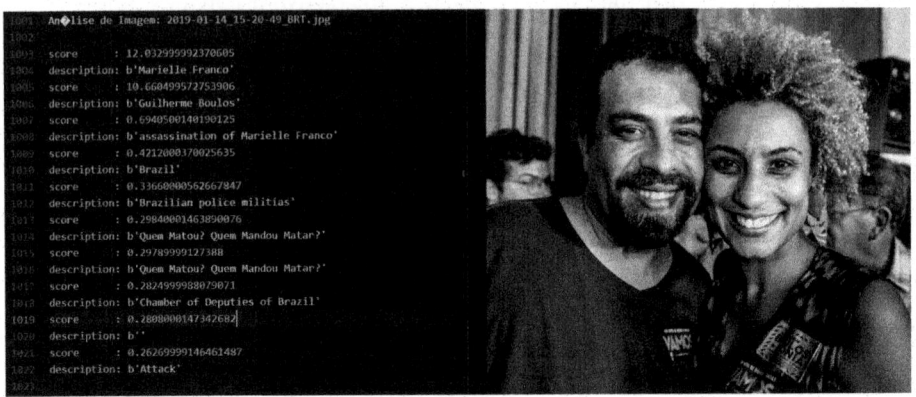

Fig. 17: Even though results in Portuguese are rare in GCV, the two questions most associated with the protests break this linguistic exclusion and appear in their native language: 'Quem matou? Quem Mandou Matar?' Credits: @guilhermeboulos.oficial.

The way in which algorithms overseeing user interactions operate, especially algorithms of public relevance (Gillespie 2014), is fundamental to understanding why activism was able to easily migrate online. Such tools ensure that users are shown content with which they would likely interact. This logic fosters engagement otherwise not possible in other media. Activism such as that related to Marielle's death and Black Lives Matter merged with social media in such a way that it may no longer be possible to think about activism without online platforms. In this sense, activism is now inextricably dependent on the platforms' services, as no alternatives provide the same impact (Srnicek 2019: 70).

This merging may have bitter and ambivalent consequences for protesting. The same online environment that allows militancy to flourish also sets the stage for anti-democratic movements, while profiting from both of them. This suggests that it is not the image content, but rather the "more profitable" metadata, like tags and interactions, that count when determining the spread of an image. Also, as the main source of income for online platforms flows through the abundance of behaviour surplus gathered from a large number of users, there is no rush for those platforms to suppress anti-democratic activities and risk losing groups of users (Zuboff 2019: 476). Therefore, although online activism has seen increased mobilisation to its causes, their very existence online keeps its causes from reaching beyond the borders of their communities, increasing polarisation. Moreover, algorithms of public relevance are not playing the role of mere observers, trying to predict the affinities of each group. Those algorithms control what users see and consume, helping communities grow into niches evermore fitting to their predictions (Brito/Jurno 2020; Gillespie 2014). Consequently, online activism is not only curtailed in a surveillance structure, but becomes such a structure itself, where bodies watch over each other (Bruno 2013: 7).

As we celebrate an increasingly interconnected world dominated by a cute and seemingly harmless capitalism (Beiguelman, 2020), a "coup from above" (Zuboff 2019: 479) from the big tech companies expropriates human rights. Our findings related to images connected to Marielle, particularly those targeting specific audiences, illustrates how this ongoing expropriation is reinforced and poses a risk to democracy: the digital dream has morphed into a violent commercial project, to which online activism unwittingly contributes by simply generating traffic and online interaction. For Zuboff (2019: 480), this kind of "nightmare" characterises surveillance capitalism, but it is important to highlight that other scholars on contemporary capitalism corroborate this finding – sometimes using different terms. For example, Crary's (2013) considerations on 'late capitalism', where the human being must work uninterruptedly, relate directly to the idea of the loss of the right to sanctuary (Zuboff 2019: 449), as the human need for an inviolable space of refuge.

4. Other Thoughts: Black Women's Invisibilities

Empirical investigations with images for this article indicate issues related to CV/AI and how it behaves when faced with specific images about Marielle Franco, but not only that. After a year dealing with images of a black woman in a digital surveillance capitalism context, necropolitics also seemed evident to us. This is an open-ended conclusion, not only because Marielle's images continue to circulate on social media and be levelled by commercial AIs, but also because the image of a black woman only managed to break the invisibility imposed on it because she was murdered and became a symbol.

Flauzina and Freitas state that the direct consequence of structural racism is the politicisation of black people suffering through "the construction of an imaginary in which the image of black people as beings fundamentally associated with the reproduction of violence operates in a coordinated manner, but is excluded from the right to claim the suffering derived from it" (2017: 135, our translation). In Marielle's case, the AI labelling promotes an "update" of necropolitics by tempering her death into a product of capitalism, reflecting how annotations (including those offered by CVs) and informational records reproduce power (Silva 2020; Crawford 2021). The selective character of social indignation in the face of violence, allied to racism, places the victimisation and reproduction of physical or symbolic violence within the capitalistic, normative technocratic logic created mostly by white people (Gruman 2020). Therefore, it is possible to understand how Marielle Franco's death also serves as a symbol of this struggle against the naturalisation of the extermination and disposal of black bodies, now increasingly powered by AI.

References

"Adriano da Nóbrega: Qual é a relação entre acusado de chefiar milícia morto e Flávio Bolsonaro?", February 10, 2020 (https://www.bbc.com/portuguese/brasil-51447905).

Bastos, Fernanda/Guerra, Laura (2018): "Do acontecimento inesperado às ações conectivas: o impacto do assassinato de Marielle Franco". In: Congresso do Instituto Nacional de Ciência e Tecnologia em Democracia Digital 1.

Beiguelman, Giselle (2020): "Smart Cities, Smart Virus: Technoutopias of the New Normal." In: V!RUS 21 http://www.nomads.usp.br/virus/virus21/?sec=4&item=1&lang=en).

Benedito, Vera/Moreschi, Bruno (2017): "The History of _rt." (https://brunomoreschi.com/A-Historia-da-_rte-The-History-of-_rt).

"Brazil Protests over Slain Politician Marielle Franco." March 16, 2018 (https://www.bbc.com/news/av/world-latin-america-43428164).

Brito, Carlos/Jurno, Amanda (2020): "Between Partnerships, Infrastructures and Products: Facebook Journalism Project and the Platformization of Journalism." In: Brazilian Journalism Research 16/3, pp. 502-525.

Bruno, Fernanda (2013): Máquinas de ver, modos de ser: vigilância, tecnologia e subjetividade, Porto Alegre: Sulina.

Corsini, Iuri (2021): "Caso Marielle: confira a linha do tempo da investigação do crime." March 14 (https://www.cnnbrasil.com.br/nacional/2021/03/14/caso-marielle-confira-a-linha-do-tempo-da-investigacao-do-crime).

Crary, Jonathan (2013): 24/7: Late Capitalism and the Ends of Sleep, London: Verso Books.

Crawford, Kate (2021): The Atlas of AI, New Haven: Yale University Press.

Fabio, Goveia (2019): "Análise das imagens de #mariellepresente: memórias entre a dor e a esperança." April 15 (https://www.labic.net/cartografia/analise-das-imagens-de-mariellepresente-memorias-entre-a-dor-e-a-esperanca).

Flauzina, Ana Luiza Pinheiro/Freitas, Felipe da Silva (2017): "Do paradoxal privilégio de ser vítima: terror de Estado e a negação do sofrimento negro no Brasil." In: Revista Brasileira de Ciências Criminais 135, pp.49-71

Franco, Luiza (2021): "Caso Marielle e Anderson: o que se sabe sobre problemas da investigação." March 14 (https://www.bbc.com/portuguese/brasil-56378215).

Gillespie, Tarleton (2014): "The Relevance of Algorithms.'" In: Gillespie, Tarleton/Boczkowski, Pablo J./Foot, Kirsten A. (eds.), Media Technologies: Essays on Communication, Materiality, and Society, Cambridge, Mass.: MIT, pp. 167-194.

"Google Cloud Vision AI." (https://cloud.google.com/vision/).

"Google Trends." June 22, 2021 (https://trends.google.com.br/trends/explore?date=all&geo=BR&q=Marielle%20Franco).

Graf, Alexander/Koch-Kramer, André (2016): "Instaloader documentation." June 15 (https://instaloader.github.io).

Gruman, Galen (2020): "The State of Ethnic Minorities in U.S. Tech: 2020." September 21 (https://www.computerworld.com/article/3574917/the-state-of-ethnic-minorities-in-us-tech-2020.html).

"Internet Live Stats." July 25, 2021 (https://www.internetlivestats.com/).

Kharroub, Tamara/Bas, Ozen (2016): "Social Media and Protests: An Examination of Twitter Images of the 2011 Egyptian Revolution." In: New Media & Society 18/9, pp. 1973-1992.

Lin, Tsung-Yi et. al (2014): "Microsoft COCO: Common Objects in Context." In: European Conference on Computer Vision 2014, pp.740-755.

"Marielle Franco Murder: Two Rio Ex-Police Officers Held." March 12, 2019 (https://www.bbc.com/news/amp/world-latin-america-47538871).

Moreschi, Bruno/Gabriel Pereira (2020). "Recoding Art: A Coleção do Van Abbemuseum." In: Revista Farol 16/22 pp. 176-204.

Mueller, John (2021): "English Google SEO Office-Hours from February 5, 2021." February 5 (https://www.youtube.com/watch?v=cUT84ZIcLtA).

Prata, Didiana/Cozman, Fábio/Polleti, Gustavo (2020): "Using AI to Classify Instagram's Dissident Images". In: Proceedings of the ICDHS 12th International Conference on Design History and Design Studies 6 - Design and Technology, pp.695 -708.

Oremus, Will (2016): "Who Controls Your Facebook Feed." January 3 (https://www.slate.com/articles/technology/cover_story/2016/01/how_facebook_s_news_feed_algorithm_works.html).

Redmon, Joseph/Farhadi, Ali (2018): YOLOv3: "An Incremental Improvement." In: arXiv 1804/02767.

Ruback, Livia/Oliveira, Jonice (2018): Analyzing Polarization in Twitter: The Murder of Brazilian Concilwoman and Activist Marielle Franco, Rio de Janeiro: PPGI UFRJ.

Scherman, Andrés/Arriagada, Arturo/Valenzuela, Sebastián (2014): "Student and Environmental Protests in Chile: The Role of Social Media." In: Politics 35/2, pp. 151-171.

Seidman, Gwendolyn (2013): "Self-presentation and Belonging on Facebook: How Personality Influences Social Media Use and Motivations." In: Personality and Individual Differences 54/3, pp. 402-407.

Silva, Tarcízio Roberto da (2020): "Visão computacional e racismo algorítmica: branquitude e opacidade no aprendizado de máquina." In: Revista da Associação Brasileira de Pesquisadores/as Negros/as (ABPN) 12/31.

Srnicek, Nick (2017): Platform Capitalism, Malden: Polity Press.

Steyerl, Hito (2009): "In Defense of the Poor Image." In: E-flux Journal 10/11 (https://www.e-flux.com/journal/10/61362/in-defense-of-the-poor-image/).

Zuboff, Shoshana (2019): The Age of Surveillance Capitalism: The Fight for a Human Future at the New Frontier of Power, London: Profile Books.

Gaze, Normalization, Subjectivation

The Digital, Capitalist Gaze

Jens Schröter

Abstract

Today, there are surely more images in circulation and more visibility than ever before. This is due mostly to the diffusion of digital technologies in the context of global capitalism. The following paper undertakes to address this situation by relating the image/visibility to digital technologies and capitalism. The core idea is to analyse this situation on the basis of a theory of the gaze as a theory of the subject's constitutive visibility. One classical notion of the gaze, as elaborated by Lacan, will be discussed. The latter conceived the subject as always already visible. Being seen or surveilled is not something that happens subsequently to an already constituted subject; instead, it plays its part in forming the subject from the very beginning. This can explain the desire and fascination invested in images today. This approach to the gaze is historically differentiated and related to image technologies. Contrary to Lacan's somewhat ahistorical conception of the gaze, it becomes clear that historically, the gaze is dependent on the available media technologies, which means that the primordial visibility of the subject is realised in different ways. Finally, this is related to a discussion of capitalism, the socioeconomic context to which all modern image technologies belong. It is thus argued that the gaze in modern societies is a digital and capitalist gaze.

Keywords

Capitalism, Circulation, Gaze, Lacan, Subjectivity, 3D-Scanning

A functioning police state needs no police.

WILLIAM S. BURROUGHS (1966: 36)

Today, there are surely more images in circulation and more visibility than ever before. This is due mostly to the diffusion of digital technologies in the context of global capitalism. The core idea of this paper is to analyse this situation on the basis of the concept of the gaze as a theory of the subject's constitutive visibility. The first section presents a classical notion of the gaze, as elaborated by Lacan, who conceives the subject as always already visible. Being seen or surveilled is not something that happens subsequently to an already constituted subject; instead, it forms the subject from the very beginning. This can explain the desire and fascination invested in images today. In the second section, this approach to the gaze is historically differentiated and related to image technologies. Contrary to Lacan's somewhat ahistorical conception of the gaze, it becomes clear that it is historically dependent on the available media technologies, which means that the primordial visibility of the subject is realised in different ways. The third part of the paper relates the question of the gaze and its historical media manifestations to a discussion of capitalism, the socioeconomic context to which all modern image technologies belong. To the best of my knowledge, this has not been done before. It is thus argued that the gaze in modern societies is a digital and capitalist gaze. Following this theoretical discussion, two examples are presented in the fourth section. The fifth part of the paper sums up the results and draws a conclusion.

1. The Gaze

Visibility is a constitutive feature of subjectivity: "[...] I see only from one point, but in my existence, I am looked at from all sides" (Lacan 1998: 72). We are "beings who are looked at" (ibid.: 75). "The gaze in question is certainly the presence of others as such" (ibid.: 84).[1] "The picture certainly is in my eye. But I am [...] in the picture" (ibid.: 96).[2] In a famous passage, a few pages later, Lacan writes:

What determines me, at the most profound level, in the visible, is the gaze that is outside. It is through the gaze that I enter light and it is from the gaze that I receive its effects. Hence it comes about that the gaze is the instrument through which light is embodied and through which [...] I am *photo-graphed* [original emphasis]. (ibid.: 106)

Lacan distinguishes two modes of viewing: the first is one in which the subject sovereignly surveys a scene and is the bearer of the *look*. Lacan calls this mode "geometral" (ibid.: 85). Here, the visible is directed towards a point of view. However, this notion of seeing is in some ways illusory, since the subject is also the object of what can be called the *gaze*. The subject is visible, always seen, and being looked at is part of the structure of subjectivity. Everyone wants to "look good" – with the meaning of "good" being shaped by normative standards rooted in sexism, racism, ableism, classism, and so on. Bodies that do not conform to these norms become special objects of continuous visualisation (or its erasure) and visual correction (and even the refusal to conform reflects this imperative).

---

[1] Gondek points out that Lacan himself never speaks of the "gaze of the other" (cf. Gondek 1997: 184). Nevertheless, Lacan's formulation seems to me to be clearly oriented towards intersubjective visibility. See also Blümle/von der Heiden (2005).

[2] This quotation from the English translation has been corrected by the author to conform to the original French text: "Le tableau, certes, est dans mon œil. Mais mois, je suis dans le tableau" (Lacan 1973: 89).

Between the gaze and the subject is a "screen", and as one might surmise, the screen is the "image repertoire" (Silverman 1996: 3; see also Bryson 1988: 91-92) that serves human subjects as a pre-image of their own visualisation (e.g., ideals of beauty, fashion, strength, etc.).[3] Nonetheless, the screen is also a form of protection, since, one might say, by making ourselves "pleasing" and *conforming*, we protect ourselves from the shame caused by the gaze.

Lacan says that the "gaze is the instrument through which light is embodied" and that the subject is, so to speak, structurally photo-graphic. This wording, and the dispositive of central perspective and painting that he repeatedly mentions (in *Seminar XI*: Goya, Rouault, Holbein, Caravaggio, Cezanne[4]) suggest that image technologies play a *constitutive* role for the gaze (the visibility of the subject) in a way that remains to be determined. One can already speculate here that they are closely connected to the screen, which is clearly named after certain image technology procedures. This is indicated by its definition, cited above, as a "locus of mediation" (Lacan 1998: 107) and as the reservoir of *mass media*-images according to which we form ourselves.

The gaze seems superior to the subject and is associated with the "evil eye"; it is even said that "beyond appearance there is no thing in itself, [but] there is the gaze" (ibid.: 103). The gaze seems to dominate the subject, to put it to shame, and to subjectivise it in the first place; it is the "underside of consciousness" (ibid.: 83). Even though Lacan admits that one can "play" with the "screen" ("Man, in effect, knows how to play with the mask as that beyond which there is the gaze," ibid.: 107), the gaze has a "paranoid coloration" (Bryson 1988: 104).

2. The Historicity and Mediality of the Gaze

If the gaze and the visibility of the subject are so fundamental, if "the gaze [...] is as old as sociality itself" (Silverman 1996, 132), it would appear to be "transhistorical" (ibid.: 133).[5] Silverman nonetheless reintroduces historicity via the screen (ibid.:

---

3   The screen is clearly related to the mirror and to the imaginary, but that cannot be discussed here; see Jay (1993: 329-370). Significant feminist and queer theory approaches have therefore been able to draw on various aspects of Lacan's theory, though not without questioning the ahistorical and 'phallogocularcentric' character of his approach (cf. Jay 1993: 493-542).

4   Cf. Lacan (1998): "[...] certainly, in the picture, something of the gaze is always manifested" (ibid.: 101). How this relates to abstract images or those based on non-optical, e.g., parallel-perspective construction methods is a difficult question that cannot be discussed here (cf. Beil/Schröter 2011).

5   Its seemingly transhistorical character also makes it Eurocentric, since a transhistorical conception of the gaze makes different regimes of the gaze invisible. After all, Frantz Fanon's important study *Peau noire, masques blancs* had already appeared in

134), by showing that the image repertoire according to which we model ourselves is modifiable. Ideals of beauty and other "ideals" can change. So, there is at least a tension between – if you will – an anthropological and historical specification of being visible.⁶

Silverman goes even further. Referring to Lacan's mysterious expression that the subject is "photo-graphed", she wonders whether image technologies are not themselves different historical forms in which the regime of the gaze is "embodied"⁷: "At least since the Renaissance, optical devices have played a central role in determining how the gaze is apprehended, and such devices cannot simply be reduced to a set of images" (ibid.: 136). Referring to Barthes' descriptions of how one freezes in the moment of (consciously) being photographed, for example,⁸ she writes:

[T]he camera has been installed ever since the early nineteenth century as the primary trope through which the Western subject apprehends the gaze. [...] [W]hen a real camera is

---

1952. Fanon, influenced by Sartre and Merleau-Ponty, was himself a psychoanalyst, and already invoked the concept of the mask in his title, which also appears in Lacan (1998: 84, 107). In the preface to the 1986 edition of the work, Homi K. Bhabha writes: "[T]o exist is to be called into being in relation to an Otherness, its look or locus" (in: Fanon 2008: xxviii) and "[F]or Fanon, like Lacan, the primary moments of such a repetition of the self lies in the desire of the look [...]" (xxix). Here, too, the gaze plays a central role: chapter five, "The Fact of Blackness" (82 ff.) thus begins with the citation of a racist exclamation and the gaze it invokes: "Look, a [Ne***]!" In Lacan, however, the racist structuring of the screen is not mentioned, at least in *Seminar XI*. The transhistorical gaze seems to be white. Another question would be how blind people are actually conceptualized in a theory of the gaze. Blindness appears in Lacan (1998), but only negatively, insofar as the "geometrical" conception of vision describes a central-perspective projection that can also be constructed by blind people with threads (cf. 92f.). This is true, but if "that which concerns vision" (ibid.: 92) is thus missed, what status do blind subjects have? Cf. Lacan (2006): "Even a blind man is a subject [...] because he knows he is an object of other people's gazes" (56).

6   Attempts to historicise Lacan have been critically portrayed as bringing him too close to Foucault, cf. Copjec (1994).

7   Cf. Lacan (1998): "If, then, the gaze is that underside of consciousness, how shall we try to imagine it? The expression is not inapt, for we can give body to the gaze" (83f.).

8   Cf. Barthes (1981): "[O]nce I feel myself observed by the lens, everything changes: I constitute myself in the process of 'posing,' I instantaneously make another body for myself, I transform myself in advance into an image. This transformation is an active one: I feel that the Photograph creates my body or mortifies it, according to its caprice [...]" (ibid.: 10f.). On Barthes and Lacan, cf. Iversen (1994).

trained upon us, we feel ourselves subjectively constituted, as if the resulting photograph could somehow determine 'who' we are. (ibid.: 135)[9]

This is true not only regarding freezing or posing in front of the camera (cf. Owens 1994), but also with respect to such phenomena as passport photos, which in the context of identity documents serve to regulate subjectivity by linking appearance and name, and thus the political and economic performativity of the body (cf. Schröter 2016).

At around the same time as Kaja Silverman, but without reference to her, Ruth Iskin (1997) also added to this discussion: "How ha[s] the radically increased role of imaging technologies affected our notions of human subjectivity?" (ibid.: 43). She also emphasises the constitutive role of the gaze, as mediated by the screen (and its media realisations), for the subject (ibid.: 48, 52). This raises the question of whether other technologies also produce other "historically specific" forms of the gaze: "Lacan alludes to the fact that formations of subjectivities are deeply affected by specificities of the signification system, its apparatuses and media and, we might add, their historically specific articulations and roles in the social arena" (ibid.: 58).

These are important points, but Iskin does not go into detail about the different effects that "photography, film and TV" (ibid.: 58) or "cyberspace" (ibid.: 59) might have. For example, she describes computer displays as "post-industrial 'mirrors' of images that often continue to refer to photographic representation, whether they are synthetically generated or manipulated with the computer, or are transmitted from a photographically produced source" (ibid.: 53). Here, Iskin mentions very different types of images that can be produced with computers – and it seems to be important that they refer to photography in one way or another. It is true that many (but by no means all) forms of computer graphics refer to photography, up to and including the modelling of a "virtual camera" (cf. Schröter 2003; on the complex terminology of the digital image, cf. Schröter 2004). And it is true that all image media record and/or generate and/or reflect and/or radiate light, but such a general reference to light would make the intended media-historical differentiation of the gaze rather less clear. Silverman (1996: 195) also mentions "photography, cinema and video" and she connects these technologies through the fact that they all involve the dispositive of the camera. This would mean, however, that their different modalities of recording (still/moving, photochemical/electronic, analogue/digital) do not play a role.

Are being looked at, freezing, or posing transformed, depending on whether the camera records in an analogue or digital manner? Probably not. Could there

---

9   There were and are a number of media-technological metaphors for consciousness, the unconscious, memory, and so on, which are by no means always modelled on optical media (this probably also applies to Freud's often-discussed "Wunderblock"), but this cannot be elaborated on here.

then be a specific "digital" gaze? If, like Kittler (1986), we were to link the "digital" (mediated via the typewriter) to Lacan's discrete symbolic order, and the gaze (mediated via the cinema) to the imaginary, there could in fact be no digital gaze. It may be, however, that either the assignment of the gaze – to which Lacan (1998) ascribes a discretising and therefore potentially digital "power to separate" (ibid.: 115) – to the imaginary is inadequate or that Kittler's correlation of media dispositives to certain Lacanian registers is historically variable in itself. And how does this in turn relate to the economy of image technologies and to both their form and content, which constitute at least part of the screen?

3. The Gaze and Capitalism

Capitalism is a complex phenomenon of which there are several varieties (cf. Hay 2020), but here I want to focus on only some of its basic properties. Marx's *Capital* does not begin with "capitalists" as a group of people. It begins with the *commodity* – which Marx explicitly designates as the "elementary form" of wealth in "societies in which the capitalist mode of production prevails" (Marx 1976: 125). Why the elementary form?[10] Because it has two aspects: a sensuous one (use-value) and an abstract one (exchange-value). This is because it is exchanged, and in order to trade two different commodities, all their concrete and different properties must be ignored in the process of giving and taking. The only respect in which the two commodities are identical is their exchange-value. This involves an abstraction which – as Marx attempts to show in detail – results in the formation of a special, separate commodity: money. A society based on exchange is only possible with money as the objectification of abstract value (cf. Heinrich 1999: 196-251).

The division between the concrete and the abstract and the conflict that arises between these two poles form the core of the argument. This division also characterises labour, which as average socially necessary work determines the value of individual commodities.[11] *All* labour is both concrete labour, associated for example

---

10   The following basic features of the analysis of the value form are presented in detail in Heinrich (2005: 37-77).

11   Marx appears to be following the traditional labour theory of value of classical economics. However, that is not the case, although it is not possible to discuss this in detail here. Cf. on this topic (among many others) Heinrich (2001: 157-158): "If the Marxian theory of value could really be reduced to [...] a quantitative labour theory, it would indeed inhabit the same theoretical space as classical and neoclassical economics; in that case, the claim of Marxian critique to not just criticise the results of bourgeois economics but also the categorical foundations on which these results were acquired would not be upheld. It is true that a whole host of argumentative approaches can be found in Marx's own works that could be understood in terms of a quantitative labour theory of value (especially his treatment of the transforma-

with concrete skills that are required to produce a commodity in the form of a use-object, and abstract labour, which is quantified by an abstract temporal regime (cf. Postone 1993). Marx argues that abstract value tends to grow constantly. Different commodities have qualitatively different use-values, but different sums of money can only differ quantitatively. This can only make sense if, according to the money – commodity – money cycle, the result is *more* money (cf. Jappe 2004: 55). Once the relation of capital has been established, more value must be created from value through the intermediary step of commodity production: M – C – M'. And since value is purely quantitative, this movement is in principle endless. Capital is not the sum of all capitalists or the sum of all wealth (hoarding); capital is the movement of making *more* value out of value. It is the "automatic subject" (Marx 1976: 255) of society. Marx thus shows that the "competition of capital [...] is only the external form [...] in which capital's inner drive to accumulation is realised" (Deutschmann 2008: 132). But how does more value come into existence?

Since we have already touched on socially measured abstract labour, the answer is close to hand: the commodity of labour power can be used to enable the production of surplus value. Here, we might note that information production and circulation on social media is a similar process, in which users do unpaid work (cf. Fuchs 2014).

The class division developed historically in order to enable the production of more and more value. The enrichment of capitalists, however, is just a side effect of the movement of the increase in value, not its purpose. Hence, "owners of capital and, likewise, the managers, prove to be mere functionaries of the 'automatic subject,' which operates beyond their aims" (Kurz 2000). Workers and capitalists alike are "personifications of economic categories" (Marx 1976: 92). Capitalist society is a cybernetic system, whose sole purpose is to make more value out of value, more money out of money – no matter the consequences of this system for people, planet, or even for itself. Money as an expression of value is an end in itself. The process of abstract accumulation is the reality of capitalism. And the bureaucratic state is an apparatus that protects and enables this infinite process of growth (cf. e.g., Tilly 1990; Singh/Tiwana 2020).

The question that needs to be posed now, is: How does capitalism relate to the gaze? If the gaze is realised historically in and through different technologies, as discussed in the second section, and these technologies have emerged historically in capitalism (cf. Beniger 1986), could we not expect there to be a specifically capitalist structure of the gaze? In studies relating Marx and Lacan, however, we unfortunately find little to nothing relating to the gaze.

> tion problem in the third volume of *Capital*), but the central impetus of the Marxian theory of value lies precisely in its critique of the premonetary quantitative labour theory of classical economics. This impetus becomes clear if one bears in mind the manner in which Marx identifies the deficits of classical economics' value theory."

Tomšič (2015, ebook) has shown how the notion of abstraction immanently links Marx's and Lacan's respective projects. With respect to the "substantialisation of capital, the detachment of the autonomy of exchange-value from the negative it inevitably produces", his very interesting study unfortunately addresses the question of the gaze only once, and then only marginally. I shall come back to the passage in question shortly, but for now we can keep in mind that the author argues that the subject's "shameless" exhibition appears to be characteristic of the capitalist gaze. In another passage, he links capitalist subjectivity to quantification: "Lacan's placement of the subject in the position of the product signifies both the scientific isolation of labour-power in natural bodies and the consequent quantification of subjectivity, as well as the political-economic fabrication of homo oeconomicus, no less a product of the social implementation of a knowledge rooted in the imperatives of capital" (Tomšič 2015, ebook). Pierre Bruno (2020), who in a recent study analyses the relations between Marx and Lacan, also omits any discussion of the gaze.

Now, one might suspect that in these studies the gaze is still implicitly understood as ahistorical and anthropological, so to speak – and if this is the case, it comes as no surprise that it is not related to the specific historical formation of capitalism. Even in studies that historicise the notion of the gaze in Lacan, however, such as those by Kaja Silverman and Ruth Iskin discussed above, there is still little to no mention of capitalism. We can then affirm that the question of the (historicised) gaze has not yet been related to the question of capitalism.

To return, then, to the questions posed at the end of the preceding section: What form would a contemporary gaze take that is "embodied" (in Silverman's sense) through digital technologies that are themselves deeply embedded in capitalism? After all, as Silverman notes in her reading of Harun Farocki's film *Bilder der Welt und Inschrift des Krieges* (*Images of the World and the Inscription of War*, 1988): "The camera/gaze thus emerges within *Bilder* as an apparatus for the production of quantified and quantifiable images" (1996: 143). Does this mean that beyond the objectifying gaze, as described by Lacan, there is also a quantifying gaze (to which Baxandall (1988) has referred[12]), albeit in a completely different context and with different terminology? This would certainly make sense in the circumstances of the basic traits of capitalism delineated above. A capitalist gaze would have to be one that turns every object seen into a commodity, attaching exchange value to it and thereby abstracting it: "The cycle Money – Commodity – more Money – which Marx had so impeccably taken apart – is homologous to the Easter computus; by virtue of money, capitalism *virtualises all living things through money creation*" (Bruno 2020: 141; cf. Bjerg 2014 for a Lacanian theory of money). Given the fact

---

12 See especially p. 86, where he underlines how painting in the 15th century represented quantitative relations that were immediately recognisable for merchants, who often financed and/or bought the images.

that digital technologies can register traces of, measure and count almost everything, they can connect everything to abstract and discrete monetary units. This is obvious in the much discussed "like-economy" (cf. Gerlitz/Helmond 2013; Prokić 2020), where images are ranked according to the likes they are given. The case is similar for contemporary technologies of (self-)tracking (cf. Duttweiler et al. 2016). Here, the subject feels inspected by a measuring, quantifying gaze that no longer makes it solely an "object" in accordance with a screen of hegemonic appearance patterns, but rather an abstract data set that is ranked and compared, whether with its own changing performance or with that of others. Competition becomes inscribed into the subject. Discussions of the "like-economy", however, do not address the images, but only the likes that are added to the images. Instead, they do discuss their para-texts, so to speak. Accordingly, they are more about metadata than about the visual regime. In a famous essay, Sekula (1981) has related photography to capitalism, underlining both its role in the *commercial circulation of commodities* on the one hand (ibid.: 22) and in the *state apparatus* (e.g., in police photography) on the other:

[D]uring the second half of the nineteenth century, a fundamental tension developed between uses of photography that fulfill a bourgeois conception of the self and uses that seek to establish and delimit the terrain of the other. Thus every work of photographic art has its lurking, objectifying inverse in the archives of the police. (ibid.: 16)

Digital imaging technologies, born within a capitalist context from economic (cf. Beniger 1986) and bureaucratic policing-necessities (cf. Agar 2003), should thus operate in a comparable way. There should be a specific digital and capitalist gaze.

4. Two Regimes of the Digital, Capitalist Gaze

If we follow Sekula's hint, then there should be at least two operations of the digital gaze in capitalism. The first turns the subject into a commodity that is integrated into a visual circulation that exploits the desire of the subject to be seen: the circulative gaze. The second inscribes, as it were, the big Other into the subject: the centroramatic gaze. One cannot easily equate this gaze with the state apparatus, since the state often incorporates surveillance by private companies or uses the data of private actors for its surveillance.[13] What seems necessary here, however, is to separate the *commodifying* from the *policing* operations[14] of the gaze – even if

---

13 With thanks to Olga Moskatova.
14 Cf. Robinson on the "global police state" (Robinson 2020). Even if today's global digital corporations seem extremely powerful, we must not forget that their existence is based on property rights, laws and so on that have to be protected by the state. Capitalism does not work without the state and its monopoly on violence – which might

they overlap most of the time. Therefore, the difference between a circulative and a centroramatic gaze is underlined below.

4.1 The Circulative Gaze

In what sense are selfies a form of the digital gaze? Uzlaner (2017) has discussed the selfie from a Lacanian point of view (see also Raymond 2021), according to which selfies constitute a look at me from the outside and intended for others, but performed and self-staged by myself. I am "photo-graphed", but willingly, by myself. The selfie represents my desire to pose for the gaze, insofar as I, as the person photographing myself, place myself under the regime of the others as such – sometimes even (in a supremely Lacanian manner) with the help of a mirror: "The subject literally looks at herself through the gaze of the Other" (Uzlaner 2017: 283). Instagram filters, in this case, can be described as a game with the screen – a game that is supposed to serve the perfect self-staging within an economy of likes and an assertion strategy on the attention market – and yet can turn into ridicule and hate at any time.[15] The selfie is a typical form of the image in surveillance capitalism. Through the distribution of circulative possibilities to everyone (at least in principle), competition within the visual field enters our consciousness. In principle, we can all depict ourselves and let the resultant images circulate globally in digital data networks. The accumulation of "likes" introduces capital accumulation into the hegemonic screen and, as capital accumulation always does, it produces sexist and racist exclusions (cf. Noble 2018). The selfie manifests a *desire* to be *surveilled-as-the-right-one* (cf. Uzlaner 2017: 287-289). The empirical studies of large numbers of selfies conducted by Lev Manovich (cf. Tifentale/Manovich 2015), for example, reached the expected finding that these images look essentially the same. Everyone (potentially) conforms to the screen (especially women, cf. 115). "The gaze is rather the incarnation of the [capitalist] regime's power. [...] The subjects offer themselves to the regime's gaze and shamelessly exhibit jouissance, not knowing that the regime in the position they assume establishes the continuity between jouissance and labour" (Tomšič 2015, ebook). This is always problematic, however, since posing (cf. Owens 1994) and performatively embodying the hegemonic screen can be unstable and can be disrupted. They can be played

even be turned against such powerful corporations (as in the case of the breakup of AT&T in 1982).

15 Cf. https://www.for-me-online.de/beauty/haut-und-koerperpflege/instagram-filter, 13.07.2021: „Ruckzuck lassen sich Fotos optimieren und uns prompt noch besser aussehen. Damit Ihr nächster Instagram-Post die Herzen der Follower im Sturm erobert, stellen wir Ihnen jetzt unsere vier liebsten Instagram-Filter vor!" ("In a flash, photos can be optimised, making us look instantly better. Here are our four favourite Instagram filters, so that you can conquer the hearts of your followers!" [trans. JS]) In this conquering of hearts, what is clearly in question is desire.

with. But in social networks the image can also lead to "bodyshaming"; one can be ridiculed and the ideal-ego traumatically disrupted by the evil gaze.

A contemporary example here is Billie Eilish. The young singer wears baggy clothes and items such as glasses to avoid drawing attention to her body, precisely in order not to present a hegemonic image. If this does happen, however – for example if she decides to post bikini photos from a vacation – the outcry is enormous (cf. Sycha 2020). Suddenly, Eilish then makes her body visible, which leads instantaneously to objectification: "[...] [W]*hat I look at is never what I wish to see*" (Lacan 1998: 103; emphasis in original). Hate is born from the unbearable disappointment that in the end, it is only the capitalist image industry that produces the screen. This is a heavy blow for one's own "oppositional" subjectivity – and it is as such that Billie Eilish (in common with many forms of pop and rock music in the past) has been sold. A hateful look is directed at Eilish, precisely because this circulation of an invisible privacy, under other media conditions, interrupts the image that has just been (seemingly) built up against the dominant gaze. The problem is that in such moments, the illusion that we can really escape the hegemonial screen is disrupted. We should understand that "Eilish" is only a commodity, an abstract construction that lures us through the appeal of "resistance". In the scandalous moment itself, however, we have to realise that this is actually only about making money (cf. Bjerg 2014). Eilish's abstract character as commodity becomes visible, if only for a moment. The hateful reactions cannot be explained in any other way than as an effect of the traumatic disappointment that "beyond appearance [Eilish's self-staging, JS] there is nothing in itself; there is the [male[16] and capitalist, JS] gaze" (Lacan 1998: 103).[17] Such a phenomenon is then found "less amusing" (ibid.: 95).

4.2 The Centroramatic Gaze

Lacan constantly emphasizes that the subject is in the "picture" (ibid.: 106). But the "picture" we are in is not a two-dimensional picture. It is a three-dimensional scene, a three-dimensional image. For this reason alone, it is in fact strange that the gaze is described via the metaphor of the photograph, since this is a two-dimensional image. One might also ask whether Silverman's (1996: 135) historicising perspective – "[T]he camera has been installed ever since the early nineteenth century as the primary trope through which the Western subject apprehends the gaze" – does not also allow the possibility that historically new and perhaps even more appropriate "primary tropes" might emerge for the gaze. Perhaps the rather

---

16 See Jay (1993: 533), who speaks of the "screen of male representations".
17 Cf. also Lacan (1998: 112) on the story of Zeuxis and Parrhasios: "But the opposite example of Parrhasios makes it clear that if one wishes to deceive a man, what one presents to him is the painting of a veil, that is to say, something that incites him to ask what is behind it."

trivial observation that today's photo cameras (such as those in cell phones) *record* digitally and no longer analogously is not relevant at all. Perhaps there are quite different "cameras" today.

In a short section of *Seminar XI*, Lacan discusses Roger Caillois's (1984; 2007) influential reflections on mimicry. Caillois discussed the property of organisms, often noted in nature, of adapting to their background, and in doing so departed from Darwin's conception of adaption.[18] Lacan, referring to Caillois, emphasises approvingly: "Indeed, it is in this domain that the dimension by which the subject is to be inserted in the picture is presented" (1998: 99). Caillois (1984: 23) speaks in his discussion of mimicry of "sculpture-photography or better *teleplasty*, if one strips the word of any metapsychical content"[19]. Callois discusses a becoming-image of the animal through mimicry and Lacan extends this to his idea of the becoming-image of the subject through the gaze. What, then, might be considered the "primary trope" of a contemporary "camera" that turns the subject into an image?

One important technique of contemporary capitalist globalisation is the 3D body scanners installed at many airports, which generate an omnidirectional scan to ensure, for example, that no weapons are smuggled onto airplanes. They are part of the inevitable security infrastructure of crisis-ridden global capitalism. In these systems the representations of bodies are highly abstracted and mostly free of intimate details. Everyone becomes reduced to the information pertinent to security. The dispositive of the 3D scanner thus reverses that of the panoptic gaze described by Foucault (cf. Foucault 1995; Wood 2003). The subject is no longer outside and exposed to the gaze of a centre, but rather the subject is in the centre and the gaze is directed "centroramatically" (Schmidt 2002: 186, trans. JS) from the outside – which corresponds to Lacan's (1998: 106) understanding that the gaze is "outside."

Fig. 1 Panorama vs. centrorama, after Schmidt (2002)

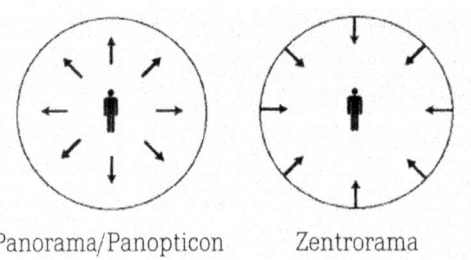

Panorama/Panopticon   Zentrorama

---

18 See Eidelpes (2018: 67-84), for a detailed and clear placement of Caillois's position in the historical context.

19 Muhle (in print) has placed this passage precisely in the context of Caillois's work and located it in the field of "millieu-esthetics".

Like Foucault's panopticon, the 3D scanner can be seen as a "diagram" or an "abstract machine" (Deleuze 1988: 34). What is important here is not any specific scanner, but the regime of visibility that dominates modern capitalism. It is important to underline that the 3D scanner is only meant as a form of metaphor (as was the panopticon in Foucault); the same principle can also be found in networked images on the Internet, for example. The 3D scanner is a very concrete example of a more general "diagram" of contemporary visibility.

The centroramatic gaze is far more radical than the panoptic gaze (cf. Foucault 1995; Wood 2003), since the latter originates from one point and therefore (at least potentially) casts a shadow in which we might conceal ourselves. But the centroramatic gaze comes from everywhere and therefore (potentially) leaves nowhere to hide. It amounts to the total visibility, the totalitarian gaze of capital. While everything is capitalised, put into circulation and valorised (cf. Szepanski 2014), everything has to be controlled. No deviation from total capitalisation is allowed. Lacan's observation that "I am looked at from all sides" (1998: 72) was never truer than today.

5. Conclusion

Digital technologies as configured in contemporary global capitalism produce at least two forms of a digital, capitalist gaze. These two forms of the digital gaze and the networked images correlated with it are two central characteristics of the reconfiguration of visibility in surveillance capitalism. Firstly, there is the *circulative gaze*, which results from the fact that the power to record images and circulate them (in principle) worldwide is now given to (potentially) everyone.[20] Potentially, everyone can follow their desire to expose themselves-as-the-right-one to the gaze of the Other: "No matter how successful the resulting image, however many likes or enthusiastic comments it gets – all the same it is not enough. The subject must again dress up, again put on makeup in the hope of finally catching that same gaze of that same Other. In this sense the selfie, like any other fantasy, is endless" (Uzlaner 2017: 288). It is as endless as the accumulation of capital. Market subjectivisation and self-commodification is enforced, but this only works because the desire of the subject is involved. Nonetheless, there is always the possibility of travesty and the danger of traumatic disappointment.

Secondly, there is the *centroramatic gaze*. This gaze radicalises the panoptic gaze, since it has no enunciative point (from which we could hide), at least in principle. On the one hand, it is of course an effect of the circulative gaze, insofar as cell phones and their cameras are everywhere, yet additional cameras such as

---

20   Although there are, of course, many regions in the world which are not connected to the Internet.

public video surveillance add to its assemblage. Its most concentrated manifestation, however – its "primary trope," in Silverman's words – is the 3D body scanner.

In the foregoing, I have stressed the commodifying and controlling aspects of the digital, capitalist gaze. The contemporary emphasis on local resistances, which is of course important, should not blind us to the current regimes of images in surveillance capitalism. There is, however, a tension between the circulative and the centroramatic gaze: While the first is about the desire to be seen, to become an attractive commodity, the second is a kind of god-like view, from which we might try to escape. The agonising between the wish to become visible and the wish to hide from the gaze is a central tension within social visibility today.

References

Agar, Jon (2003): The Government Machine: A Revolutionary History of the Computer, Cambridge/MA and London: MIT Press.
Barthes, Roland (1981): Camera Lucida: Reflections on Photography, New York: Hill and Wang.
Baxandall, Michel (1988): Painting and Experience in Fifteenth Century Italy: A Primer in the Social History of Pictorial Style, Oxford: Oxford University Press.
Beil, Benjamin/Schröter, Jens (2011): "Die Parallelperspektive im digitalen Bild." In: Zeitschrift für Medienwissenschaft 3/4, pp. 127-138.
Beniger, James (1986): The Control Revolution: The Technological and Economic Origins of the Information Society, Cambridge/MA: Harvard University Press.
Bjerg, Ole (2014): Making Money: The Philosophy of Crisis Capitalism, London: Verso.
Blümle, Claudia/von der Heiden, Anne (eds.) (2005): Blickzähmung und Augentäuschung. Zu Jacques Lacans Bildtheorie, Zürich: Diaphanes.
Bruno, Pierre (2020): Lacan and Marx: The Invention of the Symptom, New York: Routledge.
Bryson, Norman (1998): "The Gaze in the Expanded Field." In: Foster, Hal (ed.): Vision and Visuality, Seattle: Bay Press, pp. 87-113.
Burroughs, William S. (1966): Naked Lunch, New York: Grove.
Caillois, Roger (1984): "Mimicry and Legendary Psychasthenia." In: October 31, pp. 16-32.
Caillois, Roger (2007): Méduse & Cie. Die Gottesanbeterin – Mimese und legendäre Psychastenie, Berlin: Brinkmann und Bose.
Copjec, Joan (1994): Read My Desire: Lacan against the Historicists, Cambridge, MA/London: MIT Press.
Deleuze, Gilles (1988): Foucault, Minneapolis/London: University of Minnesota Press.
Deutschmann, Christoph (2008) "'Kapitalismus' und 'Geist des Kapitalismus' – Anmerkungen zum theoretischen Ansatz Boltanski/Chiapellos." In: Wagner,

Gabriele/Hessinger, Philipp (eds.): Ein neuer Geist des Kapitalismus? Paradoxien und Ambivalenzen der Netzwerkökonomie, Wiesbaden: VS Verlag, pp. 127-143.

Duttweiler, Stephanie/Gugutzer, Robert/Passoth, Jan-Hendrik/Strübing, Jörg et al. (eds.) (2016): Leben nach Zahlen. Self-Tracking als Optimierungsprojekt?, Bielefeld: transcript.

Eidelpes, Rosa (2018): Entgrenzung der Mimesis. Georges Bataille – Roger Caillois – Michel Leiris, Berlin: Kadmos.

Fanon, Frantz (1952): Peau noire, masques blancs, Paris: Seuil.

Fanon, Frantz (2008): Black Skin, White Masks, London: Pluto Press.

Foucault, Michel (1995): Discipline and Punish: The Birth of the Prison, New York: Vintage.

Fuchs, Christian (2014): Social Media: A Critical Introduction, London: SAGE.

Gerlitz, Caroline/Helmond, Anne (2013): "The Like Economy: Social Buttons and the Data-Intensive Web." In: New Media and Society 15/8, pp. 1348-1365.

Gondek, Hans-Dieter (1997): "Der Blick zwischen Sartre und Lacan. Ein Kommentar zum VII Kapitel des Seminars XI." In: Riss: Zeitschrift für Psychoanalyse 57/38, pp. 173-194.

Hay, Colin (2020): "Does Capitalism (Still) Come in Varieties?" In: Review of International Political Economy 27/2, pp. 302-319.

Heinrich, Michael (1999): Die Wissenschaft vom Wert. Die Marxsche Kritik der politischen Ökonomie zwischen wissenschaftlicher Revolution und klassischer Tradition, Münster: Westfälisches Dampfboot.

Heinrich, Michael (2001): "Monetäre Werttheorie. Geld und Krise bei Marx." In: PROKLA. Zeitschrift für kritische Sozialwissenschaft 31/123, pp. 151-176.

Heinrich, Michael (2005): Kritik der politischen Ökonomie. Eine Einführung, Stuttgart: Schmetterling.

Iskin, Ruth E. (1997): "In the Light of Images and the Shadow of Technology: Lacan, Photography and Subjectivity." In: Discourse 19/3, pp. 43-66.

Iversen, Margaret (1994): "What is a Photograph?" In: Art History 17/3, pp. 450-464.

Jappe, Anselm (2004): Die Abenteuer der Ware. Für eine neue Wertkritik. Münster: Unrast.

Jay, Martin (1993): Downcast Eyes: The Denigration of Vision in Twentieth Century French Thought, Berkeley: University of California Press.

Kittler, Friedrich (1986): Grammophon, Film, Typewriter, Berlin: Brinkmann und Bose.

Kurz, Robert (2000): Marx 2000 (http://www.exit-online.org/link.php?tabelle =autoren&posnr=104).

Lacan, Jacques (1973): Le Séminaire de Jacques Lacan. Les Quatre Concepts Fondamenteaux De La Psychanalyse, Paris: Éditions du Seuil.

Lacan, Jacques (1998): The Seminar of Jacques Lacan: The Four Fundamental Concepts of Psychoanalysis, New York/London: W. W. Norton & Company.

Lacan, Jacques (2006): "On My Antecedents." In: Lacan, Jacques: Écrits, New York and London: W. W. Norton & Company, pp. 51-57.

Marx, Karl (1976): Capital, Vol. I. A Critique of Political Economy, London: Penguin.

Muhle, Maria (in print): "'Eine Skulptur-Photographie oder besser eine Teleplastik' – Mimesen zwischen Natur und Kultur bei Caillois." In: Balke, Friedrich/Linseisen, Elisa (eds.): Mimesis Expanded, München: Fink.

Noble, Safiya Umoja (2018): Algorithms of Oppression: How Search Engines Reinforce Racism, New York: New York University Press.

Owens, Craig (1994): "Posing." In: Owens, Craig: Beyond Recognition: Representation, Power and Culture, Berkeley, Los Angeles and London: University of California Press, pp. 201-217.

Postone, Moise (1993): Time, Labor and Social Domination: A Reinterpretation of Marx' Critical Theory, Cambridge: Cambridge University Press.

Prokić, Tanja (2020): "Post, Like, Share, Submit. Visual Control and the Digital Image (13 Theses)." In: Coils of the Serpent 5, pp. 145-152.

Raymond, Claire (2021): The Selfie, Temporality and Contemporary Photography, New York/London: Routledge.

Robinson, William I. (2020): The Global Police State, London: Pluto Press.

Schmidt, Gunnar (2002): "Zeit des Ereignisses – Zeit der Geschichte. Am Beispiel der Multiperspektivität." In: Immanuel Chi/Susanne Düchting/Jens Schröter (eds.): ephemer_temporär_provisorisch, Essen: Klartext, pp. 175-196.

Schröter, Jens (2003): "Virtuelle Kamera. Zum Fortbestand fotografischer Medien in computergenerierten Bildern." In: Fotogeschichte 23/88, pp. 3-16.

Schröter, Jens (2004): "Das Ende der Welt. Analoge vs. digitale Bilder – mehr und weniger 'Realität'?" In: Jens Schröter/Alexander Böhnke (eds.): Analog/Digital – Opposition oder Kontinuum? Zur Theorie und Geschichte einer Unterscheidung, Bielefeld: transcript, pp. 335-354.

Schröter, Jens (2016): "Sich ausweisen." In: Ilka Becker/Bettina Lockemann/Astrid Köhler/ Ann Kristin Krahn/Linda Sandrock (eds.): Fotografisches Handeln, Marburg: Jonas, pp. 226-239.

Sekula, Allan (1981): "The Traffic in Photographs." In: Art Journal 41/1, pp. 15-25.

Singh, Paramjit/Tiwana, Balwinder Singh (2020): "The State and Accumulation under Contemporary Capitalism." In: World Review of Political Economy 11/1, pp. 76-94.

Silverman, Kaja (1996): The Threshold of the Visible World, New York: Routledge.

Sycha, Lisa (2020): "Billie Eilish: Beschimpfungen wegen Bikini-Fotos im Urlaub." In: Rolling Stone, April 15 (https://www.rollingstone.de/billie-eilish-beschimpfungen-wegen-bikini-fotos-im-urlaub-1968963/).

Szepanski, Achim (2014): Kapitalisierung Bd. II. Non-Ökonomie des gegenwärtigen Kapitalismus, Hamburg: LAIKA.

Tifentale, Alisa/Manovich, Lev (2015): "Selfiecity: Exploring Photography and Self-Fashioning in Social Media." In: David M. Berry/Michael Dieter (eds.):

Postdigital Aesthetics: Art, Computation and Design, Basingstoke and Hampshire: Palgrave Macmillan, pp. 109-122.

Tilly, Charles (1990): Coercion, Capital, and European States AD 990-1990, Cambridge, MA: Basil Blackwell.

Tomšič, Samo (2015): The Capitalist Unconscious: Marx and Lacan. London: Verso.

Uzlaner, Dmitry (2017): "The Selfie and the Intolerable Gaze of the Other." In: International Journal of Applied Psychoanalytic Studies 14, pp. 282-294.

Wood, David (2003): "Foucault and Panopticism Revisited." In: Surveillance and Society 1/3, pp. 234-239.

Nudged to Normal

Images, Behaviour, and the Autism Surveillance Complex

Daniela Wentz

Abstract

For Shoshana Zuboff, affective computing is one of the key technologies of "rendition" through which surveillance capitalism is realised (Zuboff 2019). An epistemic and technical condition of affective computing is the combination of facial detection and facial expression recognition, i.e., the identification of faces by computer vision and the process of measuring human emotions by identifying the corresponding facial expressions. While Zuboff criticises affective computing primarily in immediate economic contexts, particularly in market research, this article is devoted to its application in an area that she considers "innocent": the therapy of people diagnosed with autism spectrum disorder.

The focus of this paper is on wearables based on Google's smart glasses, which aim at teaching social interaction skills to children diagnosed with autism. The paper critically analyses the role of images, their operational logics and datafication for this heterogeneous human-machine constellation and shows that these technologies are hardly innocent. On the contrary, the glasses are a prime example of what Zuboff terms "rendition", and of the commercialisation of dis/ability in surveillance capitalism.

Keywords

Affective Computing; Artificial Intelligence; Autism; Autism Therapy; Behaviourism

> Think your kid might be autistic? There's an app for that!
> Want to modify your child's behavior? There's an app for that too.
>
> ANNE MCGUIRE, 2016

1. Introduction

"I was getting like a little emotional when I was seeing your presentation cause it's that amazing to me. Like it's, it's really neat." A fundraiser video for a digital assistive technology for people diagnosed with autism, called *Empowered Brain*, opens with "Colleen Matlock, chief ABA therapist at LoveU2pieces Autism Centre Missouri", speaking through tears of joy.[1]

Empowered Brain is a head-mounted wearable developed by the company Brain Power. To describe it more precisely, it is a bundle of apps that run on the hardware of Google's data glasses (which were a flop). The technical platform of *Google Glass* includes a frame worn like a pair of glasses, equipped with a camera, a whole range of sensors, a small screen above the right eye and a bone-conduction speaker, combined with various software applications. *Empowered Brain* is designed to help wearers improve social and cognitive skills, such as making and maintaining eye contact, and recognising and responding to emotional facial expressions. For example, the camera sends images to an artificial intelligence app for facial tracking and facial expression recognition, which interprets emotional expressions and sends them back to the wearer as visual feedback appearing on the glasses' screen. *Empowered Brain* is not the only one of its kind in the autism technology market. *Autism Glass*, also called *Superpower Glass* by Cognoa, a spinoff of Stanford University, operates on identical principles. In addition to the glasses, a whole range of digital technologies have emerged in recent years that pursue similar autism therapy goals. These tools vary from relatively simple learning apps for emotion recognition and explanation, to therapy approaches using social robotics and virtual reality environments. In fact, autistic people[2] are one of the

---

1 https://www.youtube.com/watch?v=CiFNiUmbZ5Q&ab_channel=BrainPower%3A EmpoweringEveryBrain%21, last accessed July 29, 2021.
2 I will use medical terminology and identity-first language in this paper when referring to individuals affected by autism rather than person-first-language. I acknowledge the arguments that have been made for each of the terminologies and their use (Cf. here for arguments for the use of person-first-language: http://www.inclusioncollaborative.org/docs/Person-First-Language-Article_Kathie_Snow.pdf; cf. here for arguments for identity-first-language: https://autisticuk.org/wp-content/uploads/2016/05/AUTISTIC-UK-KEY-TEXTS-1-WHY-I-DISLIKE-PERSON-FIRST-LANGUAGE.pdf; cf. here for the use of both terminologies interchangeably: https://autismandoughtisms.wordpress.com/2011/07/25/has-autism-versus-is-autistic-a-muddled-debate/). Individuals affected by autism, diagnosed or not, decide whether they consider autism as being

main target groups in the health sector, and emotional artificial intelligence is expected to make a ground-breaking contribution to research, diagnosis, assistance, and therapy of the condition. Emotional AI, also called affective computing, is one of the younger branches of artificial intelligence. It combines computer science, sensor technologies, biometrics, cognitive and neuroscience, psychology, robotics, and other strands of knowledge, to read, recognise, interpret, simulate, and influence human emotions. In effect, it makes human emotions manageable and operationalisable. Among its many hopes and promises is the aim to endow computerised machines themselves with feelings and emotions. Thus, the application areas of the field go far beyond the domain of said therapeutic technologies and are remarkably broad – ranging from telemedicine and telepsychology to e-learning; mobility and social robotics, to immersive and interactive (entertainment) environments; and of course, its most attractive domain, consumer research and marketing.[3]

Autistic persons are considered predestined counterparts for those emotionally intelligent, 'empathic' technologies, based on several assumptions. Autistic individuals have, according to a very influential and long-standing theory, a "theory of mind"-deficit, which means the inability to empathise with others, i.e., to assume feelings, needs, ideas, intentions and expectations in others (e.g., Baron-Cohen/Leslie/Frith 1985; Baron-Cohen 2001; Soper/ Murray 2012; Kimhi 2014; Fitzpatrick et al. 2018).[4] Those considered 'low-functioning' autists often do not acquire language at all or very late; they do not or hardly react to social signals, like gestures and facial expressions, they cannot make or maintain eye contact, etc. Furthermore, it is claimed that autistic people simply have no intellectual and emotional self-awareness (e.g., Williams 2010; Kinnaird et al. 2019) and, if at all, only "limited [...] insight into their own feelings and thought processes" (Happé 1991: 220).

---

such an essential part of themselves and their identity, that they refer to themselves as autistic, whether they consider it as something that they have or whether they choose not to refer to it at all. When I use identity-first-language I do so because I want to bring to the fore that I do not consider autism as something comparable to a disease, as something that can or must be cured. It is a political decision expressing my solidarity with the identity politics of the neurodiversity movement. Identity-first language is said to be preferred by autistic people (Kenny et al. 2016) and to prevent stigmatisation (Gernsbacher 2017).

3   Cf. McStay 2018 for a good overview of the manifold application areas of emotion AI.
4   Morton Ann Gernsbacher and M. Remi Yergeau have researched that the theory is pervasive although "the vast majority—over 75%—of the top 500 articles indexed by Google Scholar (for "theory of mind" and "autism") simply assert that autistic people lack a theory of mind rather than providing original data" (Gernsbacher/ Yergeau 2019).

Neither these assumptions about autism that underlie the development of the technologies, nor the forms of therapy in which they are (supposed to be) incorporated and their goals have gone unchallenged. Particularly from the ranks of neurodiversity studies, the pathologising of autism in general and the forms of therapy and cure have been questioned and deemed unethical.[5] Morton Ann Gernsbacher and M. Remi Yergeau, for example, have meticulously and convincingly demonstrated that the assumption of a theory of mind-deficit in autistic people is highly questionable and yet "despite these numerous empirical failures, the claim pervades psychology and well beyond" (Gernsbacher/Yergeau 2019). Nevertheless, no non-computational studies are available on these technologies yet.[6] The aim of this article, therefore, is to examine the epistemological, historical, and discursive conditions of these technologies, their rationale and functioning, and the role played by the images such technologies produce. It does so by approaching them from different but combined angles, namely media dis/ability studies and history of knowledge and science. As Anna Tuschling has argued, without the history of knowledge and reference to the development of affective computing, its scope and significance cannot be understood (Tuschling 2018: 44). I examine how behavioural theory and autism research have been informing computer science and have become the theoretical and practical undergirding of the technologies at issue. I analyse how exactly, through the images and image operations they produce and perform, they aim to condition their wearers into a predefined neurotypical type of behaviour and suppress unwanted neurodiverse behaviour. The best way to understand their scope and impact, I argue, is through the lens of Shoshana Zuboff's elaboration of the principles of what she calls "surveillance capitalism" (Zuboff 2019). Although she does not use the term biopolitics once in her analysis of the genesis and presence of surveillance capitalism, she does identify as its main feature the transference of all human experience, the body, emotions, behaviour, and thoughts, into a radical capitalist logic of exploitation that ultimately leads to a democracy-eroding new social order. Zuboff detects the aforementioned affective computing as one of the key technologies of "rendition" and "behavioural modification" through which surveillance capitalism is realised. But while she assesses the autism technologies as rather "innocent" compared to other affective technologies more directly intertwined with the logics of capitalism, I intend to show that they are anything but innocent. Rather, they are prime examples of a "datafied biopolitics" (Manschewski/Nosthoff 2021) operating on both the micro-level of the individual body and macro-level of the population.[7]

5   E.g., by Dawson 2004; Yergau 2018; McGuire 2016; Rosqvist/ Chown/ Stenning 2020;

6   Other aspects of affective computing have already been discussed in media studies: Cf. Angerer/Boesel 2015; 2016; Tuschling 2018.

7   For Michel Foucault, who introduced the concept of biopolitics as it is used here into the debate, as well as for more recent studies that move argumentatively in his

2. Rendition from the Depths

In Zuboff's analysis, human affects and emotions may be "the new frontier of behavioural surplus" (2019: 254), but ultimately "simply one more source of raw-material supply for machine rendition and analysis, all of it for the sake of more-perfect prediction" (ibid.: 282). The overarching and declared goal of affective computing or artificial emotional intelligence is the humanisation and personalisation of human-machine interfaces and the associated interactions (cf. Picard 2000 [1997]; Somers 2019). For Zuboff, the pervasive 'personalisation' and 'user-friendliness' banners under which affective computing is promoted serve only as smokescreens for companies of surveillance capitalism to greedily grab our most intimate impulses, desires, affects and emotions to tackle and nudge us, so that we end up exactly where they want us to be.

She pinpoints the origin of this "burgeoning new domain of rendition" (ibid.: 281) unerringly to the MIT Media Lab of the late 1990s, where computer engineer Rosalind Picard, whose research was far ahead of the state of the art at the time, predicted the development of computers with a sense of emotion. She made the case for the feasibility and desirability of this kind of development by envisioning a variety of application scenarios in her founding manifesto and two years later in a book of the same name (Picard 1995; 2000 [1997]). A few scenarios seem so worthy of mention to Zuboff that they find their way into her narrative of the history of affective computing. One amongst them is its application for the therapy of autistic people. For Zuboff, that area of application represents a moment of innocence for affective computing, a philanthropic idea before its fall from grace. Affectiva, the company founded by Picard and Rana El Kaliouby, an associate at MIT, used their research on emotion AI and turned it into a marketable product. Affectiva was caught in the maelstrom of surveillance capitalism only shortly after its founding, where it has been busy harvesting behavioural surplus ever since. In fact, prior to founding this company, Picard and El Kaliouby had each worked independently at first, then together for a few years at MIT from the early 2000s onwards, on several emotion detection technologies that were originally intended to primarily help autistic individuals – or at least, that is the story.

In the narrative of the development from El Kaliouby's perspective, which was published in 2015 as an article in *The New Yorker* (which Zuboff refers to at length), the technology soon caught the interest of various companies:

> footsteps, but concentrate on the analysis of a transformed economic system under the conditions of digital information and communication technologies on the one hand and recent (bio)scientific developments on the other, biopolitics and capitalism are inextricably linked and so cannot be considered separately from each other at all (Foucault 1979; 1994; 2020; Rajan 2006; Fritsch 2015; Puar 2017).

"Pepsi was curious if it could use the software to gauge consumer preferences. Bank of America was interested in testing it in A.T.M.s. Toyota wanted to see if it could better understand driver behaviour – and perhaps design a system to detect drowsiness. Inquiries flooded – from Microsoft, H.P., Yamaha, Honda, Gibson, Hallmark, NASA, Nokia.... (El Kaliouby, quoted after Khatchadourian 2019)

These companies bombarded the developers with enquiries to such an extent that they founded Affectiva. Then it quickly – at the insistence of the company's then-CEO – dropped work on assistive technologies, in favour of "myriad products based on affective computing" primarily for use in market research (Khatchadourian 2019). In Zuboff's version of the story, Picard, who "was forced out of the company after only four years", is given the role of the sorcerer's apprentice who can no longer get rid of the ghosts he called forth, and now simply comments from the side lines on the dark machinations of the "rendition from the depths" (Zuboff) – albeit without having abandoned her own research projects on emotion AI at MIT.

Picard did not foresee the market forces that would transform the rendition of emotion into for-profit surplus: means to others' ends. That her vision is made manifest in thousands of activities should be a triumph, but it is diminished by the fact that so many of those activities are now bound to the commercial surveillance project. (Zuboff 2019: 291)

3. Facial Behaviour

The fact that Picard and Kaliouby both researched "innocently enough" (Zuboff) the development of technologies related to autism at the beginning of the 2000s is by no means a coincidence, and I do not want to impute purely altruistic motives to either of them. Rather, it can be assumed that both hoped quite pragmatically for inspiration from autism research for the development of their overarching goal – emotion AI. The consistent identification of autistic people as ideal early adopters of their technologies was based on the establishment of several similarities between assumptions about the former and the logics of computers. Picard, basically echoing in her writing the widespread assumptions about autistic people, equates computers without emotional intelligence with autistic people, who are considered here as socially deficient beings:

In many ways computers are like autistic people – particularly like autistic "idiot savants," an unfortunate term that has been used to describe people who have unusually gifted abilities in certain areas – such as rapid computation of large numbers, memorizing phone listings, and precise memory of huge sets of facts and trivia, but who lack the forms of common sense and emotional intelligence that most people acquire effortlessly. [...] Unaffective computers are similarly handicapped; they are great at recalling facts and information that are semantically linked to the keyword or concept of the moment, but they are unable to determine which of all the possible linked items is the most relevant to the situation at hand. (Picard 2000: 90)

This argument, inadequately formulated in its entirety, was not revolutionary. In fact, since the beginnings of autism research, the assumed social deficits of autistic people have been counterbalanced by the diagnosis of a remarkable responsiveness in dealing with things and technologies. The latter, it seems, led to the creation of metaphorical analogies to machines time and again to describe autistic people, from Bruno Bettelheim's "mechanical boy" (1959) to the various diagnostic manuals in which 'repetitive motor behaviour' is still a diagnostic criterion, to books for children on the spectrum: "Our brains are like computers" (Shaul 2016). Even the famous autist Temple Grandin repeatedly described her mind as a web browser, computer, etc. (cf. Grandin 2000).[8]

While the history of the analogy between autistic brains and computers has taken a course leading from stigma to positive connotations and even appropriation as part of autistic identity, in Picard's case we are still dealing with a narrative of deficiency. Picard's position is strategic because factors like assumed deficient social interaction skills, ascribed lack of empathy and emotional intelligence not only define a starting point for imagined therapy, but also act as justificatory knowledge for the development of emotionally intelligent machines. In El Kaliouby's narrative, too, the apparent congruence of the autistic mind and computers comes to light through the observation of a shared deficit, although in this retelling it appears to be merely serendipitous: "During a presentation of her research goals, an audience member mentioned that the problem of training computers to read faces seemed to resemble difficulties that his autistic brother had" (Khatchadourian 2019). Following up on this hint, El Kaliouby discovered a project at the Cambridge Autism Research Centre "to create a catalogue of every human facial expression, which people on the autism spectrum could study to assist with social interactions [...] Kaliouby recognized at once that the catalogue presented an unprecedented opportunity: rich, validated data, ideal for a computer to learn from" (ibid.).

This is more than an anecdote. It is also more than just another example of how theories and experiments of autism research inform other fields of knowledge, especially computer science. Rather, it demonstrates the analogistic heuristics of the genesis of the technologies under discussion. What El Kaliouby eventually developed was a programme called *MindReader* that "could track several complex emotions in relatively unstructured settings" (ibid.). Applied the

---

[8] Cf. Peters/ Pinchevski (2015) for a reconstruction of the history of the relationship between autism and technology.

other way around, she envisioned a kind of wearable emotional or behavioural prosthesis to assist autistic people:

> As she considered its (MindReader's, D.W.) potential, she wondered if she could construct an "emotional hearing aid" for people with autism. The wearer would carry a small computer, an earpiece, and a camera, to scan people's expressions. In gentle tones, the computer would indicate appropriate behaviour: keep talking, or shift topics. (ibid.)

From today's perspective, this vision reads pretty much like a description of the autism glasses. So, it comes as no surprise that Affectiva, in association with Google and AWS, an Amazon company entrusted with web services and cloud computing, are listed as partners of Brain Power, the manufacturer of the *Empowered Brain* glasses. In fact, the emotion AI used in *Empowered Brain* for facial expression recognition comes from Affectiva (Liu et al. 2017: 2). This also means that the glasses operate with 'basic emotions', as Picard already imagined back in the 90s as the basis for affective computing (Picard 1995: 5). The basic assumption on which the principle of facial expression recognition is based is that a person's feelings are expressed physically, especially mimically, both voluntarily and involuntarily. Feelings are thus conceptualised as "observable behavioural data" (Zuboff 2019: 284) that can be classified, converted into machine-readable instances, and operationalised. Following this assumption, the way of expressing emotions is universal, transcending history and cultures, and accordingly can be read and recognised everywhere and at any time by (almost) everyone. In practical implementation, one assumes a fixed set of universal emotions, those so-called basic emotions, which are correlated with supposedly equally universal, clearly assignable physiological markers – mainly facial muscle movements, but also breathing frequencies, galvanic skin responses and the like. In the case of *Superpower Glass*, which also works according to this principle, the eight-part collection of emotions consists of "happy, sad, angry, scared, surprised, disgust, 'meh,' and neutral" (Voss et al. 2019: 447). When the camera of *Superpower Glass* is pointed at a face while it is being worn, the screen integrated into the glasses shows a green frame to indicate that a face has been identified. The image data is sent to the smartphone app connected to the glasses, which performs facial tracking and emotion classification, and stores the images and related data. Immediately afterwards, an emoji appears on the screen as feedback, symbolising one of the eight emotions that the glasses have recognised. A parallel audio classification of the recognised emotion via the loudspeaker is an additional option (cf. ibid.). *Empowered Brain* works the same way, but is based on six emotions, as Affectiva's 'toolkit' follows the *Facial Action Coding System* (FACS) already developed in the 1970s by Paul Ekman and Wallace Friesen; this classifies six supposedly universal emotional states, namely "surprise, fear, disgust, anger, happiness and sadness" (McDuff et al. 2016: 3724; cf. Ekman/Friesen 1975). Thus, it pretty much follows a catalogue of emotions that has persisted in the history of affect theory since Aristotle (cf. Weigel 2015: 91).

Sigrid Weigel examined the genesis of the *Facial Action Coding System* and undertook a detailed pictorial critique of this instrument in order to expose the "epistemic reverse side", or the unspoken presuppositions and unexplained epistemic blind spots of this system, which are still firmly established in affective computing. She shows that the FACS is a highly constructed "combinatorics" of a "(1) historical knowledge tableau in the form of a compilation of physiological expressive lore with (2) photographic records of their enacted embodiments by living models and (3) an *ars combinatoria* of gestures of the three facial parts" (ibid.: 94, my translation).

For instance, the coding system for a definitive correlation of emotions with individual regions of the face and their movements was achieved by compiling studies in physiognomics from the 19th century onwards:

> We constructed a table which listed all the facial muscles and the six emotions, entering into the table what these men had written about which muscles were involved in what way for each emotion. There were many gaps, however, where no one had said anything about the involvement of a particular muscle in a particular emotion. [...] We filled in those gaps with information from our cross-cultural studies and our shared impressions. (Ekman/Friesen 1975: 28)

The fundamental nomenclature of the FACS can thus be traced back to, amongst other sources, Guillaume-Benjamin Duchenne de Boulogne's tableau of "Expressions de Passion", which he formulated in the 19th century based on the anatomy of the facial musculature. This "semiotics of facial muscles" (Weigel 2015: 99, my translation) portrays the face as a tableau of physiologically localised emotional signs, in which the names of the individual muscles are identical to and named after the feelings they express on the face's surface, presenting as Weigel writes, an "almost ideal coding system" (ibid.: 104). Ekman and Friesen took up these and other nomenclatures, expanded them, and produced an atlas of photographs that capture the specific emotional expressions by instructing actors, actresses and others to move certain muscles. The movements of the respective single parts of the face were also documented individually to substantiate the semiotic character of the facial expressions (Ekman/Friesen 1975). In the automation of this system, in the *AFFDEX SDK* programme by Affectiva, an algorithm is trained with a data set of images and videos of the facial expressions of many people, which had been previously codified with the help of the FACS (cf. McDuff et al. 2016: 3724).

Even this brief outline clearly shows how problematic this system is, and on what unspoken presuppositions and poorly substantiated assumptions it is based. In addition to the obviously clumsy analogical conclusions and the radical neglect of the historical and cultural situatedness of feelings and their expression, there is an obvious contradiction in the system, which Ekman and Friesen do address.[9] There is a juxtaposition of 'true' feelings, expressed through involuntary, uncontrolled, possibly unconscious expressions, and the ever-present possibility of the display of false feelings, produced through controlled and thus potentially deceptive expressions of affect. This means that the expression and corresponding interpretation of a feeling says nothing at all about whether the detected feeling is actually felt. To circumvent this dilemma, Ekman later shifted his interest to micro-expressions or rapid muscle movements of the face that escape the naked eye, which are recorded technically and made visible by slow motion or other processes of analysis (cf. https://www.paulekman.com/). It is these optically unconscious micromimic behaviours that are now associated with the assumption of an uncontrollable expression of the true emotional state. Other, more recent methods of recognising feelings have moved away from image-based detection altogether and now search for feelings in the non-visible layers of the body, for example, by means of electromyography (Weigel 2015: 97). In the case of the autism technologies, on the other hand, the contradiction must be dealt with on various levels. Here, for several reasons, one is dependent on the conception of feelings as observable, unambiguous "facial behaviour" (Ekman/Friesen: 29) and the face as the authentic scene of their appearance. One must also – as it is done here – proclaim this quite confidently as an unquestionable credo:

The face is where evolution put data about people's feelings, thoughts, intentions, trustworthiness, and more. Yet, for many on the spectrum, looking at faces can be confusing, stressful, or just neglected. *Play With Faces* reverses all that. With it, your child has an excuse to look at faces, and it is fun: they get decorated in real time. (https://brain-power.com/)

This quote already reveals one of the reasons why this is accepted as a self-evident fact. In addition to the emotion assistance software already described, both glasses are equipped with so-called "engagement activity modes" (Voss et al. 2019: 448), which are designed to help people practise certain skills via graphically augmented reality elements, as in the example above, and via gamification, for example a reward system with points or stars to be won. In the example above, it is the process of focusing on the face of a counterpart or "facial engagement". In "Guessing my Emotion" by *Superpower Glass* and "Emotion Charades" by *Empowered Brain* – which illustrates the second reason – the goal is to guess the emotional facial expression of the other person. These lessons basically repeat

---

9   Weigel is not the only critic of basic emotions. Both the historian Ruth Leys (2017) and the neuroscientist Lisa Feldman Barret (2017) have fundamentally criticised basic emotions and their underlying assumptions. The cultural and historical situatedness of emotions in general has been emphasised by Sarah Ahmed (2004) and Martha Nussbaum (1999), to name but two.

Ekman's and Friesen's logic of producing the photographic atlas of emotions, insofar as the other party receives instructions via the app on the smartphone concerning which emotion s/he should express. The camera tracks the face, makes two suggestions in the form of different emojis for which emotion has been portrayed, and the wearer of the glasses must choose one. The success of the glasses wearer's learning thus depends not least on the acting talent of those who perform the visual emotion for her/him.

The third and most important reason has to do with the purpose of the glasses. For they are not simply prostheses, but highly specialised therapeutic interventions. The declared aim of the technologies is the learning effect that comes from wearing them. Without the assertion of validated knowledge and the competence of its teaching, the very purpose of the whole endeavour would ultimately be at stake. Finally, as I will show in the next chapter, the assertion that feelings are ultimately nothing more than facial behaviour opens up the full scope of these technologies. Behaviour is the key to understanding what is at stake here.

4. Nudged to Normal

Rana El Kaliouby was not the only one who envisioned the future of her technology. In her book, Rosalind Picard, too, had sketched out some ideas of what the technologies that were yet to be developed might be like. While El Kaliouby's emotional hearing aid may have been more about integration into everyday life, Picard actually imagined a therapy setting in which the emotionally intelligent computer took the place of the therapist.

One way to help autistic people is to have a trained person sit down with them and repeatedly walk-through situations to help them learn how to understand and respond. However, the helper is prone to lose patience in the tedious repetition of endless situations. The autistic requires a new explanation with each situation since he cannot easily generalize from the explanations they have previously learned. Autistics benefit greatly from this one-on-one help and could make greater strides with more of it. This is interaction that could be provided by computers capable of understanding emotion. Computers with an ability to teach this understanding – via games, exploratory worlds, virtual social scenarios, and other interactions that provide repetitive reinforcement, could be developed with present technology. Even a relatively simple computer, which just implemented a basic appraisal theory of emotion, could run a large variety of scenarios illustrating how emotions arise, and guide an autistic user towards a better understanding of socially adept responses. In the future, computers should also be able to recognize the emotional expressions of an autistic user, to help give him feedback as he tries to learn skills such as empathy. (Picard 2000: 90)

I quote this in such detail here because the description of the therapy setting also reveals the type of therapy into which the technologies were to be integrated. Picard was very clearly thinking of ABA therapy, Applied Behaviour Analysis Therapy. ABA therapy, as the name suggests, is the application of the research, experiments, and ideas of the founder of radical behaviourism and behaviour analysis, B.F. Skinner. Skinner did his famous conditioning experiments with mice, rats, and pigeons in the 1940s and 50s to find out how behaviour can be explained, predicted and ultimately controlled. During the experiments, he found that observable behaviour is not solely dependent on prior stimuli, as Pavlov, Watson and others had shown, but can also be produced by the consequences of observable behaviours (cf. Skinner 1938; 1953).

This process of bringing about desirable behaviour in a predictive way by reinforcing a specific action and eventually entire chains of actions is what he called "operant conditioning". His primary aim was to use "behavioural engineering" to continuously reinforce some actions at the expense of others. He then transferred his findings from the behavioural analysis of animals to humans and finally built an entire social theory on operant conditioning. In essence, he was interested in applying this engineering to entire populations. He elaborated this vision for the first time in a novel called "Walden Two" (1948), which describes a peaceful, happy society based on operant conditioning and its technologies. Later, in writings such as "Beyond Freedom and Dignity" (1971), he put the same ideas into more science-conforming prose.

In Zuboff's analysis of the genesis and present manifestations of surveillance capitalism, Skinner is the key thinker, and his operant conditioning the core technology through which surveillance capitalism is realised. The logic underlying surveillance capitalism is the discovery and conceptualisation of our experiences, feelings, and behaviour as raw material in the value chain; their systematic observation, tracking and extraction; and the transformation of that into data and finally products that are traded or used, not only to predict but also to guide our future behaviour. Zuboff sees this as a realisation not only of Skinner's operant conditioning, but also of his vision of society. Surveillance capitalism automates behaviour modification through the development of digital technologies such as fitness trackers and the like, but also through social engineering, as Zuboff analyses using the example of Facebook's social contagion and mood experiments. Drawing on Skinner, Zuboff paints a gloomy picture of the present, where she sees a new, anti-democratic power at work, which threatens human rights:

With this reorientation from knowledge to power, it is no longer enough to automate information flows about us; the goal now is to automate us. In this phase of surveillance capitalism's evolution, the means of production are subordinated to an increasingly complex and comprehensive "means of behavioural modification." In this way, surveillance capitalism births a new species of power that I call instrumentarianism. Instrumentarian power knows and shapes human behaviour toward others' ends. Instead of armaments and armies, it works its will through the automated medium of an increasingly ubiquitous computational architecture of "smart" networked devices, things, and spaces. (Zuboff 2019: 8)

While radical behaviourism, following Zuboff's thinking, appears to be making it big for the first time in surveillance capitalism, it has been the chief ideology for the treatment of autism for more than half a century. Applied behaviour analysis as a form of therapy was developed as early as the 1960s by psychologist Ivar Loovas at UCLA, as an intervention for treating not only autistic, but also gender-nonconforming children. In the so-called "Feminine Boy Project", which Lovaas carried out in the 1970s with his doctoral student at the time, the foundations were laid for the repulsive and cruel treatment that is now called conversion therapy (cf. Gibson/Douglas 2018). While conversion therapy is now a banned treatment method in many countries for good reasons (in Germany only since 2020), ABA therapy is still the most widespread form of therapy in the field of autism. If carried out according to the textbook, children spend twenty to forty hours a week with their therapists and parents in this type of treatment. Its objective is the increase of desired social behaviour and the inhibition of unwanted or "challenging behaviour". It is based on Skinner's operant conditioning, which means that desired behaviour is positively reinforced through methods like praise and rewards, while unwanted behaviour is sanctioned. In the early years, not only positive reinforcers were used, but also aversive ones like electric shocks, beatings, or verbal rebukes.

It may have become clear by now that the autism glasses pursue behavioural therapy goals like those of ABA. The glasses are not only meant to accompany and/or extend ABA therapy into families, they *are* the therapy: "Your child looks through a wearable computer screen and gets points for performing social behaviours with you and others. The real-time reinforcement builds social-emotional skills and self-confidence and creates data for progress reports" (https://brainpower.com/demo-s/).

In the case of the autism glasses, the "automated behavioural modification" that Zuboff sees at work in surveillance capitalism is primarily evoked by the gamification of images that they produce, which act as nudges. It has often been argued that both nudging and gamification in general are methods based on behaviourist assumptions and principles. As shown above, in the case of the autism devices, it is a combination of attention-seeking through graphic elements that appear on the screen and ludic elements to achieve the goal of the learning unit. The goal could be a reward system in the form of stars or points to be earned, and the integration of levels of varying 'difficulty' that are reached through desirable behaviour, such as holding eye contact.

If one were to believe the publications of the developers and the statements of the 'testimonials' quoted on their websites, this method seems to work quite well. So well in fact, that it brings tears of joy to the eyes of not just the ABA therapist quoted at the beginning of this article: "I cried when he used *Empowered Brain*, because he was looking at me differently. I realised he had never really looked at me before in his life," reads one mother's quote on the website (https://brainpower.com/families/).

This kind of idolisation and repeated drilling of the importance of eye contact can be found everywhere. One does not have to retrace the cultural history of the gaze to understand how exchanges of looks are hardly innocent, or what constellations of power and even violence are embodied in them. The simple sentence "Look at me when I'm talking to you" shows the whole scope of the gaze in all its clarity. Why autistic people have difficulties with eye contact is neither the problem nor the therapeutic approach of ABA. It asks about the symptoms, not the causes. Its aim is to stop autistic behaviour, not to alleviate a condition.

As I hope to have shown, the technologies analysed here for the therapy of autistic people are uncannily illustrative of the attempt to automate operant conditioning along the lines of B.F. Skinner's radical behaviourism. But does that also make them technologies of surveillance capitalism? For if one agrees with Zuboff, "[a]lthough it is still possible to imagine automated behavioural modification without surveillance capitalism, it is not possible to imagine surveillance capitalism without the marriage of behaviour modification and the technological means to automate its application" (Zuboff 2019: 296). As I will show in the following section, it is not only through Zuboff's derivation of automated behavioural modification that the rationale and operational mode of these technologies can be unlocked; in fact, it is simply not possible to imagine such technologies without surveillance capitalism.

5. The Autism Surveillance Complex

At least from today's perspective, El Kaliouby and Picard's narrative of having abandoned research into autism technologies as it lacked any promise of profit seems somewhat counterintuitive. And not just because both never really gave up working on these ideas. One does not have to do much research to conclude that "in short, autism is currently big business" (Broderick/Roscigno 2021: 3). In recent years, several studies have examined aspects of the political economy of autism, or at least stated the capitalist nature of autism as a prerequisite for other issues. Some scholars analyse autism as a commodity (Mallet/Runswick-Cole 2016), others even speak of an autism industry (Milton/Moon 2012). Anne McGuire (2016) was the first to invoke the term "autism industrial complex" to highlight the sheer diversity of "public and private investment interests that benefit economically from, and indeed whose very fiscal survival is reliant upon" autism and autistic subjects. Numerous new and highly specialised jobs have emerged around autism including diverse, more or less scientific forms of therapy; products for the prevention of autism, such as prenatal supplements for brain development; products for treatment as toys and tools like our glasses in question here; and hundreds of meters of advice literature. This commodification of autism can also be observed in popular culture. It has become a veritable 'brand' that can turn any product into, one could say, 'autism merchandise': "One can, for example, purchase a pair of Autism Speaks skate shoes or a bag of puzzle piece shaped pretzels. The autism 'brand' can be found anywhere from clogs to candles. It marks cufflinks, keychains, frying pans, wine bottles, baseball caps, T-shirts, balloons, bumper stickers, champagne glasses, and thongs" (McGuire 2016: 126-128). Alicia Broderick and Robin Roscigno use the concept of the autism industrial complex in order to make it productive for the analysis of the questions of "how autism came to be successfully commodified" and of "the nature of the intersecting social, historical, cultural, political, and economic infrastructures that both produce and sustain it as a lucrative commodity" (Broderick/Roscigno 2021: 8). Drawing on the concept of the 'military industrial complex' first invented by Dwight D. Eisenhower and since then transferred and adapted to describe many different spheres, Broderick and Roscigno identify a tripartite intersection of components, namely ideology, technology, and profit, which comprise the autism industrial complex. In other words, the autism industrial complex is not a monolithic block or a single entity, but overlapping networks of entities not necessarily pursuing the same agenda, which "seek not only to promote their products and services in order to generate profit, but that simultaneously seek to promote their ideas and beliefs (which is just as central to the ultimate goal of generating profit)" (ibid: 10). The plutocrats of the autism industrial complex, the main players in the autism market, have one thing in common, that they are "intimately connected with [...] behaviourism" (ibid.: 11). According to this account, the authors consider behaviourism in general and operant behaviourism in particular to be the ideology that undergirds the autism industrial complex. "It has been the deployment of behaviourism as an ideology – driven through its applied technologies of aba – that has enabled the development of a large-scale and complex technocratic infrastructure for generating profit from autism over the course of the last seventy-five years" (ibid.: 13). Despite this compelling analysis, the authors conclude that the role of behaviourism in the development and cementing of the autism industrial complex has been merely "serendipitous", a historically contingent trend that could just as easily have been taken up by Freudian psychoanalysis or neuroscience. "As a pure thought experiment, entirely removing behaviourism from the mix still leaves autism and capitalism. This, we argue, is (and will continue to be) the crux of the matter" (ibid.: 20).

However, things are not that simple. For if behaviourism is taken out of the equation, it alters the character of (contemporary) capitalism – recall Zuboff's "it is not possible to imagine surveillance capitalism without the marriage of behaviour modification and the technological means to automate its application" – as much as it alters the character of 'autism'. Autism without behaviourist research, diagnosis and therapy would be a completely different phenomenon, with different perceived symptoms, assumptions, approaches, subject understandings. In this respect, the autism industrial complex, if it existed at all without behaviourism, would certainly have a different face.

Broderick and Roscigno also stop short of taking the next logical step in their argumentation, the question of the specific historical conditions for the rise of behaviourism as the chief ideology of the autism industry. Instead, they leave it at the rather vague statement that capitalism and behaviourism developed at the same time – the same could probably be said for almost everything. While it may not be possible to discuss this at length here, it is at least possible to make some assumptions, considering my argumentation so far, as to where we might look in order to understand the historical entanglement of the factors that led to the development of the autism industrial complex or what I believe would be a more precise term, an *Autism Surveillance Complex* as it appears today.

The parallel development of capitalism and behaviourism is a gross understatement, because the fact is that behaviourist theses have been so pervasive in economics for decades that behaviourism may as well be regarded as its dominant orthodoxy. Second, we should ask about the media of behaviourism. As I have shown above, regarding the connection between autism and (media) technologies, we must speak of a mutual production in which the media involved in research, diagnosis and therapy are constitutively involved in the determination of what autism is. Conversely, the findings and assumptions of autism research migrate as sources of knowledge into the developments of technologies and their disciplines. In a historical perspective, film, and the method of so-called microanalysis, as developed in the context of behavioural research and developmental psychology at least since the 1920s, would be particularly relevant. It was meant to give what was still a relatively young discipline scientific legitimacy through objective observability and analysable data. In fact, the founder of behaviourism, John B. Watson, was the first psychologist ever to produce a film in the context of his research. The film shows the infamous "Little Albert" experiment, which Watson used to prove his classical conditioning thesis by teaching a baby to fear animals by associating them with a loud, unpleasant noise (cf. Curtis 2011). The use of film as a diagnostic instrument and research method in behavioural research, psychology and thus also in autism research continues even now, where the evaluation of the film sequences produced is carried out increasingly by means of machine learning (cf. Curtis 2011; cf. Joice 2020; cf. Condon 1981; cf. Tardif et al. 1995; cf. Taric et al. 2018). Still, in the absence of clear biological markers to diagnose autism, observing, documenting, analysing and ultimately modifying behaviour remains a near obsession for the autism industry. This is also in part thanks to technological developments that allow ever finer gradations and classifications of behaviour. In her analysis of the biopolitical frameworks that produce and define autism, Anne McGuire has poignantly expressed this intertwining of the production of autistic behaviour and the simultaneous attempt to contain it:

Paradoxically, [...] such timely actions and reactions [...] surveil particular kinds of behaviours, notice particular behaviours as signs of 'deviance,' discipline and restrict these behaviours, [...] but they are also entrepreneurial, creative, and creating-uncovering more ways of noticing and charting the minutiae of human difference, generating more ways of classifying behaviours as abnormal or deviant, coming up with more and more ways of treating or preventing autism, more and more ways of raising awareness about its pathological state of underdevelopment. As it both stimulates and regulates conducts beyond the norm, the neoliberal 'now' is a time for ('good') autism advocacy. (McGuire 2016: 142)

The autism glasses are also part of this double-edged logic. Unsurprisingly at this point, they collect all the behavioural data while being worn, which are then processed and displayed in extremely detailed dashboards for tracking, meticulous analysis and feedback from the therapists and caregivers. For example, sensors directed at the wearers of the glasses themselves are used to track the behaviour of their eyes to provide information about attention and the extent of fulfilment of the requested behaviour, and possible progress or regression about the predefined goal by means of the dashboard. On the other hand, at least in the case of *Empowered Brain*, the collected data are used to conduct unspecified big data driven studies. The developer's site reveals only this much: "Our aim is to uncover data-driven subtypes of autism, and to customize the experience for each unique child and adult. By being part of the Brain Power family you are also part of perhaps the world's largest humanitarian study of autism and related conditions. You can benefit your community."[10] One can conclude from this statement that by signing the user agreement, the patients' caregivers' consent to the former's observed behaviour being used as a training set for machine learning algorithms aimed at the automated diagnosis of autism and related conditions, such as ADHD. Likewise, the fact that the actual business of the company building the *Superpower Glass* is the development of digital diagnostics for autism spectrum disorder leaves little room for doubt. That this approach represents a prime example of the migration of the data-driven practices of surveillance capitalism to the health market and to health management, in which "personalized medicine", algorithmic diagnosis and above all prevention and behavioural change constitute the declared goals, hardly needs to be explained at this point and can be described as surveillance-capitalist biopolitics or "datafied biopolitics" (Maschewski/Nosthoff 2021, my translation; see also Meier 2020; McStay 2018: 133-135).[11]

10 This does not read like Facebook's *data for good* mission statement by accident: "We empower partners with privacy-preserving data that strengthens communities and advances social issues" (https://dataforgood.facebook.com/).
11 Felix Manchewski and Anna-Verena Nosthoff, for example, show vividly and in great detail how the major tech companies Google, Apple, Facebook and Amazon have recently been able to exploit the Covid pandemic to massively intensify their efforts in the health sector, to open up new business segments, and to make themselves vir-

This transference can also be observed in other spheres that have so far not been suspected of profit orientation. In their analysis of the datafication of learning, Jeremy Knox, Ben Williamson & Sian Bayne, quite in line with Zuboff, note that behaviourism, principles associated with it, and techniques based on it are also making a comeback in the field of learning and education. In the datafication of human learning, the authors note, nudging technologies are increasingly being applied, and more so those of emotion AI. As they note, referring to Karen Yeung's concept of the 'hypernudge', it is

[t]he logic of such devices [...] that they can read mood from the student's voice, body, brainwaves, or face and deliver feedback which is supposed to prompt the student to shift to a more positive and rewarding state. These technologies are pedagogic variants of the 'hypernudge' techniques employed by social media and web companies to influence users and maintain consumer engagement. [...] In this way, learning itself is reconceptualised in terms of psychologically quantifiable affective characteristics which are both detectable as autonomic bodily signals and amenable to being changed and modified in line with particular theories about what constitutes the 'correct', 'preferable', or 'desirable' behaviours for learning. (Knox/ Williamson/ Bayne 2019: 11)

Skinner's reinforcement learning, which we know from glasses therapy, in turn migrates into artificial intelligence, where it is applied as a training principle of machine learning algorithms. For example, the algorithm of the now well-known program Alpha Go, developed by Google's Deep Mind, evolves exclusively through reinforcement, namely through the rewards it receives by winning. The statement of the authors, that "this strong vision of learning may be able to train machines towards 'superhuman' capabilities, but there is certainly no suggestion that such a brutal regime would be suitable for human learners", suggests no apparent knowledge of ABA-therapy and its automation by smart glasses. Considering the impulses of autism research for computer science and the development of (digital) technologies, and taking seriously the statement of Verily CEO[12] Derek Dunfield, according to which, "Most people can't recognize their emotions and don't have the vocabulary. If my watch could tell me why I feel bad and what to do about it, we would have a better society" (cited in McStay 2018: 135), this is not only a transfer of the deficiency narrative associated with autism to almost the entire population, but also an idea of how this deficiency could be remedied on a micro and macro-level.

---

tually indispensable in the fight against the pandemic by cooperating with various public health institutions (Maschewski/Nosthoff 2021).

12 Verily is a subsidiary of the Alphabet/Google Group, which is entrusted with Google's health business.

References

Ahmed, Sara (2004): The Cultural Politics of Emotion. Edinburgh University Press.

Angerer, Marie-Luise/Bösel, Bernd (2016): "Total Affect Control. Or: Who's Afraid of a Pleasing Little Sister?" In: Digital Culture & Society 2/1, pp. 41-52. DOI: https://doi.org/10.25969/mediarep/824.

Baron-Cohen, Simon (2001): "Theory of Mind in normal Development and Autism". In: Prisme 34, pp. 174-183.

Baron-Cohen, Simon/Leslie, Alan M./Frith, Uta (1985): "Does the Autistic Child have a 'Theory of Mind'?" In: Cognition. Vol. 21, 1985, pp. 37-46.

Bettelheim, Bruno (1959): "Joey: A 'Mechanical Boy'." In: Scientific American 200, no. 3 (March 1959), pp. 116-27.

Bösel, Bernd/ Angerer, Marie-Luise (2015): "Capture All, or: Who's Afraid of a Pleasing Little Sister?" In: Zeitschrift für Medienwissenschaft. Überwachung und Kontrolle, 7, no. 2, pp. 48-56. DOI: https://doi.org/10.25969/mediarep/1563.

Broderick, Alicia/Roscigno, Robin (2021): "Autism Inc.: The Autism Industrial Complex." In: Journal of Disability Studies in Education, pp. 1-25.

Condon, William (1981): Sound-film Microanalysis as a Technique for the Assessment of Dysfunctional Behavior, Dissertation, Boston College.

Curtis, Scott (2011): "'Tangible as Tissue': Arnold Gesell, Infant Behavior, and Film Analysis." In: Science in Context, 24, pp. 417-442.

Dawson, Michell (2004): "The Misbehaviour of Behaviourists", https://www.sentex.ca/~nexus23/naa_aba.html.

Feldman Barret, Lisa (2017): How Emotions are made. The Secret Life of the Brain, New York: Houghton Mifflin Harcourt.

Fitzpatrick, Paula/Frazier, Jean/Cochran, David/Mitchell, Teresa/Coleman, Caitlin/ Schmidt R.C. (2018): "Relationship Between Theory of Mind, Emotion Recognition, and Social Synchrony in Adolescents With and Without Autism." In: Frontiers in Psychology 9: 1337, doi: 10.3389/fpsyg.2018.01337.

Foucault, Michel (1979) [1976]: The History of Sexuality Volume 1: An Introduction, London: Allen Lane.

Foucault, Michel (1994): "La naissance de la medicine sociale." In: Dits et Ecrits, Vol. III, Paris: Gallimard, pp. 207-228.

Foucault, Michel (2020): Society Must Be Defended: Lectures at the Collège de France, 1975-76. London: Penguin.

Fritsch, Kelly (2015): "Gradations of Debility and Capacity: Biocapitalism and the Neoliberalization of Disability Relations." In: Canadian Journal of Disability Studies, 4(2), pp. 12-48. https://doi.org/10.15353/cjds.v4i2.208.

Gernsbacher, Morton Ann (2017): "Editorial Perspective: The Use of Person-first Language in Scholarly Writing may Accentuate Stigma." In: Journal of Child

Psychology and Psychiatry, and Allied Disciplines, 58, pp. 859-861. https://doi.org/10.1111/jcpp.12706.

Gernsbacher, Morton Ann/Yergeau, M. Remi (2019): "Empirical Failures of the Claim that Autistic People Lack a Theory of Mind." In: Archives of Scientific Psychology, 7(1), pp. 102-118.

Gibson, Margaret F. /Douglas, Patty (2018): "Disturbing Behaviors: Ole Ivar Lovaas and the Queer History of Autism Science." In: Catalyst: Feminism, Theory, Technoscience, 4(2), pp. 1-28.

Grandin, Temple (2000): "My Mind is a Web Browser: How People with Autism Think." In: Cerebrum, Winter Vol. 2, Number 1, pp. 14-22.

Happé, Francesca (1991): "Autobiographical Writings of three Asperger Syndrome Adults: Problems of Interpretation and Implications for Theory." In: Uta Frith (ed.), Autism and Asperger Syndrome, Cambridge University Press, pp. 207-242.

Joice, Katie (2020): "Mothering in the Frame: Cinematic Microanalysis and the Pathogenic Mother 1945–67." In: History of the Human Sciences, pp. 1-27.

Kenny, Lorcan/Hattersley, Caroline/Molins, Bonnie/Buckley, Carole/Povey, Carloe/Pellicano, Elisabeth (2016): "Which Terms should be used to describe Autism? Perspectives from the U.K. Autism Community." In: Autism, 20, pp. 442-462. https://doi.org/10.1177/1362361315588200.

Khatchadourian, Raffi (2015): "We Know How You Feel. Computers are Learning to read Emotion, and the Business World can't wait." In: The New Yorker, January 12, https://www.newyorker.com/magazine/2015/01/19/know-feel.

Kimhi, Yael (2014): "Theory of mind abilities and deficits in autism spectrum disorders." In: Topics in Language Disorders 34, pp. 329–343.

Kinnaird, Emma/Stewart, Catherine/Tchanturia, Kate (2019): "Investigating alexithymia in autism: A systematic review and meta-analysis." In: European Psychiatry, 55, pp. 80-89, https://doi.org/10.1016/j.eurpsy.2018.09.004.

Knox, Jeremy/Williamson, Ben/Bayne, Sian (2019): "Machine behaviourism: future visions of 'learnification' and 'datafication' across humans and digital technologies." In: Learning, Media and Technology, pp. 1-15, https://doi.org/10.1080/17439884.2019.1623251.

Leys, Ruth (2017): The Ascent of Affect. Genealogy and Critique, Chicago: University of Chicago Press.

Liu, Runpeng/Salisbury, Joseph P./Vahabzadeh, Arshya/Sahin, Ned T. (2017): "Feasibility of an Autism-Focused Augmented Reality Smartglasses System for Social Communication and Behavioral Coaching." In: Frontiers in Pediatrics, Vol. 5:145, pp. 1-15, doi: 10.3389/fped.2017.00145.

Mallett, Rebecca/Runswick-Cole, Katherine (2016): "The commodification of autism: What's at stake?" In: Katherine Runswick-Cole/Rebecca Mallett/Sami Timimi (eds.), Re-thinking autism, London and Philadelphia: Jessica Kingsley.

Manchewski, Felix/ Nosthoff, Anna-Verena (2021): "Big Tech und die Pandemie – Smarte Retter in der Not." In: Luxemburg. Gesellschaftsanalyse und linke Praxis, https://www.zeitschrift-luxemburg.de/big-tech-und-die-pandemie/#sdendnote3sym.

McDuff, Daniel/Mahmoud, Abdelrahman/Mavadati, Mohammad/Amr, May/Turcot, Jay/el Kaliouby, Rana (2016): "AFFDEX SDK: A Cross-Platform Real-Time Multi-Face Expression Recognition Toolkit." In: Proceedings of the 2016 CHI Conference Extended Abstracts on Human Factors in Computing Systems (CHI EA '16). Association for Computing Machinery, New York, NY, pp. 3723–3726, https://doi.org/10.1145/2851581.2890247.

McGuire, Anne (2016): War on autism: On the cultural logic of normative violence, University of Michigan Press.

McStay, Andrew (2018): Emotional AI. The Rise of Empathic Media, London: Sage.

Meier, Christian (2020): "Google macht sich zum Schwerezentrum der Medizin von morgen." July 31, https://www.riffreporter.de/de/technik/google-macht-sich-zum-schwerezentrum-der-medizin-von-morgen.

Milton, Damian/Moon, Lyte (2012): "The normalisation agenda and the psycho-emotional disablement of autistic people." In: Autonomy, the Critical Journal of Interdisciplinary Autism Studies, 1(1).

Nussbaum, Martha (1999): Sex and Social Justice, New York: Oxford University Press.

Peters, John Durham/ Pinchevski, Amit (2015): "Autism and new media: Disability between technology and society." In: New Media and Society, pp. 1-17, DOI: 10.1177/1461444815594441.

Picard, Rosalind (1995): "Affective Computing." M.I.T Media Laboratory Perceptual Computing Section Technical Report No. 321.

Picard, Rosalind (2000): Affective Computing, Cambridge MA: MIT Press.

Puar, Jasbir (2017): The Right to Maim: Debility, Capacity, Disability, Durham: Duke University Press.

Rajan, Kaushik Sunder (2006): Biocapital. The Constitution of Postgenomic Life, Durham: Duke University Press.

Rosqvist, Hanna Bertilsdotter/ Chown, Nick/ Stenning (2020): Neurodiversity Studies. A New Critical Paradigm, London: Routledge.

Shaul, Joel (2016): Our Brains Are Like Computers! Exploring Social Skills and Social Cause and Effect with Children on the Autism Spectrum, London and Philadelphia: Jessica Kingsley.

Skinner, B. F. (1938): The behavior of organisms: An experimental analysis, New York: Appleton-Century.

Skinner, B. F. (1953): Science and Human Behavior, New York: MacMillan.

Skinner, B.F. (1948): Walden Two, Indianapolis: Hackett.

Skinner, B.F. (1971): Beyond Freedom and Dignity, Indianapolis: Hackett.

Somers, Meredith (2019): "Emotion AI, explained." In: https://mitsloan.mit.edu/ideas-made-to-matter/emotion-ai-explained.

Soper, H. V./Murray, M. O. (2012): "Autism". In: Noggle, C.A/Dean, R. S./ Horton, A. M. (eds.): The Encyclopedia of Neuropsychological Disorders, pp. 125–128. New York, NY: Springer.

Tardif, Carole/Plumet, Marie-Hélène/Beaudichon, Janine/Waller, Delphine/ Bouvard, Manuel/Leboyer, Marion (1995): "Micro-analysis of Social Interactions between Autistic Children and Normal Adults in Semi-structured Play Situations." In: International Journal of Behavioral Development, 18 (4), pp. 121-141.

Tariq, Qandeel/Daniels, Jena/Schwartz, Jessey/Washington, Peter/Kalantarian, Haik/ Wall, Dennis (2018): "Mobile detection of autism through machine learning on home video: A development and prospective validation study." In: PLoS Med 15(11): e1002705.

Tuschling, Anna (2018): "Die Kunst des Überlistens: Über Affective Computing." In: Andreas, Michael/Kasprowicz, Dawid/Rieger, Stefan: Unterwachen und Schlafen: Anthropophile Medien nach dem Interface, Lüneburg: meson.

Voss, Catalin/Schwartz, Jessey/Daniels, Jena/Kline, Aaron/Haber, Nick/Washington, Peter/Tariq, Qandeel/Robinson, Thomas/Desai, Manisha/Phillips, Jennifer/ Feinstein, Carl/Winograd, Terry/Wall, Dennis (2019): "Effect of Wearable Digital Intervention for Improving Socialization in Children With Autism Spectrum Disorder. A Randomized Clinical Trial." In: JAMA Pediatrics, 173(5), pp. 446-454. doi:10.1001/jamapediatrics.2019.0285.

Williams, David (2010): "Theory of own mind in autism: Evidence of a specific deficit in self-awareness?" In: Autism, 14(5), pp. 474–494, https://doi.org/10.1177/1362361310366314.

Yergeau, M. Remi (2018): Authoring Autism: on rhetoric and neurological queerness, Durham: Duke University Press.

Zuboff, Shoshana (2019): The Age of Surveillance Capitalism. The Fight for a Human Future at the New Frontier of Power, London: Profile Books.

Methodological Reflections

Detained through a Smartphone
Deploying Experimental Collaborative Visual Methods to Study the Socio-Technical Landscape of Digital Confinement

Carolina Sanchez Boe and Henry Mainsah

Abstract

The facial recognition software SmartLink is being increasingly deployed as an "alternative to detention" by ICE (US Immigration and Customs Enforcement), along with other surveillance technologies such as voice recognition and electronic ankle shackles. Rather than being a proper "alternative" to immigrant detention, these technologies have become an addition to the ever-increasing detention numbers, spreading confinement into immigrant communities and homes. These new forms of enforcement technologies constitute an understudied aspect of surveillance capitalism, as they are deployed with the active involvement of private companies with for-profit motives.

This article draws on an experimental collaborative visual methodology enacted by an anthropologist, a design scholar, a lawyer and a participant with personal experience seeking asylum and being monitored through SmartLINK®. Together, we revisit visual material generated as part of ethnographic fieldwork on "digital confinement". Using a walkthrough method, we proceed to conduct a collaborative analysis of Smartlink, its technological features, data generation, and cultural representations. Conducting research with someone who is constantly under surveillance through her cell-phone raises specific methodological and ethical issues, and in our article we call for participatory alliances and relational ethics when researching regimes of digital confinement.

Keywords

Facial Recognition Apps; Immigration Enforcement; Digital Confinement; Collaborative Visual Methodologies; Walkthrough Method

"The official said that the alternative would be better than detention, but it is nasty. Very nasty", says Lorena about her experience of subjection to electronic monitoring through a facial recognition app. Like 225,000[1] other foreign-nationals in the USA, Lorena, an asylum seeker who has fled violence in Guatemala, is submitted to so-called "alternatives to detention" (ATD) under the "Intensive Supervision and Appearance Program" (ISAP), which combines GPS tracking with electronic ankle monitors, voiceprint verification and facial recognition apps. After crossing the southern border to the USA, Lorena was detained in an immigration detention centre by ICE (US Immigration and Customs Enforcement), and was released with an ankle monitor. She was later submitted to voiceprint verification (VoiceID), then required to install facial recognition app SmartLINK®. Besides weekly "check-ins" where she has to take a photo of herself in a certain way and at a precise moment, she is required to have her smartphone on her, her battery charged and her GPS turned on at all times. She does not know when her supervision will end, nor whether she will be granted asylum or be deported today, tomorrow, in a month or after several years.

Experiences such as Lorena's are an illustrative example of new forms of enforcement technologies which produce and uphold internal borders within the USA. They constitute an understudied aspect of surveillance capitalism, as much research has focused on extractions of data for consumption and elections that target the middle-class in the global North (Zuboff 2019), or on surveillance technologies deployed on citizen minorities (e.g., Browne 2015; Eubank 2019). However, the use of facial recognition technologies for border enforcement is a major and expanding market. Between 2006 and 2021 alone, budgets for digital alternatives to detention have increased from $28m to $440m, while the budget for detention increased from $1 billion to $2.8 billion, as shown by a recent report by Just Futures Law and Mijente (2021). In February 2022, President Biden asked Congress to validate a budget that would increase the number of immigrants submitted to alternatives to detention from 169,000 to 400,000 within a year, with a clear tendency towards an increased use of the facial recognition app SmartLINK® at the expense of electronic ankle monitoring and voice verification.

The deployment of electronic monitoring as an alternative to confinement behind physical walls and fences is not a new phenomenon. In the late 1970s, Judge Jack Love, a New Mexico district court judge, read a Spiderman comic, where Spiderman's nemesis, the Kingpin, strapped a transmitter onto the superhero's wrist in order to track him anywhere he went (Lyon 1994: 42). Judge Love found that a similar transmitter could help relieve jail and prison overcrowding, and a Colorado-based company, BI Incorporated, developed the device. BI Incorporated was later bought by GEO Group, one of the world's largest prison and detention contractors (Schenwar/Law 2020: 41). Electronic ankle monitors spread

---

1 According to figures from www.ice.gov, April 2022.

in the criminal justice systems of the US and beyond; however, in most instances, it was not an alternative to prison but an additional form of control (Schenwar/Law 2020). ICE started contracting with BI Incorporated in 2004, when the agency initiated its Alternatives to Detention program, first monitoring foreign-nationals who had been sentenced to prison, then detained, and who, for various reasons, could not be deported (Boe 2020a). The program has since expanded to include persons who would otherwise never have been detained, including asylum seekers apprehended at the southern border, like Lorena.

Rather than being an "alternative" to immigrant detention, these technologies have become an addition to ever-increasing detention numbers, spreading confinement into immigrant communities and homes, ensuring great wealth and lobbying power for private prison companies. These re-invest some of the resulting profit to influence detention policy, ensure more government contracts, and impede reforms that would hurt their interests, as Gilman and Romero's (2018) research shows. Today, GEO Group profits from *both* the expansion of detention *and* of digital alternatives to detention, just as the for-profit company benefited from the parallel expansion of prisons and of electronic monitoring for probation. Tech companies are also rapidly moving into immigration enforcement as a new market for their products.

The use of applications such as SmartLINK® for monitoring migrants since 2017 is part of a wider trend in recent times involving the steady use of networked information technologies in emerging policing practices, sometimes coined as "predictive", "smart", "big data" and "platform" policing (Brayne 2017; Byler 2022; Ferguson 2017; Jefferson 2020; Wood 2019). Researchers in the humanities and social sciences have underlined the need to devise methods for addressing the realities of the "computational turn" (Rogers 2019). How can we understand and map the socio-technical landscape that shapes the deployment of forms of extractive surveillance capitalism such as digital confinement and border control? How do monitored subjects experience these forms of digital enforcement through the images and other data extracted from their cell phones?

Our aim, in this article, is to propose an approach for studying how facial recognition technologies of confinement function and are experienced through an experimental collaborative visual methodology. Our methodological approach consists of a "walkthrough method" (Light et al. 2016) enacted within a collaborative reflexive ethnographic framework involving an anthropologist (Boe), a design scholar (Mainsah), a participant with personal experience of using the app SmartLINK® (Lorena) and her lawyer, occupying changing roles as researcher and research subject. Drawing on an interdisciplinary approach, our proposed methodology enables us to uncover different digital traces left by the deployment of SmartLINK®; analyse the production of and the imaginations of digital archives; and examine embodied experiences of extractive surveillance shaped by technological structures and infrastructures.

1. Methodological Concerns

Studying such enforcement technologies and how they operate in situated contexts of use constitutes a considerable methodological challenge. Software applications (apps) are a prevalent aspect of our digital everyday lives used across different domains from health, entertainment and finance to policing. Apps are relatively closed technical systems (Light et al. 2016) often created by commercial actors who want to protect trade secrets and design architecture. The source code of apps are often not shared publicly, meaning that researchers cannot easily examine their underlying technical structures. Thus, a major obstacle to studying technical systems such as algorithms and software applications is that, given the systems' obscure nature, researchers might not know the right questions to ask and where to begin with their inquiry (Hargittai et al. 2020).

When researching apps, unlocking the "black box" of back-end systems that shape their use requires some level of technological literacy. The app as a material environment opens itself up to a multiplicity of readings as to what is its "expected use" (Light et al. 2016). The readings might depend on the researcher's existing knowledge of app design. They might also depend on the researcher's knowledge of what genre the app belongs to, and her expectations about its conventions and norms. Thus, there is a need for methodological approaches that acknowledge the multiplicity of reading strategies for understanding the app's design and use among researchers, research subjects and other stakeholders.

Further, apps such as SmartLINK® come into use within wider ecologies and assemblages (Pearce et al. 2020) of users, platforms, infrastructures, software, devices, algorithms, data and regulatory regimes, among others. Their use is governed by numerous institutions, authorities and agencies within and across borders at local, regional, national, and international levels. This implies that researchers might find it difficult to define the boundaries of their empirical research field, and constantly need to reflect on the empirical object of their research (Marres 2017).

Finally, the material-technical aspects of these technologies are closely connected with the social and the corporeal. These technologies can routinise bodies, actions and identities through design choices, programming and connected infrastructures (Wood 2019). It is thus hard to separate the use and experience of these technologies from their design and representation. It is equally important to be attentive to the ways in which users can resist these arrangements through processes of appropriation in use.

Developing an Approach

To address the challenges outlined above, we explore the use of a walkthrough method developed by Light and colleagues (2016), which we enact using an experimental collaborative visual methodological approach. The walkthrough method involves engaging with an app's interface and related production information to understand its technical mechanisms and embedded cultural references, to appreciate how it shapes user experience. The researcher logs onto the app and mimics everyday use, observing and noting the app's screens, features and menu functions. The researcher contextualises this process by reviewing the representations and operational environment connected to the app.

The walkthrough method combines perspectives from STS (Latour 2005) and Cultural Studies. The principles of Actor-Network Theory (ANT) highlight the influence of non-human actors by looking at a technology's materiality and the affordances it extends, as well as the role the social and the material play in how users perceive their actions in relation to a technology. Equally, the walkthrough draws on methodological approaches from Cultural Studies used to understand material culture and the everyday practices of technology consumers. These approaches involve the study of technologies both as material artefacts and sites of cultural struggle through a combined focus on how a technology is represented, what social identities are associated with it, and how it is produced and consumed (Du Gay et al. 2013).

In our case, this method is enacted through two walkthrough iterations, one between an anthropologist and a research participant accompanied by her lawyer, and another between two researchers, the anthropologist and a design scholar. The enactment of the walkthrough method builds on interdisciplinary collaboration, whereby the anthropologist, Boe, draws on expertise built through extensive research on the anthropology of confinement and migration control, with particular focus on deportation, prisons, electronic monitoring and facial recognition. The design researcher, Mainsah, draws on his knowledge of digital media, technology design and collaborative research methods. The participant provides insight into a situated context of use, drawing on personal experience using the SmartLINK® app during her asylum process in the United States, and her lawyer ensures the best interest of her client, while taking part in the process, both by asking questions and contributing with her extensive knowledge of immigration law and practice.

The first walkthrough involves an exploration of the app's interface and experience of use in the context of an interview recorded on video by Boe, in which Lorena takes the anthropologist on a verbal and kinetic "guided tour" of the app, highlighting her experience of use, and the anthropologist, lawyer and participant together analyse the different features and digital traces generated through the process of use. The walkthrough was video recorded in Austin, Texas, in the fall of 2019 as part of the Borders without Fences and Confinement without Walls project, which involved collaborative ethnographic fieldwork and the making of a documentary film on "digital confinement". The project was led by Boe, and studied the spread and experiences of electronic monitoring, and how digital confinement compares with experiences of incarceration and detention behind physical walls and fences. It is based on fieldwork carried out in New York and

Texas among asylum seekers and migrants who are electronically monitored (Boe 2020b).

The second walkthrough took place between Boe and Mainsah. It consisted of looking at marketing materials produced by the owners of the app to understand how their discourses frame users and use. It involved engaging directly with the app's interface to examine its technical features and watching the video of the first walkthrough together. The first walkthrough was about engaging with the app by focusing mainly on experience of use in a situated context, through the eyes of Lorena. The second walkthrough aimed at adding new layers of insight by placing closer focus on the technical aspects of the app and the cultural meanings embedded in the app's interface and its marketing discourse, combining Boe's anthropological gaze with Mainsah's understanding of interaction design. The second walkthrough also provided the opportunity to review the first with fresh eyes and multiple perspectives. Knowledge generated through the walkthrough of the app's interface, and the participant's account of user experience is contextualised by analysis of online material produced by ICE and BI Group, to triangulate it with the experiences of the user.

We highlight the experimental and contingent way in which the enactment of the walkthrough method, that we describe, played out. An ideal research design for implementing such a fully collaborative visual methodology would have involved the researchers Boe and Mainsah, and research participant Lorena all being present in the same room sitting round a table and going through the SmartLINK® app and website, analysing together. However, COVID-19 pandemic social distancing restrictions and the closing of US borders for EU citizens made this impossible.

Fig. 1: Image of the participant holding a smartphone with the screen showing the app. Credit: Carolina Sanchez Boe

In the end, the walkthrough method that we present reflects a collaborative process of knowledge production (Ajjawi et al. 2020) spanning over two years and involving dialogue, reflection and sharing across different geographical and virtual locations, different languages, and different forms of experiential, scientific and technological expertise. It involves multi-sited ethnography (Austin, Texas; Paris, France; Oslo, Norway; online) and analysis (Marcus 1998) across time (2019–2021), and is carried out in three languages, Spanish, English and French. Our experience enables us to produce new layers of knowledge with video and audio archives, through iterative cycles of reflection and interdisciplinary collaborations.

2. The Walkthrough

The first enactment of the walkthrough method took place in the fall of 2019 between the anthropologist, Boe, and the participant, Lorena, with her lawyer present.

Fig. 2: Screenshot of Lorena's fingers navigating through a menu function of the SmartLINK® app. Credit: Carolina Sanchez Boe

Lorena logs on to the app, while describing how once a week she is required to take a photograph of herself in the app, and she has to have the phone on her and turned on at all times, with a full battery and the GPS on, so that ICE can follow her every step. She explains that she was asked to give her email address to the officer who had downloaded the app onto her phone. She also had to give contact information for six people living in the USA to ICE, spurring a reaction from both the lawyer and the anthropologist. Few asylum seekers know six persons in the USA, leading asylum seekers' friends and family to ask some of *their* friends to agree to give their contact information to the asylum seeker. Lorena adds that in case there are issues with the phone, such as a disconnection with the GPS, a problem with the photo, or if the phone runs out of batteries, ICE can call the contact persons to ask where you are and if you have run away, which is disruptive for the contact person and stigmatising for the person being monitored. The lawyer comments that there is also an issue of whether the contact person's information is kept by the Department of Homeland Security and for how long.

When Boe had interviewed Lorena's lawyer a few days earlier, she suggested setting up a meeting with Lorena, who also agreed to be filmed anonymously during the interview. The choice of filming is both a dissemination tool to understand and convey the reconfigurations of confinement and of internal borders through remote control and a method of inquiry in its own right. Audio-visual methods open up the possibility to create collaborative knowledge outputs and initiate exchanges with participants on how to raise awareness about their concerns, hereby acknowledging their role as full collaborators in the project, while establishing a "civil contract" with participants which, in this research, involved making sure to continuously protect their anonymity for obvious reasons (Azoulay 2008; Köhn 2016).

In the Summer of 2019, Boe had started directing a documentary on the use and experiences of electronic monitoring for internal border control, filmed with Austin-based videographer Jessie Rodriguez. The two developed a filmic approach which would anonymise the participants, while acknowledging the humanity of the person. This approach gives the viewer a sense of closeness to the subject and conveys sensorily how it feels to be forced to have a device on at all times, whether it is an electronic ankle monitor or an app on a smartphone.

In the process of filming Lorena on her own in the fall of 2019, Boe positioned the camera in a way that captured the app which Lorena was walking her through, but also tried to film her so that her hair, her skin, her clothes, her bag, would give the viewer a sense of the person, even though her identity could not be disclosed, striving to highlight her presence while protecting her against recognition and possible retaliation. While Boe's camera provides a GPS service and the possibility to connect it to the web, she has never made use of these possibilities, due to concerns about privacy and unwanted surveillance. Lorena chose "Lorena" as the name under which she would appear in the material. During this performative action that demonstrates the functionality of the app, Lorena and the anthropologist deliberately put the anthropologist's camera into the gaze of Lorena's phone camera, and into the frame where Lorena takes her selfie every week, while Lorena made sure to cover Boe's face.

Fig. 3: Boe's camera captured in the facial recognition software of Lorena's phone. Credit: Carolina Sanchez Boe

A Multi-Layered Memory Process

The walkthrough serves not only as a means of going through the app's interface but also as a form of visual elicitation (Bagnoli 2009; Pink et al. 2017; Rose 2001; Liebenberg 2018). A visual artefact, such as a smartphone app, can be mobilised to encourage memories and uncover layers of past experiences that might not be readily articulated through language alone (Sheridan et al. 2011).

As Lorena walks us through the app, it spurs a memory process, where the app serves as a memory object. She recalls, for instance, how she was initially relieved to get her ankle monitor off, until she was required to give ICE access to her email account, which connects to her social media, and install the app on her own smartphone, which holds photos of her family and friends along with other personal information and memories. As she opens the calendar function for appointment reminders, she remembers how the calendar failed to notify her of an appointment with a judge, which is confirmed by her lawyer. Lorena is also reminded of the first time she had to take a photo on her own, of how nervous she was, and remembers several instances where she was interrupted in her work by the app and had to hastily find a background which was sufficiently neutral for the requirements of the facial recognition software. She explains how her smartphone vibrates if she is not sufficiently quick at meeting the requirements, and how this can ultimately lead to one of her contacts being called on the phone to ask whether she has escaped. Going through the app enables Lorena to reconnect with embodied experiences such as the vibrations of the app, which in turn triggers memories of the monitor she once had on her ankle.

Fig. 4. Close-up image of the photo-taking function of the app with detailed instructions. Credit: Carolina Sanchez Boe

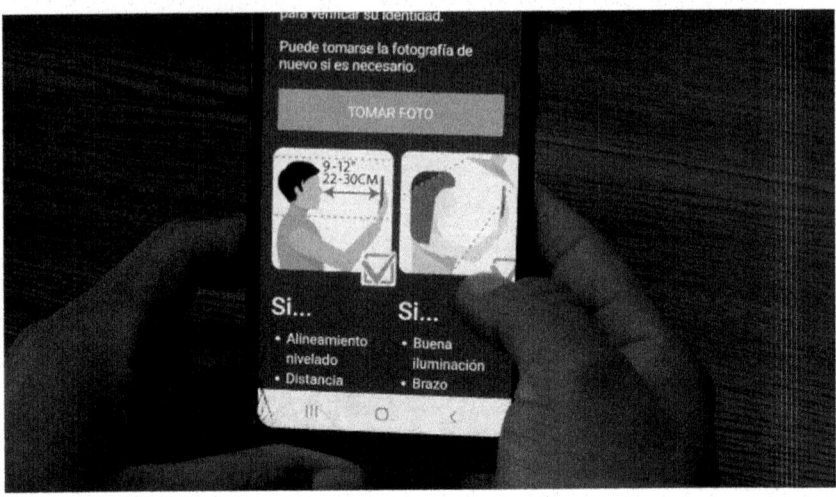

Lorena compares the three geolocalisation devices used for digital detention, saying how she first had an ankle monitor, then voice recognition, where she would get phone calls and have to state her name three times, which would be compared to her voiceprint, before getting the SmartLINK® app. The electronic ankle monitor would run out of battery often, especially in cold weather and a loud "Battery low!" would sound from her ankle. She recollects how the bulky plastic device is very "uncomfortable" *(incomodo)*, as it blinks and is difficult to hide, causing a sense of criminalisation and isolation in public spaces, and difficulties accessing the labour market. Increasingly, these so-called "alternatives" cause stigmatisation within immigrant communities themselves, due to a growing awareness that people around the person who is monitored are also subject to surveillance (Boe 2020b). In this sense, digital detention, whether materialised in an ankle monitor, voice recognition or a biometric facial recognition app, is equally "uncomfortable" and "nasty" *(feo)*, as it opens up the possibility to be even more intrusive than immigration detention.

Enacting the walkthrough with Lorena gives us insight into how surveillance technological systems produce what Ellis and colleagues refer to as "affective atmospheres" such as moods, emotions, feelings, thoughts, judgments, perceptions, sensations and all manner of social relations and associated practices (Ellis et al. 2013: 718). In this regard, they call for methods that are sensitive to the affective impacts that they produce in everyday embodied encounters.

The Fear of Endangering Others

SmartLINK® is often referred to as "de-escalation", a word that has connotations with the abolitionist word "decarceration", which is very misleading. It is the alternative to the alternative and is often implemented along gendered lines, with concerns for the potential dangers of electronic ankle monitoring for pregnant women or for their foetus and future child, or to counter the bodily harm, such as chafing, sores and allergies generated by ankle monitors. To Lorena, SmartLINK®, however, is just as "incomodo" as the ankle monitor in the sense that she is never allowed to leave it, not even to go to the bathroom: "They told me that I had to have my phone on at all times, and that I shouldn't have another phone or phone-line, only the one where the application is installed." Lorena has also been told that she is not allowed to use another phone, which means that every time she calls someone or uses her phone to take photos or surf on the internet, she is compelled to do so with the phone that the app is installed on. This enhances the fear that the SmartLINK® app might be able to extract data from other services on her smartphone. Why else should she not be allowed to use another device? As with the ankle monitor, Lorena fears that she may endanger others through her cell phone.

This fear of endangering others has intensified since August 2019, when ICE conducted the largest immigration raid in recent US history, arresting 680 workers at seven poultry manufacturing plants, detaining and deporting hundreds of couples, leaving their children to come home from school to empty houses (Glenza 2019). In the weeks and months that followed, some were deported while others were released with ankle monitors (Fausset 2019). The Mississippi raids marked a new era of immigration enforcement, as a key part of the operation involved the use of data harvested from digital monitoring of asylum seekers for the preparation of the raids with the active participation of Silicon Valley tech giant Palantir (Mijente 2019), which is also involved in the management of refugee camps and in WHO food programs.

The affidavit of the arrest, which is available online (AP 2019), reveals how ICE had been using surveillance data extracted from the electronic monitors of three women from Guatemala, one of the women having been "de-escalated" to SmartLINK® in February 2019. The warrant teaches us about the working hours of the women, that they work shifts from 4.43 am–1.17 pm, and implicitly about their conditions of labour, which anthropologist Angela Stuesee (2016) has written about extensively. We also learn that one of the women had arrived in the US in 2014 and had been monitored for 5 years, which shows how indefinite electronic monitoring, as detention, can last for years, with an average time of 837.8 days according to a recent report from Just Futures Law and Mijente (2021).

Technologies for digital confinement have become an addition to ever-increasing detention numbers, spreading confinement into immigrant communities and homes indefinitely, and they open up opportunities to submit other immigrants and citizens to surveillance beyond the individual who is being monitored. Other research participants that Boe has interviewed, who have experienced both detention and electronic monitoring, explain how the latter, despite the restrictions in their spatial mobility, gives a "taste of freedom", which, they say, makes them comply more than they would in detention (Boe 2020b). Lorena is no different, in that she accepts her situation in the hope that she will obtain asylum and secure a safe future for her children, "It is for them that we are fighting, that I am fighting, for my children". *(Es por ellos que nosotros luchamos, que lucho yo por mis hijos)*.

One way of complying is through the forms of forced participation that are required for SmartLINK® to work. Barassi (2019: 414) argues that surveillance capitalism depends on "the systematic coercion of digital participation, which forces citizens to comply with data technologies". She suggests how, in our technology-saturated cultures, citizens are constantly compelled to comply through the use of digital services or by providing personal data. Sometimes forced compliance happens in physical ways, such as through facial recognition technologies at airports. At other times this occurs simply because we live in data-driven environments that rely on automated decision making. Coercion of digital participation highlights "the violence of digital profiling and the fact that data traces *speak for and about individual lives* in ways that go beyond individual choice or control" (Barassi 2019: 415, original emphasis).

Fig. 5: Interface of the facial recognition function. Credit: Carolina Sanchez Boe

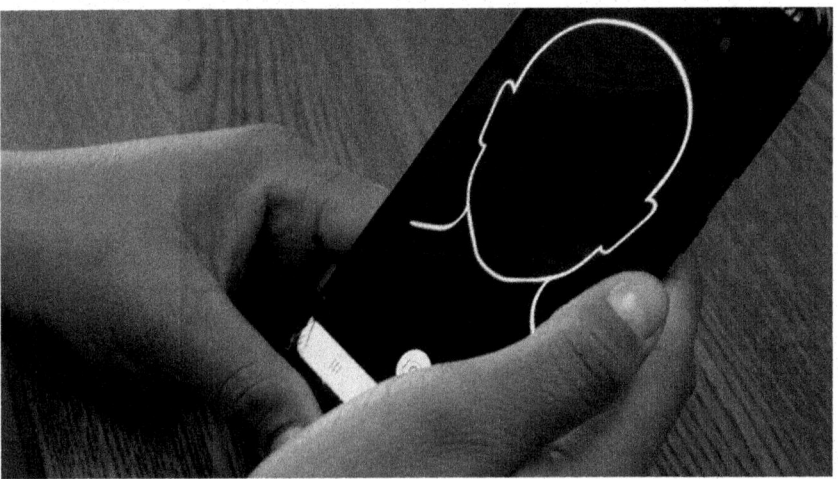

Asylum seekers are required to take part in their own surveillance, to self-report, to keep the device that detains them charged at all times, and are hence to perform the function of being their own prison guard. This specific form of digital labour saves the companies that profit from digital detention expenses for labor, on top of the savings made on buildings, uniforms and food, when compared to detention behind physical, not digital walls. Furthermore, surveillance happens through asylum seekers' own devices, with the use of their personal smartphones, rather than electronic ankle monitors that the company produces and manages. Hence, technical breakdowns of the device become the responsibility of the user and no longer of the company that monitors them.

In November 2021, two years after meeting Lorena initially, Boe met with her again in Austin, Texas. Her asylum case was still pending, and she was still being submitted to SmartLINK®. The lack of a definite end date gives immigration enforcement a particular temporal experience that differs fundamentally from most experiences of confinement such as prison, which, most often, has a set end date. Nicholas De Genova conceptualised "deportability" and "detainability", that is, living with the constant risk of being deported or the risk of being detained (2002), which is what monitored research participants experience. Their only certainty is that if they get a negative answer to their asylum case, they will be deported, and they have no knowledge whether this life-altering event might happen today, tomorrow, in a month or in several years' time. Indefinite control and the inability to plan for the future seems, in some ways, even harsher when one is outside of detention centres, sharing an everyday life with friends, co-workers and family, than in detention, where everyone in one's close surroundings shares the same uncertainty (Boe 2020b).

3. Scrolling through Corporate Visions of Electronic Monitoring

The second enactment of the walkthrough took place several months after the encounter between Boe and the participant recorded on video, through a series of meetings between Boe and Mainsah in the spring and summer of 2021, during COVID-19 social distancing restrictions. We each sat in front of our computer screens in Paris, Aarhus and Oslo, connected through video chat.

Part of our walkthrough method involves examining what Light and colleagues (Light et al. 2016) describe as the environment of expected use, the socio-economic and cultural context of the app. This means paying attention to how the producer describes the app's vision, imagines the user and presents scenarios of use. It also involves looking at how the producer conveys and conceives of the functions that the app provides and supports. This component of the walkthrough involved the two researchers going through product information about the app on the website, on Google Play and Apple Store, as well as material provided by ICE. So, what do we learn about SmartLINK® from the marketing material on BI Incorporated's website?[2]

---

2   https://www.bi.com.

We discover that we can also access information on SmartLINK® provided by Google Play and Apple Store,[3] which feature screenshots of the interface and mostly negative user reviews in English and Spanish. We notice a "disclaimer" that warns users that "Continued use of GPS running in the background can dramatically decrease battery life", in spite of the fact that it is a requirement for users of SmartLINK® to have their GPS turned on at all times.

As we scroll through the website and product catalogue, we learn from the "About Us"[4] section of the website that: "Our products include a wide range of electronic monitoring systems, enabling agencies to apply the least restrictive or appropriate option to support compliance to conditions of release. By releasing individuals to community supervision with the support of these innovative tools, they are able to live (sic) in the community, support themselves and their families, and supervising officers understand better how a person is doing in the community."

Under the headline "Strengthening Communities Through Innovation", the photos that support this claim to electronic monitoring being the "least restrictive" show families happily enjoying leisure time, a father and son with a baseball and glove, a little girl on a playground with her father. Through words and photos, the cultural representation of the user is that of the male under criminal justice supervision, and female asylum seekers such as Lorena, or the women whose surveillance led to the Mississippi raids are not represented, as the accent is put on the companies' activities in criminal justice enforcement. The notion that users may not comply but may need enforced surveillance is present, with the product sheet for SmartLINK® highlighting features such as "Eliminates the risk of GPS spoofing"[5]. We could read this as a potential for resistance among the monitored; however, we know from Lorena's interview and Boe's wider research project that asylum seekers go to great lengths to comply with the requirements in order to get their day in court and obtain asylum.

We notice how, in spite of the omnipresence of data-driven technological solutions and promises of risk assessment, issues such as privacy, data generation, collection and storage are not mentioned. What kind of personal data is collected? What kind of personal consent is given? What data is produced?

Another issue not mentioned is the profit-driven motives of the company, which can be found in other literature produced by the company to its shareholders. Gilman and Romero quote a 2017 report from GEO, BI Group's parent company, which stated that new ICE contracts for electronic monitoring had increased revenues by 33% and constituted "milestones that have paved the way for

---

3   https://apps.apple.com/us/app/bi-smartlink/id1068021794. https://play.google.com/store/apps/details?id=com.biinc.mobile.client&hl=en&gl=US&showAllReviews=true. https://appadvice.com/app/bi-smartlink/1068021794.
4   https://bi.com/about-us/.
5   https://bi.com/wp-content/uploads/2021/05/SmartLINK-factsheet.pdf.

continued positive momentum for our company" (Gilman/Romero 2018). What we do learn is that SmartLINK® is Android & IOS compatible, and can be downloaded through Google Play or Apple Store, and that BI Incorporated has three trusted partners in T Mobile, Verizon and Google.[6] Hence, implicitly, the company website shows us how telecom and internet companies, which developed in other fields, are now getting involved in criminal justice and border enforcement, generating considerable profit for these companies, too.

Under the heading "Made in the USA", the "About Us" section further insists on the benefits that the company presents for the private work market, as it states that "BI proudly designs, engineers, and manufactures 200,000+ GPS tracking, alcohol detection, and RF monitoring units annually in Colorado". The company prides itself in creating jobs in the private sector, while implicitly stressing that it saves man-hours in the public sector. According to the product catalogue, "alternatives" to detention such as SmartLINK® and the "biometric check-ins" and "remote case-management" through BI's TotalAccess® "reduces time spent on administrative work".[7] Finally, we know from previous research that the monitored are no longer spending time in offices, queuing or waiting, which offered potentials for sociability with others in similar situations. In this sense, the "alternatives" produce a sense of atomisation, with individuals getting disconnected from others who share the same experiences (Boe 2020b). Hence, rather than "strengthening communities", as the marketing material suggests, SmartLINK®, like other digital alternatives to detention, resonates with other infrastructures that make the presence of detention and internal borders of the nation-state invisible, while rendering border violence hyper-visible at sites located at the national borders, as shown by anthropologist Nicholas de Genova (2013).

Exploring the Interface

Gaining an overview of the technical features of the app is a central component of the selected method. In the second walkthrough, besides examining marketing material, another key task for Boe and Mainsah involved studying the features of the app and engaging with the app's interface, examining the screens, exploring menus and testing buttons. This implies experiencing how to download the app, log in and out, register and set up an account. For Boe, this was a repeat with Mainsah of the process previously carried out with Lorena.

We download the app onto our phones and start the walk through. However, doing all this as an outside user in the case of the SmartLINK® app is not possible because of institutional restrictions. When you download SmartLINK® without being on probation or enrolled in the ISAP program, you cannot get beyond the login. There are other secondary sources that give an idea of the app's interface.

---

6   https://bi.com/about-us/.
7   https://bi.com/mobile-monitoring/.

Representations of the app on the company's website and on Google Play offer a partial preview of the interface with four screenshots showing the login page and key menu functions. The menu functions, which are featured on the app store screenshots of the interface, are the "check in" buttons, where you are asked to take a picture of yourself that will be compared with your enrolment picture to verify your identity, and the calendar function for appointment reminders. Together with the content of the website, the menu items featured on the app store serve as a way of conveying the app owner's preferred user practices and expectations of use. However, logging into the app as researchers to view its interface provides very little information when compared to reviewing the video and photographic archive produced in 2019, with Lorena and her lawyer.

Multiple Gazes

Given the status of apps as relatively closed technical systems that are open to multiple cultural readings, enacting the walkthrough involved looking in from multiple perspectives and different subjective positions. Watching the video together enabled us to notice different types of details and develop new reflections. For example, we noticed that Lorena writes her appointment down on a sticky note placed on her ISAP photo ID card, which is issued to all persons released from detention under the ATD program. We wonder why she chooses to note an appointment manually rather than open her app to see when she has an appointment.

We also read a transcript of the interview translated from Spanish to English (Mainsah does not speak Spanish). In itself, the process of translation is a method that generates knowledge, as we translate both the language and the meaning behind what is said. *"Incomodo"* can be translated to "uncomfortable", "embarrassing" or "cumbersome", while *"feo"* can be translated to "foul", "awful" or "nasty".

For the anthropologist, watching the footage again in 2021 with her colleague became a very different experience from interviewing and filming itself. During this collaborative process of watching, remembering and reflecting, the video footage served as a memory object in its own right, enabling the creation of new layers of knowledge. This is akin to Lincoln and Robards' experience of "scrolling back" and walking through the timeline of Facebook together, creating a memory process that benefits from different kinds of situated knowledge and different gazes (Haraway 1988; Robards/Lincoln 2017). The design researcher has a complementary reading of the app than the anthropologist, drawing on competences such as technical knowledge of apps, how facial recognition software works, and an eye for the cultural representations embedded within the interface.

Conclusion

The digital detention technology landscape comprises a complex assemblage of wearable devices, identification cards, app stores, physical locations and apps that collect information about the users, all of which pose questions about privacy and consent. The involuntary wearing of the devices has its own types of affective, embodied consequences. What we suggest is that these methods provide a good foundation for generating further research data for understanding how monitored subjects experience these forms of digital enforcement, and how they imagine that the images and other data extracted from their cell phones can be used against them, their families, their colleagues, employers or communities.

The walkthrough shows major differences between the discourse of the company's marketing material and the experiences of users who are forcibly submitted to new forms of surveillance capitalism. In this article, we have addressed some of the methodological challenges we encounter when studying surveillance technologies deployed on vulnerable populations. Among the difficulties for researchers, there is the issue of understanding assemblages of enforcement tech, how the device connects to other apps, devices and legal regimes. This is a cross-disciplinary field that requires different forms of expertise and types of knowledge. Another difficulty is the question of getting access to this tech, which, in turn, poses the challenge to anonymise research participants who are being monitored at all times.

There are major ethical issues related to studying technologies with users who are detained through their smartphone. In the article, we call for participatory alliances and relational ethics when examining regimes of digital confinement. During the process, Lorena was accompanied by her lawyer, who works in the best interest of her client. Collaboration with lawyers is a necessity in order to protect our research collaborators when examining enforcement technologies in digital carceral contexts, which imply engaging with participants in vulnerable situations. Besides the safety of participants, our inquiry generated discussions among us relating to researcher safety, given the increased surveillance and criminalisation of immigrant rights activists (Boe 2020b). Could there be consequences for non-US citizens carrying out critical research on border enforcement, who at the same time depend on border agencies to obtain a visa to enter the USA? We need to have ongoing discussions about the possible implications of putting others and ourselves in danger, and here, collaborative research is a necessity.

Such collaborative endeavours, we argue, are also necessary when we draw from interdisciplinary methods and theories, and collaborate with the monitored to understand the embodied experiences of digital confinement. By creating alliances between different approaches and disciplines, and with the people who are experiencing enforcement tech or are witnesses to it in their daily practice, we can contribute to rendering invisibilised forms of violence against minorities visible, along with new forms of punitive and profit-driven surveillance capitalism.

Deploying the walkthrough method with people subjected to electronic monitoring opens the possibility of witnessing the manifestation of a carceral continuum, or the notion that bodies are controlled and disciplined beyond prison walls through forms of governmentality that are similar to the ones deployed in carceral institutions (Foucault 1995: 303). In this case, technologies from the criminal justice system are being implemented in immigrant communities, expanding detention and surveillance beyond the individual, monitored person to their co-workers, neighbours and friends. Just as electronic monitoring for criminal justice purposes expanded carceral spaces into the city, digital 'alternatives' create immigration detention in communities, multiplying internal borders within urban and rural spaces. The Mississippi raids showed how the surveillance of three women, whose data had been stored, was analysed and used months later for the arrest of several hundred undocumented workers by ICE. So-called "alternatives" to detention open new possibilities for the retroactive surveillance of hundreds of persons through the devices of a few individuals. We are now moving into a new era when immigration control and for-profit extraction of migrants' time and mobility is no longer carried out only by actors from the for-profit prison industrial complex, but increasingly so by tech companies that are investing in new data markets.

While digital alternatives are highly intrusive to users and dangerous for their communities, some immigration advocates still perceive the deployment of digital tools as a welcome substitute for immigration detention, also during the various campaigns to release detainees during the pandemic that started in early 2020. No human rights defenders would ever support opening more prisons or more immigration detention facilities, but many still perceive electronic monitoring as a "more humane" alternative to the terrible conditions of detention in the USA. This is *not* an alternative to detention; it *is* detention in another form. Digital confinement, whether through ankle monitors or through a smartphone, causes considerable stress for their involuntary wearers and puts whole communities in danger through the presence of a single person. To Lorena as to others, facial recognition is worse than detention and electronic ankle monitors, as it is an even more invasive form of confinement.

These developments within border enforcement are not only important for immigrants, their support networks or the US taxpayers who finance for-profit detention, but are of relevance to us all, also the seemingly most protected citizens. We may think twice about the corporate interests, privacy concerns and user consequences of the deployment of similar technologies to SmartLINK® during the pandemic, to subject the sick or the quarantined to surveillance, or to track the interactions between contaminated and healthy citizens. Research shows how identification and tracking and confinement technologies are commonly tested with experiments on the most vulnerable and marginalised first, often non-citizens, before being generalised to the population (Noiriel 1988), especially in times of crisis.

Acknowledgements

Carolina Sanchez Boe wishes to thank Lorena, Stephanie Taylor (J.D.) and professors Denise Gilman and Elissa Steglich from the immigration clinic at the University of Texas Austin Law School; Andreas Roepstorff at Interacting Minds Center, Aarhus University, Olivier Martin and Eric Dagiral at Université Paris Cité and Université Sorbonne Nouvelle, CNRS, CERLIS, David Brotherton at SADR, CUNY, Camilo Avendano for his assistance with the intricacies of Central American Spanish; videographer Jessie Rodriguez, as well as the Carlsberg Foundation for its funding of the project "Digital Confinement: The Reconfigurations of Borders and Detention Through New Technologies" (2021–2023) and Independent Research Fund Denmark for its funding of the project "Borders without Fences and Confinement without Walls" (2018–2021). Henry Mainsah's work in this article was partly funded by the Research Council of Norway (Project No. 288663, titled RELINK).

References

AFP (Associated Press) (2019): "Immigration Raid Affidavit - PH Food. Sworn Statements Supporting the Search Warrants that Led a Judge to Authorize Immigration Raids in Mississippi. United States District Court for the Southern District of Mississippi." August 5 (https://www.documentcloud.org/documents/6251347-Immigration-Raids-Affidavit-PH-Food.html).

Ajjawi, Rola/Hilder, Joanne/ Noble, Christy/ Teodorczuk, Andrew/Billett, Stephen (2020): "Using Video – Reflexive Ethnography to Understand Complexity and Change Practice." In: Medical Education 54/10, pp. 908-914.

Bagnoli, Anna (2009): "Beyond the Standard Interview: The Use of Graphic Elicitation and Arts-based Methods." In: Qualitative Research 9/5, pp. 547-570.

Barassi, Veronica (2019): "Datafied Citizens in the Age of Coerced Digital Participation." In: Sociological Research Online 24/3, pp. 414-429.

Boe, Carolina. Sanchez (2020a): "Institutions of Confinement as Sites of Passage: The *mètis* of Foreign-Nationals caught in the Wars on Terror, Drugs and Immigration." In: Cambridge Journal of Anthropology 38/1, pp. 70-87.

Boe, Carolina. Sanchez (2020b): "Fighting Border Control in Three Sites of Confinement: The Uses and Experiences of Prison, Detention, and Electronic Monitoring for Foreign-Nationals in New York." In: Champs Pénal 21 (https://journals.openedition.org/champpenal/12273).

Brayne, Sarah (2017): "Big Data Surveillance: The Case of Policing." In: American Sociological Review 82/5, pp. 977-1008.

Browne, Simone (2015): Dark Matters: On the Surveillance of Blackness, Durham/London: Duke University Press.

Byler Darren (2022): Terror Capitalism: Uyghur Dispossession and Masculinity in a Chinese City, Durham/London: Duke University Press 2022.

De Genova, Nicholas (2002): "Migrant 'Illegality' and Deportability in Everyday Life." In: Annual Review of Anthropology 311/1, pp. 419-447.

De Genova, Nicholas (2013): "Spectacles of Migrant 'Illegality': The Scene of Exclusion, the Obscene of Inclusion." In: Ethnic and Racial Studies 36/7, pp. 1180-1198.

Du Gay, Paul/Hall, Stuart/Janes, Linda/Madsen, Anders Koed/Mackay, Hugh/Negus, Keith (2013): Doing Cultural Studies: The Story of the Sony Walkman, London: SAGE.

Ellis, Darren/Tucker, Ian/Harper, David (2013): "The Affective Atmospheres of Surveillance." In: Theory & Psychology 23/6, pp. 716-731.

Eubank, Virginia (2019): Automating Inequality: How High-Tech Tools Profile, Police, and Punish the Poor, New York: Picador, St. Martin's Press.

Fausset, Richard (2019): "After ICE Raids, a Reckoning in Mississippi's Chicken Country." In: New York Times, December 28 (https://www.nytimes.com/2019/12/28/us/mississippi-ice-raids-poultry-plants.html).

Ferguson, Andrew Guthrie (2017): The Rise of Big Data Policing: Surveillance, Race, and the Future of Law Enforcement, New York: New York University Press.

Foucault, Michel (1995): Discipline and Punish: The Birth of the Prison, New York: Vintage Books.

Gilman, Denise/Romero, Luis (2018): "Immigration Detention, Inc." In: Journal on Migration and Human Security 6/2, pp. 145-160.

Glenza, Jessica (2019): "US Arrests 680 Workers in Immigration Sting before Trump Visits El Paso." In: The Guardian, August 8 (https://www.theguardian.com/us-news/2019/aug/07/us-arrests-680-workers-in-immigration-sting-before-trump-visits-el-paso).

Hargittai, Eszter/Gruber, Jonathan/Djukaric, Teodora/Fuchs, Jaelle/Brombach, Lisa (2020): "Black Box Measures? How to Study People's Algorithm Skills." In: Information, Communication & Society 23/5, pp.764-775.

Harraway, Donna (1988): "Situated Knowledges: The Science Question in Feminism and the Privilege of Partial Perspective." In: Feminist Studies 14/3 pp. 575-599

Jefferson, Brian (2020): Digitize and Punish: Racial Criminalization in the Digital Age, Minneapolis/London: Minnesota University Press.

Just Futures Law/Mijente (2021): "ICE Digital Prisons." June 1 (https://www.flipsnack.com/JustFutures/ice-digital-prisons-1u8w3fnd1j.html).

Jørgensen, Kristian Møller (2016): "The Media Go-along: Researching Mobilities with Media at Hand." In: MedieKultur: Journal of Media and Communication Research 32/60, pp. 32-49.

Latour Bruno (2005): Reassembling the Social: An Introduction to Actor-Network-Theory, Oxford: Oxford University Press.

Liebenberg, Linda (2018): "Generating Findings That Are Able to 'Stand on Their Own Feet' Exploring Innovations in Elicitation Methods." In: International Journal of Qualitative Methods 17/1, pp. 1-3.

Light, Ben/Burgess, Jean/Duguay, Stefanie (2016): "The Walkthrough Method: An Approach to the Study of Apps." In: New Media & Society 20/3, pp. 881-900.

Lyon, David (1994): The Electronic Eye: The Rise of the Surveillance Society, Minneapolis: University of Minnesota Press.

Marcus, George Emanuel (1995): "Ethnography in/of the World System: The Emergence of Multi-Sited Ethnography." In: Annual Review of Anthropology 24/1, pp. 95-117.

Marres, Noortje (2017): Digital Sociology, Bristol: Polity Press.

Mijente Support Committee (2019): "Breaking; Palantir's Technology Used in Mississippi Raids where 680 were Arrested." October 4 (https://www.mijentesupportcommittee.com/post/breaking-palantirs-technology-used-in-mississippi-raids-where-680-were-arrested).

Møller, Kristian/Robards, Brady (2019): "Walking Through, Going Along and Scrolling Back: Ephemeral Mobilities in Digital Ethnography." In: Nordicom Review 40/1, pp. 95-109.

Noiriel, Gérard (1988): Le Creuset Français. Histoire de l'immigration XIXe-XXe Siècles, Paris: Seuil.

Pearce, Warren/Özkula, Suay/Greene, Amanda/Teeling, Lauren/Bansard, Jennifer/Omena, Janna/Rabello, Eliane (2020): "Visual Cross-Platform Analysis: Digital Methods to Research Social Media Images." In: Information, Communication & Society 23/2, pp. 161-180.

Pink, Sarah/Sumartojo, Shanti/Lupton, Deborah/Heyes LaBond, Christine (2017): "Empathetic Technologies: Digital Materiality and Video Ethnography." In: Visual Studies 32/4, pp. 371-381.

Robards, Brady/Lincoln, Siân (2017): "Uncovering Longitudinal Life Narratives: Scrolling Back on Facebook." In: Qualitative Research 17/6, pp. 715-730.

Rogers Richard (2019): Doing Digital Methods, Los Angeles, CA: Sage.

Rose, Gillian (2001): Visual Methodologies, London: Sage.

Schenwar, Maya/Law, Victoria (2020): Prison by Any other Name: The Harmful Consequences of Popular Reform, New York/London: The New Press.

Sheridan, Joanna/Chamberlain, Kerry/Dupuis, Ann (2011): "Timelining: Visualizing Experience." In: Qualitative Research 11/5, pp. 552-569.

Stuesee, Angela (2016): Scratching Out a Living: Latinos, Race, and Work in the Deep South, Oakland, CA: University of California Press.

Wood, Stacy (2019): "Policing through Platforms." In: Computational Culture 7, October 21 (http://computationalculture.net/policingthrough-platform/).

Zuboff, Shoshana (2019): The Age of Surveillance Capitalism: The Fight for a Human Future at the New Frontier of Power, New York: Hatchett.

Urban Data Analytics as Research Topic, Method and Ethical Concern[1]

Daniel Trottier, Ju-Sung (Jay) Lee and John Boy

Abstract

Local and global business interests assemble images of neighbourhoods from localised knowledge, including disparate forms of public data such as reviews, blog posts, and open data from municipalities and other organisations. (In)visible forms of working with and worrying about neighbourhood data can be understood as an engagement with the neighbourhood's reputation, or rather its symbolic trajectory: a set of tangible and intangible indicators through which an urban space is known and treated accordingly over time. This paper addresses ethical concerns that emerge from contemporary datafied urban ethnography. We consider a combination of large-scale and bespoke, quantitative, and qualitative analyses of available sources with sustained ethnographic engagement with a Dutch neighbourhood coping with a troubled reputation. While the latter activities can mitigate ethical issues stemming from the former, ethnography in turn raises further concerns of exploitation and risk exposure and should not be treated as a kind of 'ethical panacea' for big, open, or public data projects. A multifaceted and interrogative approach to data collection may offer a more rounded account of contemporary urban data practices by drawing upon distinct and possibly conflicting accounts of social life. The challenge is to prioritise under-represented and otherwise marginalised voices in both the design and the dissemination of research on urban data analytics.

Keywords

Data Analytics; Urban Data; Big Data; Digital Ethnography; Surveillance of Neighbourhood

---

[1] This research was funded by a grant from the Leiden-Delft-Erasmus Centre for BOLD Cities.

Introduction

At the time of writing, a Google News search of the Dutch neighbourhood Moerwijk revealed terms like 'rattenoverlast', 'rattenplaag', and 'ratten zo groot als katten' (*rat nuisance, rat plague* and *rats as big as cats*). For a prospective resident, this may be one of many encounters with digital content that paints an unflattering account of the community. While the rat problem may be a demonstrable fact (as would be the case elsewhere), its prominence online is evidence of this neighbourhood's embattled reputation. Public records and newspapers have long remained a means to render urban spaces meaningful, generating knowledge that serves to exclude disadvantaged communities (Gutsche 2015). The domestication of the internet has augmented this knowledge production, notably through user-generated and geo-located content on social platforms. A potential democratisation of open source dataveillance (van Dijck 2014) is shaped by the uneven adoption of data services. Many actors play a role in producing, circulating, and exploiting data, even in neighbourhoods that are not considered 'hot' or otherwise relevant. Neighbourhoods far removed from flashy 'smart city' initiatives are nevertheless heavily datafied.

This paper is informed by ongoing research on Moerwijk, a residential and partly post-war neighbourhood located in the south-western reaches of The Hague. Our case study of this neighbourhood considers both beneficial and harmful uses of (personal) information technologies in making neighbourhoods openly legible. As researchers, we must consider the potential impact of our own data gathering activities on the individuals and communities who are implicated. Our datafied urban ethnography aims to contextualise aggregate data gathered from platforms. Addressing ethical and data protection concerns is increasingly an administrative and legal obligation for scholarly research, and one which we also address in other ongoing analyses (Lee et al. 2021). Beyond filling in forms when seeking approval from a governing body, ethical concerns should orient researchers in relation to their subject of analysis, ideally as an ongoing dialogue. Ethical reflection in this context accounts for how data is collected, the scholarly and broader public exposition of findings, and how they may be translated into other contexts and practices.

Our case study makes use of various sources of data about Moerwijk – notably public and openly accessible data – as a means to understand how the neighbourhood is generally represented. We take an open-ended and multi-sectoral approach to data collection. This includes statistical data from the CBS (Het Centraal Bureau voor de Statistiek), the Dutch census agency, digital platforms like Twitter and Instagram, and real estate data, including publicly available data on platforms like Funda.nl. These sources provide a multi-contextual account of Moerwijk as an urban space that generates data. Critical analysis driven by surveillance studies literature provides insights into the socio-cultural and political implications of this data, notably on the long-term symbolic trajectory of the neighbourhood. Yet a reasonable understanding of this trajectory – and its impact on those who depend on the neighbourhood – can only be acquired through sustained ethnographic engagement. Not only are field work and interviews necessary counterpoints to large scale data analysis; they are a guiding source of insights on their own. Ethnography serves to follow up on hunches generated from the above analysis, while centring the experiences and perceptions of stakeholders.

This paper aims to acknowledge and begin to address the ethical concerns that emerge from contemporary datafied urban ethnography, in which so-called 'public' data is critically interrogated and contextualised through qualitative engagements with local stakeholders. After localising our ethical concerns below, the following section situates urban data in terms of mediated visibility, with geodemographics as a relevant antecedent. This is followed by methodological and ethical dilemmas in researching these data practices, focusing on various data sources and possible interactions between them. Here, we consider necessary steps that might not otherwise arise during ethical screening following conventional protocols. These considerations stem from our ongoing multimodal research on Moerwijk. Our focus aligns with broader concerns about the reproduction of stratification through the widespread adoption of digital platforms, the cumulative effects of these practices for disadvantaged communities (Gandy 2016), and the risk of gentrification of newly desirable neighbourhoods in times of mounting wealth disparity.

Some of these ethical concerns are easy to recognise. There is the ongoing risk of processing and publishing data that may identify or even stigmatise individuals. There is also the more aggregate and less tangible concern of bringing harm to disadvantaged communities. Beyond these risks, we can question the appropriate and desirable use of large pools of public, semi-public, and non-public data that shape our analyses (cf. Zimmer 2010). This paper is written in response to a rise of open data initiatives among research communities that advocate free access to scientific data, including data pertaining to urban environments and populations. There may be a net social benefit if certain forms of aggregate data are rendered accessible and legible to all. Yet making a broad range of data available to anybody with sufficient resources inevitably allows for abuse and exploitation, much of which we may only learn about when coping with its impact. While as-yet-unknown abuses of aggregate data may not be reasonable grounds to opt out of open data initiatives, they speak to the importance of assessing the ethical and broader societal impact of information-based infrastructures.

While such concerns may be distinct from digital media technologies and data, the latter form a surveillant infrastructure through which managers and owners can monitor essential services, labour, and other economic and cultural activities. Public discourse often states that particular neighbourhoods, residents and other stakeholders may be left behind in these developments. Presumably this means that existing disadvantages experienced by residents of such neighbourhoods would be exacerbated as surrounding – and competing – communities undergo digitalisation. There is also a potential, more tangible fear of abuses or instrumentalisation of digital platforms within neighbourhoods like Moerwijk. Residents and local merchants may turn to Google, Amazon, and Meta-affiliated platforms to generate positive attention and revenue, even if residents and most stakeholders are in no position to own or fully grasp these tools. Yet in practice, these are clearly not equally allocated or equally exploitable services, especially when addressing profit-driven social media platforms that bear no responsibility for the communities that use them.

Urban Data and Symbolic Trajectories

Discrediting Google news alerts are part of a broader process by which a neighbourhood's reputation is reshaped through digital platforms. Local and global business interests integrate localised knowledge from disparate forms of public data. These include reviews of amenities such as restaurants and lodgings, blog posts, as well as open data from municipalities and other organisations. Urban data collection and analysis by a loose assembly of local actors and global platforms thus expand in terms of data sources and practitioners who generate cultural capital that "enhances the flow of visitors and developers" (Zukin et al. 2017: 475). This data may be framed as assisting residents and others who interact with Moerwijk, a residential neighbourhood in The Hague. Yet as seen above, its often-disproportionate focus on spectacular and stigmatising events and characteristics harms those who are dependent upon the neighbourhood, or who may otherwise be preoccupied with its standing. Data-based scrutiny and assessment of neighbourhoods – whether conducted by residents, investors, or academics – offer a disproportionate account of events, reducing multi-contextual accounts to specific measures by obscuring the interpretation that "always prefigures data analysis" (van Dijck 2014: 201). Simultaneously, an uneven uptake of digital media across stakeholders[2] may facilitate misrepresentations of marginal communities and the reproduction of systemic biases (O'Neil 2016). Yet even accurate and flattering portrayals are data practices that can either exclude or marginalise local participation in image construction.

Working with and worrying about data, considering surveillance capitalism, can be understood as an engagement with the neighbourhood's image, or rather its symbolic trajectories: a set of tangible and intangible measures through which an urban space is known and treated accordingly over time (Lee et al. 2021). These measures embody a collective process, as many actors are involved in the ongoing public standing of a neighbourhood. These include residents, elected officials and

---

2   For the purpose of our research, we define stakeholder as any individual or organisation who has a vested interest in and/or depends on the well-being of Moerwijk as a neighbourhood.

local businesses, but also global platforms – particularly social media – that enable those actors to embed their discourse in (and connect it to) similar concerns across the globe. Public discourse about the digitisation of urban spaces might centre on corporations like Alphabet's own endeavours (de Vynck/Wong 2020). Yet these platforms also enable others to engage in information collection, analysis, and exploitation, with social and organisational consequences.

Neighbourhood reputations are a form of "contemporary image ensembles", which local and global stakeholders routinely contribute to and draw upon (Mackenzie 2019: 5). These efforts are mobilised through "observation events distributed throughout and across devices, hardware, human agents" in addition to "artificial networked architectures such as deep learning networks" (ibid.). Image ensembles are mediated in a way that fuses routine social media practices with wider-reaching speculation about the value and commodification of neighbourhoods. Urban data analytics is a means for local actors and global platforms to generate capital, mobilising others to provide pervasive yet reductive accounts of services and spaces. Digital media is thus pervasively (ab)used in the symbolic trajectory of urban neighbourhoods. Our concern with the misuse of data compels us to address the ethical dimensions in mediated relations between residents, businesses, and global digital platforms. This includes identifying harmful uses of digital media, especially for those who may suffer from either gentrification or living in a stagnant and stigmatised neighbourhood. Freely available tools that pervade social and digital life but may remain restricted to residents in terms of the required media literacy and other access issues function to either improve or maintain the reputation of a neighbourhood. As urban data analytics rely extensively on (and thus advance) monitoring practices, particularly of disadvantaged communities in urban spaces, surveillance and visual studies can help address the mobilisation of data about neighbourhoods on digital platforms.

A mixed method approach is necessary because symbolic trajectories are composed of numerous data practices, diverging in terms of context and purpose. Large-scale data analysis by researchers in media, sociology, geography, and informatics (among others) begs for *qualitative* interrogation to critically question the arrangement of data as "'natural' phenomena" (van Dijck 2014: 202; emphasis in original). Moreover, researchers who study urban data from a surveillance studies lens are a (perhaps modest) part of this image ensemble and should shape their own data collection and analysis along often-conflicting ethical concerns. These include the potential misuse of available data, as well as the impact we may have in shaping the way data about these neighbourhoods (and neighbourhoods like them) are understood and utilised. As van Dijck remarks, academics risk being complicit in transferring "the power over data-collection and interpretation from the public to the corporate sector" (ibid.: 203). In observing and reporting on digital media practices in this context, researchers may impact those under study. They may strive to make their findings open to all, and these interventions distribute data that could reinforce inequalities within the spaces under study.

Researchers may be critical of surveillance practices in urban spaces while reproducing their harms, including assumptions about data and representation that carry through their analysis. Scholarship should aim to locate embodied, situated knowledge in a manner that does not facilitate its colonisation by the very practices we may critique, for instance in advancing new ways to measure and eventually commodify local (digital) cultural practices. The challenge is to refine mixed methods protocols that neither neglect situated knowledge and experiences, nor make them ripe for exploitation.

Surveillance of Neighbourhoods: Precedents of Data Technologies as Methodology

Surveillance technologies reshape relations among those who inhabit and/ or invest in urban spaces, often by making aspects of a neighbourhood visible at the expense of its reputation. Public discourse frames these technologies as empowering for individuals, who may monitor and transmit information about their neighbourhoods. Readers could even expect that digital media may disrupt relations with employers, landlords and governments. Such visions suggest the possibility of residents' being visible on their own terms (cf. Albrechtslund 2008), but also collecting and disseminating information about more powerful actors (Mann et al. 2003; Reilly 2015). Under conditions of new and ubiquitous visibility (Thompson 2005), virtually any social phenomenon may be more easily monitored and scrutinised. Yet while data-led surveillance practices persist through the growth of platforms like Google, they can be characterised as volatile, as they are "not permanent but temporary, not equally imposed on everyone, and oscillating between appearing and disappearing" (Bucher 2012: 1177). Residents of marginalised neighbourhoods may cope with asymmetrical relations of surveillance, as well as asymmetrical relations regarding their knowledge of how this surveillance operates (Brighenti 2007). These concerns compel residents and others to engage in digital self-preservation of locational reputation (Kien 2020).

These demands on residents, merchants and other potential urban data stewards fuel a shared belief "in the objective quantification and potential tracking of all kinds of human behavior and sociality through online media technologies" (van Dijck 2014: 198), a tacit endorsement of continuous forms of data-based surveillance. Shared beliefs in objective urban data analysis may reproduce existing inequities (Gandy 2016) including racial, economic, and virtually any grounds upon which communities may be marginalised. While in principle there are minimal barriers to adopting localised online platforms and mobile devices, not all forms of access are equal, notably in contrasting local businesses and individual residents against global platforms and multinationals that purchase their services. Premium and paid versions of platforms typically offer greater analytic insights as well as greater bandwidth, compared to free and 'open-to-all' services.

An unpaid volunteer and a successful realtor may use the same tools in name, but in practice their affordances and outcomes may differ tremendously. Both free and premium services pose privacy concerns. No-cost versions of services like Google or Facebook typically generate and retain more data about neighbourhoods than they disclose to users. The continued ubiquity of these and other platforms in urban spaces raises persistent questions about privacy for stakeholders (van Zoonen 2016). While privacy may be framed as an individual concern, we can also interrogate how particular communities may be (dis)advantaged when profiled and assessed through persistent data collection.

As surveillance technologies with tangible research offerings for much social scientific research, geodemographic services coupled with GIS serve as a precedent to how neighbourhoods are monitored in diverse sectors (Burrows/Ellison 2004). GIS may still be in use, yet it has been supplemented with (a) social platforms on mobile devices in the domestic sphere, and (b) other localised data collection practices in other established sectors, including public services, real estate, and the hospitality sector. Geodemographics can be understood as a "social profile for the postal code" (Dalton/Thacker 2015: 3) which in turn interacts with a more abstract reputation of an area that is both ephemeral (difficult to 'pin down' and operationalise) and persistent (equally difficult to alter when more objective measures of reputation improve). Neighbourhood reputation is thus reproduced through datafied profiles. It is tempting to distinguish these in terms of quantitative (in the case of datafication) versus qualitative (in the case of a generalised reputation), while any single knowledge practice alone may be understood as holistic and multi-modal.

Many of these technologies are also effectively black boxes (ibid: 6), meaning that their functioning – including how they may assist in allocating outcomes to people – is not sufficiently understood, either as an abstract concept or in applied practice. The concept of the black box in this case is scalable. We can refer to any single platform, algorithm, or sensor as potentially unknowable to those who use or are otherwise impacted by it. At an aggregate level, the way in which these various tools are interoperable (or may be temporarily aligned) can also be rendered opaque as it gains prominence:

Spatial Big Data is the logical outcome of long-running attempts to resolve these two built-in uncertainties of geodemographics. It does so through the promise of representing a fully measured, quantified, geolocated individual, rather than the homogenized, quantified areal units of geodemographics. (ibid.: 7)

These technologies work simultaneously with data from people and locations (both with comparable epistemological salience). GIS is assembled from disparate sources, but also framed as a singular tool that an administrator or public servant can wield (Haque 2003) – even while framed as "not a single system or database organizer as found in traditional statistical software" (ibid.: 43). There are other actors in the GIS public servant scenario, yet it is typically restricted to public servants and private service providers. In comparison, the current data landscape in locations like Moerwijk is assembled even more in terms of the actors involved. In framing this phenomenon broadly, we include several different organisations that share conflicting concerns about Moerwijk, or concerns that happen to touch on Moerwijk.

Prior research also identifies "[s]ources of ethical misconduct" in practitioner use of GIS:

(1) actions of the GIS user that could be deemed unethical due to the technical incompetence leading to biased decisions (limited knowledge in cartography); (2) misinterpretation of results due to lack of information or understanding of the true nature of the real-world phenomenon; and (3) concerns regarding the quality of data as public managers, because of high demand, are increasingly relying on private vendors and other alternative data sources. (ibid.)

While these are indeed examples of abuse of geodemographic data, there is an implication that greater technical competence, a greater volume of data, greater processing power, or fine-tuned algorithms will grant access to the "true nature" of urban life processes, which could in turn absolve practitioners from ethical concerns. Focusing on these risks overlooks concerns over whether data should be processed in the first place, alongside social harms that may arise from ever more refined surveillance of urban spaces.

Data Practices and Ethical Concerns: Tensions Between Open Data and Ensuring Anonymity

Datafied engagements of neighbourhoods like Moerwijk are informed by several principles in terms of accessing and handling public data. While commendable on paper, in practice they may provide conflicting or even contradictory guidance. Prominent calls by research clusters, disciplinary organisations and funding agencies promote open research data (e.g., NWO 2021). This involves not only making research findings open to the public, but also the datasets that underpins these findings. Such calls are especially salient when the data is about public spaces, and when it can potentially be of service to 'the public', however they may be defined. Open research data can benefit urban initiatives and may even directly benefit those who reside in otherwise underserved neighbourhoods. Yet extending the shelf life of this data also extends the possibility of misuse and unanticipated harms stemming from this collection. Calls for open data must be tempered by the prioritisation of privacy and data protection. As a starting point, this involves ensuring the anonymity (or pseudonymity) of those who may otherwise be identified in our data collection. Yet after addressing what we may consider the 'low hanging fruit' of privacy concerns, there may be a lingering risk of reidentification, through the combination and processing of multiple data sources, as well as the aggregate identification of clusters of people through (as an example) postal codes. Setting aside these specific concerns, making a neighbourhood 'knowable' in the aggregate may also bring unanticipated harm, for instance when providing empirical accounts of the grounds for its troubled reputation.

Datafied urban ethnography aims to be "as open as possible, as closed as necessary" (Landi et al., 2020) by providing and prescribing a socio-cultural context in which urban data is understood. This involves positioning digital data about neighbourhoods as a point of inquiry for ethnographic research, rather than strictly as research data that can simply be extracted. It also demands critical inquiry and assessment for data collection and dissemination, all the while remaining open to the possibility of accessing new data sources, which would warrant a reconsideration of these concerns. This potential conflict between open and protected data raises questions about what right we have to collect and mobilise data about Moerwijk, as well as alternative arrangements. By providing the context (and narratives) of those whose lives are implicated in this data, we aim to allow those who depend on the neighbourhood to speak to the data, rather than the other way around. Yet researchers must acknowledge that they cannot control how open research data is later utilised, and qualitative contextualization can be overlooked by stakeholders who do not share our concerns about humanising data. We struggle with these dilemmas in the context of the ongoing datafication of urban spaces, and social scientists otherwise risk being left at the margins of these transformations if they adopt blanket measures of self-exclusion on ethical grounds. It is therefore perhaps best to see transparency not as a binary decision – to disclose or to mask – but as a "toolkit" (Reyes 2017).

Digital Data Sources

Any identifiable details from digital content, from Twitter or other data sources, could obviously be omitted in processing raw data. While we analyse and report on public tweets from various stakeholders, any details that would identify a private (non-public) individual are not included by default in reports or public datasets. These would be user accounts that, based on biographical or profile metadata, do not represent an organization, business, or public figure. If researchers wish to identify an individual via their Twitter content, they should seek permission from that individual directly. Depending on the context of the tweet, we employ a range of measures to ensure that non-public individuals are not identifiable (e.g., quoting only a portion of the tweet; paraphrasing; translating the tweet from Dutch to English). As for non-private actors (user accounts), because these are affiliated with the marginalised neighbourhood, not identifying them may incur a disservice by, for example, robbing them of (sympathetic and potentially beneficial) public attention that they do not typically receive. This point is further elaborated upon below in a section that discusses explicit identification of neighbourhoods themselves.

We stress that our digital research activities, including the above privacy considerations, endeavour to maintain "contextual integrity" (Nissenbaum 2010). We, and other internet researchers, would argue that adhering to this standard should neutralise concerns surrounding some digital practices that are legal but nevertheless debated, such as data scraping that does not fully observe a platform's terms of service (AoIR 2019). The ethical consideration of such practices always needs to consider contextual factors (Fiesler 2020).

One ongoing challenge involves how to manage the possibility of as-yet unknown data sources during the course of the project (e.g., wearable data, new type of or newly emerged access to an app or platform, new forms of interoperability between existing data sources). These may provide novel insights into the symbolic trajectories of neighbourhoods, as expressed through the most recent iterations of embedded urban surveillance. Yet an unreflexive incorporation of additional sources risks displacing residents' accounts further, especially if they are unlikely to be early adopters of these technologies. In fact, our research has already had to contend with a shift in data sources. Prior to the availability of Twitter Academic, tweets were obtained through the standard and limited Search API and the Twitter web interface, both of which yield less than comprehensive data. In this case, the new data source can be considered an improvement over the status quo ante since Twitter as a well-known and popular platform provides insights into how multiple stakeholders frame the neighbourhood.

Ethnographic Field Work

As stated above, stakeholders comprise of residents, civil servants, employees and volunteers for local civic organisations, visitors to the community, representatives of small businesses, and public officials. Such engagements centre their experiences with how digital media and technologies shape and assess their neighbourhood, alongside their perceptions and judgements of these practices and their impacts on their lives, professions, and on the neighbourhood. Our preliminary impressions suggest that short-term engagement with communities (e.g., one-time visits to collect data, followed by complete disengagement) are not well received, and that a more prolonged dialogue with residents and other stakeholders is preferred. While this may be an uncontroversial statement, it also brings considerable staffing costs and possible delays in terms of publication targets. Moreover, a nearby neighbourhood (Schilderswijk) is dealing with what may be described as 'participant fatigue' after being the subject of several research projects (cf. Mandel 2003). Residents may want to share their opinions about the stigmatisation of their neighbourhoods; yet a disproportionate emphasis on these themes by well-meaning ethnographers can be dispiriting to the subjects, who may come to internalise the very same stereotypes about their homes that the research set out to subvert.

On a global scale, neighbourhoods like Moerwijk are currently gripped by the COVID-19 pandemic. In the short term, this has limited urban mobility as well as the ability to congregate, furthered economic anxieties, and compounded other existential needs such as access to food, health care and other essential services. From an academic perspective, COVID-19 also poses distinct ethical challenges to researchers, as ethnographic engagements, face-to-face interviews and focus groups pose clear risks of infection for researchers and participants. The ongoing pandemic has of course complicated our fieldwork plans. While the Netherlands did not experience the strictest forms of lockdown seen in neighbouring countries, public health policies heavily restricted non-essential travel within the country. Moreover, it would have been possible to comply with these guidelines and still put researchers and participants at risk of infection, for instance, if an asymptomatic carrier of COVID-19 was in prolonged contact with others during field work. In the interest of minimising any such risks, we have opted for remote work during this period, including further engagement with the above-mentioned data sources. Most ethical evaluations of projects do include accounting for environmental risks to researchers and participants, so these concerns are by no means new. Rather, the troubling novelty is the global scale upon which such concerns have become a part of ethics planning, coupled with the uncertainty about immediate as well as longer-term data collection. At the time of writing, it remains unclear when sustained in-person field work will revert to a low-risk or no-risk endeavour.

When engaging with many kinds of stakeholders, there is the risk of encountering and exploiting power relations between members of the broader community, as well as an overdependence on key informants. While first contacts, well-connected insiders and even gatekeepers may serve an important role in reaching individuals, researchers need to ensure that their reliance on these links does not distort their account of the neighbourhood (O'Reilly 2009). Rather than identifying a single contact person as an entry point to the community, we propose treating field engagement as a series of iterative first encounters with contacts who are unaffiliated with one another and diverse in terms of demographics and opinion (in addition to following up already existing contacts). This enables researchers to be attentive to marginal and under-represented understandings of technological norms, complicating what would otherwise be concise ethnographic accompaniments to urban data analytics.

When contacting property developers, entrepreneurs, landlords and employers, their relations of power via clients, employees, and other individuals could potentially provide researchers with privileged and even coercive access to them, or their digital presence. Scholars should be especially mindful of these dynamics and account for these power relations in their reporting. To mitigate power imbalances between stakeholders, we recommend actively avoiding situations where a more powerful respondent or gatekeeper will directly benefit from recruiting others. This includes assessing one's own involvement with business improvement districts and comparable entities, to assess the possibility that the knowledge utilisation that universities and funding agencies enjoy could disproportionally benefit already capital-rich entities.

More recent studies propose "innovative methodological approaches" (Fransham 2020: 2), including machine learning (Reades et al. 2019), to understand and predict gentrification through large-scale data sets. Mobilising localised data can be both a means to understand, as well as a manifestation of surveillance capitalism. In considering Moerwijk and neighbourhoods sharing similar features, we advocate a sustained ethnographic presence, not only to supplement the data activities, but also to consider how residents and others make sense of these activities. Ethnographic research may address ethical issues stemming from quantitative analysis by mitigating biases and preconceptions. Yet ethnography also furthers concerns of exploitation, exposure and misrepresentation (Wacquant 2002; Bratich 2017), and should not simply be treated as a kind of 'ethical panacea' for big, open, or public data projects. A multifaceted approach to data collection offers a rounded account of contemporary urban data practices by drawing upon distinct and possibly conflicting accounts of social life, but it also augments the risks of bringing harm to the community under scrutiny. This includes unintended consequences of drifting away from the principle of data minimisation, through the exposure of participants. Hence, a delicate balance between the benefits of data heterogeneity and these risks must be reached. This research thus invokes the ethical implications of using data in studying people and neighbourhoods, notably when focusing on these subjects' own use of data.

Linking Data and People

Bringing together these two types of data facilitates an understanding of the relations between the data infrastructures of urban spaces, and the individuals who depend upon them. Digital data in the case of Moerwijk can provide guidance to ethnographic work, by helping identify trends and reputational concerns that may or may not be of relevance to stakeholders. Preliminary findings can also be critically interrogated through ethnographic work. Data yielded from platforms like Twitter and Instagram present a vision of neighbourhoods like Moerwijk that may not align with the residents' own experiences. When our methodology reflects facets of surveillance capitalism that we may otherwise critique, it is imperative to incorporate and centre perspectives that are underserved by digital platforms, in part by sharing preliminary findings with residents, and allocating space for their interpretation of these findings in subsequent work.

Gathering online data and qualitative approaches should be treated as complimentary yet separate activities. As stated above, a mixed methods approach is best suited for studying multi-contextual and potentially conflicting practices. In cases where qualitative fieldwork alerts researchers to local web resources that are relevant to data analysis (for example, a representative of a local initiative flags their organisation's website), scholars may seek permission to make use of any data on these sites, while ensuring that no individuals are identifiable in the process. While interviewees may be recruited during observations, these interviews should be treated as distinct research activities, and the relevant protocols (e.g., informing participants; finding an appropriate location) should be adhered to.

The collection and analysis of digital data sources will contribute to field work activities, including interviews and focus groups. This data serves as an account of Moerwijk and allows us to identify potential concerns for stakeholders, which they may or may not be aware of (for example, in the event that we identify a pattern of comparatively lower review ratings for local businesses and services). Yet we do not want data to speak on behalf of people, nor do we want it to guide our conversations with residents and other stakeholders exclusively. To this end we advocate that the substantive focus of our (and comparable) research is also guided by stakeholders. Practically speaking, this can be accomplished on site through semi-structured and open-ended interview guides. It can also occur in a more sustained manner, for example, by encouraging participants to raise local concerns that will in turn shape the types of questions we ask, and even our choice of data collection and knowledge utilisation activities.

Evaluating Risks of Identifying Neighbourhoods

Anonymisation and pseudonymisation are common practices for reporting research findings that focus on individuals, especially if dealing with sensitive or stigmatising topics. Our case study focuses on an aggregate – a neighbourhood. Identifying a neighbourhood could facilitate the identification of individuals when combined with other details about those people, such as their profession. While this is a risk, a separate and arguably more perplexing concern is the broader impact that research and reporting have on the reputation and public standing of Moerwijk itself.

The simplest approach would be to omit any direct mention of the neighbourhood in the published results. Yet this can do a potential disservice to the neighbourhood, which would be excluded from broader dialogue and engagement linked to the project. If Moerwijk were anonymised in a peer-reviewed publication, a press release on that publication would also need to exclude any mention of the neighbourhood, as would any knowledge utilisation activities that put these research findings to use. Although comparable research may concern neighbourhoods that experience stigmatisation, data collection and analysis should critically assess the processes through which such stigmatisation is digitally enacted, to provide residents and other stakeholders with opportunities to correct or counter undesirable perceptions. It can therefore be justified to include the names of target neighbourhoods in publications and other knowledge utilisation activities. While talking about a neighbourhood that is coping with a troubled reputation could potentially lead to further stigmatisation, scholarly and societal framing of this topic may rest on the observation that this reputation is largely unwarranted (empirically, both in quantitative measures as well as qualitative accounts) and that residents and other stakeholder voices should feature more prominently in public discourse. Thus, by default we believe it will do a disservice to communities like Moerwijk if they are omitted from publications and knowledge utilisation initiatives.

Despite these recommendations, we may consider whether addressing categorical discrimination through dispersed urban surveillance contributes to a more prevailing bifurcation of 'good' and 'bad' neighbourhoods. Coupling residents' experiences with digital metrics may privilege the former over the latter but can also lead to additional ways to quantify and rate an urban area's market value. In situating our research in a broader context of coalescent surveillance practices, we may inadvertently contribute to the financial and cultural revaluation of neighbourhoods like Moerwijk. For this reason, researchers must consider whether the most ethical step we can take for a neighbourhood is simply not to study it?

Conclusions and Recommendations: Ethics Beyond Ethical Approval

In accounting for how urban data surveillance shapes the reputation of embattled and neglected neighbourhoods, we propose a datafied urban ethnography that situates local data practices in terms of local data handlers. We also acknowledge that such an approach must strike a balance between finding (and using) the best data available and any potential harm that reporting on such data might incur. In our case study, this compels our own research team to consider the ethical implications of our efforts. This leads us to generate data in ways that mean residents have early access to our findings, and a first word in interpreting them. This prioritisation is reflected in our ethnographic work, but also public outreach efforts that are centred on Moerwijk and its residents.

Mixed methods approaches to urban data collection uncover vulnerabilities caused by information technologies when they contribute to the symbolic re-shaping of neighbourhoods. Researchers are often outsiders to the communities under study. While this should not exclude the possibility of critical insights or positive interventions on their part, when it comes to drawing upon a normative understanding of what a neighbourhood like Moerwijk 'ought to be', researchers need to defer to those who reside in, depend upon, and invest in these spaces. This can be accomplished throughout the course of a project, informing ethnographic encounters and interviews. Knowledge utilisation activities – whether they target a localised audience, an audience of professionals at a national scale, or an audience abroad – should also centre on and prioritise how local stakeholders understand public data and digital platforms. Of course, this is not to say that researchers should not contribute to these conversations. Inasmuch as they develop knowledge and expertise on these matters through field work and prior research, they are expected to offer external insights to conversations with stakeholders. But in doing so, they need to ensure that these encounters remain a dialogue.

Researchers must also recognise that the first account, the loudest voice, or the majority perspective they encounter does not necessarily represent the opinions and needs of the community under study. While dependent on those who set aside time to offer an account of their neighbourhood, we recognise that they may present locally contested accounts of its digital presence and may have their own interests in doing so. At its core, our case study is concerned with the development of a 'positive' digital presence for urban spaces. Such a presence is made up of an assemblage of automated and deliberate forms of dataveillance. We need to reflect further on what is meant by 'positive' in this context, and consider who benefits from normative understandings of a favourable symbolic trajectory.

Contemporary data practices force a reconsideration of the terms we use to describe social actors and their practices. Both researchers and residents appear to be engaged in (or at least beholden to) data handling practices. A normative and orthodox account of what 'proper and professional' data handling is like might mean that we delegitimize or overlook certain practices involving urban data. A qualitative, ethnographic and above all curious approach to data use in urban spaces should help us to recognise how those at the margins may live with data. Yet researchers must also question assumptions that our recognition of these practices is inherently good – for marginal communities more generally and for the subjects of our research. Researching and publishing about otherwise neglected data practices can easily impact these practices – for example, by making such communities even more self-conscious than they might be already, and consequently tentative of their practices, and in this way, risk furthering existing asymmetries of access, capital, and power.

We must therefore address normative assumptions about what a good online presence should be like (for individuals and organisations alike), as well as expectations of optimal digital media usage. Our own research is formulated in a way that suggests that Moerwijk's digital media configuration is sub-optimal, disadvantageous, or dysfunctional. This can be framed from the perspective of those who are most dependent on the neighbourhood, who are typically also those who are most disadvantaged more generally (e.g., low-income residents with limited opportunities for upward or even lateral mobility). Yet because of the multi-sector nature of this topic, coupled with normative assumptions that shape the use of technology (e.g., what elements should be included in a 'functional' Google Review for a small business; what remedies should be in place if these are absent?), what begins as a concern for those who are marginalised or excluded may end up largely benefiting those with a comparative advantage such as entrepreneurs, property developers, and global digital media platforms. Ideally, scholarly concern with those on the margins should align with their interests and voices. Further, residents' having these interests met and having their voices heard should bring minimal risk or burden upon themselves. This paper aims to contribute to translating these lofty ideals into practical steps for urban data scholars and ensuring that these steps may be of value for comparable data practices.

References

Albrechtslund, Anders (2008): "Online Social Networking as Participatory Surveillance." In: First Monday 13/3 (https://firstmonday.org/ojs/index.php/fm/article/view/2142).

Association of Internet Researchers (2019). Internet Research: Ethical Guidelines 3.0. https://aoir.org/reports/ethics3.pdf.

Bratich, Jack Z. (2017): "Observation in a surveilled world." The SAGE Handbook of Qualitative Research, edited by Norman K. Denzin and Yvonna S. Lincoln, 5th ed., Thousand Oaks, Calif.: SAGE, pp. 526–45.

Brighenti, Andrea (2007): "Visibility: A Category for the Social Sciences." In: Current Sociology 55/3, pp. 323-342.

Bucher, Taina (2012): Want to be on the Top? Algorithmic Power and the Threat of Invisibility on Facebook. In: New Media & Society 14/7, pp. 1164-1180.

Burrows, Roger/Ellison, Nick (2004): "Sorting Places Out? Towards a Social Politics of Neighbourhood Informatization." In: Information Communication & Society 7/3, pp. 321-336.

Dalton, Craig M/Taylor, Linnet/Thatcher, Jim (2015): "Inflated Granularity: Spatial "Big Data" and Geodemographics." In: Big Data & Society 2/2, pp. 1-15.

De Vynck, Gerrit/Wong, Nathalie (2020): "Alphabet's Dream of a Smart City in Toronto Is Over" In: Bloomberg May 7 (https://www.bloomberg.com/news/articles/2020-05-07/alphabet-s-dream-of-a-smart-city-in-toronto-is-over).

Fiesler, Casey/Beard, Nathan/Keegan, Brian C. (2020): "No Robots, Spiders, or Scrapers: Legal and Ethical Regulation of Data Collection Methods in Social Media Terms of Service." In: Proceedings of the International AAAI Conference on Web and Social Media 14, pp. 187-196.

Fransham, Mark (2020): "Neighbourhood Gentrification, Displacement, and Poverty Dynamics in Post-Recession England." In: Population, Space and Place 26/5, pp. 1-13 (online first).

Gandy, Oscar (2016): Coming to Terms with Chance: Engaging Rational Discrimination and Cumulative Disadvantage, London: Routledge.

Gutsche Jr. Robert E. (2015): "Boosterism as Banishment." In: Journalism Studies 16/4, pp. 497-512.

Haque, Akhlaque (2003): "Information Technology, GIS and Democratic Values: Ethical Implications for IT Professionals in Public Service." In: Ethics and Information Technology 5/1, pp. 39-48.

Kien, Nguyen Trung (2020): "Care of the Self in the Age of Algorithms: Early Thoughts from a Foucauldian Perspective." In: Ho Chi Minh City Open University Journal of Science - Social Sciences 10/1, pp. 79-90.

Landi, Annalisa/Thompson, Mark/Giannuzzi, Viviana/Bonifazi, Fedele/Labastida, Ignasi/da Silva Santos, Luiz Olavo Bonino da Silva Santos/Roos, Marco (2020): "The "A" of FAIR–as Open as Possible, as Closed as Necessary." In: Data Intelligence, 2/1-2, pp. 47-55.

Lee, Ju-Sung/Boy, John, D./Trottier, Daniel (2022): "Symbolic Trajectories in Action: Digital Technologies and Representations of a Stigmatized Neighborhood." Under review.

Mackenzie, Adrian/Munster, Anna (2019): "Platform Seeing: Image Ensembles and their Invisualities." In: Theory, Culture & Society 36/5, pp. 3–22.

Mandel, Jennifer L. (2003): "Negotiating Expectations in the Field: Gatekeepers, Research Fatigue and Cultural Biases." In: Singapore Journal of Tropical Geography 24/2, pp. 198-210.

Mann, Steve/Nolan, Jason/Wellman, Barry (2003): "Sousveillance: Inventing and Using Wearable Computing Devices for Data Collection in Surveillance Environments." In: Surveillance & Society 1/3, pp. 331-355.

Nissenbaum, Helen (2010): Privacy in Context: Technology, Policy, and the Integrity of Social Life, Stanford: Stanford University Press.

NWO (2021): "Open Science" (https://www.nwo.nl/en/open-science).

O'Neil, Cathy (2016): Weapons of Math Destruction: How Big Data Increases Inequality and Threatens Democracy, New York: Broadway Books.

O'Reilly, Kare (2009): "Key informants and gatekeepers." Key concepts in ethnography. London: SAGE, pp. 132-137.

Reades, Jonathan/De Souza, Jordan/Hubbard, Phil (2019): "Understanding Urban Gentrification Through Machine Learning." In: Urban Studies, 56(5), pp. 922-942.

Reilly, Paul (2015): "Every Little Helps? YouTube, Sousveillance and the 'Anti-Tesco' Riot in Stokes Croft". In: New Media & Society 17/5, pp. 755-771.

Reyes, Victoria (2017): "Three Models of Transparency in Ethnographic Research: Naming Places, Naming People, and Shar-ing Data." Ethnography 19/2, pp. 204–26.

Thompson, John B. (2005): "The New Visibility." In: Theory, Culture & Society 22/6, pp. 31-51.

Van Dijck, José (2014): "Datafication, Dataism and Dataveillance: Big Data Between Scientific Paradigm and Ideology." In: Surveillance & Society 12/2, pp. 197-208.

Van Zoonen, Liesbet (2016): "Privacy Concerns in Smart Cities." In: Government Information Quarterly 33/3, pp. 472-480.

Wacquant, Loic (2002): "Scrutinizing the Street: Poverty, Morality, and the Pitfalls of Urban Ethnography." In: American Journal of Sociology 107/6, pp. 1468-1532.

Zimmer, Michael (2010): "But the Data is Already Public": On the Ethics of Research in Facebook." In: Ethics and Information Technology 12/4, pp. 313-325.

Zukin, Sharon/Lindeman, Scarlett/Hurson, Laurie (2017): "The omnivore's neighborhood? Online Restaurant Reviews, Race, and Gentrification." In: Journal of Consumer Culture 17/3, pp. 459-479.

Biographical Notes

Mark Andrejevic is Professor at the School of Media, Film, and Journalism at Monash University, where he directs the Automated Society Working Group. He is also a Chief Investigator with the Australian Research Council's Centre for Automated Decision Making and Society, a multi-university research consortium.

Alexandra Anikina, PhD., is Balzan Postdoctoral Fellow at Sorbonne Nouvelle University Paris 3 and Associate Researcher at the Centre for the Study of the Networked Image, London South Bank University.

Vinicius Ariel is an undergraduate student on the Computer Engineering course at the Polytechnic School of the University of São Paulo (Poli USP) and a researcher in the Group on Artificial Intelligence and Art (GAIA). He is currently working as a developer at VR Monkey.

Armin Beverungen is Junior Professor of Organisation in Digital Cultures at the Institute for Sociology and Cultural Organisation at Leuphana University of Lüneburg.

Carolina Sanchez Boe, Carlsberg Foundation post.doc. at IMC, Aarhus University, works on the anthropology of confinement and migration control.

Cornelia Bogen, academic assistant for culture and media education, Ludwigsburg University of Education.

John D. Boy is an Assistant Professor of Sociology at Leiden University.

Peter Gentzel, Ass. Prof. Dr. (Friedrich-Alexander-University Erlangen-Nürnberg) is Assistant Professor for Digital Transformation of Media and Communication, Department for Media Research and Art History.

Michelle Henning is Professor for Photography and Media in the School of the Arts, University of Liverpool.

Sascha Hosters is a writer and creative producer based in New York. Since finishing his PhD in Media Studies at Rutgers University, he has been working as a freelancer for the New York Fashion Week and other clients in the film and fashion industries.

Amanda Chevtchouk Jurno holds a PhD and a Master's Degree in Communication from the Federal University of Minas Gerais (UFMG). An academic researcher and professor, she is also a journalist, having graduated from the same university. Media researcher at R-EST Sociotechincal Network Studies and at Group on Artificial Intelligence and Art (GAIA).

Ju-Sung (Jay) Lee is an Assistant Professor in the Department of Media and Communication at Erasmus University Rotterdam.

Monique Lemos is a post-graduate in Digital Anthropology, having graduated in Social Sciences at the School of Sociology and Politics of São Paulo Foundation (FESPSP). Researcher at Group on Artificial Intelligence and Art (GAIA at INOVA-USP) and researcher on computer vision and necropolitics. Founder and CEO of Topograficas.

Henry Mainsah, Consumption Research Norway (SIFO), Oslo Metropolitan University, conducts interdisciplinary research on digitization, consumption, and creative research methods.

Bruno Moreschi is a researcher and multidisciplinary artist. Postdoctoral Fellow at the Faculty of Architecture and Urbanism at the University of São Paulo (FAUUSP), PhD in Arts at the State University of Campinas (Unicamp) with a Capes Scholarship.

Lucas Nunes holds a Bachelor's Degree in Molecular Sciences from the University of São Paulo (USP) with emphasis on Computer Sciences and Artificial Intelligence. He is now a Computer Science Master's Degree student at the Institute of Mathematics and Statistics at the University of São Paulo (IME-USP), studying Computer Vision and Natural Language Processing.

Gabriel Pereira is a Visiting Fellow at the London School of Economics and Political Science, funded by the Independent Research Fund Denmark International Postdoc grant.

Didiana Prata is a graphic designer, image curator and adjunct professor at the University Centre of Fundação Armando Alvares Penteado. She is a Phd candidate in Design at the University of São Paulo. Her investigation is focused on multimedia design for different interfaces, database aesthetics and A.I. as curatorial strategies.

Silke Roesler-Keilholz is a research assistant in Media Studies at Regensburg University. Her research focuses on media of surveillance, postfeminism and fashion media studies.

Ruben Schlagowski, M. Sc. (University of Augsburg), is a researcher at the Faculty of Applied Computer Science.

Jens Schröter is Chair for Media Studies at the University of Bonn.

Daniel Trottier is an Associate Professor at the Department of Media and Communication of Erasmus University Rotterdam.

Zala Volcic teaches at Monash University, Melbourne, Australia, and works on issues to do with media, (digital) cultures, nationalism, borders, class and gender. She has researched and written on global media, transitional justice, class and social media.

Daniela Wentz is a postdoctoral researcher for the research project INTERACT! New Forms of Social Interaction with Intelligent Systems at Ruhr-Universität Bochum.

Jeffrey Wimmer, Prof. Dr. (University of Augsburg), is Professor for Media Reality at the Department for Media, Knowledge and Communication.

Medienwissenschaft

Florian Sprenger (Hg.)
Autonome Autos
Medien- und kulturwissenschaftliche Perspektiven auf die Zukunft der Mobilität

2021, 430 S., kart., 29 SW-Abbildungen
30,00 € (DE), 978-3-8376-5024-2
E-Book: kostenlos erhältlich als Open-Access-Publikation
PDF: ISBN 978-3-8394-5024-6
EPUB: ISBN 978-3-7328-5024-2

Tanja Köhler (Hg.)
Fake News, Framing, Fact-Checking: Nachrichten im digitalen Zeitalter
Ein Handbuch

2020, 568 S., kart., 41 SW-Abbildungen
39,00 € (DE), 978-3-8376-5025-9
E-Book:
PDF: 38,99 € (DE), ISBN 978-3-8394-5025-3

Geert Lovink
Digitaler Nihilismus
Thesen zur dunklen Seite der Plattformen

2019, 242 S., kart.
24,99 € (DE), 978-3-8376-4975-8
E-Book:
PDF: 21,99 € (DE), ISBN 978-3-8394-4975-2
EPUB: 21,99 € (DE), ISBN 978-3-7328-4975-8

Leseproben, weitere Informationen und Bestellmöglichkeiten finden Sie unter www.transcript-verlag.de

Medienwissenschaft

Ziko van Dijk
Wikis und die Wikipedia verstehen
Eine Einführung

2021, 340 S., kart., 13 SW-Abbildungen
35,00 € (DE), 978-3-8376-5645-9
E-Book: kostenlos erhältlich als Open-Access-Publikation
PDF: ISBN 978-3-8394-5645-3
EPUB: ISBN 978-3-7328-5645-9

Gesellschaft für Medienwissenschaft (Hg.)
Zeitschrift für Medienwissenschaft 25
Jg. 13, Heft 2/2021: Spielen

2021, 180 S., kart.
24,99 € (DE), 978-3-8376-5400-4
E-Book: kostenlos erhältlich als Open-Access-Publikation
PDF: ISBN 978-3-8394-5400-8
EPUB: ISBN 978-3-7328-5400-4

Anna Dahlgren, Karin Hansson, Ramón Reichert,
Amanda Wasielewski (eds.)
Digital Culture & Society (DCS)
Vol. 6, Issue 2/2020 – The Politics of Metadata

2021, 274 p., pb., ill.
29,99 € (DE), 978-3-8376-4956-7
E-Book:
PDF: 29,99 € (DE), ISBN 978-3-8394-4956-1

**Leseproben, weitere Informationen und Bestellmöglichkeiten
finden Sie unter www.transcript-verlag.de**